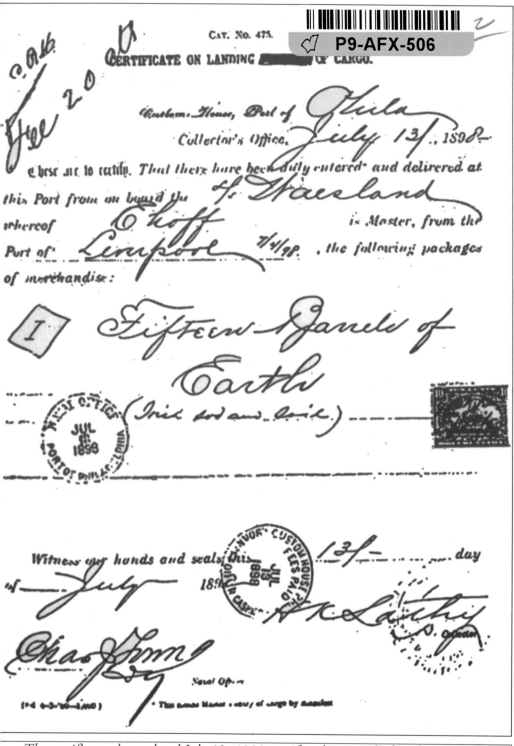

The certificate above, dated July 13, 1898, verifies the arrival of "Fifteen Barrels of Earth (Irish sod and soil)," shipped from Liverpool, and ordered by a canny Irish undertaker to serve clients who wanted to be buried under the Old Sod, and would pay well for the privilege.

IRISH CALIFORNIANS
HISTORIC, BENEVOLENT, ROMANTIC

National Convention Ancient Order Of Hibernians
In America And Ladies Auxiliary Banquet
In Exposition Auditorium
San Francisco Cal July 1st 1919

53528.

*Overleaf: The National Convention of the
Ancient Order of Hibernians in America,
and Ladies' Auxiliary Banquet,
in Exposition Auditorium (Civic Auditorium),
San Francisco, July 19, 1919.*

IRISH CALIFORNIANS
HISTORIC, BENEVOLENT, ROMANTIC

PATRICK J. DOWLING

SCOTTWALL ASSOCIATES
San Francisco
1998

Library of Congress Catalog Card Number: 98-061475

Cataloging in Publication Data:
Dowling, Patrick J.
    Irish Californians: Historic, Benevolent, Romantic
    by Patrick J. Dowling
    1. Irish immigrants (biographies) 2. California history
    3. Irish Catholicism   4. Irish name origins   5. Irish nationalism
    6. Irish Politics   7. Ancient Order of Hibernians   8. Fenians (Sinn Fein)
    9. DeValera, Eamon   10. Doheny, Edward   11. McKenna, Andrew J.,
    Supreme Court Justice   12. Sweeny, General Thomas William
    13. Toland, Dr. Hugh   14. San Francisco   15. San Diego
    16. San Jose   17. Los Angeles   18. Sacramento   19. Eureka
    20. Siskiyou County   21. San Bernardino

Book and cover design: James Heig
Editor: Susan Little
Scanning: Kathleen Chen

First Edition: 5 4 3 2 1
Copyright ©1998 Patrick Dowling

Scottwall Associates, Publishers
95 Scott Street
San Francisco, CA 94117
Telephone (415) 861-1956

Printed in Canada

ISBN 0-942087-16-X

DEDICATION

To my wife, Maureen Dowling,
and my daughters, Patricia, Kathleen,
Colleen, and Cecilia, for their constant
support and encouragement. And to my son,
Michael, who kept reminding me
that life is fleeting.

Acknowledgments

To name all who shared in this literary endeavor would be well nigh impossible, but a number of people deserve special mention. Had it not been for their support and encouragement, this work might never have reached fruition. To all those who contributed in any way, I thank you from the bottom of my Irish heart, and I beg forgiveness from those who have helped and whom I have neglected to mention. My thanks go to the following:

—Richard Coyer, a leading authority on the history of San Diego, for sharing his work on the Irish contribution to that delightful City of the Sun.

—Jim Kelly, former journalist athe the *San Francisco Progress*, and a longtime spokesmen for thle University of San Francisco, for his valuable editorial suggestions.

—Eileen Murphy, San Francisco educator, who corrected many misspellings and grammatical errors.

—Jim Toland, Professor of Journalism at San Francisco State University, erstwhile copy editor for the *San Francisco Chronicle*, who shared his knowledge of the life and times of Dr. Hugh Toland.

—Kerry Daly, for information about her forebears , who founded the great Daly mercantile family.

—Dr. Albert Shumate, a longtime friend and confidant, for sharing his vast knowledge of San Francisco history.

—Mrs. Mary Russell, founding member of the San Diego Historical and Genealogical Society, for her help in obtaining information about San Diego pioneers.

—Jack Rosenbaum, whose delightful column in the *San Francisco Independent* repeatedly gave heart to this writer.

—Mrs. John F., Delury, who graciously provided a copy of lher late husband's thesis on the Irish in Sacramento.

—Branagh Mullan, a gifted and tenacious young lady who obtained vital information relative to my interests from sources in Washington, D.C.

—John Concannon, Flushing, New York, Historian of the Ancient Order of Hibernians in America.

—Michael O'Connor, Dublin, Ireland, goodwill ambassador, for his constant support and encouragement.

—Sister Winifred Mary White, S.N.J.M., for sharing her dissertation on Eugene Casserly.

—Jim Callaghan, Pleasant Mount, PA, a history writer without equal, for his tilmely advice.

—Father Henry P. Johnson, Pastor of St. Patrick's parish in Angels Camp, who provided photographs and information about the church.

—Matthew Brady, columnist for the *San Francisco Independent*, for sharing his great collection of anecdotes about San Francisco.

—Sister Anne Curry, Historian, Sisters of the Presentation, San Francisco.

—William Carr, Fresno, who keeps alive the Irish traditions in the California heartland.

—Tom Wrinn, who provided material about the life and work of Michael Wrin, benevolent San Franciscan.

—Jim Norris, who provided pictures and information about pioneers in the Santa Inez Valley.

—Walter McConnell, Director of the Humboldt County Historical Society, who provided information about James Talbot Ryan, founder of Eureka.

—Harry Wassmann, historian of Benicia, for information about the illustrious Judge Joseph McKenna.

—Dr. Jeffrey Burns, Archivist of the Archdiocese of San Francisco, for his help and advice.

—Sister Anne Curry, Historian, Sisters of the Presentation, for her valued assistance.

Many Historical and Genealogican Societies also contributed very generously to this chronicle:

Belmont Historical Society
Boys Town Hall of Fame, Omaha, Nebraska
Calaveras County Historical Society, San Andreas
California Historical Society, San Francisco
Contra Costa County Historical Society, Martinez
El Dorado County Historical Society, Placerville
Gilroy Historical Society
Goleta Historical Society
Humboldt County Historical Society, Eureka
Marin County Historical Society, San Rafael
Mendocino County Historical Society, Ukiah
Murphy Museum, Murphy, Idaho
Nevada Historical Society, Reno
Orange County Historical Society, Santa Ana
Sacramento Discovery Museum
Sacramento Historical Society

San Bernardino Historical Society
San Diego Historical Society
San Jose Historical Museum
San Mateo County Historical Association
Santa Barbara Historical Society
Santa Inez Historical Society
Santa Maria Historical Society
Siskiyou County Historical Society, Yreka
Society of California Pioneers, San Francisco

To these and all other people or organizations
who have helped me in this work, I am deeply grateful.

—Patrick J. Dowling, San Francisco, September 1998

TABLE OF CONTENTS

FOREWORD

IN 1988, when Patrick Dowling published his much-acclaimed *California: the Irish Dream,* his many friends and admirers hardly suspected that at his age, Pat would find the time or the energy to produce another book on the fascinating history of the Irish in California. Fortunately, Pat's boundless enthusiasm for his adopted state and native land have defied the sands of time.

Moreover, Patrick's new book, *Irish Californians: Historic, Benevolent, Romantic,* is more than a worthy sequel to his first work. Whereas *California: The Irish Dream* focused primarily on the Irish-born pioneers in Northern California, the stories told in this new book sweep across the entire state, from San Diego to Eureka, and relate the lives not only of Irish immigrants such as Eleanor Martin, the Irish Czarina, from County Roscommon, and James Talbot Ryan, the Founder of Eureka, from Tipperary, but also of American-born Irishmen and women such as James Cunningham, the "boy wonder" of San Bernardino, and Abigail Parrott, the Irish philanthropist from San Mateo.

Lovers of Patrick's first book will be enchanted anew, for the stories told in *Irish Californians* are as colorful and dramatic as those which galvanized readers of the earlier book.

However, this new book is more than just an engaging history of the Irish in the Golden State—although that history alone is a vitally important one. Because the Irish were so extensively involved in California's economic, social, cultural and political development, their history is, to a remarkable extent, the history of the state itself during the nineteenth and twentieth centuries.

California was really the first state in the Union to develop a large and prosperous Irish-American business and political class. To be sure, there were in the Golden State large numbers of poor Irish-born and American-born Irish workers, who played major roles in the history of California's labor and radical movements—often in conflict with the state's Irish-American as well as native Protestant elites.

However, the Irish enjoyed a much larger share of wealth and power in California than elsewhere, producing conservative Republican politicians such as Ronald Reagan, as well as liberal Democrats such as Pat Brown and his son, Jerry Brown. For the Irish, California was a mecca of opportunity compared to Eastern states such as Massachusetts and Pennsylvania. For example, in 1855 James Dixon, from County Wexford, complained bitterly of the nativist prejudice which thwarted his ambitions in Philadelphia, but by the time he wrote his next surviving letter, from Marin County in 1868, he had become a prosperous cattle rancher and lumber baron.

Likewise, in the 1920s Hollywood offered young Tim O'Brien, the runaway son of an Irish policeman, the chance to realize all his boyhood dreams of riches and romance: "California is going to be my home," he wrote excitedly to his mother in Belfast. And although O'Brien's own fantasies of becoming a movie star turned to ashes, the screen success of other Irishmen and women, such as Brian Donleavy, from County Mayo, and the American-born Maureen O'Hara, glamorized the lure of California for the Irish and, indeed, for the whole nation.

A few years before the beginning of the Great Depression, a penniless young Irish immigrant named Patrick Dowling also decided that California was going to be his home. Without reiterating John Riordan's story of Pat's remarkable life, of his rise from "rags to riches," we can say that it was exceptionally fortunate for California, for the California Irish, and for his people's neglected history that Pat made that decision. The United Irish Cultural Center of San Francisco, its extensive Irish Library, and his two wonderful books stand as monuments to his love for both his adopted state and his native land. It was also very fortunate for me, personally, as from the time we first met, back in the mid-1970s, when I was a struggling graduate student at Berkeley, Pat taught me that history is much more than impersonal statistics and cold theories of social change. Rather, history, and especially Irish-American history, comprises the stories of individual human beings, with all their virtues and vices, humor and pathos, dreaming and struggling against the odds to better themselves and their communities—sometimes mistakenly or unsuccessfully, but nonetheless courageously.

These are the stories that Patrick Dowling relates in *Irish Californians: Historic, Benevolent, Romantic.* Like Pat himself, they are a tribute to his own people's past and an inspiration to all Californians in a period of renewed immigration to the Golden State.

—Kerby Miller, Professor of History, University of Missouri Author of *Emigrants and Exiles* (Oxford University Press, 1985), and *Out of Ireland,* a television program which has received world-wide acclaim.

INTRODUCTION

WOODROW WILSON, President of Princeton University, once wrote, "I would never read a book if it were possible for me to talk half an hour with the man who wrote it." But a renaissance man and a historian such as Patrick Dowling is not accessible to most of us.

Still, in reading this book we have the feeling that the author is talking directly to us, as though Patrick Dowling were sitting in the chair opposite us.

Mr. Dowling hit the mark he was aiming at: to present a clear and lucid book bringing to life the history of the Irish in California. This volume is much more than a book of facts—it is more useful than that. It is an integrated guide to the role and place of the Irish in the march of California history.

A hundred years ago the great California historian Hubert H. Bancroft, in his *History of the Pacific States*, assessed the pleasure given to the modern historian in using the tools of historiography to blend in, trace, and analyze the legends and stories and myths and poetry of a people. Surely it is a difficult but highly satisfying task and a rewarding one, as Mr. Dowling's work demonstrates.

Mr. Dowling embraces this challenge with vigor and enthusiasm. His relish for his job and successful and rewarding results are found in his pristine and engrossing *Irish Californians*. He brings his enormous resources—intellectualism, common sense and pesky inquisitiveness—to print. Mr. Dowling does well here. He has a knack of interviewing a formal historian with tools that are those of the oral story teller. The thin line separating storyteller from scholar has been straddled by the likes of Will Durant and Carl Sandburg. Now Patrick Dowling joins their ranks.

This is Patrick Dowling's second volume surveying the Irish in California. His first, *California: The Irish Dream*, is an appropriate companion to his new book. Each volume is self-contained and can be read in either order. And in no way are these two volumes provincial or isolated from the history of California and the nation. As a matter of fact, the reverse is true: they are part and parcel of the development and growth of California and the nation as a whole.

Irish Californians deals with a host of persons, some well known, some slightly known, and some virtually unknown, from Michael M. O'Shaughnessy and Supreme Court Justice Joseph McKenna to Senator John Barry Curtin, Thomas Sweeny, baseball hero Lefty O'Doul and a host of others. Mr. Dowling has been heard to complain that he has neither time nor space nor pencil and paper to write about all those justifying inclusion in a moderate size volume. He finds it is harder to exclude than to include.

He has selected well in the volume before us. He has tried to provide geographical equity, has striven for accurate analyses, and has given us stories of real people, not just the rich and heralded.

The English historian George Macaulay Trevelyan faced Mr. Dowling's dilemma while writing his classic English Social History. He asked: "How far can we know the real life of men in each successive age of the past when there is much in libraries, but not about the millions who forswore or never achieved fame. Or shall we be content that part of the loaf may be better than no bread."

In some cases Mr. Dowling had to weave an accurate fabric from scanty threads. Unfortunately, the sweet annals of the poor are often too short. But by careful research, including oral histories and many obscure sources, he has managed to bring to life many heretofore unknown contributors to the fascinating history of the state.

Here is included a healthy balance of Irish Californians: women, teachers, farmers, artists, politicians and athletes. The vastness and the fastnesses of the State, from the Mexican border to Eureka, are handled with the skills of a juggler. Mr. Dowling's books emphasize the Irish story, but not in an isolated and non-harmonious way. They blend in and march with the history of the United States and California, from pre-gold rush well into the 20th century.

Implicit in this study is what some call the "Dowling conundrum." This is the question of why the hundreds and thousands of Irish persons coming to California fared so much better than did those immigrating in the same numbers at about the same time to the Eastern seaboard of the United States.

Whether it was because the Irish came to an already extant Catholic tradition in Spanish California; whether California was a more tolerant and receptive land generally to immigrants; whether the lack of Puritan roots counted; whether land distribution and ownership were strongly influenced by the Roman Catholic Church—whatever the reasons, Mr. Dowling provides conclusive evidence that economic, political and social advancement was a virtual open door for the Irish in California.

Carlyle remarked once that he would first know the history and background of the writer/historian before judging the book at hand, since the author's life and experience shape the book.

Mr. Dowling's good judgment, scholarship, prudence, and wisdom were honed by his many experiences, occupations, and by the innumerable persons he has spoken to in his life. And Patrick Dowling is a good listener.

Patrick Dowling was born in Ireland March 12, 1904, on a farm in a county called Laois (then Queens County), in the shadow of the beautiful Slieve Bloom Mountains. He left to come to the New Ireland some seven decades ago.

In California he shared the experience of most Irish, working a host of jobs from laborer to retail merchant. He studied economics, saved his money, invested prudently, and became the owner of a substantial supermarket in San Francisco. After spending a quarter century in the retail food business, with long hours and quite often no days off, he decided it was time for a change.

After much consideration he chose the real estate business, which would allow him greater freedom and more time to spend with his growing family. He sold the supermarket, took a brief vacation and then became a real estate salesman for a local firm. Already well versed in selling, he found the new business very much to his liking. His financial investment was much less as were his worries.

Better yet, Mr. Dowling discovered that, according to the California real estate code, he was eligible for a real estate broker's license based on his years as a successful retail merchant (that law has since been changed). While working he took an evening course, passed the examination, and got his license.

Shortly thereafter Mr. Dowling opened an office on Market Street, the city's main thoroughfare, a short distance from his former retail enterprise. Little wonder then, that his first clients were Mr.. and Mrs. Martins, longtime customers of his supermarket nearby.

Customer loyalty was endemic to Mr. Dowling's enterprises, perhaps because he remembered and valued each one. "In 1936, when I opened for business as a food merchant, Mrs. Catherine Lowe, who is still hale and hearty, was my first customer."

Mr. Dowling's Horatio Alger-like personal history may have a lot of bearing on what he brings to his concept of history, but it doesn't make a historian. A real historian also needs compassion, intelligence, the ability to listen and to know what to retain, discard and develop in telling a story. Patrick Dowling has these qualities, and has combined them with years of study of historical literature. His home attests to his scholarship: his study is filled with both electronic equipment for research and writing, and with hundreds of first-edition tomes on Irish history dated back as far as the 18th century. It is the lair for a historian at ease with his work.

In step with Irish tradition Mr. Dowling devotes considerable time and energy to charitable and Irish activities. He was one of the founders and architects of the United Irish Cultural Center in San Francisco. This institution is a remarkable place: in the 1960s and 1970s most fraternal organizations in this country were in decline, but not so with the Center. It is a resource that has prospered and grown.

The crown jewel of the Center is the library, the son and heir of Patrick J. Dowling, if you will. In 1972 he set aside a lucrative real estate business to devote full time to the development and maintenance of an All-Irish Library and Archives, the first and only one of its kind in America. The energetic bibliophile traversed the American West in pursuit of books and artifacts, from San Diego to Seattle.

In the following year he traveled to Ireland with his daughter, Kathleen, on a similar mission. While there they set up collection depots where interested parties could deposit books, historic documents and family keepsakes for shipment to San Francisco. At the same time Patrick made arrangements with the proprietor of an Irish shipping firm whom he had befriended during a visit to San Francisco, and who was so taken with the idea that he offered to ship the collection free of charge.

The question remained where to house the collection during the construction of the Center. Mr. Dowling solved that problem by agreeing to store the prized collection at his home until the Center was completed. In the meantime he had the books catalogued under the supervision of Mary Green, a professional librarian .

When the day came, the collection was transported to its permanent home by a volunteer crew, with trucks and cars, and was reshelved in proper order, all within a period of forty-eight hours.

Innovative displays of local and international Irish history and lore are exhibited. There are current Irish periodicals and more than 3,000 volumes on Irish literature and history, all available to members, guests and especially college students engaged in research. The library is designed to be user-friendly and helpful to both the casual reader and the scholar.

For many years Dowling served as Library Director. To savor this monument is to know Dowling. A colleague of Patrick Dowling is the historian George Rush at the University of California, Berkeley, who has said of his friend, "Dowling has definitely done a service for the Irish community, and the Irish have made a contribution to our history. It is a shame historians have left a void in this area but heartening to know that he is filling that void."

From this volume the reader can learn and grow. But a warning is in order: do not begin this volume late at night, for it may be so engrossing that you will not put it down at a reasonable hour. Each chapter is self contained, crisply written, and each has Dowling's signature pleasant literary Irish lilt. My favorites are the chapters about Eleanor Martin and Dr. Hugh Toland, but all hold hidden treats for the reader.

As for Patrick Dowling, he can be encouraged to begin his third volume and add further to Irish scholarship and understanding. California State Senator Quentin Kopp best describes the author's work: "His study has the immense merit of being never dull. There is no contemporary historian who could not learn something from Dowling in the skill and art of interesting the reader."

—John Riordan, native San Franciscan

Executive Council member, Irish Historical Society
Past President, San Francisco Community
College Board

PROLOGUE

Here's to you, our brothers true,
 Who freedom's slogan crave,
The gallant bands in foreign lands,
 The Gaels beyond the waves.

Throughout the globe in every soil
 Where human foot hath trod,
You'll find the hardy sons of toil
 From the dear old verdant sod.

And 'neath the friendly Stars and Stripes
 That many times they died to save,
They're here and there and everywhere
 The Gaels beyond the wave.

So let's not forget the exiled ones,
 Our brothers stout and brave,
The gallant bands in foreign lands,
 The Gaels beyond the wave.

And away out west in the Golden Land
 Betwixt sun and moon and mirth,
The exiles found a land more fair
 Than anywhere else on earth.

On mountains high, in valleys fair,
 They sing and dance and rave;
They're here and there and everywhere,
 The Gaels beyond the wave.

True indeed, the Gaels are everywhere in America—and their influence on America, and on California in particular, is there for all to see.

The Irish were in the forefront of everything for the betterment of America; in peacetime from colonial days to the landing on the moon, and in wartime from Lexington and Concord to Viet Nam.

America is a nation of immigrants—men and women from every land came to these shores in search of freedom, opportunity and a better way of life. Each in turn gave of their time and talents for the good of all, and by working together, built the greatest nation in the history of mankind. In all of this mass assimilation of diverse cultures, the Irish were particularly noticeable because of their larger numbers. Little Ireland gave more of its people to America in proportion to its population than any other nation. They and their numerous offspring played a major role in the making of America.

French General Marques de Chastellaux, a leading historian who took an active part in the American War of Independence, had this to say about the Irish: "An Irishman, the moment he sets foot on American soil, is ipso facto an American. On more than one occasion Congress has owed its existence, and America possibly her preservation, to the fidelity and firmness of the Irish."

There is ample proof of his stirring words in the heroic part the Irish played in the American struggle for national independence. For example, 38% of George Washington's troops were Irish by birth or descent, a number that included fifteen hundred officers who served with distinction. In General Washington's Virginia Regiment alone, the records list Timothy Conway, Mathew Doran, Patrick Galoway, David Gorman, William Hogan, Robert Murphy, William McAnulty, Denis McCarthy and Nathaniel Barrett. At that same time, 89 enlisted men in Washington's Virginia command gave Ireland as their Birthplace.

WHEN George Washington took over as Commander of the Revolutionary Army, the following Irish officers became his most trusted leaders: John Sullivan, his Aide de Camp, who countersigned Washington's orders as need be; Richard Montgomery, who led commanded the Canadian campaign until he lost his life at Montreal; General Stephen Moylan from County Cork, secretary to the Commander-in-Chief and commander of the Virginia Cavalry; John Shee from County Meath, commander of the famed Pennsylvania Line; and Brigadier General Richard Butler, a Dubliner. Among other Irish leaders of note were Secretary of War James McHenry, from County Antrim; Major General Edward Hand, County Offaly; Commander of the Western Frontier, William Irvine, County Fermanagh; a leader in the Monmouth, New Jersey, campaign and the "Father of the American Navy," Commodore John Barry of County Wexford.

The Irish took part in many of the major engagements during the war; at Lexington, Concord and Bunker Hill, at King's Mountain, North Carolina, and Lookout Mountain in Tennessee.

In Savannah, Georgia, there stands a massive monument erected to the memory of a courageous Irish-American, Sergeant William Jasper, who lost his life in the defense of that city, and died a patriot's death embracing the regimental banner.

The Irish were at Valley Forge in 1775, where they were given time off to celebrate St. Patrick's Day. General Washington took the occasion to make "St. Patrick" the password for that day.

At Yorktown, one can well imagine the jubilation in the Irish ranks when the British Commander, General Cornwallis, surrendered, and the Union Jack bit the dust on American soil. In that moment of victory, not only did American history change course, but currents were set in motion with consequences for the rest of the world.

The truth is that Yorktown was life or death for George Washington and the forces under his command. Had the rebels lost, there would have been little future and no freedom for those who bore muskets, particularly the Irish. In all likelihood, General Washington would have suffered the fate of Robert Emmet, who paid with his life on the scaffold.

THE IRISH played an equally meritorious role in the building and development of the nation, which was at a standstill during the protracted conflict. The early canals, linking river to river and lake to lake, forming the nation's first transportation system; the first railways, reaching places the barges could not reach and at a greater speed; the mills, foundries and factories providing work for willing hands; the roads and bridges, the whole infrastructure of a nation coming together; the schools and churches dotting the landscape in generous measure, all became monuments to Irish ingenuity and determination.

Countless Irish laborers worked their hearts out on road construction, which culminated in the building of a National Road, the brainchild of George Washington himself.

Over the years President Washington developed a fondness for the Irish, some of whom were among his most trusted associates, like Hercules Mooney, a little known tailor, who on one occasion saved Washington from being captured by the British. Washington gave vent to his feelings, by becoming a member of the Friendly Sons of Saint Patrick in Philadelphia. His letter of acceptance reads as follows:

> George Campbell Esq..
> President of the Society of
> the Friendly Sons of Saint Patrick
> in the City of Philadelphia.

Sir;

I accept with singular pleasure the Ensign of so worthy a fraternity as that of the Sons of Saint Patrick in this city, a Society distinguished for the firm adherence of its Members to the glorious cause in which we are embarked. Give me leave to assure you, Sir, that I shall never cast my eyes on the Badge with which I am honored, but with a grateful remembrance of the polite and affectionate manner in which it was presented.

I am with respect and esteem, Sir,

> —Your most obedient servant, G. Washington

Perhaps nothing before or since has so pleased the Irish! In Irish lore, two of the greatest men who ever lived were St. Patrick and George Washington, the former in legend, who drove the snakes out of Ireland, and the later in fact, who drove the British out of America.

ONE OF THE most fascinating chapters in American history is that of the wandering Irish schoolmasters who taught the children of the colonists all the way from Maine to the Carolinas. Those learned men were the victims of the Penal Laws enacted in Ireland in 1695, a diabolical scheme to bring the Gaelic Irish under subjugation, quench the lamp of learning and keep the Irish children in darkness and ignorance.

A reward was placed upon the head of any schoolmaster found guilty of practicing his profession. Guilt brought quick passage by convict ship to the West Indies or to American plantations as indentured servants, slaves in all but name.

Good fortune for them and for their adopted land brought the largest number to the shores of America, there to set history's courage. Ireland's loss was America's gain, for they were men possessed of a good education, with the ability to impart it. In fact it was Irish schoolmasters who imbued the children of the colonists with the understanding and appreciation of the blessings of liberty and independence.

In their young charges they instilled a spirit of resistance to tyranny, as when the Old World laid claim to America again in the war of 1812. As for their distaste for everything British, Yankee philosopher Alex Graydon wrote, "As to the genuine sons of Hibernia, it was enough for them to know that England was the antagonist."

In a period of pride in new-found liberty and contempt for any who would attempt to take it away, American freedom had no more resolute proponents than the Irish schoolmasters of the time. In New Hampshire John Sullivan put aside his books to reenlist in the Army. He was of a breed with Margaret Healy from County Cork, who took up teaching in Cambridge, Massachusetts, in 1680, and Maurice Lynch, from County Limerick, another schoolroom pioneer. In New York City, James McGrath began teaching in 1748 and Thomas Flynn in 1774 on Cortland Street.

In New Jersey those stalwarts of learning and liberty included Timothy Murphy and Charles Kelly. In Philadelphia, Mary McAllister established the first school for girls in 1767. Out in Columbia Ohio, John Reilly from County Cavan established what was called "the first school in the American settlement on the Ohio" in 1690. To Pennsylvania's city of Chester, from Letterkenny in County Donegal, came the renowned Doctor Francis Allison, who went on to become president of the College of Philadelphia, now the University of Pennsylvania.

Down In Charleston, South Carolina, three classic Irish schoolmasters, Felix O'Hanlon, John Dillon and Daniel Shanley left their imprint on the youth of the Palmetto state.

SOME OF America's noblest and best came under the spell of Irish schoolmasters. Daniel Webster, the famous statesman and orator, was taught by Edward Evans of County Sligo, a school teacher in Northfield, New Hampshire. Alexander Hamilton, America's outstanding political genius, was brought up under the care of Dr. Hugh Knox from County Armagh at his school in the Island of St Croix. Hamilton later studied medicine in New York under the tutorship of Dr. Samuel Clossey, an Irish teacher and physician. John Randolph of Roanoke, acclaimed as "Virginia's wisest statesman, truest patriot and most devoted son," stated that he was educated by Master William Cochran at the Columbia College in New York in 1784. Cochran, a native of Tyrone, Ireland, was said to be a highly accomplished and elegant scholar.

To every student of American history the signature of John Hancock stands immortal on the Declaration of Independence, but few are aware that he acquired his classical education and unique penmanship from an Irish schoolmaster named Peter McLouth, who taught at Quincy, Massachusetts.

And in Old Kentucky who can speak of the wandering Irish schoolmasters with such verve as one of the state's very own, Irwin S. Cobb, a legend himself for his way with words. "The children of the pioneers of Kentucky, almost without exception, learned their first lessons in log cabins, under the teachings of that strange but gifted race of men, the wandering Irish schoolmasters who founded the old field schools of the south, and to whom the south is largely indebted for the seeds of its culture.

Last but scarcely least, a youngster named Abraham Lincoln and his sister learned their first lessons at Riney's School in Hodgenville, Kentucky. Master Riney, an Irish Catholic, was extremely popular with his students. The great President in later years spoke of him in terms of appreciation and respect.

NOT ONLY Irishmen but Irishwomen as well made great contributions to the land of their adoption. Before the American Civil War there were no trained nurses, and consequently neither the North nor the South was prepared to cope with the casualties of war. In desperation the government authorities, at the urging of President Abraham Lincoln, turned to the Catholic Sisterhoods for nurses. The good Sisters agreed to serve whenever and wherever needed.

All told, 572 intrepid, compassionate religious women cared for the sick and wounded on the battlefield while the bullets flew all around them. They served in makeshift hospitals, in huts, and on boats carrying men with torn bodies and missing limbs, screaming out with pain. No ordinary women could have nursed the sick, the wounded and the dying as they did, but one amongst them did stand out. She was the black-capped, five-foot-two-inch, little slip of a nun, Sister Anthony O'Connell, whom the men in grey and the men in blue alike called the "Angel of the Battlefield."

Sister Anthony (Mary O'Connell) was born in the townland of Loughgur, in County Limerick, on August 15, 1814. Following the death of her mother she was brought to America and placed in the care of Ursuline Sisters at Charlestown, Massachusetts. At the age of twenty she entered the Sisters of Charity in Emmitsburg, Maryland, where she made her novitiate. She was sent to Cincinnati, where she arrived on March 3, 1837. Immediately she began helping the sisters take care of the orphans of the city.

When Archbishop Purcell established an orphanage for boys in nearby Cumminsville in 1852, Sister Anthony was placed in charge. In 1855, when the Orphanage was taken over by Saint John's Hospital for the care of invalids, Sister Anthony was appointed procuratrix of her community, a position she held until the outbreak of the Civil War. (St. John's infirmary was in a building which Harriet Beecher Stowe previously used as a private school.)

At war's outbreak the Sisters of Charity not only offered their services as nurses, they turned over their beloved St. John's to the authorities for use as a hospital for the care of the sick and the wounded. In effect it became an Army base hospital, harboring men from several fighting fronts. In the meantime Sister Anthony and her companions served on the grim battlefields of Cumberland, Murfreesboro, Shiloh, Harper's Ferry, Richmond, Nashville and Winchester. They tended wounded soldiers who were being transported from Shiloh along the Ohio River to Cincinnati for more extensive care by the Sisters of Charity at St. John's Hospital. Sister Anthony and her band also accompanied the wounded who were being transported on rail flat cars, all the way from Cumberland to Washington D.C., for treatment and rehabilitation.

"I was rather ugly," Sister Anthony once said of herself. By ordinary standards that may have been true enough; her sallow face was haggard and streaked with weariness as a result of the long hours she worked without relief. Despite her appearance, the sick and the lonely saw only kindness in her deep-set Irish eyes and ready smile. Some whispered shyly to her, "You remind me of my dear mother! You're beautiful." Her goodness was contagious, spreading among Protestant and Catholic alike. In her works of charity she knew no country, no religion, no race or color.

A T THE CLOSE of the Civil War, when the government offered the well equipped hospital for sale, two Protestant gentlemen, Joseph Butler and Lewis Worthington, deeply impressed with the Sisters' work, purchased the property outright, and deeded it forthwith to Sister Anthony. Butler suggested the name "Good Samaritan," and so it has been called ever since. Sister Anthony retired to the motherhouse in 1880 and there celebrated her Golden Jubilee in 1885. She visited the Good Samaritan Hospital frequently, making her last gift to the suffering. She was called to her eternal reward on December 8, 1897.

At her requiem Mass spacious St. Peter's Cathedral was filled, with hundreds crowding the aisles and hundreds more unable to gain admission standing shoulder to shoulder on the broad stone steps and everywhere about to bid farewell to one of the Church's heroic daughters.

A S WE HAVE SEEN, the Irish in America helped plant the "Tree of State" and often nourished it with their blood. It was not until they settled in the Golden Land of California, however, that they could rest beneath its shade, and reach up and pick the fruit thereof.

It is time now to pause and reflect on the deeper meaning of the historic contribution of Irishmen and Irishwomen to America, California and our local communities. In fact, the Irish influence on California history was so powerful that we might appropriately call California the "New Ireland," a state with the largest Irish population in the United States, numbering nearly four million. This book hopes to pay tribute to the large tribe of Erin's sons and daughters who have left us a colorful and patriotic legacy.

One might say, being Irish is a mixed blessing. We're a most peculiar people. There's a tremendous variety among the Irish; we include saints as well as sinners, tycoons and paupers, the learned and the wacky. Those qualities most of us have in common are being colorful and outspoken, in having an abiding love of liberty, a lively imagination and most certainly a way with words.

One Irish-American, Bishop Fulton Sheen, a man of profound and poignant words, some years ago trotted out three psychologically essential traits to define the Irish: love of a fight, humor, and blarney.

Sheen said, "The difference between blarney and baloney: blarney is the varnished truth, while baloney is the unvarnished lie. Blarney is flattery laid on so thin that you love it. Baloney is flattery laid on so thick that you hate it."

Put it this way: if you tell a women who is in fact forty, "You look sixteen," that's baloney. In Irish blarney it would be, "Tell me how old you are—I want to know at what age women are most beautiful."

The other two traits also help define the Irish. Irish love a fray, as in the "Fighting Irish." It's said that humor on the other hand, is what helped the Irish survive the "dark and evil days," when the early Gaels were at the mercy of the marauding Saxon hordes.

We Irish have a "never say die" attitude, along with a sense of humor that sees laughter through the tears of suffering. In truth, these Irish traits are universal to humanity, among the noblest characteristics of the human spirit.

We can throw in a fourth mark of the Irish: we are the dreamers of dreams and seekers of the proverbial pot of gold at the end of the rainbow, romantic Celts ever wandering in search of life's fulfillment.

And so it was on the western frontier of California that countless Irish realized their hopes and dreams in every field of endeavor. Take politics as an example. The venerable politico Sean T. O'Kelly, President of the Irish Republic, once piously declared: "Politics is man's most noble profession." If we are to take O'Kelly at his word, there must have been quite a roster of "Irish Noblemen" on the California scene.

One ambitious Irish-American, David Broderick, was so frustrated in his many attempts to gain a foothold in New York City that he quit his home turf and departed for California in 1849. Already well-versed in politics, Broderick quickly identified with the more politically ambitious Irish and won election to the state senate the following year. He made such an impression on his colleagues that he was elected president of the senate the very next year, in 1851. In 1857, barely eight years after his arrival in the Golden State, Broderick ran for the position of United States Senator, representing his adopted state and was swept into office.

David Broderick's political acumen paved the way for other aspiring Irish political figures like John Downey from County Roscommon who became the first Irish-born Governor of California and indeed the first Irish-born Governor of any state in the Union. John Conness of County Galway served for six years as a United States Senator and became one of the most renowned legislators on the national scene as President Abraham Lincoln's right hand man and Eugene Casserly from County Westmeath took the seat of the retiring Senator Conness.

THE CHAIN of political leadership remained in Irish hands for a period of twenty two years, from Broderick's election in 1851 through Conness' six-year term, until Eugene Casserly's early retirement in 1873. California owes a dept of acknowledgment at least to these Irishmen who served their adopted state with dignity and honor during its earliest years. They proved their loyalty and fidelity to the United States by holding California firm to the Union during the divisive years of the American Civil War.

Despite all that has been written and widely debated about the Civil War, California's decisive contribution to that conflict has not garnered the general attention of American historians. In point of fact, when California sided with the Union it helped turn the tide of battle in favor of Abraham Lincoln's hard pressed Northern Army, for that show of support came at a time when there were thirteen free states and an equal number of slave states. Moreover, the infusion of California gold into the Union coffers helped bolster a near worthless currency and provided the funds to prosecute the war.

As the saying goes, "An army fights on its stomach." It was true then and still is...ask any man who ever wore an army uniform. California gold had more to do with winning the Civil War than most American are aware of.

IT WAS A HANDFUL of scholarly Irishmen who formulated the State Constitution, adopted at the first State Convention held at Monterey in 1849. Men like Philip Augustus Roach from Fermoy, County Cork, who by all accounts was the right man in the right place at the right time. He was a scholarly young man who was well grounded in American policy and values. He served as U.S. Vice Consul at La Harve in France and as Consul at Lisbon, Portugal. During his stay in Europe he became fluent in French, Spanish and Portuguese. In Monterey, Roach was the only person at the convention who could conduct the proceedings in both English and Spanish.

William Shannon from Ballina, County Mayo, was chairman of the all-important rules committee. In light of the slavery question that was foremost in delegates' minds, his responsibility seemed almost providential. Among other things, Shannon's powerful oratory helped persuade the delegates to bar human slavery from the Pacific region.

John Ross Browne came from Dublin. His father was editor of an Irish Journal, the Dublin Comet. For his outspoken criticism the elder Browne was arrested and imprisoned and had his holdings confiscated. In sheer desperation son John set out for America with his wife and family and settled in Louisville, Kentucky. Brilliant like his father, he completed his education in that city and found employment as a roving reporter for a Louisville newspaper. His next move was to Washington D.C. where he received an appointment as Senate reporter. The experience proved advantageous when he came to California as a government revenue agent for the Pacific Coast Region in 1849.

Barely settled into his new job he won a plum from the newly-elected President Zachary Taylor. He was named Postal Inspector for the San Francisco district which embraced the old Spanish colonial capital of Monterey. By sheer coincidence he arrived in Monterey just as the first State Constitutional Convention got underway. He was singled out shortly thereafter by Robert Semple, president-elect of the convention, to record the historic proceedings. Had it not been for the scholarly Dubliner, John Ross Browne, the story of California's beginnings under American rule would have gone unrecorded.

IN A LIGHTER VEIN, we can salute the many Irish showmen and entertainers who brought joy to California, the nation and the world. There have been thousands and thousands over the years, but perhaps the following represent the best: crooner Bing Crosby; funny man Fred Allen; curmudgeon Barry Fitzgerald, film actor Pat O'Brien "with the wind at his back;" Helen Hayes, of stage and screen fame; dapper little Mickey Rooney; Maureen O'Sullivan, from the woodlands of County Roscommon; singer Dennis Day; fiery Maureen O'Hara; gentleman Gregory Peck; and the showman supreme, Ronald Reagan.

ALTHOUGH a sizable number of Irish politicians held important positions statewide, San Francisco was the epitome of Irish political power. The election of Irish-born Frank McCoppin as Mayor of San Francisco in 1867 rolled out the Kelly Green carpet on which the Irish marched to the power that lasted for well over a century. As late as 1967 the heads of every department in City Hall were Irish by birth or descent, and their names read like a litany of Irish Saints:

Mayor	John Shelley
City Attorney	Tom O'Connor
Assessor	Joseph Tinney
Treasurer	Tom Scanlon
Controller	John Farrell
District Attorney	Thomas Lynch
City Planning	James Kearney
Civil Service	William Fitzpatrick
Sheriff	Mathew Carberry
Police Chief	Thomas Cahill
Fire Chief	William Murray

Board of Supervisors: James Halley, Francis McCarthy, Joseph Casey, John Ferdon, Leo McCarthy, Clarissa McMahon, and J. Eugene McAteer.

The roster of Irish judges is equally impressive: Frank Shaw, (my good neighbor and longtime friend, proud of his Irish heritage), Melvin Cronin, Raymond O'Connor, Edward O'Dea, Francis McCarty, William Mullins, Daniel O'Hanlon, Lucy Kelly McCabe, Eugene Lynch, Timothy Reardon.

NOT EVERY IRISHMAN in San Francisco had a halo around his head. Believe it or not, politics had its Irish rascals. Case in point: Christopher Augustine Buckley, better known as "Blind Boss Buckley," who through graft wielded enormous power in the Democratic Party for a decade or more. The colorful politico caught the attention of Rudyard Kipling, who said of him: "Today the City of San Francisco is governed by the Irish vote under the rule of a gentleman whose sight is impaired, and who requires a man to lead him about the streets. He is officially called Boss Buckley and unofficially, the Blind White Devil." There was also a visiting English journalist at the time who eulogized Buckley in his novel, "The Wrecker." Buckley apparently relished this notoriety, however uncomplimentary: "Politics is not a branch of the Sunday School business," he noted. Buckley himself never sought public office, yet he held more power longer than any of his Democratic peers.

Irish-Californians were the first national group in America to form their own political party, appropriately called "The Workingman's Party." It was founded by the Blind Boss in one of his better moments, with the help of an Irish-born rabble-rouser named Denis Kearney. A self-made Irish activist, Kearney earned his spurs in the byways and sandlots of the city's Mission District. There he proclaimed the "rights of working men" while perched atop an Irish teamster's flatbed dray. Kearney was at his best, however, high atop Nob Hill (which he called Snob Hill), where he fearlessly confronted the establishment on their own turf.

In that light, one can say, San Francisco hasn't changed very much. It's still the place where anybody can proclaim a cause and find others to cheer him on.

IRISH SUCCESSES in politics were matched by their achievements in every field of endeavor, from building and banking to merchandising, education, sports and entertainment. In construction, it may be said that San Francisco is the only major world city that was both planned and built, for the most part, by the Irish (Dublin was built by the Danes). Few, however, are aware that "America's favorite city" owes its charm and singularity to Irish architects, engineers and craftsmen, like Irish-born Jaspar O'Farrell, who laid out a street plan unique among American cities. The Mahoneys, the Cahills and other Irish built it, the Phelans, the Tobins and the Sullivans financed it. The world-famous Palace Hotel, the Phelan building, the Hibernia Bank, the Flood Building, the Bank of California and Saint Mary's Hospital all were built by the indomitable Mahoney Brothers, and all are monuments to Irish talent and hard work.

Building was in the blood of the Irish in San Francisco. In the 1970s there were enough successful Irishmen in the construction industry to build the contemporary United Irish Cultural Center by donating their time, energy and talents. A visit to the center has its rewards, chief among them being a pint of Guinness which will cure all your ills, momentary and otherwise, and can be had without a doctor's prescription. For sure it can bring out talents unbeknown to the quaffer until that moment.

LIKE THE LEGENDARY Irish schoolmasters who taught the children of the early American colonists, the Irish were also the first teachers in California. Patrick O'Brien led the way, teaching in the first public schoolhouse in the state, established by Martin Murphy at his ranch near Sacramento in the 1840s. The Murphy children were among the first pupils when the school opened. O'Brien was housed, fed and paid by Murphy, who was already a man of considerable wealth and influence as a result his investment in California land. All went well at the new schoolhouse until the arrival of General William Tecumseh Sherman, who arrested O'Brien as a supposed army deserter. On learning that O'Brien was the only qualified teacher in that part of the country, Sherman released the Irishman forthwith and sent him on his way. O'Brien made his way back to the Murphy farmhouse the following day and nonchalantly took up where he had left off.

Among the first teachers in San Francisco were the Sisters of the Presentation, who arrived in early 1854. Their first schoolhouse was located on Powell Street in North Beach. Among their pupils were a number of Italian and Hispanic youngsters. Neither they nor their parents could converse in English. So the good sisters, in addition to their regular assignments, took on the added role of teaching the children to speak English. As a consequence, young Latins went about the city speaking English with an Irish Brogue.

THE COMMUNITY of Irish farmers in old San Francisco was so huge and so successful that they founded their own organization, the "Crispin Guards." A partial list of the fraternity included Twomey & Sons, O'Dea, Tierney, Casey, Healy, Doran, Foley, Ford, McCarthy, McDevitt, Cronin and Cummins. They were said to be one of most colorful groups of marchers in the St. Patrick's Day Parade, with their flamboyant Sergeant of Police, Pat McGee, leading the way. Arrayed in Green and Gold and sporting the tools of their trade, they wooed the spectators along the line of march with their antics, clapping to the clang of cymbals and the beating of drums. An alert San Francisco reporter said they were "Noisy enough to make Old John Bull tremble in his hob-nailed boots."

Incidentally, with horses an absolute necessity for everyone at the time, the Irish also predominated in horse-shoeing, a highly lucrative trade in pioneer days.

As I work with the publisher on the final stages of this book, I am deeply grateful to be thriving well into my 94th year, and to have contributed in some small way to the history of the Irish in this glorious city, in the wonderful state of California, in the greatest nation in the world.

—Patrick J. Dowling
San Francisco, 1998

Philip Crosthwaite
Courtesy San Diego Historical Society

— I —

Irish Pioneers in San Diego

In 1915 John Steven McGroarty wrote "The place of San Diego de Alcala, the Harbor of the Sun, is the Place of First Things, where California began." He went on to say that "San Diego lures the wanderer and the traveler from every land, as well by the charm of her wondrous beauty and her gateway to opportunity as by the glamour and fascination of a past rich in romance as a lover's dream." And so the story of Irish pioneers in California begins at the Harbor of the Sun.

The men and women of Irish heritage came to San Diego not because of her romantic past, which they probably had no knowledge of, nor by the lure of gold, for there weren't any gold deposits like those of Northern California, but for opportunity and adventure, fortune, farmland, avoidance of military service, or some other reasons that perhaps they themselves could not put into words. A number of them dwelt here for only a short time and moved on. But others stayed and devoted their lives to the building and enriching of life in the little pueblo glistening in the Harbor of the Sun. There was one Irish pioneer in particular, the first one to settle in San Diego, whose life and work would be inextricably intertwined not only with San Diego itself but also with the lives of Irish settlers who came after him. Ironically, this pioneer came to San Diego not by design but by mistake, and he ended up staying because of a flip of a coin.

Philip Crosthwaite, 1825 - 1903

The Irishman in question was Philip Crosthwaite, whose parents, Edward and Rachel Crosthwaite from County Kildare, immigrated to America in the early 1800's. In 1825 they returned to Ireland to visit their relatives in the legendary town of Athy, near the Currah of Kildare. During their stay Rachel gave birth to Philip on

December 27, 1825. When the Crosthwaites decided to return to the United States they left young Philip with his grandparents in Athy for the time being. In 1841, at the age of sixteen, Philip came to America to live with his parents in Ohio. Following a two-year stay he returned to Ireland to continue his education at Trinity College in Dublin. During his second year at Trinity his grandmother died, and Philip decided to return once again to the United States.

While making his way through Philadelphia in the spring of 1844, Philip Crosthwaite struck up an acquaintance with Richard Rhead, who convinced Crosthwaite that they could make good money fishing off the Newfoundland Banks. He agreed to the plan, and the two men set out for Newport, Rhode Island, where they joined the crew of the *Hopewell.* However, when the ship set sail on August 1, 1844, they discovered that it was bound for San Francisco. They informed the ship's captain of their plight; and in order to make amends, he promised the two men that he would allow them to board the first ship they met headed for an American port. Unfortunately they never met any other ships, and so Crosthwaite and Rhead were stuck on the *Hopewell* on the long voyage around Cape Horn to its destination in San Francisco. When the ship arrived in the Pacific Ocean the crew set out on a whale hunt and were successful in capturing eight whales. In mid-October 1845, the *Hopewell* docked in San Diego, which was under Mexican rule at the time, for supplies. In the meantime Crosthwaite saw a chance of getting back to the United States. While the whaler was anchored he, Rhead and six other crewmen jumped ship and hid out in the Mexican pueblo until the *Hopewell* set sail again.

A few weeks later an American ship came to San Diego for supplies before embarking on its return voyage to New England. Crosthwaite and Rhead asked the captain about joining his crew, but unfortunately there was only one berth available on the ship. The two men flipped a coin to see who would get that berth, and Rhead won the toss. Philip Crosthwaite was now on his own, stranded in the little Mexican pueblo of San Diego and forced to await another ship bound for any port in the United States.

From *Hopewell* to Hopelessness

To support himself in the meantime he worked bringing supplies to nearby Mexican ranches. Weeks turned into months, and he despaired of ever returning to the United States or to his own dear native land. In the spring of 1846 he got a job hunting sea otters, earning the equivalent of $40 a pelt. For the next eight months Crosthwaite and a number of other men lived in canoes while they hunted the elusive otter in the kelp beds. In October they came ashore in Baja (lower) California, where they met Pio Pico, the governor of Alta (upper) California. Pico informed them that Mexico and the United States were at war and that he was fleeing to escape capture. Taking the news as a warning, they decided to abandon the otter hunt and return to San Diego.

The men reached San Diego late at night, sometime in early November, and being so tired from their journey went right to bed. It was like the old adage, "out of the frying pan into the fire." Early the next morning they were awakened by Captain Archibald Gillespie, of the United States army, who told Crosthwaite and his companions, "There can be no neutrals in this country; you must enlist for three months or be imprisoned." Crosthwaite and his companions readily enlisted.

Things had changed dramatically in Southern California while the men were away in the Pacific hunting otters. On July 29, 1846, the American forces seized San Diego and from there marched northwards to Los Angeles, which they captured on August 15, where Captain Gillespie was appointed commander of that pueblo. However Gillespie and his troops apparently mistreated the citizens of Los Angeles, and the Californians rose up and drove the Americans out.

Gillespie was obliged to return to San Diego and seek recruits to retake Los Angeles. Shortly thereafter the Army command learned that Andres Pico, (Governor Pico's brother), with a force of fifty men, was encamped some thirty miles away. Captain Gillespie's force set out to engage the Mexicans in battle. On their way they encountered two deserters from Pico's camp, who informed them that his command now numbered over one hundred men. Soon thereafter another man rode up and said that Brigadier General Stephen Kearny, with a hundred dragoons, had arrived from Santa Fe, New Mexico, and needed an escort to San Diego. With that, Gillespie and his men changed direction and set out in haste to meet Kearny.

The Battle of San Pasqual

AFTER MAKING contact with Kearny's Army of the West, Gillespie informed the General that Pico's men were camped nearby at San Pasqual. The Americans joined forces and prepared to make a surprise attack. In the early morning hours of December 6, 1846, the

American troops, with Gillespie's men on the left flank, moved on Pico's camp. Unfortunately the dragoons made so much noise that the element of surprise was lost. All of this, in addition to misunderstood commands, led to confusion within the American ranks and provided the Californians time to get ready for the assault. At that same moment other Californians were hiding behind rocks and ambushed Crosthwaite and others from the flank and rear.

Trying to fire effectively from horseback was impossible, and the dragoons' short swords were no match for the Californians' lances. Some of Pico's men recognized Captain Gillespie and went after him, stabbing him several times and leaving him on the field for dead. He later recovered from his wounds and was able to drag himself to safety. Crosthwaite managed to come through the skirmish unscathed. He even took one of Pico's men prisoner. The battle of San Pasqual, Mexico's only victory during the war, was a brief affair, but a costly one for the Americans, who lost eighteen men. The grim task of gathering the dead and wounded for the return march to San Diego fell to the lot of Crosthwaite and his companions. Because Pico's men harassed the Americans as they tried to leave the area, progress was slow. Kearny and his weary troops were forced to camp a short distance from San Pasqual with little food and water. He sent Kit Carson, who had accompanied Kearny's Army of the West from New Mexico, to get help. Finally, at 4 a.m. on December 12, Carson, with 180 sailors from San Diego, arrived in time to rescue Kearny and his men.

With the debacle of San Pasqual over, the American forces returned to San Diego for rest and rehabilitation. While there, General Kearny reorganized his command and marched on Los Angeles, which, with the help of Major John Fremont they retook on January 13, 1847. Crosthwaite, however, was not involved in this takeover. Instead he was a part of a regiment assigned to protect San Diego, where his principal duty was guarding the Army's livestock.

Although California was under martial law, the military authorities decided that the territory should continue to be governed according to Mexican law. New elections were held in San Diego for the offices of first and second alcalde; the successful candidates, respectively, were Captain Henry (Delano) Fitch (a distant ancestor of President Franklin Delano Roosevelt), and the pragmatic Irishman, Philip Crosthwaite. These two men were now the highest civilian officials in San Diego.

Crosthwaite's post as second alcalde was similar to that of sheriff.

His responsibilities included looking after public safety, maintaining peace, and enforcing the branding regulations of cattle. He held this important office throughout the year 1847.

Crosthwaite Takes a Bride

THE FOLLOWING YEAR, on June 10, 1848, Crosthwaite married a fourteen-year-old senorita, Maria Josefa Lopez, and from that day forward played a leading role in the future development of the Gateway City. A month after his marriage he signed a lease for Mission San Diego de Alcala. Besides the Mission property, the deal included 53 cattle, 44 goats, 42 horses, 33 sheep, and 13 asses. Although most of the buildings were in decay, the one wing, where the brown-robed Franciscans lived, was still in good condition, and it was in these rooms that the newlyweds set up house in that memorable year, on August 6, 1848.

Meanwhile, there was tremendous excitement elsewhere in the state following the discovery of gold in Northern California in January 1848. Soon tall tales of vast fortunes made their way southward. Crosthwaite was not immune to these catchy stories; in late 1848 he turned his mission property over to his father-in-law and set sail for San Francisco. Although he was lucky enough to find a small amount of gold in the diggings, Philip became disillusioned and returned home to San Diego on August 24, 1849. Shortly after his return he learned that the United States, led by Major Samuel Heintzelman, had taken possession of Mission San Diego to garrison their troops, in spite of the fact that Crosthwaite's lease still had two years to go. As a result he and his wife were forced to sell their livestock and move in with her father.

The following year California was caught up in a period of tremendous change politically and financially. In the hectic year of 1849, the state sought admission into the United States, and by October 13 a State Constitution had been drafted and ratified. The constitution called for elections for public offices to be held throughout the state, with one in San Diego scheduled for April 1, 1850. Because of his experience as second alcalde, Philip decided to run for sheriff. He lost the election by a landslide, 107 to 45 votes. As luck would have it, the man who had been elected, unopposed, for county treasurer had a change of heart and made it known that he did not want the post. And so the newly elected city council, meeting in session, picked their favorite hometown boy, Philip Crosthwaite, to be San Diego's first county treasurer.

As treasurer Crosthwaite was required by law to appear in person at the state capital to pay the money due the treasury. The state reimbursed him for his travel expense. The transaction turned out to be a windfall for Crosthwaite, as the taxes from San Diego that first year amounted only to $200, while Crosthwaite's expenses were $300, so he came home with more money than he left with. Such an arrangement was too good too last; the next year the law was changed, allowing taxes to be mailed to the state treasury.

Four months after the elections one council member resigned his seat, and in a special election held shortly thereafter, Philip Crosthwaite won the vacant post. The following year, 1851, he was appointed deputy county clerk, and, because of his command of the Spanish language, he also served the new government as an interpreter. Crosthwaite was well on his way to becoming one of the most important figures in the life and times of Southern California, only six very eventful years since his arrival in San Diego.

An Indian Uprising

A CONFLICT AROSE with the local Indians when the sheriff, who was also the tax collector, notified the tribes that their livestock would be taxed. One group, under the leadership of Antonio Garra, was vehement in refusing to pay any taxes and encouraged other tribes to oppose the measure. The conflict became so heated that the white settlers feared an Indian attack at any moment. On November 11, 1851, several sheep herders were attacked at night near Fort Yuma. Eleven days later, a group of invalids bathing in the hot springs at John Warner's ranch were murdered. The next day Warner's ranch was burned to the ground.

To put an end to the uprising the men of San Diego formed a volunteer company, the "Fitzgerald Volunteers." Crosthwaite joined the company as "third sergeant." His first assignment was to take a detachment of men and ride into the back country to pick up a herd of horses that had been offered to the volunteers.

On November 27 the Fitzgerald posse left San Diego and cautiously made their way eastward until they reached Warner's ranch five days later. From there they went to a nearby Indian village, and finding it abandoned, set it on fire. The men then returned to San Diego to await further developments.

On their way back home the volunteers learned that William Marshall, who was considered one of the powers behind the uprising, was camped in the area; they took a detour to capture him. Ironically,

Marshall had been on the same ship that brought Crosthwaite to California in 1845. Marshall had also jumped ship. He ended up marrying an Indian woman, and took a job working on Warner's ranch.

When the posse reached San Diego a court-martial was set up to try Marshall for his supposed part in fostering the uprising. During this trying episode, Crosthwaite showed friendship toward the accused man. After being tried and sentenced to death, Marshall asked one of the Fathers at Mission San Diego to be baptized in the Catholic faith, and Crosthwaite came forward to be his godfather. He even accompanied Marshall to the gallows on the day of his execution. These gestures of Philip Crosthwaite's kindness were truly courageous in light of the fact that Marshall was one the most hated men in the Southland.

A short time later another hated man, Antonio Garra, was captured by an Indian who was friendly to Californians. Garra was turned over to the military authorities in San Diego, where he was court-martialed and executed by a firing squad. This put an end to the Garra uprising, which was followed by a period of peace and reconciliation.

A Man for All Seasons and Community Projects

WHEN THINGS settled down in San Diego Crosthwaite continued wholeheartedly in the service of his adopted community. When his term as county treasurer ended he took over in a dual capacity as county clerk and recorder. On August 24, 1852, he even recorded a deed to himself for a lot he bought adjacent to the old Plaza in San Diego; the property included a house and one outbuilding. This enabled him to move his family out of his father-in-law's home and into one of their own. With the help of his father-in-law he began to acquire a herd of cattle, which helped supplement his meager income from the public sector. In due course he opened a grocery store and butcher shop, with the meat coming from his own herd. At other times he furnished meat to the local Indians, assisted by the local Order of Masons of which he was a member.

As time went on Crosthwaite became even more involved, financially and otherwise, in the San Diego community. In the fall of 1854, along with other influential men, he started the San Diego and Gila, Southern Pacific and Atlantic Railroad Company. The plan was to build a rail line from the Colorado River to San Diego. He served as one of the company directors and pledged four thousand dollars to

the effort. In that same year he won election as school superintendent. The following year he was elected by three votes as justice of
the peace, and was appointed deputy sheriff for the county.

The First White Settler in Historic Poway

THE IRISH success story in California is a result of their settling on
the land, which is the primary source of wealth everywhere in the
world. This held particularly true for the Irish in California. Philip
Crosthwaite was no exception. Shortly after becoming deputy sheriff
he purchased one half of the Rancho Paui, now known as Poway, the
site of downtown San Diego. Four days later he acquired an additional one hundred acres adjoining his Paui property. On this land he
built an adobe residence, thus becoming the first settler in Poway.

The outbreak of the Civil War led to hard times, financial and
otherwise. The conflict between the states dashed any hopes of building a rail line across the southern part of the country and ending in
San Diego. The war put an end to the planned San Diego and Gila
railroad. These problems were compounded by a continued drought
which forced some local ranchers to abandon their holdings. On
August 6, 1861, Crosthwaite gave up his 160 acres in Poway and
moved his family to Baja California, where he purchased the 18,000-
acre Rancho San Miguel, fifty five miles south of San Diego. The climate in Baja was humid, and there was sufficient water for crops to
flourish. The natural vegetation was capable of supporting livestock
year round. Besides raising 2,500 head of cattle and a variety of
crops, Crosthwaite made money delivering supplies to the miners in
the region.

Seven years later, in 1868, Crosthwaite moved his family back to
his beloved San Diego to live on the five hundred acres he owned in
Mission Valley, while leaving the bulk of his livestock in at San
Miguel.

Birth of the *San Diego Union*

THAT SAME YEAR Crosthwaite was most instrumental in bringing a
new newspaper to San Diego. The *San Diego Herald,* the town's
first newspaper, ceased publication on April 7, 1860, and for the next
eight years there was no local paper. In the fall of 1868 Crosthwaite
traveled to Northern California to visit his sister Mary, wife of Colonel
William Gatewood, publisher of the *San Andreas Register.* He evidently
wanted his sister near him; here was a chance to get her and a newspaper for San Diego at the same time. He convinced his brother-in-law

to come back with him and see for himself the opportunity for a newspaper in San Diego.

Gatewood was so impressed by the community's enthusiasm for a newspaper of their own that he decided to relocate in the southland. He stopped publication of his other paper, shipped his press and type to the new location, and on October 10, 1868, published the first issue of the *San Diego Union,* which is still San Diego's premier newspaper. Gatewood, an ardent unionist, called his paper the *Union* because of the North's victory in the Civil War.

Crosthwaite once again became involved in business and civic affairs in San Diego. In January 1869 he was appointed deputy county clerk, and the next month he formed a partnership with an associate and opened a general store. In September of the same year he was appointed the honored position as chief of police in San Diego. When his term as police chief expired Crosthwaite was appointed deputy sheriff in 1871, and re-appointed the following year. The *San Diego Union* glowingly endorsed these appointments, saying "[Crosthwaite] has been an efficient and useful officer; his thorough knowledge of the country and its people make his assistance invaluable. We are glad to see him retained in office."

On April 20, 1872, a fire swept through the heart of Old San Diego, destroying several buildings. This catastrophe proved to be the death blow for the old Mexican Pueblo. Rather than rebuild their premises, businesses, including the *Union* newspaper, decided to move to the New Town. The fall of old San Diego spelled hard tines for businesses and for Philip Crosthwaite himself. A flood swept through Mission Valley in January 1874, destroying his old adobe house and a number of improvements he had made to his ranch. Having lost everything at the age of 49, he gathered up his growing family and moved back to his Rancho San Miguel in Baja California.

Although his home was now in Mexico, Philip kept in touch with longtime friends in San Diego and transacted business for them across the border. And on May 30, 1882, he traveled north to participate in a ceremony commemorating the Battle of San Pasqual. As the last survivor of that historic battle he was the honored guest.

By the turn of the century, traveling between San Miguel and San Diego became too much of an effort for Crosthwaite, now in his seventy-fifth year of an active life. So he rented an apartment in New San Diego to reminisce with his old cronies, and to enjoy the friendship of his fellow Masons and the celebrity of being one of the oldest pioneers in the Gateway city.

In February 1903, soon after his 77th birthday, Crosthwaite developed complications from a cold and became seriously ill. When his condition was discovered he was rushed to a hospital. A week later he appeared to be recovering; then he suffered a relapse and died on February 19, 1903.

Philip Crosthwaite's funeral brought out one of the largest gatherings in the history of San Diego up to that time. He left Maria, his wife of 55 years, seven sons, three daughters, forty-seven grandchildren and a host of friends to mourn his passing. In his 57 years as a resident of San Diego he made countless contributions to his community's civic, legal and fraternal institutions. His legacy lives on in his many descendants who still reside in San Diego and Baja California.

George Lyons, 1823 - 1908

A YEAR AFTER Philip Crosthwaite arrived in Southern California, another Irish pioneer came to San Diego. Like Crosthwaite, he settled in the area and eventually had a major influence on local politics, law, architecture, business, and mail service. This man was George Lyons.

The son of Daniel and Catherine Kirkpatrick Lyons, George was born on June 15, 1823, in County Donegal. He came to the United States as a boy and later learned the carpentry trade. Sometime in the 1840s he joined the crew of a whaler as a ship's carpenter. The whaling expedition eventually brought Lyons to San Diego in December 1846. He settled down in the small Mexican pueblo and married Maria Bernarda de Villars, the daughter of a former Mexican army officer.

Lyons' first involvement in the community was as a merchant. In 1850 he opened George Lyons & Co., Variety Store, in which he offered San Diegans "a large and well-selected stock of general merchandise." Three years later he took his first steps into local politics, aided by Crosthwaite and his friend from the Masonic Lodge, Lieutenant Derby.

In 1853 the editor of the *San Diego Herald* left town on business and placed Derby in charge of the paper during his absence. It turned out Derby's politics were the opposite of the editor's, and the *Herald* was soon supporting candidates the editor would have opposed. One of these candidates was George Lyons for county assessor. Despite Derby's help, Lyons did not win the election, but that same year he was made a city trustee. The following year, 1854, Lyons was appointed postmaster of San Diego, and was re-appointed in 1857. One of the first things he did as postmaster was to journey to San Francisco to see how their post office operated. He then used what he saw to make the San Diego post office as efficient as possible. Besides his duties as postmaster, Lyons also found time to build and operate a saloon and bowling alley with "some of the best arranged alleys in the southern country," according to a newspaper report.

Lyons apparently planned to continue his career as a public servant. On June 30, 1855, he announced his candidacy for sheriff, but less than a month later he withdrew from the race without giving any reason. Later that year he got into trouble with the law. He was brought before the local court of sessions, presided over by Justice of the Peace Philip Crosthwaite, for obstructing and injuring a pedestrian on the street "by causing a large quantity of dirty and offensive water to be conveyed from his said premises" upon the street. Because of a lack of evidence he was acquitted of the misdemeanor offense.

Despite his minor brush with the law Lyons continued to serve the San Diego community. In March 1856 he was elected as a delegate to the Democratic Party's state convention. Over the next twenty years he would serve the Democratic Party as a delegate to local and state conventions and in other capacities. The same year he became involved with the San Diego and Gila Railroad Company as a stockholder; later he would serve as a director.

On July 25, 1857, Lyons once again announced that he was a candidate for sheriff. Among his opponents was Philip Crosthwaite. But there was soon to be trouble. On August 22, the *Herald* published a letter claiming that Lyons was not a naturalized citizen and was therefore ineligible for public office. A week later the paper published Lyons' reply, in which he asserted that he was indeed a citizen and "eligible to hold the office of Sheriff or any other the people may see proper to confer" upon him. Lyons, however, did not offer any proof of his citizenship. Recent research has shown that Lyons declared his date of naturalization as August 28, 1857, six days *after* the letter questioning his citizenship appeared.

Despite this controversy Lyons won the election by 62 votes. Six months after being sworn in as sheriff he resigned the job as postmaster. His term as sheriff turned out to be rather dull, with no bank holdups, gunfights, or other such Wild West excitement. Mostly Lyons presided over court-ordered sales of property. On May 15, 1858, for example, Sheriff Lyons announced the sale of some of

Philip Crosthwaite's property to satisfy a debt. When his term as sheriff expired Lyons applied for, and received, another appointment as postmaster of San Diego.

Using his knowledge of carpentry, Lyons teamed up with another man sometime in the late 1860s and started a construction business. The partnership apparently lasted only a few years, but was responsible for a number of buildings in Old San Diego. Their motto, as stated in advertisements, was, "Promptly and neatly executed. Our work speaks for itself." Lyons was also involved in road construction in the county during the 1880s; one project was building a road between San Diego and Poway.

Lyons did not own large tracts of land, as Crosthwaite did, but he and his family did have a nice house on some land across the river from Old San Diego. One visitor to the Lyons' home in the 1850s left this description: "The garden was surrounded by a live fence of willows, which provided abundant foliage." The *Herald* reported in 1855 that Lyons had succeeded in growing tobacco on his property and felt the crop could be raised in the region. Lyons had a setback, however, during the winter of 1861-62, when the river flooded and washed his garden away. This did not stop him from planting a new garden which ten years later impressed the *San Diego Union*: "One of the most beautiful places in this vicinity is that of Mr. George Lyons near the river at Old Town. The pepper trees are the finest we have seen this side of Los Angeles, and their graceful foliage is gladdening to the eye of the wayfarer."

Lyons' last job as a public servant was once again connected with the post office. In 1885 he served as the assistant to the postmaster in Old Town, and one of his sons had the job of mail carrier.

In November 5, 1899, his wife of 53 years died. Almost nine years later George Lyons died on March 10, 1908, after being ill for forty days. He was survived by nine of his ten children. Sixty-two years of faithful service and contribution to Old San Diego had come to an end.

Joshua Sloane, 1814 - 1879

ANOTHER IRISH pioneer to settle by the Harbor of the Sun was also briefly involved with the local post office and party politics, but in Joshua Sloane's case it was the Republican Party. Joshua Sloane was born in Ireland in 1814 and came to San Diego sometime in the first half of the 1850s. His first known job in the town lasted only about two months. On January 26, 1856, he was hired as a teacher.

Joshua Sloane
Courtesy San Diego Historical Society

The local school board, upset with Sloane's methods of discipline, fired him on March 1, charging him with brutality. The teacher would sometimes take his shoe off and force the unruly student to smell the "fetid stocking."

After his brief stint as a teacher Sloane operated a windmill used to grind grain. Located on the hill overlooking Old San Diego, the mill stood about forty feet high and had six blades, each twenty feet long. Sloane was able to turn out three grades of flour: "superfine,

fine and middling." Since this was the only mill for a hundred miles around, Sloane had a very successful business for himself. But in April 1859 he sold the mill for $900; the *Herald* claimed the mill was worth three times that amount.

Sloane may have sold his mill because about this time he started his career in public service. In 1857 he was appointed deputy county treasurer. Later he was appointed deputy postmaster, and in 1859 he stepped up to postmaster. Since Sloane was a Republican, and San Diego at that time was solidly Democratic, the citizens did not want to see him re-appointed and sent a petition voicing their opposition. Talk about Irish shenanigans! When the letter arrived in the post office where he was postmaster, Sloane opened the envelope, and saw what the petition said. He wrote a new petition asking for his re-appointment and then cut off the signatures, pasted them onto his new petition, and sent it on its way. The people of San Diego probably wondered why their plea went unheeded.

During the 1856 Presidential election Sloane's political preference came to the forefront. He supported the Republicans because they were against the spread of slavery into the western territories. He tried to organize a Republican rally in San Diego, but only he and his dog Patrick showed up. This didn't discourage Sloane, who wrote to the Republican National Headquarters, saying he had been unanimously chosen local party chairman, with "Mr. Patrick" as secretary.

With the election of Abraham Lincoln in 1860 things improved for Sloane. For 1861-62 he was appointed collector of customs for San Diego. Some stories claim he placed his dog on the payroll, but this is not substantiated. Evidently it didn't need to be; just being Irish covered a multitude of sins in California's halcyon days. Other stories report that Sloane used to spy on disembarking women with binoculars, and that he allowed his dog to sniff around baggage and cargo looking for food. When San Diegans, disapproving of his antics, suggested he court one of the widows in town, Sloane's reported reply was "I'd rather kiss a rat than an old woman!"

Founder of Balboa Park

JOSHUA SLOANE did make one major, lasting contribution to San Diego: Balboa Park. This large area of land had originally been set aside many years earlier for public use, with the approval of King Charles of Spain, as some would have it. It wasn't until 1868, however, that a resolution came before the board of trustees asking that this land be used for a public park. When the board hesitated, Sloane, as secretary of the board, harangued and badgered them until, to shut him up, they agreed to preserve 1400 acres for a public park. Thanks to Joshua Sloane, San Diego has Balboa Park with its world-famous zoo, award-winning Old Globe Theater and several museums.

Joshua Sloane died on January 6, 1879, still a bachelor. Although many stories and anecdotes circulated about his behavior, he was actually a very shy man who preferred the company of dogs and cats to people. All the stories aside, Sloane did make a very real and lasting contribution to San Diego.

James McCoy, 1821 - 1895

WHILE MANY of San Diego's Irish pioneers came here of their own accord, others arrived as members of the United States Army. The 1850 census shows 36 families having at least one member born in Ireland, and the majority of these listed "soldier" as their occupation.

Among the dead at the Battle of San Pasqual are the names Kennedy and McNanny. Scanning the rosters of the regiments stationed in San Diego turns up officers and men with names like Dwyer, Gallagher, Kearny, Murphy, Murray, O'Connell, Quinn, Ryan and others. The great majority of these men did not stay, but left when their regiments were reassigned. But there was one soldier who did stay and went on to make his mark on San Diego's law enforcement and politics. This was Sergeant James McCoy of the first U.S. Artillery.

McCoy was born in County Antrim on August 12, 1821. Like his parents, he worked at farming, but that changed when he turned 21 years of age. In 1842 he boarded the *Alexander* for America, arriving in Baltimore on July 9.

McCoy first made his living in Baltimore working in a market garden and later as a laborer in a distillery. About seven years later he enlisted in the U.S. Army, and in 1850, on a ship filled with other recruits, he left for California. Upon his arrival in San Diego, McCoy was assigned to Company I, first U.S. Artillery, commanded by Lieutenant Colonel John Bankhead Magruder.

Magruder's command was set down among the ruins of Mission San Diego, Philip Crosthwaite's former home. McCoy, working his way up to the rank of sergeant, later left as part of a 12-man detachment for Mission San Luis Rey to the north, replacing two companies of dragoons that had been transferred. Some time later he was sent with fourteen men to Jacumba, about 60 miles east of San Diego

James McCoy
Courtesy San Diego Historical Society

on the Mexican border, to protect the mail route to Fort Yuma. One story that has circulated over the years, and is highly suspect, claims that McCoy and the other soldiers were attacked by 500 Indians, whom they successfully beat back.

McCoy's enlistment ended in 1853, and for the next six years he held various jobs in Southern California. At one time he took part in surveying the desert along the Colorado River for possible future townships. For two months in 1859 he carried mail between San Diego and Fort Yuma.

Also in 1859, McCoy settled down and became part of the San Diego community. In that year he won election (by 70 votes) as county assessor. He also began raising sheep; by 1860 he had a flock of five hundred. He soon began raising cattle, and eventually became one the leading stock raisers in San Diego county.

But ranching did not occupy all of McCoy's time. In 1861 he ran for sheriff and won. This started a ten-year career of maintaining law and order in San Diego. Being a bachelor at the time, McCoy shared a place with his deputy. For amusement they used to have boxing matches, with the loser having to cook breakfast.

McCoy made his first real estate purchase in Old San Diego in 1866. Three years later this property came in handy, because on April 27, 1869, he married Winnie Kearny of Los Angeles. While the sheriff and his bride went to San Francisco for a honeymoon, George Lyons' construction company was building an elegant two-story house for the newlyweds. The McCoys moved into their new home on September 8. According to the *San Diego Union* McCoy's house "loomed up over the rest of the houses in the neighborhood in about the same proportion that its owner did over his late competitors in the race for sheriff."

At the same time McCoy also served as president of the city board of trustees. On September 24, 1869, he and the other trustees appointed Philip Crosthwaite as San Diego's Chief of Police.

McCoy was now well established in San Diego life, and like his fellow countryman Crosthwaite, was not pleased with the fact that Old San Diego was losing ground to New Town. By 1871 the citizens of New Town felt the courthouse and public records should be moved to their community. The battle eventually reached the state supreme court, which ruled in New Town's favor. McCoy formed a posse to resist the relocation of the papers, but late on a Sunday night in March 1871 the documents were secretly gathered up and taken to New Town.

After ten years as sheriff McCoy decided to move up in the world of politics. He submitted a statement to the *San Diego Union* announcing he would not seek reelection as sheriff. Instead he ran for and won the state senate seat from San Diego. The first bill he introduced to the senate, just four days after the session began, asked to "legalize, ratify, and confirm deeds of conveyance and grants of land made by the municipal authorities of the City of San Diego." The bill passed on March 9, 1872, giving the San Diego board of trustees the right to sell, grant, and deed city land for a possible railroad. McCoy may have had ulterior motives for the bill, since he also served as a director and stockholder in the San Diego and Gila Railroad Company.

During his third and fourth years in the senate McCoy served on committees for commerce and navigation, state prisons, agriculture and internal improvements. Everyone back home seemed pleased with McCoy's performance in Sacramento. The *San Diego Union* even went so far as to say "the sound democracy of McCoy is unquestioned, and the [Democratic] party should consider the Senator for Congress." But McCoy had other plans, and when the session adjourned in March 1874 he retired from the state senate.

A year later McCoy ran for his old job of sheriff, but lost the election 915 votes to 657. His health began to fail in late 1884, and in January 1885 he traveled to San Francisco for treatment. After a two-month recuperation McCoy took another stab at politics, applying to President Grover Cleveland for the post of collector for the port of San Diego. The appointment never came through.

By 1885 McCoy may have been permanently out of politics, but his involvement in San Diego had not ended. During his 45 years in Southern California there were nearly two hundred deeds recorded in McCoy's name, and over half of these were transacted after 1885. Although some of this land speculation was profitable, McCoy sold much of it at a loss.

McCoy's health continued to be poor, and on November 8, 1895, he died in the house he had built for himself and his wife in Old San Diego.

James McCoy contributed to the San Diego community through his military service, ten-year career as sheriff, and service in the state senate. And in a way McCoy will soon make another contribution to San Diego. The state of California has recently reconstructed The James McCoy house for use as a visitors' center for Old Town State Park.

Andrew Cassidy, 1817 - 1907

WHEN THE Army came to San Diego, civilians also came to work for the military. Andrew Cassidy was a civilian who accompanied the Army to the Harbor of the Sun.

Cassidy was born in County Cavan in 1817 and emigrated to the United States 17 years later in 1834. Although little is known about his early life, Cassidy must have received a very good education, because around 1850 he was employed by the Army engineers at West Point. Three years later he went to work for the Coast Survey Office at Washington, D.C.

By August 1853 Cassidy found himself in San Diego as a member of the Topographical Engineers. His job was to measure the tides in San Diego Bay. The first thing he did was to remove the existing manual tide gauge and replace it with a self-registering one which he built himself. For seventeen years he kept a record of the tides and other observations: barometric pressure, temperature, wind, rain, clouds. These observations, filling nine journals, are now in the possession of the San Diego Historical Society. Besides recording the tides, Cassidy also collected specimens for the Smithsonian Institute.

Life on the beach was very boring and dull. Cassidy lived in a small building with an Irish housekeeper. A visitor said Cassidy did nothing "save watch the ebb and flow of the tide." To break up the monotony he would often take a trip into Old San Diego. He would "come to the saloon, finish a game of billiards, take a drink, then a smoke, pass the time of day with a little cheerful conversation and before sunset return to the solitude of [his] home. This, all year round."

Besides his duties recording the tides at San Diego, Cassidy managed to find time to get involved in the local community. In 1857, for example, he served on the local grand jury, along with fellow Irishman George Lyons. Three years later he was appointed deputy collector of customs. The next year he was re-appointed, serving under Joshua Sloane.

He moved to Old San Diego in 1863, when he was 46, after his marriage to the 15-year-old Rosa Serrano. The next year he acquired 1,000 acres of land in Soledad Valley and began raising livestock and cultivating olives, pears, figs, and pomegranates. During the early years on this ranch Cassidy and his wife lived in an adobe house that belonged to Philip Crosthwaite's father-in-law. It wasn't until many years later that he built his own home on the ranch. Also at this time Cassidy took over the Paula Rancho, which belonged to his father-in-law, and bought two lots in Old San Diego, one of them near James McCoy's property.

Cassidy retired from his job as tide gauge keeper in 1869, and in June of that year he, along with James McCoy, was appointed to the committee to organize the festivities for the upcoming Fourth of July.

In 1870 his wife died, and Cassidy seemed to throw himself more deeply into local politics and activities. In 1871 the local Democratic Party nominated Cassidy for supervisor of the Third District; he won the election, 70 votes to 39. Two years later he was nominated again for the same office and this time won 131 to 68.

Sometime in the late 1870s he married again, this time to Mary

Providencia Smith, and in 1877, when Cassidy was 60, they had a daughter, Mary Winifred Cassidy. The next year his wife died of cholera at the age of 20.

Cassidy continued his agricultural pursuits at Soledad, although as the years passed he occasionally rented the property to others. In 1882 he left San Diego for a three-month visit to the east coast. He finally gave up ranching and sold Soledad in 1887.

Andrew Cassidy died on November 25, 1907 of "senile debility." For 54 years in San Diego he lived "a long life of usefulness in a humble, kindly, lovable way." In his honor, to mark the quiet contributions he made, there is a Cassidy Street in Oceanside and an historic marker at the site of his tide gauge.

The Growing Irish Population

THE CITY by the Harbor of the Sun continued to grow, and so did its Irish population. In 1860 the census showed 84 natives of Ireland plus their families. Many of these were still connected with the military. Ten years later, 134 people with Irish surnames could be found on the census list. By 1880 San Diego could no longer be considered a frontier town, but the Irish influence continued. In January 1882, for example, a local branch of the Irish National Land League was started.

The Irish influence has remained constant in San Diego down through the years. James Duffy, who arrived in the city in 1870, became a leading entrepreneur and served as superintendent of the County Hospital for over seventeen years. He played a leading role in organizing the Cuymaca Horticultural Society in 1889, and was one of the most ardent proponents of the San Diego Fair. His wife of many years, Mary Jane, was a native Californian, born in Placer County in 1855.

Then came the Whalen family, with roots in County Tipperary. Edward, patriarch of the Whalen clan, was born in 1872, and some years later, as an orphan, worked his passage to the United States. He enlisted in the army and served for a time at Fort Omaha. He enrolled in Creighton University, where he played on the first of its football teams, and graduated in 1894 with highest honors. Edward removed to O'Neal, Nebraska, where he became principal of the public high school, and met his future wife, Susan Quilty, who was teaching there at the time. At age 45 he accepted a commission in the Army. Soon after his discharge Captain Whalen moved with his family to San Diego, where he practiced law until his death in 1937.

Whalen's children played a major role in various aspects of life in San Diego, and in the judicial system in particular. Edward D., an accountant, served, like his father, in the U.S. Army, and afterward for many years was chief clerk in the District Attorney's office. Thomas served as district attorney of San Diego County for fifteen years (1931-1945). Vincent A. became a superior court judge and a member of the Court of Appeals (1959-1975). Francis C. (b. 1907) became a judge of United States district court. Charles Quentin (b. 1909) was a lawyer practicing in San Diego.

Mary Catherine Whalen (b. 1911), the youngest of Edward Whalen's children, came to San Diego in 1920 and worked in the offices of her father and her brother, Vincent. In 1936 she married Roy Fitzgerald, a San Diego Municipal Court judge. They had four children: James, Michael, John and Clare, who became Sister Clare Patrice of the Sisters of Saint Joseph of Corondelet. Also the Fitzgeralds had six grandchildren to carry forward the Irish tradition of the home and family as the center of everyday life. Besides her many domestic duties, Mrs. Fitzgerald was active in many religious, charitable and civic organizations. She received of the medal Pro Ecclesia et Pontifice from Pope Pius XII.

The Jack Murphy Stadium

A VIVID MEMORIAL to the Irish in San Diego is Jack Murphy Stadium, named in honor of the late Jack Murphy, Sports Editor for the *San Diego Union*. Murphy was described as a savvy politician who knew the right people and the right things to say at the right time. He was also a gifted writer who could write about his dog in the sports page and people would read it. He led the bond drive for a new stadium, approved by over 72% of the voters. The stadium is now the home of the San Diego Chargers, thanks to Jack's persuasiveness. In 1968 the San Diego Padres baseball team gained major-league status, also thanks to the efforts of Jack Murphy, a witty Oklahoma-Irishman.

The O'Connors of San Diego

A ND LAST but surely not least, Maureen O'Connor was elected mayor of San Diego in 1986, continuing a long tradition of Irish participation in San Diego politics. At age 25, in 1971, she had won a seat on the city council, the youngest councilwoman in the history of the city.

Maureen was one of twelve children of Jerome and Frances

Maureen O'Connor, the progressive, popular, and pretty mayor of San Diego.

Shinnick O'Connor. The O'Connor family lived for a period in the palatial home of the late Roman Catholic Bishop Charles Buddy in Mission Hills. The Bishop moved to the Alcala Park campus of the University when it was finished and wanted someone to live in the home. Mrs. O'Connor said,. "It was ideal for a large Catholic family like ours." When they went out on the town the O'Connors were a force to be reckoned with. On election day they could put an O'Connor in every single precinct.

Maureen and her twin, Mavourneen, were champion swimmers and all-around athletes, like the rest of the family. When the two girls defeated all competitors in a swimming meet and then were declared ineligible for the prize because they were women, Maureen decided to run for political office in order to change things. She won a seat on the city council and served several terms.

Maureen O'Connor, as a populist candidate for mayor, campaigned on the promise she would erase the taint of scandal from city government, and made good on her promise. She pioneered "meet the mayor" sessions to which everyone was invited. She cruised the streets with police officers and picked up garbage with the scavengers to show that she was no "cocktail mayor."

"I have been out there, riding in police cars, visiting recreation centers, and riding with the firefighters," she told a reporter. Yet she didn't please everyone. "She was outspoken and tenacious, a provider of leadership," declared Gordon Luce, who was considered part of San Diego's old-line establishment. "Overall, I think she has been a good Mayor."

As one with the courage of her convictions, the Mayor singlehandedly persuaded the City Council to reverse itself and support

The O'Connor family celebrates father Jerome's 80th birthday in Dublin,
Ireland. Back row, left to right (standing): Thomas, Colleen, Timothy,
Dianne, Michael, Sheila, Patrick,Karen, Shawn. Seated: Mavourneen,
faher Jerome, mother Frances, Sharon. Maureen O'Connor was the only one
missing. Courtesy Colleen O'Connor

voluntary water conservation rather than imposing mandatory
restrictions. This was at a time when almost every major elected official in the state supported government-imposed curbs. O'Connor
was called irresponsible for her stance, but that didn't seem to phase
her.

At the close of her second term O'Connor vigorously defended
her record and ticked off a list of accomplishments, including two-
term limits for elected municipal officials, improvements to Balboa
and Mission Bay parks, building a city jail, solving the overflow of
Tijuana sewage, passing the Human Dignity Ordinance and outlaw-
ing discrimination on the basis of race, religion, nationality and sexu-
al orientation.

If there is a central point to the story it is that the Irish, as elsewhere in California, have left a major imprint in San Diego, the
"Harbor of the Sun."

James Talbot Ryan
Courtesy Humboldt County Historical Society

– 2 –

James Talbot Ryan

Founder of Eureka

1822-1875

James Talbot Ryan takes pride of place in John T. Young's early historical sketches of Eureka, California. "I feel impelled," Young wrote, "to pay a tribute of friendship to that energetic, enterprising, public-spirited, liberal-minded, open-handed pioneer, James T. Ryan. Jim Ryan is a man to whom in my opinion, the early residents of Humboldt County generally, and of Eureka especially, are more largely indebted than to any other man." It was a long way from Tipperary, his birthplace, to the rugged coast of Humboldt Bay for a man who was destined to play a major role in the development of early California.

In the turbulent years of the American Civil War, Alexander McDougall, the senior senator from California, invited Jim Ryan to Washington to meet President Abraham Lincoln. On the appointed day he escorted Ryan to the White House and introduced him to the President as a longtime friend and fellow Californian. "Mr. President, this is General Ryan, a loyal neighbor of mine, who can build a cathedral and preach in it, a ship and sail in it, or an engine and run it, and, Mr. President, he can make a better stump speech than either you or I can do."

James T. "Jim" Ryan was born in County Tipperary, on October 8, 1822, one of nine children of Joseph Ryan. By all accounts the Ryans were a well-to-do family in the Old Country who fell on hard times, and like so many of their countrymen were forced to emigrate. On arrival in the New World, the family settled in New Brunswick, Canada. During their stay in the latter city Jim met and married an

Irish lass named Nora Connally. The newlyweds removed to Boston at the first opportunity and settled down to married life.

While residing in Boston Nora gave birth to a son whom they named Joseph, after his grandfather, an age-old Irish tradition. The Ryans had four more children, James, Nora, Mary and Milton, who were born after they settled in California. According to the 1860 U.S. census the Ryans were living in Eureka with their next of kin, the Duff family, James and Margaret Duff and their children Margaret, Louise, James R., Kate, Emma and Nelly.

A Renowned Clan

According to Mac Lysaght, the renowned Irish genealogist, Ryan is among the ten most numerous surnames in Ireland. One of the outstanding literary figures in Irish history was Edmond O'Ryan, the Gaelic poet and erstwhile "Rapparee" (rebel) who created the romantic character, Eamonn a Chunic (Ned of the Hill). A lesser known "Ryan the Poet," of the Leinster Clan, has his epitaph inscribed on a granite slab over his grave in the old churchyard in Camross, County Laois, alongside that of the author's father, Michael, who died in 1907. The first line, "Here Lies in a Tomb a Bard Sublime" is all that I can remember. John Phelan, an Irish-Californian, was the only man I knew who could recite the poetic epitaph word for word.

The Ryans were as tenacious as they were learned and poetic. For example Luke Ryan, a daring Irish smuggler, was the darling of Benjamin Franklin's "Privateers" who played havoc with the British naval fleet during the American Revolution. He had gained considerable experience as an officer in the Irish Brigade, which prepared him for the hazardous life of a privateer on the high seas. His cohorts, Irish-born Edward McCatter and Patrick Dowling, proved themselves equally courageous in time of adversity. All three were commissioned by Franklin, who was the American Minister Plenipotentiary in Paris at the time. The swift cutters, French-owned, were acquired by the American authorities and manned for the most part by fearless Irishmen. Their mission was to foray against British trade by sea and take as many prisoners as possible, to be traded for captured Americans, or in Franklin's words, "to redeem our poor countrymen."

Luke Ryan, Patrick Dowling and Ed McCatter were given command of the cutters *Black Prince, Black Princess* and *Fearnot*, respectively, and sent out on one of the most daring adventures in the history of naval warfare. Franklin's Irish privateers were ill-equipped to take on the mighty British Navy, which was master of the sea in that period of world history. Their orders were firm and deliberate "Gentlemen, you are now on their own. Do as you have been commanded, but don't get caught."

Nothing further was heard from them until they arrived in the Port of Le Havre with their spoils: British sloops, crews and supplies. The indomitable Luke Ryan, captain of the *Black Prince,* had eighteen Britishers confined as prisoners in the ship's hold. His all-Irish crew, Tom O'Connor, Michael Morgan, Bartholomew Mulvaney, Brian Rooney, Ned and Tim Duff, John and Chris Kelly, dared the impossible, knowing full well that if caught, they would soon grace the gibbets in Plymouth or Portsmouth.

This is only a small part of the intriguing tale of Ben Franklin's Irish privateers. The rest will have to wait another day.

The Ryans in America

ALL WENT WELL for the Ryans in the booming port city of Boston, where Jim's father, Joe, eventually became a successful building contractor. He resided continuously in Boston until his death at the age of seventy. Jim learned the building business from his father and became a successful builder and contractor in his own right. He worked at this trade for seven years, from 1842 to 1849, during which time he constructed a number of substantial buildings, some of which are still in use.

Despite his success in Boston, his heart was set on the new country where gold had recently been discovered. Ryan booked passage on the brig *Crescent City,* bound for Panama. He crossed the Isthmus by muleback, planning to sail to San Francisco. The vessel lay at anchor, but its crew was nowhere to be found, all hands having deserted en masse. As a way out of this dilemma, a number of well-to-do passengers like Messrs. Scranton and French pooled their resources and chartered a coaling brig at a cost of $27,000 to transport the passengers to their destination.

A charge of $250 per person seemed prohibitive, but under the circumstances they had no choice; it was either pay up or stay put. When the overcrowded vessel got underway there was such shortage of food and water that a number of passengers, including Jim Ryan, abandoned ship as it set anchor at Aqua on the coast of Baja (lower) California.

From there the party set out on foot, and after a three-day march in the wilderness, reached a Mexican rancho, where they bargained for horses to carry them to San Diego. Here they waited impatiently for three weeks until the steamship *Oregon* arrived in the harbor. Following a period of intense bargaining and the payment of $40 each, they were permitted to board the overcrowded vessel bound for San Francisco.

Despite the hardships the weary passengers were overjoyed when they caught sight of the Golden Gate in the spring of 1850. Their ship moved slowly into the inner bay and dropped anchor in the sheltered cove beneath Telegraph Hill at Clark's Landing, near where the landmark Transamerica Pyramid building now stands.

In Search of Gold

THE RYAN PARTY'S primary interest was in the rich mines in Trinity and Humboldt Counties, where gold was said to be plentiful. Unlike their Irish counterparts who had arrived penniless a year or so earlier, the Ryan party included a number of wealthy prospectors. Sam Brannan, the Mormon leader who was returning to California, was on the ship. So were William Howard, a wealthy merchant for whom Howard Street is named; Duer Teshmaker, of the newspaper *Alta California*; James Duff, the first qualified civil engineer in those parts, and last but not least the indomitable Jim Ryan himself.

In order to facilitate the business at hand a company was formed which called for an initial investment of $500 each. With the proceeds therefrom it was agreed to charter a schooner, the *General Morgan*, in San Francisco to transport the prospectors to Humboldt County's mining region. After an uneventful voyage up the coast the vessel dropped anchor near the mouth of the Eel River, and from there the men set out in rowboats to explore the shoreline and the extent of Humboldt Bay and inner harbor.

They camped overnight, and on the following day went on foot through the rugged terrain to observe the surrounding country from the pinnacle of the hill.

As it turned out, on that memorable day in 1850, the Ryan party were the first white men to lay eyes on the vast groves of giant redwoods (Sequoia sempervirens) that rose from the water's edge and stretched across the horizon as far as the eye could see. They were awesome to behold, one of the Wonders of the World, trees that had begun to grow before Christ was born in Bethlehem. In later years these giants of the forest would be immortalized by Joseph Strauss, architect of the Golden Gate Bridge, in a poem:

THE REDWOODS

Here sown by the Creator's hand,
In serried ranks, the Redwoods stand;
No other clime is honored so,
No other lands their glory know.

The greatest of earth's living forms,
Tall conquerors that laugh at storms;
Their challenge still unanswered rings,
Through fifty centuries of Kings.

The nations that with them were young,
Rich empires, with their forts far flung,
Lie buried now their splendor gone;
But these proud monarchs still live on.

So shall they live, when ends our day,
When our crude citadels decay;
For brief the years allotted man,
But infinite perennials span.

This is their temple vaulted high,
And here we pause with reverent eye,
With silent tongue and awestruck soul,
For here we sense life's proper goal.

To be like these, straight true and fine,
To make our world like them a shrine,
Sink down, Oh, traveler on your knees,
God stands before you in those trees.

Jim Ryan was so taken by the awesome grandeur of the terrain and the tranquil surroundings that he would go no farther. There he stood on the pinnacle of the hill looking in every direction, and seeing no one about, staked his claim, crying out with Archimedean fervor, "Eureka! Eureka! Eureka!"

He then had the land surveyed and mapped by his brother-in-law, James Duff, the first qualified engineer to settle in Humboldt County.

The following year, in 1851, Ryan returned to San Francisco to make preparations for the development of his newly acquired property. In order to get the project underway he formed a partnership under the trade name of Ryan and Duff, and acted as the company's first president. Subsequently the firm purchased a steamboat, the *Santa Clara,* in San Francisco to transport workmen and equipment to Humboldt Bay. Jim, a capable mariner, took over as captain and hired a number of qualified seamen to assist him on the voyage.

On arrival at Humboldt Bay the crew set anchor and bided their time, waiting for the incoming tide to carry them to the shore, and then for the outgoing tide, which left the *Santa Clara* standing on solid ground. In this way the ship's engines would provide the power to operate the machinery when the proposed sawmill was constructed.

In the meantime the *Santa Clara* provided housing for the workers during the construction of the sawmill. When the pioneer mill went into operation it was capable of cutting one hundred thousand feet of lumber per day, a far cry from the saw pit and the manually operated cross-cut saw which had to be pulled up and down by two brawny operators.

An Irishman named Charles McKernan, a mule skinner from County Leitrim, hauled timber from the redwood forests to the Ryan sawmill in Eureka with his twenty-mule team. McKernan, the legendary "Mountain Charlie," in later years moved to Santa Cruz County, where he farmed and raised stock. He lost part of his skull and almost lost his life when he was attacked by a ferocious grizzly bear. Luckily a companion arrived in the nick of time and shot the bear. The doctor who attended him gave him up for dead, but fortunately he survived, minus part of his forehead and with his bright blue Irish eyes somewhat disfigured. Eventually McKernan became a man of means, the owner of an elegant house in San Jose, where he raised a large family and lived to an advanced age.

For a number of years the sawmill was the principal source of employment in Eureka, the hub of Humboldt County. Local residents were elated when the first three ships were loaded with lumber and set out with their precious cargoes, bound for San Francisco. Their joy, however, was short-lived: all three ships were wrecked in the turbulent waters of the outer harbor.

Captain Ryan was so disheartened by the tragedy that he promised to do everything in his power to make sure that nothing like this would ever happen again. He traveled to San Francisco, where he purchased a tugboat for the purpose of escorting ships safely in and out of Humboldt Harbor. When the deal was completed he threw a party and invited all his friends to the christening of the tug, which he named the *Mary Ann,* after his youngest daughter.

When it came time to return to Eureka Jim took over as captain, accompanied by his wife, Nora, and his sons, Joseph and Robert, who had followed him to California, as well as his sister-in-law, Margaret Duff. All went well for a year or more, with regular shipments of lumber going down the coast to the burgeoning city of San Francisco. Then the sawmill caught fire and burned to the ground. The tragedy affected everyone for miles around, for the mill was the principal source of employment in Eureka.

Jim, however was not a man to call it quits. As soon as the smoke cleared away he called together all his employees and vowed that, with their help and cooperation, he would build a bigger, better sawmill in its place. True to his word, Ryan, Duff & Company, under his supervision, cleared the site and constructed a more substantial mill, which employed more workers than ever before.

The Ryans had four more children, James, Nora, Mary and Milton, who were born after they settled in California. According to the 1860 U.S. census the Ryans were living in Eureka, with their next-of-kin, the Duff family, James and Margaret Duff and their children.

Ryan' s Political Career

"THE POLITICAL IRISHMAN is always a power among his associates. The Irishman who is not a politician has not yet been discovered," said Joseph Gorman, who arrived in California in 1868 and won election in his first bid for political office. Apparently Jim Ryan was no exception to this rule. When he first ran for political office he was elected to the state senate, representing Humboldt and Trinity Counties. He served two terms, from 1860 to 1864, with such vigor and distinction that he was appointed Commissioner of Indian Affairs by John Downey, governor of California during the Civil War.

While serving in that honorable post Senator Ryan traveled to Washington to meet with the two California congressmen, John Conees and James McDougall, hoping to get a bill enacted to provide money to pay off debts incurred by the State of California in the prosecution of the Indian Wars. Following a lengthy debate an amount agreeable to the concerned parties was set aside for that purpose.

Upon his return to California, Senator Ryan was greeted with tremendous enthusiasm when he showed up in Sacramento. In order to show their appreciation, California legislators meeting in a joint session enacted a bill to compensate Ryan for his work as War Bond Commissioner. An amount of $2,000, a hefty sum in those days, was unanimously approved.

Politics was in the blood of the Ryans. Jim's brother, Pierce, had an even more enviable record as a California legislator, serving as senator from 1870 to 1875. He was also a highly respected and successful businessman in Eureka, as the proprietor of the Ryan's Dry Goods Company. However, when the firm was sold to the Abrahamson brothers, the store was renamed the White House. Pierce, like his brother, was active in community affairs and was the prime mover in the development of a well-organized fire department in Eureka, which became a model for other communities in Northern California.

The distaff side of the family were also very much involved in Eureka. Marie Ryan married Doctor Jonathan Clark, the first physician to practice in Eureka. In the ensuing years he served as surgeon for Fort Humboldt, when Captain Ulysses Grant became commander of the fort in 1853. Doctor Clark was also appointed surgeon at Fort Gaxton in nearby Hoopa during the Indian Wars. The Clarks resided in one of the most fashionable homes in Eureka, built by Jim Ryan.

Josephine Ryan became the proprietor of a millinery business, the first of its kind in Eureka. She designed and wove exotic ornamental tapestries, for which her establishment became famous. Samples of Josephine's handwoven fabrics are on display in the Humboldt Museum in Eureka.

Eloquence and initiative were the qualities that the Ryans possessed in abundance. Pierce Ryan, Jr., was said to be one of the most eloquent lawyers in the history of Humboldt County. It was said of him, as a criminal lawyer, "If Pierce Ryan takes a case it's as good as won."

The *Comanche* Story

ON HIS THIRD TRIP to Washington, Senator James Ryan pleaded with Congress to build an ironclad like the U.S.S. *Monitor* that beat back the Confederate armored *Merrimac* in early 1862, during the Civil War. Ryan maintained that San Francisco's artillery batteries at Fort Point and Alcatraz were not powerful enough to repel a Confederate assault on the western metropolis. Following a heated debate as to its merits and the cost involved the project was overwhelmingly approved.

Senator Ryan promptly formed a partnership with Peter Donahue, the San Francisco industrialist, and Francis Secor, a leading New Jersey shipbuilder, with the idea of building a more powerful *Monitor* in the Jersey shipyards. The plans were drawn up by John Ericsson, the naval architect who had designed the previously mentioned Ironclad.

The new model was much larger and more heavily armed than its prototype, 200 feet long, with two 15-inch guns mounted in its turret, and two steam boilers capable of driving nine engines at the same time. Her coal bunkers were enormous, capable of storing enough fuel for more than a week at sea. The outer frame was of wrought iron six inches thick.

When it came time to award the contract to build the ship, the Ryan-Donahue-Secor firm was the only one to submit a bid, on account of the enormity of the project and the risks involved. Their bid in the amount of half a million dollars was accepted at once.

The iron monster was constructed at Secor's Shipyard in Jersey City and commissioned the *Comanche* after the Indian tribe by that name. The *Comanche* had a displacement of 1,875 tons and required a crew of eight officers and fifty seamen to maintain her on the high seas.

An immediate problem arose: how to transport the *Comanche* to its home base in San Francisco at a time when the nation was engulfed in a dreadful Civil War. After much discussion it was decided to dismantle the *Comanche* and ship the parts in the hold of a mighty warship called the *Aquila*. The whole affair was a closely guarded secret. The *Aquila* set sail under cover of darkness with its precious cargo, bound for San Francisco by way of Cape Horn. Even local authorities were not aware of its coming until the *Aquila* cleared the Golden Gate and anchored at the weather-beaten Hathaway's Wharf in late November 1863.

Tragedy Strikes the *Aquila*

THE AFTERNOON FOLLOWING the big ship's arrival in San Francisco, a mighty storm arose, striking the *Aquila* with such force that she capsized and sank in the bay with the makings of the *Comanche* in her hold. And there she remained, collecting rust, until the following spring.

Jim Ryan was not a man to give in. When word of the disaster got out, concerned citizens came forward with proposals for the raising of the *Aquila,* among them Horace Cole, a wealthy local contractor. But it fell to one of San Francisco's very own, Peter Donahue, to raise the big warship, retrieve the parts and put the *Comanche* together again. It was a tall order, but Donahue proved equal to the task.

Instead of trying to raise the mighty *Aquila* he hired experienced divers who went down and cut into the hull in order to retrieve the parts of the *Comanche.* These were then hoisted onto the wharf to be cleaned and made ready to assemble. When that job was out of the way plans were drawn up for the raising of the *Aquila,* which took place on May 27, 1864. On that day people converged on the waterfront in droves to catch sight of the mighty *Aquila* as it was lifted out of the muddy waters.

Peter Donahue and his associates began the task of reassembling the *Comanche* as soon as money was made available. Jim Ryan was on hand to offer his support if needed. In the spirit of the occasion he vowed that he would not shave his whiskers until that ship was reassembled and in working order.

Launching the *Comanche*

WHEN IT CAME TIME for the launching of the *Comanche,* an overflow crowd of some 25,000, including such eminent Californians as Captain John Sutter, packed the reviewing stands erected by the water's edge at Third and King Streets. The gala affair was said to be the greatest public celebration ever staged "South of the Slot," as the area south of Market Street was known.

The spectacular event was presided over by Peter Donahue, a South O' Market Boy himself. The mood of the gathering was ecstatic, enhanced by inspiring speeches, patriotic intonements, a salute from naval cannons and the stirring music of an Army band.

The entertainment was followed by a lavish banquet prepared under the direction of Peter Donahue and his wife, Annie. The party ended on a patriotic note: everyone arose and sang "The Star Spangled Banner," at which point Jim Ryan jumped on the platform and ceremoniously shaved off his lengthy whiskers.

Shortly thereafter workmen got the ironclad ready for a trial run to Mare Island Naval Base to be outfitted with the proper armaments. On her maiden voyage along the bay, the *Comanche* was escorted by tugboats and a U S Revenue Cutter, a fitting tribute to the old master, Peter Donahue, and his workmen who had labored long and hard to make the iron monster seaworthy.

A Great Day for the Irish

AT LONG LAST the Irish had something to shout about: a powerful warship, the brainchild of one of their very own Jim Ryan, from Tipperary. It was manned by a crew whose names were Irish to the core: Commander Mc Dougal, seamen Flynn, Farley and Flanagan, Berry, Brennan and Barrigan, O'Brien, O'Donovan, Brophy and Muldoon.

Jim Ryan was so elated that he journeyed to Washington for a fourth time, on another important mission. He lobbied Congress to enact a bill to reimburse local contractors for the difference between the United States currency, which had been depreciated during the Civil War, and what they themselves had paid for labor and material in gold coin. The bill was carried through Congress by California Senators James McDougall and John Conness, and duly enacted into law.

Ulysses Grant at Fort Humboldt

THE ARRIVAL IN EUREKA of a brash Army Captain Ulysses S. Grant, went almost unnoticed in the sparsely populated western wilderness. Following his graduation from the U.S. Military Academy at West Point in 1843, Grant was commissioned a second lieutenant in the Fourth Infantry Regiment. One of his first assignments was in the war with Mexico, where he was decorated for bravery under fire. This engagement was followed by ordinary garrison duty in Michigan and Fort Vancouver, Washington, whence he was promoted to the rank of captain in 1847.

In 1854, Captain Grant was given command of Fort Humboldt on California's rugged northwest coast, one of the most isolated posts under the Army's far-flung command. One could well understand how lonely and frustrated the young officer must have been, a continent apart from his loving wife and children. His sheltered upbringing, surrounded by family and friends, did little to prepare him for an assignment such as this, where there were scarcely any inhabitants at that period in time, save a few Indians. His parents, Jesse and Hannah Simpson Grant, had provided their children with the best society had to offer in the way of education and environment. Little wonder then that Grant felt lonely, with his nearest neighbors miles away.

Had it not been for Jim Ryan, Captain Grant might have resigned his commission forthwith and returned home to his loving wife and children. The Ryans invited Grant into their home and showered him with Irish hospitality. They made him acquainted with their many friends and did everything in their power to make him feel at ease. They even threw a party for him, inviting Irishmen for miles around to come and bring their friends. This was the first time that Grant had been invited to an Irish shindig, which was a far cry from his sedate upbringing in Ohio.

Jim's wife Nora, a perfect hostess, entertained the gathering with her delightful singing. She regaled her listeners with a repertoire of old Irish melodies and sentimental ballads and asked everyone to join in the chorus.

Grant, who was known as one who liked a drop, felt at ease among his new Irish friends, whose parties were never known to be dull or dry. The Ryans provided a lavish banquet for their guests and everyone ate and drank to their hearts' content. In later years when word got around that General Grant was fond of his liquor, newspaper reporters claimed he had acquired the habit as a result of his association with the Irish in Humboldt County.

As to General Grant's drinking habits there's a humorous story that bears repeating. When General George McClellan, Commander of the Union Army, called on his Commander-in-Chief, Abraham Lincoln, to report on the progress of the war and his plans for the future, he apparently had other things in mind as well. During the course of their conversation McClellan brought up the subject of Grant's drinking and carousing while on duty, and insisted Grant should not be given a position of leadership in the Union Army. The President hesitated for a moment and then turned to General McClellan and said, "General, my advice to you is to speak with General Grant and find out the brand of liquor he drinks." Apparently President Lincoln had already made up his mind to replace McClellan for his lack of aggressiveness in prosecution of the war. After Grant's sensational victories at Vicksburg and Chattanooga, the President appointed him Commander of the Union Army in March 1864, replacing General McClellan.

In retrospect it was Senator Jim Ryan who was responsible for the turn of events that placed Ulysses Grant in the right place at the right time. Ryan convinced Captain Grant that he was duty bound to fulfill his assignment at Fort Humboldt until the base was in proper order, which would take time. He persuaded Grant to stay on for another year or more. This protracted service enabled him to resign with the consent and good wishes of his superiors in Washington

At the outbreak of the Civil War, Ulysses Grant was working as a clerk in his father's store in Galena, Illinois. His proven record of service as commander of Fort Humboldt made him eligible for re-enlistment in the Union Army with the rank of Colonel.

Although the story of Ulysses Grant, Union Army Commander and eventually President of the United States, has been written and rewritten, few indeed are aware of the important role Jim Ryan played in his career. The companionship and understanding of these two men helped change the course of American history.

JAMES TALBOT RYAN is well remembered for his lifelong contribution to Humboldt County and especially to the City of Eureka, of which he was the founder. Everything for the betterment of Eureka involved the Ryans and their next of kin, the Duffs, the Clarks and Kellys. They pioneered in the development of the lumber industry, building and banking, medicine, merchandising, shipbuilding and transportation.

David Gordon, founder and editor of the *Weaverville Journal*, paid a lasting tribute to Jim Ryan as part of an obituary in 1875: "He was known for his indomitable will and energy, meeting all the vicissitudes of life without flinching, and was a true and reliable friend when his friendship was once acquired. The flags floated at half mast on Monday in honor of his memory. Peace to the ashes of the dead pioneer."

M. Theodore Kearney
Courtesy Fresno City & County Historical Society

− 3 −

MARTIN THEODORE KEARNEY
THOMAS E. HUGHES
FRESNO'S CELTIC LAND BARONS

RESNO'S EARLY DEVELOPMENT and prosperity can well be attributed to two tenacious Irishmen, born over three thousand miles apart, who by fate or a bit of Irish Luck crossed paths on the sun-drenched plains of Central California. Their joint efforts led to the development of the Colony Farm System of land distribution, which lured wealthy investors from all over America. The prescient Colony scheme was further enhanced by a massive irrigation system that provided farmers with an adequate supply of water at a rate they could afford. Whereas Kearney's efforts in land division were confined to Fresno and the vicinity, Tom Hughes's activities involved a much wider area, including the adjoining counties of Madera and Merced. All in all their accomplishments in the heartland of California are a major example of the Irish contribution to the state.

In his day Theodore Kearney was acknowledged as one of the most energetic and powerful agricultural leaders in California. Besides the pioneer Colony Farm System in Fresno County, he founded the California Raisin Growers Association and developed his splendid Fruitvale Estate, the model for raisin production in the central valley. Kearney belongs in a class with such enterprising Irish entrepreneurs as John Downey, pioneer Southern California developer; Thomas Hope, of Santa Barbara, whose flocks of sheep were so immense no herdsman could count them; Martin Murphy, pioneer wheat farmer, who owned more arable land in California than in all his native county Wexford; and Patrick King and Bill Murray, who acquired a 1,233-acre spread, the site of the twin cities of Larkspur and Corte Madera in Marin County.

A self-made man, Kearney, the oldest son of an Irish laborer, went on to carve for himself the image of a refined, educated and well-mannered gentleman, and to gain access to the inner chambers of high society in San Francisco. Unlike Eastern cultural environments, acceptance into the city's elite was dependent not on wealth as such, nor proof of blue-blooded antecedents, but rather as a recognition of a valued newcomer, someone with a touch of class and influence, who could invent and promote schemes for the betterment of all. And who was better suited for that role than the flamboyant promoter Theodore Kearney? He was the right man in the right place and at the right time.

The Kearney Family Tree

THEODORE KEARNEY was born in Liverpool, England, in 1842, the son of immigrant Irish parents, James and Ann Kearney. With little prospect for advancement in that city, the Kearneys, like so many of their peers, set their sights on America in 1854, when Theodore was only twelve years old

Following their arrival in the New World the family settled in Malden, Massachusetts, the home of thousands of Irishmen and women who fled from starvation during the potato famine. In Malden the Kearney's found conditions to be more advantageous, with work for every willing hand and a greater opportunity for advancement by the more ambitious. The Irish immigrant families lived mostly in blocks of tenement houses, convenient to the mills and foundries where the men folk labored; the women worked mostly as domestic servants.

Little is known of the family during their five-year stay in Malden. In fact, Theodore Kearney, for whatever reason, kept their involvement on the local scene a closely guarded secret. In later years, he distanced himself from the Irish, perhaps on account of his father, who was a habitual drinker and abused his mother on a number of occasions, a behavior that he vehemently detested. Theodore was so fearful that he might succumb to his father's drinking habits that he took the temperance pledge at the age of fourteen.

The Kearneys' Elite Celtic Clan

ACCORDING TO Edward MacLysach, the leading Irish genealogist, the surname O'Kearney (Kearney) is renowned in Irish annals, and rates a splendid coat of arms to match the clan's high standing. Unlike other leading families who stayed in their ancestral home counties, the Kearneys scattered in every direction, which accounts for the fact that today the name can be found almost everywhere throughout Ireland.

The Kearney offspring in America have left a record of accomplishments in various fields of endeavor. Five stalwarts by the name of Kearney grace the pages of the Dictionary of American Biography in such fields as literature, government and war.

General Stephen Kearney commanded the Army of the West, whose celebrated march across the continent to Santa Fe New Mexico, and thence to Monterey, was the predecessor of General Sherman's march through Georgia during the Civil War. General Philip Kearney, Stephen's nephew, was equally noteworthy in his day. A graduate of a renowned military academy in Saumeur, France, and America's West Point, he proved his mettle as a military leader in the war with Mexico, in which he lost an arm. A fighting Irishman bar none, Philip Kearney was dubbed "The One-Armed Irish Devil" by the Mexicans after he charged their ranks with his mount's reins in his mouth.

Theodore Kearney, the subject of this narrative, had a totally different outlook on life. In fact, he harbored a distaste for military service, and somehow managed to avoid the draft during the American Civil War. He was said to be in sympathy with Confederates, a number of whom were his closest associates in the business community. In the ensuing years, Kearney engaged in a period of self-education, specializing in German, French and elocution, and took up dancing to enhance his social image.

At the age of nineteen, having completed his studies, he removed to Boston in search of employment and began a new life on his own. And what an engrossing a life it turned out to be. Kearney lived and worked in the big city for a period of some seven years until he got the urge to try his luck in far-off California. He came by way of Panama, taking some three months to reach his destination in San Francisco in February 1869.

From the moment of his arrival in the Gold Rush city Mr. Theodore Kearney acted like an invited guest, one eagerly awaited— by whom it didn't matter. The flamboyant newcomer presented himself as a gentleman, fit to be seen, well bred, highly educated and elegantly mannered. He spoke with a polished Boston accent as if he were a native New Englander, and was altogether the epitome of an educated chevalier, which assured him a place in high society.

To prove his financial worth, Kearney deposited a substantial

sum of money, which he had acquired from previous business deal-
ings, in one of the leading San Francisco banking houses. This display of wealth caught the immediate attention of well-heeled
prospective investors like William Chapman, from Ohio.

About that same time the erstwhile Bostonian formed an alliance
with Doctor Edward Perrin, a man well versed in irrigation, whom
Kearney had met onboard ship on his way to California, Dr. Perrin
convinced Kearney that the great San Joaquin Valley was capable of
producing bounteous crops if properly irrigated. As proof of his con-
viction Perrin traveled to Fresno, where he purchased an 8,640-acre
parcel, securing it with a down payment of $8,000. A short while
later he increased his holdings by purchasing an additional 1,000
acres in that vicinity.

William Chapman, a shrewd investor, acquired vast sections of
public land through the manipulation of government-issued agricultural scrip, entitling the holder to a minimum 160 acres of land per
scrip. Scrip was issued to people who had somehow established a
claim against the government, either for services rendered or in
return for releasing a claim against some federal property. The scrip
could be bought, traded or sold, so that one man could accumulate a
considerable quantity of it and then use it to claim open land in the
sparsely settled state.

Speculators in the know, like Frederick Roeding, for whom
Fresno's Roeding Park is named, purchased a considerable amount of
unappropriated lands in similar fashion. Others, like Henry Miller of
the agricultural mega-firm of Miller and Lux, also took advantage of
the scrip method of land acquisition. The previously unclaimed lands
were offered for sale on the open market at a very attractive price of
$1.25 an acre. Apparently, the scrip method of acquiring land in
California was within the law at the time.

Both Chapman and Kearney had an abiding interest in
California agriculture, which they envisioned as a way to wealth and
influence on a grand scale. Their enthusiasm attracted other wealthy
investors like William Martin, a wealthy San Francisco capitalist, and
Thomas Hughes, who was already well established in the real state
business in the central valley.

Chapman was so taken with the idea of the proposed Colony
Farm System that he appointed Kearney as manager and chief promoter of the newly formed Central California Colony. They had the
land surveyed by Bernard Marks, a former school teacher who was in
a financial bind as a result of his failed investment in mining stocks,

and who hoped to retrieve his losses by investing in agriculture. The land was divided into 192-acre parcels and offered for sale at $1,000 on easy purchase terms of $105 down and $12.50 a month, interest free until paid in full. The Fresno Colonists may have taken a cue from John Downey's pioneer Southern California land division scheme some years previously. Downey offered plots of fifty acres and upwards at ten dollars an acre, with ten percent interest per annum, with one tenth to one fifth of the purchase price in cash, according to location. In that light, The Good Old Days were all they were said to be, and more.

THE FRESNO PROJECT, however, was more conducive to permanent settlers, many of whom had struck it rich in the gold fields and were eager to settle down and build homes for themselves and their families. Kearney's plan made it all the more attractive by having the streets and roads laid out through the tracts, with canals to supply water as needed for irrigation and household use. He also added a homey touch by naming the broad avenues Elm, Fig, Peach, Walnut and Cherry to match the trees about to be planted. The landmark scheme lured settlers from throughout the nation, many of whom were accustomed to living in cramped quarters in East Coast cities, and who, without a moment's hesitation, set out for the open spaces.

The exuberant enterprise caught the attention of the *Fresno Expositor* newspaper in August, 1875, which ran this glowing account of the first colonists:

> We have been favored with an insight into the character of the first 30 to 40 settlers of homesteads in this suburb of Fresno. The prospect afforded for the near future is extremely gratifying. We find them all of the most intelligent class of our people; some of them are residents of San Francisco, engaged in various branches of business, and are deliberately investing in fruit-raising and drying business as others invest in dividend-paying mines.

Those early settlers, many of whom had lived in more adverse climes, were amazed at how fast the crops grew to maturity in sunny California. They could scarcely believe their eyes when in less a year's time the newly planted grapevines were flourishing in the virgin soil, nourished by an abundance of clear water flowing through the newly constructed irrigation system. The vast plains which were once a sandy desert were transformed into a veritable Garden of Eden as if by magic.

Theo Kearney's promotional brochure, in which he speaks of real estate as the basis of all wealth and of California's unequaled soil, climate and irrigation projects, is a fitting introduction to one of the most successful ventures in the history of agriculture in America.

Old-time San Franciscans can recall how the venerable columnist, Arthur Brisbane, preached a kind of gospel from the pulpit of the San Francisco *Examiner,* and those fortunate enough to heed his advice became wealthy as a result. The same proved true in the case of four former San Francisco school teachers, who took his advice. The "tree ladies" combined their assets to purchase a one hundred-acre parcel in the Fresno Farm Colony, which proved to be a lucrative investment. Three years later they marketed 30 twenty-pound boxes of sun-dried raisins. In their seventh year of operation their well-appointed vineyard produced a whopping 7,500 boxes.

Theodore Kearney, never one to miss a beat, cited the erstwhile schoolteachers as an example in his catchy promotional announcements, which appeared in both San Francisco and Fresno newspapers. *The Fresno Expositor* of January 24, 1877, tells it best:

> Why will you go on year after year planting grain, trusting to the uncertain rainfall, and invariably losing in a dry season the hard-earned savings of several years, when right at your very doors in the CENTRAL CALIFORNIA COLONY, you may secure land and an abundance of water to irrigate it at a moderate price and on easy terms of payment. One-quarter cash, and the balance in monthly, quarterly, or semi-annual payments extending over four years, no interest charged on deferred payment. With that land and water you are independent of the season, you are sure of one crop at least, and if you are industrious may raise two, and even three crops of some products. If you combine intelligence and industry with the land and water offered, you can make more money in cultivating one of those twenty acre farms than your average profits in cultivating five hundred acres of grain during the past five years. Besides, you have the certainty of providing enough for the support of your family, and the gratifying prospect of having, in a few years, an orchard and raisin vineyard which will yield you an income from $3,000 to $5,000 per year.

Further information could be obtained by visiting the Colony, by calling on the agents in Fresno, Dixon & Fayetteville, or by writing to the CCC, 306 Pine Street, San Francisco—M. Theo. Kearney. For the land-hungry settlers the "Land Rush" of the 1870s was almost the equal of the Gold Rush of 1849.

The Fresno project was such a success that Kearney became a wealthy man within a few years' time. He could then live the life of a country gentleman, which had been his life's ambition.

Alas, greed and self interest intervened; The Chapman-Kearney partnership was abruptly dissolved as a result of a dispute over future investments when Kearney laid plans for a new venture that did not include Chapman. Shortly thereafter, Kearney was obliged to sell a portion of his holdings in Northern California in order to satisfy his indebtedness in the partnership.

A More Comprehensive Scheme

IN THIS NEW VENTURE Kearney purchased a much larger property, the 2,560 acre Easterly Rancho, in joint ownership with an investor named N.K. Masten. In order to retrieve a part of their original investment as quickly as possible, the partnership sold off several substantial plots to large-scale vineyardists. The remainder they divided into twenty-acre parcels to suit less affluent investors. Kearney presciently reserved the coziest location for himself, a 390-acre plot which he named The Vineyard. At the end of the Vineyard Colony's first year in business Kearney was able to buy out his partner in the Easterly Rancho, leaving himself in complete control of future developments.

The success of this latest Farm Colony venture merely whetted Kearney's appetite for something on a grander scale, more inspirational and utopian. The years of patient effort, business acumen and salesmanship paid off handsomely. At long last the flamboyant promoter could live the 'Life of Riley' as the saying goes. Kearney's social calendar blossomed with lavish banquets at the famed Palace Hotel, the landmark Cliff House and the ultra-fashionable Lick House in San Francisco, where the menus were so expensive that the skinflint proprietor, James Lick, took his meals in a nearby cafe catering to the laboring class.

In the meantime Kearney spent his evenings attending live performances in theaters and concert halls and in Tom Maguire's lavishly decorated Opera House, where he held a reserved seat at major events.

In order to hobnob with the elite he traveled to Old Monterey, and spent a month-long vacation at the fashionable Del Monte Lodge, built in 1880, with an occasional visit to the posh communities of Carmel and Pacific Grove. Kearney liked to see and be seen in the company of wealthy and influential Californians. He planned

*Theodore Kearney's house, Fruit Vale, also called "Chateau Fresno," served
as a showplace for California agriculture as well as for its owner.
Courtesy Fresno City & County Historical Society*

everything with an eye for comfort by spending the spring and fall in
Fresno, to avoid the oppressive summer heat, and the summer in cool
San Francisco, where he leased a suite in the luxurious Palace Hotel.

Fruit Vale Estate: A Lifelong Ambition

IN EARLY 1883, Kearney visited Fresno as usual and toured the area
in search of land suitable for his pet project, an estate with amenities fit for a king. In order to facilitate his plans Kearney purchased a
huge tract of rich land west of the town, measuring six miles east to
west and three miles across, as the sole owner. Wanting a name to
match his intended dynasty, he called it "Fruit Vale Estate."

In order to carry out his plan to make Fruit Vale the showplace of
California, Kearney organized a million-dollar investment corpora-
tion to finance the colossal project. The search for funds led him to
New York, and from there to Paris, Hamburg and eventually to
London, where he met one Captain Cheape, a canny Scotsman who
had already invested heavily in the successful Fresno Irrigation
Works. When the negotiations for Cheape's participation in the Fruit

*The imposing entrance gate to the Kearney estate led to a drive lined
with palm trees, eucalyptus, and many other varieties of trees.
Courtesy Fresno City & County Historical Society*

Vale project were completed, Kearney returned to California to make
plans for the construction of his lordly palace.

Captain Cheape arrived in San Francisco the following spring of
1887, where he was welcomed by Kearney and wined and dined on a
lavish scale. Shortly thereafter the two men traveled to Fresno and
stayed at the Grand Central Hotel, where they were joined by E. W.
Hilgard, head of the California Department of Agriculture, who had
prepared a report on the quality of the soil and the crops and trees
that would flourish in it. Cheape was apparently sold on the idea and
gave his immediate financial backing to the Kearney plans. The name
"Chateau Fresno" was coined by Kearney himself, for a grand castle
modeled after France's Chateau Chenonceau. The landscaped gardens of Del Monte Lodge became the inspiration for his dream park,
with tennis courts, waterfalls and sparkling fountains. Winding roads
were laid out in the pancake-flat landscape to give the illusion of
rolling hills and woodlands encircling a grand chateau.

The tree-planting Kearney initiated in 1892 outdid any similar
project ever attempted up to that time, with magnolia, camphors and

*The gatehouse at the Kearney estate resembles a miniature French
castle, quite fitting for the Prince of Fresno.
Courtesy Fresno City & County Historical Society*

olives by the hundreds, eucalyptus and acacias by the thousands,
countless evergreens, redwood, spruce and cedar, and an array of
palms, junipers, wisteria, vines and other shrubbery. When completed, the eleven-mile, tree-lined Kearney Boulevard was said to be one
of the most beautiful drives in the United States. A three-lane road-
way featuring a broad central lane was reserved for heavier traffic
including horse-drawn wagons, buggies and fancy surreys. An outer
lane was to be for pedestrian and bicycle traffic, and the third was set
aside for a proposed electric trolley line.

Little wonder Kearney was called "The Prince of Fresno." His life
is the story of Fresno.

California Raisin Growers Association

KEARNEY'S ENTHUSIASM knew no bounds in any project that
involved his beloved Fresno. In 1898, he took the lead in the
establishment of an effective raisin co-operative, an idea that had
been tried but had failed for want of a tenacious leader. Kearney
earnestly proposed an association that would define quality, set a fair
price, and do direct marketing for the California raisin industry. A

board of directors was elected forthwith with Theo Kearney as its president. A membership drive was set in motion, which induced some 90% of the raisin growers in the state to become members in its first year. Kearney was the first man with the will-power, business acumen and charisma to make such an association work for the benefit of both the growers and packers. Under his leadership, the association was able to negotiate a price of $3.08 a pound for their raisins in 1898, twice that of the previous year.

Hailed far and wide as the savior of the California raisin industry, Kearney was christened the "Raisin King of Fresno." A magnificent photograph was taken at a mass meeting of the California Raisin Growers Association in Fresno, in which over nine hundred participated, with Theo Kearney as "High King" seated at the head table.

Despite his accomplishments, the flamboyant promoter incurred the wrath of some members of the association as a result of disagreements between himself and Chester Rowell, editor of the *Fresno Republican.* A conflict as to who was right and who wrong about the future of the raisin industry grew more bitter with each passing day. Kearney was upset when the newapaper reported that Kearney came from Ireland and had changed his name from Michael to Martin. He became furious when the paper claimed he was related to Denis Kearney, the San Francisco rabble-rouser. Claiming that this "public joking" would endanger his future plans for Fresno, Kearney demanded an apology. Instead Rowell stepped up the attack, and Kearney struck back by urging his followers to boycott the newspaper. There the matter rested temporarily.

In the heat of battle, Kearney resigned and hastened to San Francisco for a brief rest. Apparently he changed his plans and returned to Fresno, where he met with his longtime friend, Thomas Hughes, at his headquarters, the Hughes Hotel. He withdrew his resignation without comment and nonchalantly took over as president again.

Despite the hassle with the local press and disagreements with a number of his associates in matters of administration, Kearney held firm in his support of the California Raisin Growers Association as a means of protecting their basic interests.

The Sunmaid Raisin Cooperative

WITH THEODORE KEARNEY long gone, a new organization, the California Associated Raisin Company, was formed in 1909 to protect growers' rights following the chaotic conditions and resultant low prices that prevailed in the 1907-08 season. The organization held firm to its commitment to ensure a set price on raisins that would bring growers an equitable return on their investments. In 1914, a banner year for the Associated Raisin Company, the members received $2,275,000 more than for the previous year's crops, an amount that represented three times their total cash investment in the company. On this optimistic note the company announced a new brand name for its raisins, "Sun-Maid", explaining that it was "because choice raisins are a product of our marvelous California sunshine."

The Raisin Queen

AMONG THE MANY SUGGESTIONS to promote the sale of raisins was the idea of a pretty maid in appropriate surroundings. Lorraine Colette, a dark-haired lass working in the packing house, was chosen, along with two other young ladies. The girls wore the traditional worker uniform with blue bonnets and white blouses with blue trimmings. Their first assignment was at the Pan-Pacific International Exposition in San Francisco in 1915. On that auspicious occasion, Lorraine rode in a light plane, dropping baskets of raisins on the crowded fairgrounds below. Following her return to Fresno to take part in the home town parade she was asked to pose for a painting by local artist Fanny Scafford. Out of several sittings, came the final choice, a portrayal of the young model wearing her blue bonnet and white blouse holding a wicker basket overflowing with green grapes and, in the background a brilliant sunburst.

This catchy Sun-Maid trademark became a familiar sight to generations of Americans and millions throughout the world who relished the taste of sun-kissed California raisins. The painting, mounted in a golden frame, was donated to Sun-Maid in 1974 by Lorraine, and now graces the head office of the Kingsbury processing plant. The distinctive bonnet, trimmed in blue, adorns a wall at the Smithsonian Institution in Washington.

Americans nationwide, and Californians in particular, mourned Lorraine Collette's demise in March, 1983, following a long and fruitful life of ninety years. She had been a part of the Sun-Maid Raisin family for more than three generations. Her memory lingers on in one of the most widely recognized trademarks in the modern world: friendly, smiling Fresno Queen Lorraine Collette, with her black curly locks, white blouse trimmed in blue and her dazzling blue bonnet.

Thomas E. Hughes
Courtesy Fresno City & County Historical Society

Thomas E. Hughes

IN 1882 THEO KEARNEY made the acquaintance of a fellow Celt, Thomas Hughes, a transplanted North Carolinian, who traveled to California in 1853 to join his father and an older brother, William. Hughes came by way of Batesville, Arkansas, where the family first settled after leaving North Carolina. While there he met and married Mary Rogers, who along with his brother and sister accompanied him on the precarious westward journey. To ensure their safe arrival in the new country, William met the party at the California state line with provisions for the rest of the journey and fresh teams of horses and wagons to carry them to their destination at his ranch in Stockton.

Following the birth of their two sons, the couple paid a return visit to Arkansas to visit Mary's parents, who were no doubt thrilled to see their grandchildren. During that stay, a third son was born, whom they named William after the boy's uncle in California. When Mary's health began to deteriorate following the birth, they decided to return to California hoping that she would regain her health in the state's salubrious climate.

Their plans were nullified however, by an accident as the party neared Fort Laramie, Wyoming. The wagon in which Mary was traveling overturned while crossing a river, throwing her into the cold water. As a result her health deteriorated, and she passed away on the arrival of the Hughes party in Fort Laramie, Wyoming. Hughes, though terribly shaken by the tragedy, carried her lifeless form into the trading post and procured the necessary ingredients to prepare the body of his beloved for shipment by wagon to Stockton, California. Mrs. Hughes was finally laid to rest following what was said to be the longest funeral march in the history of the west.

When the days of mourning were past, Hughes removed to Merced County, with his three sons, where he purchased seven thousand acres and engaged in large-scale wheat farming This very successful venture induced him to settle in Merced County.

In 1862 he remarried, taking for his second wife a local belle, Anne Yoakum, who bore him his only daughter. Discouraged by crop failures due to lack of rain, Hughes sold out and moved with his family to San Francisco, where he engaged in the real estate business.

This turn of events led to his meeting with another successful land developer, Theodore Kearney, who induced him to locate in Fresno, where Kearney was already well established. Hughes and his sons made an agreement with Doctor Perrin to herd his sheep on Perrin's lands in Fresno in 1878. The Hugheses moved to Fresno in the month of June, and while his sons looked after the sheep, Hughes opened a real estate office.

In their separate ventures, the two businessmen complemented each other. While Kearney, a seasoned veteran of land distribution, played it safe, selling only to investors with abundant capital, Hughes, believed it would be more advantageous in the long run to sell on credit, in order to open up the market to all who were desirous of investing in Central California land.

To put his land scheme to the test, Hughes purchased a 6,080 acre parcel for $40,000, and sold a 640-acre section to acquire enough cash to provide a system of irrigation for the remaining 5,440 acres. About this time, he hit on a novel idea to attract prospective buyers, by offering round-trip railroad tickets from San Francisco to Fresno to induce well-heeled capitalists to visit his acreage.

The first excursion brought hordes of land-hungry buyers to Fresno; they purchased the available land faster than Hughes and Sons could prepare the agreements of sale. They did "A Land Office Business," as it came to be known. The enterprise was so successful that the Hughes firm was obliged to open a branch office in San Francisco the following year to meet the ever-increasing demand for land.

Within a year's time the firm set a record volume for the Fresno area by selling some 36,000 acres of land, realizing over $300,000 for rural properties and over $18,000 for properties in the city of Fresno. The *Fresno Weekly Expositor* tells it thus:

> There is perhaps no man, firm or set men that have done more for the advancement of Fresno County than the firm of Thomas Hughes and Sons - the efforts of these owners to scatter abroad reliable information relative to Fresno County lands, has done more than any other one thing to give the colony system rapid growth and permanent settlers.

IN ORDER to meet the demands of the new settlers, Hughes took the lead in 1881 in organizing the pioneer Fresno County Bank, which a year later became the First National Bank. And again in 1885 Hughes sought to enlist San Francisco's wealthy capitalists in the construction of a first-class hotel on his property in the heart of Fresno. Failing to enlist investors, he set out in a new direction to implement the project. His friend Theodore Kearney was so involved in the development of his holdings that he was not in a position to engage in any new enterprise, for the time being at least.

To carry forward his building plans Hughes founded the Fresno Hotel Association with a capital investment of $10,000, with Hughes and Sons controlling half the stock. Despite an uncertain future, the building proceeded as planned. The ground-breaking ceremony took place on April 1, 1887, and in May the foundation was laid. However by midsummer only the first floor of the building had been completed. Perturbed by the laxity of effort, Hughes offered the contractors a thousand dollars a month for each month the hotel was completed prior to April 1, 1888. The builders, accepting the incentive, completed the magnificent hotel in record time. In the interim the Hughes family properties near the hotel, which had averaged several thousand dollars in value before the hotel was built, now had an assessed valuation of over $327,000.

The lavish hotel, Fresno's tallest building at four stories high, was enhanced by the city's first elevator, with electricity throughout, generated by the hotel's own power plant. The hotel had its own ice-making plant, which ensured a $200 a month saving for the owners.

The first floor, along Tulare street, was divided into eight handsome stores faced with plate glass fronts. The main entrance on I street had an ornamental archway and recessed vestibule and variegated mosaic tiling. Three double doors led to the main lobby, stair case and elevator. To the left and right of the grand lobby were reading rooms, a smoking room and the hotel office, as well as the entrance to the main dining room, which, in connection with the breakfast room and private dining room, could accommodate 450 people in comfort at one seating.

The architect, James Seadler of San Francisco, spared no effort in making the hotel as quiet and comfortable as possible. The billiard room with six tables, the barroom and the adjoining wine cellar on I Street, were separated from the hotel entrance so as to prevent any unusual noise from disturbing guests.

THE GRAND OPENING of the Hughes Hotel was set for June, 9, 1888. However a fire broke out a few days earlier, and although damage to the hotel was minimal, the Hughes stables close by were totally destroyed. Fortunately the horses were all set free in the nick of time by the stable foreman, Mr. Childs, who risked his life in the effort. The grand opening was put on hold for the time being. Finally, on the evening of July 11, 1888, what was described by the press as "The Most Brilliant Social Gathering of the Year," and by others as the most delightful social event in the history of Fresno, got underway.

Nothing was overlooked by the welcoming committee. Arriving guests were met at the railroad depot, serenaded by a uniformed band, and escorted up the streets of the city to the shimmering Hughes Hotel. The grand ballroom was gaily decorated with stars and stripes bunting, interspersed with banks of green ferns and California evergreens. The Grand March began at 8 p.m. in the main lobby, led by one of Hughes's sons and his lady fair. All together over one hundred couples attended the house-warming party, which honored the grandest structure anywhere between San Francisco and Los Angeles.

This was only one of Hughes's many efforts to benefit his beloved Fresno. In 1887 he pioneered in the establishment of a streetcar line running from the train depot to the fairgrounds. And the following year he formulated a plan for a new Opera House. The edifice was to be a three-story brick building consisting of two stores on the ground level, fifteen or more offices for commercial use, and a theater with a seating capacity of 1,300 people. However, nothing ever came of the grandiose proposal. It fell to the lot of a man named Robert Barton to build Fresno's first Opera House, which was still functioning in the 1930s.

By December 1889 the assessed valuation of Fresno County made it the sixth richest county in the state. Hughes was its seventh largest taxpayer, holding property with an assessed value in excess $350,000. The actual market value, of course, was much higher.

The 1890 January edition of the *Fresno Expositor* declared:

> While [Hughes] has amassed $1,000,000 or more in the past ten years he has not acquired a dollar of it by oppressing creditors or taking advantage of those whom he has dealings with. Always approachable and unassuming, he is pre-eminently the leading spirit and useful man of Fresno County.

Through the efforts of Hughes, Kearney and others, the population of Fresno grew from a village of less than two thousand inhabitants to a thriving city of ten thousand within a period of eight years. Fresno is now a vibrant city with a population of over 400,000 inhabitants.

What the federal government is doing today—underwriting loans to help people buy their own homes—Thomas Hughes, the "Father of Fresno," and Theodore Kearney, the "Prince of Fresno," did many years before, on a smaller yet firmer scale.

Thomas Hughes and Theodore Kearney did much to build Fresno into a mighty agricultural empire, supplying virtually all of the raisins consumed today in the United States.

Eleanor Downey Harvey Martin
from a miniature portrait
Courtesy Society of California Pioneers

– 4 –

ELEANOR DOWNEY MARTIN
THE IRISH CZARINA

1826 - 1928

IRISH-BORN ELEANOR DOWNEY MARTIN, the queen of high society in old San Francisco, was a genteel and gracious charmer, an exemplar of Victorian respectability, who ruled San Francisco society with a firm hand for more than five decades. At her splendid house on Broadway, the "Irish Czarina," as she was called, entertained three Presidents of the United States: William McKinley, Theodore Roosevelt, and William Howard Taft. For generations, no function, social, benevolent or charitable, was complete without her presence. She could hold an assemblage in the palm of her tiny hand, with her imperious manner and emphatic Irish wit.

Heiress to three great fortunes before she reached middle age, Eleanor Martin could bestow social success with a nod and a smile. Her first husband, Walter Harvey, left her a large fortune. Through the Downey family she inherited a sizable amount. Her second husband, Edward Martin, left an estate said to be one of the largest in California. She inherited more money and property on the death of her sister, Annie Downey Donahue, in 1896.

When Eleanor Martin chose a steamboat excursion for an outing on the inviting waters of the Bay, rather than the customary drive down the Peninsula, proper ladies and gentlemen immediately chartered colorful sailing craft and motor boats to ferry them to Sausalito for a sumptuous lunch of early California cuisine. When rested and refreshed, they climbed the steep hills to have their photographs taken against the panorama of the Golden Gate.

For more than half a century a fashionable mix of local notables, foreign dignitaries, churchmen, princes, potentates, business tycoons, uniformed officers, musicians, artists, literati and a host of longtime friends moved through the elegant Pacific Heights mansion of Eleanor Martin. Unlike the so-called magic circle of the Astors, the Rockefellers and Ward McAllister of New York, whose gatherings were often prudish, humorless and puritanical, the San Francisco society functions were relaxed, witty and entertaining. To Eleanor Martin, a friend was a friend, regardless of his station in life—butcher, baker or banker.

Mrs. Martin's combined assets of unlimited wealth, natural beauty, and graceful hospitality enabled her, with the help of her friend, Ned Greenway, to establish the standards of high society in old San Francisco. Her elegant mansion at 2040 Broadway, with gas lamps shining brightly from every window, was the center of social life in the new metropolis.

Neighbors looked on in wonderment as gaily decorated surreys and handsome coaches pulled up to the curb, disgorging lovely ladies, escorted by top-hatted cavaliers into the mansion, to be greeted by the radiant Czarina in person. Sumptuous dinners of eighteen courses often began at 6:30 and lasted until midnight. Such occasions were typical in the Gilded Age, when fashionable ladies wore flowing dresses with sleeves full and fluffy, and broad-brimmed hats which cast shadows as they moved about. To be invited to such glamorous affairs was considered a badge of honor in San Francisco's halcyon days.

Eleanor Martin was one of a kind, a gifted society leader who looked and acted the part, always courteous and generous. Over the years she donated large sums of money and goods to various charities and civic institutions for the betterment of society in general. Her ornate residence on Broadway became the center of life from which all good things emanated. For her there was no generation gap between young and old, even as she approached her ninetieth birthday. She loved youth with a passion, and always surrounded herself with spirited young men and women. Many indeed were young ladies of modest means whom she took under her wing and helped up the social ladder.

High society in early San Francisco was a complex phenomenon. In the 1860s the city was still so new that no one could claim to be a member of an "old family." Connections to aristocratic or wealthy families in the East or the South were the most solid bases for social leadership. No matter how humble one's birth, a vast fortune, whether from gold mining, commerce, shipping, or agriculture, was usually sufficient to gain admission to the top social circles of the city. But there was no clear organization or pattern; one couldn't be sure whether a new acquaintance was entirely respectable, or exactly what the basis of his claim to respectability might be. Eleanor Martin felt a duty thrust upon her that had to be fulfilled. She would organize high society, establish rules for membership and conduct.

In order to more fully understand how all of this came to be, one has to know something of Eleanor's upbringing in Ireland, in that challenging period in Irish history.

Eleanor Martin's Irish Roots

BORN ELEANOR DOWNEY in Castle Sampson, County Roscommon, in 1826, she was one of four children whose parents were Denis and Bridget (Gately) Downey. She had two brothers, John and Patrick, and a sister, Annie, all of whom emigrated to America and eventually settled in California. Patrick died young.

Castle Sampson lies close by the River Shannon, adjacent to the historic town of Athlone, birthplace of the beloved Irish tenor John McCormack. The locale was an area of small farms whose occupants fell on hard times, and as a result the majority of them, like the Downeys, were forced to emigrate.

John Downey, an ambitious young man, arrived in California almost penniless, established a business, invested in real estate, and eventually became governor of California. Annie Downey married Peter Donahue, San Francisco's leading industrialist, owner of the Union Iron Works, builder of railroads and steamboats, the man who installed the first gaslights in the city.

As a young girl Eleanor traveled with her sister Annie to Baltimore, Maryland, where they were welcomed by two older half-sisters who operated a fashionable boarding school in that city. Their brother John, who had preceded them to America, was living with these enterprising ladies when his sisters arrived. His presence made them feel very much at home in a strange land.

Little else is known of their stay in Baltimore. The discovery of gold in far-off California altered the lives of countless Irish immigrants, including the Downey family. John Downey prospered in Los Angeles, and urged his sisters to join him there. This was not a journey to be undertaken lightly by two young women traveling by themselves. Nevertheless, in 1856, Eleanor and Annie sailed to Panama, crossed the Isthmus, and arrived in San Francisco May 22 of that year. Eleanor was then 30 years old.

Their arrival coincided with one of the most memorable occasions in the history of San Francisco. It was a church holy day, the feast of the Ascension of Christ into heaven, according to Catholic tradition. A solemn High Mass was being celebrated by the most Reverend Joseph Sadoc Alemany, first Archbishop of San Francisco and second Bishop of California, at old St. Mary's Cathedral, still standing at California and Grant. The ceremony was said to be so glorious and inspiring that it lured people from every walk of life, religious or otherwise. Four other Catholic Churches—Mission Dolores, founded in 1776, Saint Francis, which served as the city's first cathedral, Saint Patrick's, San Francisco's Irish Bethlehem, and the French Notre Dame Des Victoires celebrated Christ's Glorious Ascension into heaven with equal fervor. The prayerful celebrations lent an air of joy and tranquillity to the rambunctious Gold Rush city. The religious atmosphere had a lasting effect on the Downey sisters, who themselves were devout Catholics.

By sheer coincidence it was also the occasion of the burial of James King of William, whose funeral procession slowly wound through the streets of the city in the afternoon. King, the controversial editor of the *San Francisco Call*, was gunned down in broad daylight by James Casey, whom he had maligned in the columns of his newspaper. Casey and an accomplice paid with their lives for the murder at the hands of Vigilantes, a self-appointed, self-anointed group of reformers who took the law into their own hands and meted out justice without the consent of judge or jury.

Shortly after her arrival California Eleanor enrolled in the Convent of Notre Dame in San Jose, majoring in French and Academic studies, which she put to proper use in later life. Notre Dame, despite the name, was very much an Irish-oriented institution from its beginning in California. Martin Murphy, a pioneer Irish-Californian, was an important contributor to the school.

Eleanor Downey Marries

L ATER that same year Eleanor and Annie Downey paid a visit to their brother John in Los Angeles, who was already well established in business and land development. During their stay Eleanor met Major Walter Harvey, a dashing United States Cavalry officer who had distinguished himself during the war with Mexico eleven years earlier. Two years later they were united in marriage by the Right Reverend Thaddeus Amat, C.M., the first bishop of California.

Major and Mrs. Harvey moved north to take up residence in the booming city of San Francisco. Their first home was on Rincon Hill, a fashionable residential district which looked down on the bustling port. Here Eleanor gave birth to their only son, John Downey Harvey, and a daughter who died in infancy. The Harveys' first home was destroyed by fire, a common occurrence in those days. For a short while they lived with a Mrs. Skidmore, a widow, on Minna Street in Happy Valley, near today's Market and Third Streets. Mrs. Skidmore's daughter, Harriet, was the reigning poetess laureate of San Francisco in that period.

Major Harvey, a prominent figure in California's early history, was a flamboyant man. He was also a controversial figure, especially when word leaked out in 1852 that he had mistreated the Indians who lived beside the Kings River in the San Joaquin Valley. The affair led to a quarrel between himself and Major James Savage, Commander of the Mariposa Battalion, a trusted friend of the local tribes. The outcome was a brawl—some called it a duel—in which Savage was gunned down by Major Harvey and died almost instantly.

ACCORDING TO Irish genealogist Edward MacLysagh, the Savages were a renowned clan in Ireland at the time of the English plantation of Ulster. As for Jim Savage, he was proud of his Irish heritage. In fact he taught Irish history to the Mariposa tribes; he equated the trials and tribulations of the Irish under English rule with the plight the Indians under American rule. Thanks to Savage's influence, a group of Tulare Indians even came to San Francisco in 1852 to celebrate St. Patrick's Day.

In spite of the controversy, Major Harvey was never held accountable for Savage's death. In 1861, Harvey was appointed superintendent of immigration at the port of San Francisco, a position he held until his death in August of that same year. His wife was then 35.

Eleanor remained a widow for nine years; then she met and married Edward Martin, one of the founders of the Hibernia Bank in San Francisco, and a leading figure in the city's financial circles. Martin's fortune was said to be one of the largest in California in the 1870s. A native of County Wexford, Martin had come over the mountains to California with the Murphy-Miller-Townsend party in 1844. Their marriage proved to be a turning point in the life of Eleanor Martin. Of that union three children were born Peter, Walter and Andrew.

Annie Downey Donahue
Author's collection

All three received classical educations and married into families of wealth, high standing and influence. Peter married a fashionable young lady, Lily Oelrich of New York. Andrew married Genevieve Goad, and Walter married Mary Scott. Peter and Andrew died young, but their children and grandchildren later gathered round the festive table at their grandmother's palatial residence in Pacific Heights. Walter lived to a ripe old age and remained a constant companion of his mother, following the death of his father in 1880.

The Heavenly Twins: High Society Comes to San Francisco

ANNIE DOWNEY married Peter Donahue, a widower with two children, and San Francisco's leading industrialist, owner of the
Union Iron Works, builder of railroads and steamboats, the man who
installed the first gaslights in the city. The marriage brought together
two of the leading families in early California. Wealth being the high
road to influence, Annie, like her sister, soon became a leader of high
society in San Francisco.

While her older sister Eleanor was better suited for the role as San
Francisco's social arbiter, Annie also played an important part in
establishing social standards and sponsoring events. The two Irish
charmers became known as "The Heavenly Twins." In dignity and
elegance they both lived the part, through the challenging 1870s, the
rip-roaring 80's, and the Gay 90s.

Coincidental to the establishment of High Society in old San
Francisco, was a chance meeting between Eleanor Martin and Ned
Greenway, the San Francisco representative for Beau Brummel
Mumm's champagne. Greenway suggested that the two of them
should organize San Francisco society and make it the equal of New
York's Four Hundred, which was the number Mrs. Astor's ballroom
could accommodate. Eleanor Martin agreed wholeheartedly.

The first order of business was to make a list of the most desirable
aspirants for membership in the posh society. It was mutually agreed
that Mrs. Martin's immediate circle of friends would have first choice,
in addition to certain obligatory personages such as the Crockers,
Huntingtons, Hopkinses, and others with a known thirst for Mumm's
champagne. As a precaution against outside interference, the two
friends further agreed that they alone would have the final say, the
absolute right to veto undesirable candidates for membership in their
circle. Eleanor Martin and Ned Greenway took themselves very seriously, and they expected everyone else to take them seriously as well.

Eleanor Martin truly enjoyed her role as social arbiter, and was
fully prepared to fulfill it in every manner possible. For Mr.
Greenway, the rotund champagne dispenser, it was good business.
And he enjoyed being in the limelight for the first time in his life.

San Francisco's First Cotillion Ball

AS THE prima donna of high society in San Francisco, Eleanor
Martin held firm to the Irish tradition that the home was central
to everything in life. Mrs. Martin's home was her castle in a special

and somewhat peculiar sense. She believed in the home as woman's time-honored career, and frowned on women's suffrage, though after it was achieved she considered it her duty to vote in every election. She believed that a woman's proper place was in the home, where she was the source of hospitality and the focus of attention. But a new problem arose when she and Ned Greenway began planning the first Cotillion Ball. She realized her Broadway mansion would be unable to accommodate such a large gathering. She and Ned Greenway instead chose the Odd Fellows Hall, the only building large enough to house Eleanor's extensive list of high society's Who's Who.

Mrs. Martin and Mr. Greenway carefully reviewed the debutante lists in preparation for the Cotillion. Their edict was final. Gate crashing was impossible. On the night of the premier Bachelor's Cotillion in 1887, the dapper Ned Greenway and Lady Eleanor led the Quadrille—Greenway blowing a whistle and calling out the intricate steps and figures for the dancers to follow.

Michael de Young, owner of the *San Francisco Chronicle*, was so entranced by the grand affair that he hired Ned Greenway to write a society column in his newspaper. Not to be outdone, William Randolph Hearst engaged William Chambliss, a former Mississippi riverboat captain who had a way with words, to write a similar column for the San Francisco *Examiner*.

The journalists devoted most of their energies to deploring each other's tastes and habits, and belittling the subjects of each other's column. Chambliss in particular loathed the Greenway-Martin list of worthies invited to the Bachelor's Cotillion ball. His reference to Michael de Young as being a Jew led to his undoing. San Franciscans were in an ecstatic, optimistic mood at the time and wanted none of the Mississippi Boatman's vitriolic pen.

John Downey Harvey, 1858-1947

JOHN DOWNEY HARVEY, the only son of Walter and Eleanor Downey Harvey, was an active clubman who personified a forgotten era of graciousness and good fellowship in old San Francisco. Born in Los Angeles, he removed to San Francisco with his parents. He attended Saint Ignatius School, which at that time was located on Market Street, where the Emporium department store was later built. Upon completion of his studies at the Jesuit institution young Harvey enrolled at Santa Clara College, majoring in business and administration.

After graduation he became involved in various business enterprises which his father had pioneered and developed. In the ensuing years Harvey became a successful entrepreneur and noted sportsman. He was an active member of the Bohemian Club, the Olympic Club and the Pacific Union Club. An ardent golfer, he held a membership in almost every golf club in the Bay area.

He is best remembered, however, for his part in the development of the famed but ill-fated Ocean Shore Railway, of which he served as president for a number of years. The Shoreline Company, formed in 1905, led to development of the most unusual railroad in the history of California. It was a thrilling ride while it lasted. The rail line ran from the Twelfth Street terminal in San Francisco out to Daly City, and then hugged the rugged coastline down to Tunitas, below Half Moon Bay. The board of the company consisted of a blue-chip line-up of officers, including such industrial giants as J. A. Folger, the legendary California Coffee King.

There was an air of excitement as fun-loving San Franciscans by the thousands headed down the sea coast aboard the train, enjoying the spectacular scenery. The railroad produced a gigantic land boom on the Peninsula, with lots near the various stations being snapped up at an astounding rate. The excitement was short-lived; the new line was plagued with delays, disruptions and devastating landslides which combined to deflate the once beautiful dream. Great chunks of the railroad bed tumbled with a mighty roar and fell into the Pacific Ocean.

Gone but not forgotten after twenty years, the Ocean Shore Railway was still a topic of conversation among old-timers when this writer arrived in San Francisco in 1926. History buffs can still trace the route of the scenic railroad through the many signs, collapsed trestles and side-hill cuts that are still visible. Surprisingly, the Ocean Shore Railroad was listed in local telephone directories until a few short years ago.

John Harvey died at the his home at 1100 Union Street in 1947, at the age of 89.

The Declining Years

M<small>RS.</small> M<small>ARTIN</small> dearly loved the chatter, the laughter and the warmth of friends and neighbors about her. She presided over splendid dinners until well into her nineties, although she sometimes dozed off between courses, according to newspaper reports. Although she had lived for years with her memories of San Francisco's delightful past, Eleanor Martin had also kept in touch with the world around her and kept pace with the changing times. She remained active in charitable affairs, and following the earthquake and fire of 1906 she turned over her beautiful home to the government to be used as a headquarters for Army personnel during the crisis.

According to Sister Margaret Redman, presently living in retirement at the Convent of the Sacred Heart in Albany, New York, when the Order removed from Menlo Park to San Francisco in the 1920s to await the completion of the new College for Women on Lone Mountain, Mrs. Martin allowed the Sisters to teach school in her home on Broadway. Sister Margaret spent her last two years in college as a boarder at Sacred Heart Convent.

Mrs. Martin gradually retired from her reigning position in society in her advancing years, but she never lost interest in the world she knew so well. Following her retirement from active affairs, many regal banquets and delightful performances were given at her home, and no charity ball or welfare fete was complete without her presence.

Eleanor Martin, the Irish Czarina, reigned in San Francisco for over half a century. It could only have happened in California: an Irish Catholic setting the standards of high society. During the same time period, employers in New York and Boston posted signs reading "No Irish Need Apply."

ELEANOR MARTIN died on July 6, 1928, in the stately mansion where she had entertained Presidents, princes and potentates, the high and the mighty of the earth and the low and lonely. Had she lived another six weeks she would have been 102 years old. She died in the evening as the sun set over the Golden Gate and the big Presidio cannon boomed the close of another day. The years crept over her so softly that she retained her blithe spirit almost until the last, her body becoming gradually frailer, but her faculties remaining normal to the end. The doyenne of San Francisco died so peacefully that her two sons John Downey Harvey and Walter Martin, who were at her bedside, were scarcely aware that she had passed away.

Telegrams and cables poured in from all over the world, for her charm and hospitality were a legend to all who visited San Francisco.

As in the age-old Irish tradition Eleanor's wake was held at her elegant residence at 2040 Broadway, where she had been a gracious hostess to three generations of San Francisco society.

At the funeral on Monday, July 9, 1928, Archbishop Edward Hanna delivered the eulogy. He spoke feelingly of Eleanor Martin's great fidelity, of her high ideals, of her help to the needy, and of the remarkable example of the Catholic heritage her life had afforded. Although she had been a lifelong parishioner and benefactor of Saint Brigid's church, she was given the higher honor of being buried from the city's pioneer cathedral, Old St. Mary's, where she had worshipped on her arrival in San Francisco in 1856.

The interior of the church was bedecked with flowers of every color. Monsignor Charles Ramm celebrated a requiem mass before the modest coffin. Civic leaders and society figures like Senator James D. Phelan, General Hunter Liggett, and Philip Paschal, who had known Mrs. Martin for many decades, bowed their heads as they bore her to her final resting place. Mrs. Martin was laid to rest in the family plot in Holy Cross Cemetery.

Other pioneer Irish families also became civic and social leaders—the Phelans and Sullivans, the Tobins and Martins, the Casserlys and Doyles, the Murphys and Riordans, among others. The "Silent City," Holy Cross Cemetery, is a constant reminder that the Irish who were together in life are now together in death. Eleanor Martin, one can be sure, reigns as queen of the Silent City.

Joseph McKenna

- 5 -

Joseph McKenna

Small Town Lawyer
to High Court Justice

1843 - 1926

"WHERE IS THAT YOUNG MAN who at twenty-two can prefix an Honorable to his name? I want to meet him," said Leland Stanford, the newly elected Governor of California. The man he was referring to was Joseph McKenna, one of the youngest men to pass the California State Bar and practice law in Solano County. In the ensuing years, 1885-1925, McKenna served as congressman, United States Circuit Court Judge, Attorney General and Supreme Court Justice.

Joe McKenna was born in Philadelphia on August 10, 1843, to John and Mary Ann Johnson McKenna, both of whom emigrated from Ireland. One of the faceless multitude of Irishmen who immigrated to America, John McKenna, a baker by trade, settled in the Irish quarter of that city. Incited to leave Ireland in massive numbers by religious persecution, the evils of English absentee land ownership embedded in a feudal economic system, and the awesome potato famine of the 1840's, the Irish arrived on America's eastern seaboard by the thousands.

With the help of friends, John McKenna opened a small bakery in Philadelphia and shortly thereafter married Miss Johnson, who had come over a few years earlier. The income derived from the business was scarcely enough to provide for his growing family, which increased almost yearly. Besides enduring economic hardships the Irish-Catholic McKennas were faced with vicious threats by the Know Nothing movement which became a formidable force in Philadelphia in the late 1840s. In 1844 bloody fist fights led to riots and gun firing in the vicinity of the McKenna residence, which placed an increasing burden on a struggling young immigrant like John McKenna.

Despite his ethnic and financial difficulties the elder McKenna never lost faith in the American Dream. Fully determined that his children would enjoy the many benefits which had been denied him by time and circumstances in Ireland, he managed to pay the tuition for his eight year old son Joseph in the newly refurbished Catholic institution of Saint Joseph's College in Philadelphia. In the meantime he was on the lookout for a better environment in order to escape from the frustrating arena of that city's Irish ghetto.

It was then he learned of a broad new land away in the west, where there was no deterrent to advancement save that of the limitation of ability and lack of determination to succeed, and where Catholicism was an asset rather than a liability. The only obstacle that stood in the McKennas' path was the cost of transporting such a large family to far off California.

The stiff one-way fare of approximately $150 per head on the safest and swiftest route, by ship to Panama, thence across the Isthmus to catch the first vessel bound for San Francisco, was too costly for lower-class people like the McKennas. But as Irish Luck would have it, a rate war broke out between the competing shipping companies with the result that fares dropped dramatically. It was then that the McKennas were able to scrape up the passage money and without a moment's hesitation they set out for New York to board the first available ship bound for San Francisco.

The hardy clan survived the long and hazardous journey in third class accommodations, and early in 1855 the McKennas arrived in the Golden Gate City penniless, but nonetheless happy to be there.

Shortly thereafter the McKennas removed to the little port town of Benicia, which had served for a period as state capital in 1853. With the help of friends, John scraped up enough money to start a bakery business of his own. Joseph worked with his father after school and on weekends which kept the operating expenses at a minimum. At long last, this proud Irishman could boast that his children were properly attired as they trotted off to Sunday mass and as pupils in a private school, a luxury that others could not afford.

For the McKennas it was like a dream when, in 1861, their oldest son Joseph enrolled in the Benicia Collegiate Institute, a private school operated by Professor C. J. Flatt, and later incorporated as Benicia College, which offered the only law course in the State at the time. For the next three years Joseph studied hard, and in 1864 he graduated with honors from that pioneer institution. George Lamont, an attorney of long standing in Solano County, graduated in the same class and became a law partner of Joe McKenna under the firm name of McKenna and Lamont, with offices in Fairfield.

AN ARDENT PRACTITIONER with political ambitions, McKenna was appointed District Attorney of Solano County two years later. In that position he served for two consecutive terms, from 1866 to 1870. The experience seemed to whet his appetite for higher political office, and in 1875 McKenna ran for election as state assemblyman for Solano County and won election by a comfortable majority. While serving in that position his name was put forward as a Republican candidate for the office of Speaker of the State Assembly. He was soundly defeated by the Honorable G. J. Carpen of Placerville, the Democratic candidate.

In 1872 McKenna ran for a seat in the House of Representatives on the Republican ticket and failed in the attempt. In 1878, and again in 1880, he was a candidate for that same office and failed to win on both occasions.

Shortly thereafter he returned to Fairfield and took up where he left off in 1866. He was a practicing attorney for the next four years, biding his time until the political climate seemed more favorable.

When it looked as if the Republicans were about to regain control in Congress, McKenna became a candidate for the House of Representatives for the fourth time. In the Republican sweep of 1884, he was elected by a sizable majority and took his seat in the United States Congress March 4, 1885.

Four times in succession he was re-elected to that body, where he served with dignity and distinction from March 1885 to March 1892. Toward the end of his term in Congress, McKenna resigned to accept an appointment by President Benjamin Harrison as United States Circuit Judge. The fact that he was chosen to succeed the venerable Judge Lorenzo Sawyer, who had held that office for twenty two years, made the appointment all the more significant.

Attorney General of the United States

SHORTLY AFTER William McKinley's election as President of the United States in 1897, he asked Judge McKenna to become a member of his Cabinet, which he at first refused for family and other reasons. However, after the pleading telegrams from the President, "I want you and I need you," McKenna traveled to Canton, Ohio, to talk it over man to man, with the result that when the portfolio of

Attorney General was offered to him, he gratefully accepted. It was a day that history was made as Joseph McKenna was the first man west of the Mississippi to serve in a President's Cabinet.

The question of his confirmation by the Senate, however, was another matter. Judge McKenna was a Catholic at a time when there was strong prejudice against the Church of Rome. Protests that seemed but feeble whispers at first became more vocal, with the intent of barring an honorable man from holding such high office because of his religious beliefs. One of the boldest went so far as to intimate to President McKinley that the Senate might not confirm Judge McKenna's appointment because of his religion. "What then, Mr. President?" he asked. The President, evidently irked by the suggestion, replied, "Very well, then, I'll send Judge McKenna's name to the Senate until it is confirmed." The President's firm stand was effective, and on March 5, 1897, Judge McKenna's nomination as Attorney General was duly confirmed by both Houses of Congress.

When the good news was publicized in the press, congratulatory messages by the hundreds came pouring into McKenna's office in Washington. The first telegram he received came from fellow Irish-Californian John Mackey, one of the four Bonanza Kings. The message was quite lengthy, a good four pages, ardent in content and befitting the master of telegraphy himself. The second telegram came from his old friend, Congressman Tom Reed in Washington, and contained but one word: "Immense," which was adopted by others as a token of approbation.

An elaborate celebration to honor his cabinet appointment was planned by his friends to be held at the world-renowned Palace Hotel in San Francisco. The engraved invitations prepared by the welcoming committee stand as a tribute to McKenna who rose to fame on the national scene and in so doing won the respect and admiration in the hearts of his fellow Californians.

The invitations read as follows:

PALACE HOTEL, SAN FRANCISCO
FEBRUARY 15, 1897

Dear Friends:
The citizens of California will give a banquet at the Palace Hotel, on Tuesday evening, February 23rd, to Honor Joseph McKenna, United States Circuit Court Judge, in appreciation of the compliment paid this State by his appointment to a cabinet position; and in testimony of his worth as our most acceptable and honored representative.

Your presence on that occasion, with participation in the festivities of the hour is cordially requested.
By request of the committee on invitations.

> Henry P. Sonntag, Chairman,
> Barry Baldwin,
> A.A. Watkins,
> Cornelius O'Connor,
> Hugh Hume.
> Invitation Committee.

According to press reports it was the grandest party ever staged in San Francisco.

Shortly after Judge McKenna became Attorney General, he was confronted with a perplexing problem. Secretary of State Alger, a Protestant, had granted a plot of public land to the Catholic Prelate of West Point Academy on which to build a Chapel. As the attorney for the Government, McKenna filed a request for the return of the property, claiming that it belonged to the United States and, therefore, could not be conveyed to any church or individual whatsoever. This act was frowned upon by some over-zealous Catholics who proclaimed that McKenna should be held accountable. At this point McKenna sought the advice of Cardinal Gibbons, the most learned and just prince of the Catholic Church. The kind-hearted Cardinal grasped both the judge's hands in his and said, "My son, my business is the salvation of souls. Yours is in the unraveling of weighty legal questions, and I know of no man better qualified to do so. And may God bless your task." That was all McKenna needed. He remembered the parable in Christ's own words: when asked whom he should pay tribute to, Caesar or God, He asked the man for a coin and asked whose inscription was on it. "Caesar's," came the reply. Then he said to the man, "Render to Caesar the things that are Caesar's and to God the things that are God's."

Joe McKenna held this occasion dear for the rest of his mortal life. He was now at ease with his own conscience and with every American whom he was sworn to serve regardless of their state in life.

Associate Justice of the Supreme Court

PRESIDENT MCKINLEY'S NOMINATION of Joseph McKenna as Associate Justice of the Supreme Court, written by hand, was forwarded to the Senate on December 6, 1897. This time, however, no one challenged his nomination as all were in agreement that Joseph McKenna was one of the most honorable lawmen that ever graced

Back row: Justices Peckman, Shiras, Chief Justice White, McKenna
Front row: Brewer, Harlem, Fuller, Gray, Browne. The panel of Judges are
pictured here in their robes of office on the memorable occasion when Judge
McKenna took his seat as a member of that august body.

the American scene. A month or so later in January 1898, Associate Justice Joseph McKenna was duly confirmed by both Houses of Congress and took his seat on that honorable tribunal, replacing Justice Stephen Fried who had retired.

On the day the President sent his nomination to the Senate, McKenna's daughter Isabel was keeping company with Mrs. McKinley in her study in the White House. At five o'clock in the evening the President came in and tenderly embraced his invalid wife. He was wearing the traditional red carnation in the button hole of his jacket. Turning to Isabel he said, "Is your carriage below?"

Taken by surprise, Isabel rose from her seat and replied in the affirmative, "Yes, Mr. President." Taking the flower from his jacket he continued, "I have just this moment sent to the Senate your father's appointment to the Supreme Court. I want you to go straight to the Department of Justice and congratulate him. I myself would much rather have been a Justice of the Supreme Court than President of the United States," he added. "Take this carnation to him from me, with my love."

The Supreme Court Justices were men who had proven their

ability and trustworthiness and were held in high esteem by the vast majority of Americans: Chief Justice Fuller, who looked the part of a father figure; Justice Peckman, the sage; Justice Harlem, renowned for his wit and wisdom; Justice White, who would later become Chief Justice; Justice McKenna, President McKinley's first appointee; Justices Shiras, Brewer, Grey and Browne who added dignity and balance to the august panel.

WASHINGTON SOCIETY reached a high point during President McKinley's administration. Mrs. McKinley was a gentle, beautiful hostess, though quite frail and often unable to take as active a part as she would have liked. Mrs. Howard, the Vice President's wife, presided over many notable functions in the absence of the first lady. The cabinet members' wives, however, filled the void as needed, graciously and skillfully guiding the many official festivities which were an integral part of the McKinley Administration. Mrs. Howard took the lead, ably assisted by the Secretary of State's wife, Mrs. Alger, Mrs. John Hay, wife of the erstwhile Ambassador to the Court of Saint James, Mrs. Justice McKenna, Miss Long, daughter of the Secretary of the Navy, Mrs. Gray of Baltimore, wife of the Postmaster General, and Miss Wilson, daughter of the Secretary of Agriculture.

However, the President's favor fell on Justice McKenna's daughter Isabel, a young lady of great beauty and charm, who stood in for the First Lady when she was too ill to attend in person. A constant visitor at the White House, Isabel was ready, willing and able to assist the President at any time of the day or evening. Only on rare occasions did McKinley make any demands on his gentle wife to assist him at the various public functions and receptions. William McKinley was the kindest, friendliest and most caring President this nation has ever had. Mrs. McKinley would remain seated by her husband's side, holding in her hand a bouquet of orchids or violets as armor against the fatiguing ordeal of shaking hands.

Once when Isabel was asked to assist the First Lady, she was compelled to stand by her chair for so long she wondered how the President himself could stand there smiling, shaking every outstretched hand and calling each person by name without letup. "Aren't you weary, Mr. President?" she asked. "Not very," he replied, "for I never permit anyone to clasp my hand first. I do all of the shaking myself."

Congressman Tom Reed, whose lifestyle could be likened to that of G.K. Chesterton, commented on his political rival, William McKinley: "McKinley is loved even by his enemies. The spirit of

Brotherly Love dominated his life and illuminated his character with the strength and charisma that gave to it a quality of the highest order. This quality endeared him to men and women of good will everywhere and devastated his adversaries so completely."

When in mortal agony after having been struck down by an assassin's bullet in the city of Buffalo during the latter part of his second term, he whispered to the medical attendants, "It must have been some poor misguided fellow. Don't let them hurt him."

THE HONORABLE CHARLES SMITH, in his memorable address before a joint session of the New York Legislature in 1902, speaks of those elements which President McKinley possessed in abundance:

> He went over the land and across the continent, and his engaging personality and rare powers of oratory won their persuasive way. A face of sweetness and light; deep set, piercing eyes under a Websterian brow; a personal fascination took hold of all who came within its influence; a voice sympathetic, resonant and full of vibrant memory; a style of limpid clearness and simplicity, tipped with a divine flame of eloquence; an almost unrivaled power of seizing the central and controlling facts, and presenting them with sharp, luminous, and convincing force; the allied faculty of clarifying and crystallizing a truth or an argument in a phrase or an epigram; the capacity to take the tumbler from the table on the platform and make it the illustration, lucent as the sunbeam, of a theory, or policy, so the simplest child could understand, and the memory carried forever; and all over that subtle and indescribable charm of sincerity and servility which is irresistible — such were the rare attributes which swayed and carried vast multitudes.

William McKinley may not be numbered among our most revered presidents, but nonetheless he deserves to be. And by his appointment of the high-minded Irish Californian to his cabinet he made known the kind of men he wanted in his administration, men of impeccable character and ability.

As news spread that McKenna was chosen to be a member of the Supreme Court, messages of felicitations came pouring in from all over the West to the first man west of the Mississippi to be so honored. A committee made plans for a gala celebration before his departure for Washington. The journey from San Francisco to the Capital was marked by celebration after celebration as crowds gathered at every stop along the way. People gave expression to their feelings with prolonged applause, speech making, flag waving and fireworks.

The Telephone and Its Founder, Alexander Graham Bell

FROM THE RESEARCH available about United States Supreme Court Justice Joseph McKenna emerges a vignette little known to students of American history. Thanks to his daughter's diary, we have evidence that Alexander Graham Bell put his telephone to its first successful test, not in Boston, but in communication with a convent of Roman Catholic sisters in Washington, D.C.

It was in the silent halls of the Visitation Convent in Georgetown that the first "Hello" went skipping along a wire strung from Doctor Bell's workshop to the office of the Mother Superior of the Convent. The peace and quiet of the neighborhood were conducive for the delicate project. Doctor Bell's neighbors were nuns in the strictest cloister; Bell's wife was mute, and his laboratory far removed from the din of traffic. It was in this ideal retreat that the somber seer of Georgetown worked through many patient experimental years.

A sympathetic alliance existed between Bell and the good sisters, who rendered spiritual help and comfort with their devout daily prayers for the success of his labors. To his critics, however, the very thought of transporting the human speech along a strand of wire seemed impossible. They whispered that only a demented person would harbor such an idea. But the kindly nuns continued their prayers.

Mother Superior, the first to hear the magic word "Hello" at the other end of the wire, was so overcome by the success of Doctor Bell's invention that she called the congregation to join her in prayer and thanksgiving on that memorable occasion.

And so on a bright and miraculous day in the spring of 1876 the *Te Deum* was sung by the Georgetown Visitation Choir in sheer joy for what the Lord had wrought. At long last Alexander Graham Bell could rest from his labors, knowing that he had discovered the secret of transmitting the human voice over a strand of wire.

The McKennas in Washington

JOSEPH MCKENNA was a major figure in one of the most engrossing periods in American history. The McKenna residence was on Rhode Island Avenue, just a short distance from the White House. The McKennas were surrounded by a number of the most influential families on the Washington scene. Their next door neighbors were the Lowndes of Maryland, whose residence was a perfect example of the Colonial style, with many fine specimens of early American furniture.

Isabel McKenna Duffield

In the middle of the block on the same side of the street was the brick residence of Chief Justice White, a Democrat and former Confederate Army officer. There was a tender bond of friendship between White and Justice McKenna that endured until their deaths. Close by lived the gracious widow of General Philip Sheridan and her three charming daughters. On the opposite side of the street was the French Embassy and its noteworthy occupant, Ambassador Jules Combon. It was he, acting under the authority conferred on him by the Queen Regent, who with Secretary of State, William Day, negotiated the peace treaty that ended the Spanish-American War.

The welcome mat at the White House was always out for McKenna and his family. For them it was like dropping in for a chat with a next door neighbor. Their coming at any hour of the day or evening was welcome, especially Isabel, a constant visitor with Mrs. McKinley in the Blue Room.

Isabel, who became Mrs. Pitts-Duffield, wrote endearingly of her experiences in Washington in a zestful and convincing style worthy of her distinguished father.

Maggie Maloney's Sunday Hash

PRESIDENT MCKINLEY was a very humble man with simple tastes. One of the little pleasures he allowed himself was to take a Sunday morning stroll over to the residence of Assemblyman Mark Hanna to partake of Maggie Maloney's mouthwatering hash and chat with those who came by. When the word leaked out as to the President's whereabouts on Sunday mornings, those in the know conjured up excuses for being on hand at the same time. As the numbers increased Mr. Hanna was obliged to add extra leaves to his already large dining table.

Whether it was the novelty of having breakfast with the President or the brisk morning air that whetted their appetites, all were in agreement that Maggie Maloney's hash was the most delicious they had ever tasted. Maggie herself took it all in stride, although it meant getting up much earlier on Sunday mornings to meet the increasing demand for her sumptuous breakfast.

This wonderful story came to light in an article titled "Maggie Maloney's Hash" which appeared in the San Francisco *Monitor* on December 10, 1921. As I previously stated, "History is never dull or boring where the Irish are involved."

As for Joe McKenna, despite his rise to fame on the national scene, he never forgot his humble upbringing in Benicia and returned there at every opportunity. Benicia, which has been acclaimed as the "Athens of California," has its own unique history. It was co-founded by General Mariano Vallejo and Doctor Robert Semple, both of whom believed that it would become the Queen City of the Pacific. After much consideration they decided that it should be named "Francisca," in honor of General Vallejo's wife. Subsequently the agreement was translated and recorded in San Francisco, on January 19, 1847, by the presiding Alcalde (Mayor), Washington Bartlett.

In the meantime, Semple started advertising the "City of Francisca" in his newspaper *The Californian* at a time when the proposed city was only a supposition. "Francisca," he noted, "is situated thirty miles from the mouth of the Bay...far enough from the seaboard to make the climate as pleasant as any part of California. Persons passing from north to south, may cross at Francisca and travel thus from one end of California to the other without difficulty. The city is surrounded by the most fertile and beautiful portion of California and possesses all the requirements to make it the great city of the West."

The catchy advertisements caught the attention of the equally enthusiastic proponents of "Yerba Buena" who saw the new town as a rival. An alarmed citizenry called a meeting to forestall this blatant infringement by having the Alcalde proclaim that "San Francisco" was the official name of the city, and it was to be referred to as such forevermore.

When the news reached the proponents of Francisca, they were caught by surprise and called a meeting to plan their next move. It was unanimously decided to drop the name Francisca and give it another name chosen from amongst Senora Vallejo's other daughters: (Maria, Felipa, Benicia and Carilla). Their favor fell upon "Benicia," meaning "blessed."

Less there be any further confusion about the name, Doctor Semple ran an editorial in *The Californian* on June 19, 1847:

> NAME CHANGED—The name of the city of Francisca, recently laid out on the Straits of Carquinez on the bay of San Francisco, has been changed to Benicia City. The reason for the change is that this town of Yerba Buena, is, by order of the Alcalde, called San Francisco and it was thought that the names being so much alike, could cause confusion. Truly the Alcalde is the law.

The original "Official Map of Benicia," bearing the names of founders Mariano Vallejo, Thomas Larkin and Robert Semple, was published by Benjamin Barlow of New York in 1851. Benicia caught the attention of visitors from across the nation when a facsimile of the original map was given a prominent niche in the Library of Congress.

As further proof of his faith in Benicia as the future Metropolis of the West, Doctor Semple came to San Francisco on July 4, 1847, and patriotically gave away a lot he owned in the city.

IN ITS GLORY DAYS Benicia lured such notables as Mr. Von Pfister, who arrived from the Sandwich Islands (Hawaii) with a cargo of goods for a store he planned to open in San Jose, but changed his mind at the insistence of Doctor Semple and settled in Benicia instead. The enterprising newcomer purchased an unfinished adobe structure, put it in good order and opened a trading store in early August of that memorable year. The business flourished despite a lack of cash. The standard currency was hides, valued at $1.50 each, which were jokingly listed as "California Bank Bills." Wheat, barley, Indian corn and other commodities were readily accepted in lieu of coin. Alas for the "good old days," when it was possible to live the good life without a penny in the bank.

As elsewhere in California it was the Irish who set the pace in this new town. Jasper O'Farrell of engineering fame was commissioned by the City Fathers of Benicia to lay out their new town.

Another Irishman who left his mark in Benicia was Captain John Walsh, a robust seafaring gentleman who fell in love with Benicia when he arrived there in 1849. His house at 235 L Street of a Gothic Revival design is still in use. From an architectural standpoint it is said to be one of the most important dwellings in the city, a replica of General Vallejo's home in Sonoma, which is now a historic landmark.

Lieutenant Colonel Silas Casey was another prominent Irishman who supervised the construction of the Benicia Barracks in 1850, the year California became a State. It was one of the first military posts in the new state, which provided ample quarters for two companies of the Second United States Infantry Division. The Benicia Barracks was renamed the Benicia Arsenal in an official proclamation of April 1852. An Ordinance Depot was added shortly thereafter along with a gunpowder magazine with walls four and a half feet thick. The addition was completed in 1857 at a cost of $35,000.

Another Irishman associated with Benicia was Tom Maguire, a dapper showman and erstwhile saloon keeper from New York. Maguire shared Doctor Semple's belief that Benicia would become the city of the future. In fact Maguire established a branch of his San Francisco theatrical enterprise there and an elegant saloon to quench his patrons' thirst.

From a very humble beginning Benicia became a thriving community almost overnight, and the Irish, like their counterparts in Sacramento, were its most prominent residents. Stephen Cooper, who could trace his ancestors to the Emerald Isle, was appointed as the Alcalde of Benicia by Richard Mason, Colonel of the First Regiment of the United States Dragoons, and later Governor of California. The town could boast over a thousand inhabitants even in the days of James Marshall's discovery of gold nuggets in the hills and streams of the Sierras.

It was a memorable occasion when the American Fleet dropped anchors for the first time on the Benicia waterfront and prepared to make soundings in San Francisco Bay. This historic development was not lost on Doctor Semple who was quick to convey the good news to his friend Thomas Larkin, the American consulate in Monterey. "Prospects for Benicia were never better," he noted. "The commodore has selected a place for the Naval Arsenal next to Benicia. He has found fresh water for 300,000 people and a place for anchoring all the ships of the world.

Following the Naval pronouncements, the United States Army, under the supervision of General Persifer Smith, commander of the United States Pacific Division, saw Benicia as an ideal site for an Army base. General Smith toured the area on a brisk afternoon in March 1849 and was so captivated by the surroundings that he purchased a number of lots for future development. At the same time he began negotiations with two local promoters for a large tract of land adjoining Benicia as a site for Army commissaries and warehouses. An agreement was reached between the Benicia Town Council and the Army Command for the purchase of the property. When word reached the Naval Headquarters that the Army had already acquired the land they themselves wanted, the Navy hastened to find another location. Eventually they found a site to their liking in nearby Vallejo called Mare Island, where they have maintained their principal headquarters on the West Coast ever since.

Benicia's Pioneer Hospital

DOCTOR W. F. PEABODY, a pioneer medico, founded a hospital in Benicia in 1849 at 345 H Street, the first institution of its kind in Solano County. It was well patronized, primarily by the gold diggers who had struck it rich in the mines and were badly in need of medical attention. The hospital continued to function for a period of fifteen years until 1864, when it was completely rebuilt into a private residence and is now a historic landmark in downtown Benicia. Doctor Peabody's "Medical Shingle," carved in California, was purchased at a garage sale by this author and held as a memento of California's cradle days. It will be donated to the Benicia Museum.

Benicia could well boast of another historical first in its calendar of events, the arrival of the Pony Express from Saint Joseph, Missouri, on April 23, 1860, carried by a relay rider, a wiry Celt named William Hamilton. The historic occasion is commemorated by a bronze plaque at First and A Streets, a crossroads in pioneer days. The time honored memorial is now enhanced by a bust of Jack London, the youthful penman who frequented the Benicia waterfront which became the inspiration for his novel the *Fish Patrol.*

The Washington Scene

JOSEPH MCKENNA was a staunch Republican, which proved advantageous in that progressive political period. The American electorate was so heartened by the success of the Republican administration under the leadership of Abraham Lincoln during the Civil War that they elected a Republican as President of the United States for a period of twenty five years thereafter.

He was President McKinley's most trusted colleague and was addressed by the President by his first name. On one occasion, when the President and Mrs. McKinley had invited a number of his Cabinet officials and their wives to accompany them on a trip through New England, the heat was so intense that the President feared for McKenna's health, which was none too good at the time. There being only two staterooms in the private car, one for himself and the other for Mrs. McKinley, the President threatened to vacate his stateroom and put Joe into it. McKenna vigorously remonstrated, saying he simply would not have the President of the United States put out for him. The President persisted and said, "All right, Mr. Attorney General, there is nothing left for you to do but get well." "All right, Mr. President. I'll get well. If it kills me, I'll get well," replied McKenna.

Joseph McKenna's political career spanned a period of some forty years from 1885 to 1925. As Associate Justice he did not often speak for the Court, but when he did his opinions were characterized by practical sense and distinct expression. In such important matters relative to Federal Power as it applied to the States, and with reference to labor, he was highly commended for his political vision and social judgment.

In a more intimate way Joe McKenna's life proved to be a vindi-
cation of his Irish immigrant father's faith in the American Dream. In
addition to living according to the principles of hard work and determination, he also mastered the art of American politics. As an abiding and trustworthy Republican Party regular he served with much
acumen the constituency upon which his political career depended.
In like manner McKenna developed a national power base which was
built on his positive influence in Congress, numerous intimate relationships with his peers, and a proven reputation for punctuality.
With hard work and study, McKenna compensated fully for whatever
scholarly deficiencies he may have had.

FOLLOWING A LONG and fruitful life, Justice McKenna passed away
at his home in Washington on Sunday, November 21, 1926, his
four children, Major Frank McKenna, Mrs. Isabel Duffield, Mrs.
Davenport Brown and Mrs. Edward Alsop, gathered at his deathbed.
His wife Amanda preceded him in death on October 13, 1924.
Following Requiem Mass, which was celebrated at Saint Matthew's
Cathedral, Justice McKenna was interred in Mount Olivet Cemetery
in Washington.

As elsewhere in America, the Irish in Washington were together
in life and are now together in death in Mount Olivet, the oldest and
largest Catholic cemetery in the Washington Metropolitan area.
There lie the remains of many notable Americans, Irish by birth or
descent: James Hoban, Architect of the White House; Daniel
Carroll, patriot and landowner, who sacrificed much of his property
to the Government to provide the site of the Capitol and other
Federal buildings; Father Peter Keenan Guilday, renowned Church
historian; Thomas Aloysius Cantwell of baseball fame; and John W.
Hayes, an astute Labor Leader.

The map of Mount Olivet Cemetery was updated and redrafted
in October 1991 by Irish-American John McGovern, Civil Engineer-
Land Surveyor of Wheaton, Maryland.

Joseph McKenna, a great Irishman and a truly great American,
lies buried in Section 50, lot 152 on Saint Cecilia's Avenue in Mount
Olivet Cemetery, close by the Carroll Circle. He died as he had lived
in the bosom of Mother Church, a credit to America and an exemplar of his noble Irish Heritage.

James McClatchy
Courtesy Sacramento Archives and Museum, Eleanor McClatchy Collection

– 6 –

THE SACRAMENTO IRISH

IRISH PIONEERS IN THE STATE CAPITOL

I T WAS A GREAT DAY for the local Irish when Sacramento was declared the permanent state capitol in 1854. The bright prospect that the capitol city would be a center of future Irish power was no mirage: by the year 1860 the Irish would form the largest and best organized ethnic group in Sacramento.

The more ambitious Irish had struck it rich in the nearby mines and invested their earnings in farmland. Irish-born Martin Murphy, who arrived in Sacramento in 1844, was quick to plant wheat in the virgin soil of California, which brought him wealth in abundance. Unlike their counterparts who settled in the overcrowded cities of Boston, New York and Philadelphia, the California Irish prudently settled on the land.

Wheat grew so well in California soil that it became, by 1900, a glut on the market. Farmers began to convert their grain fields into orchards. This strategy was particularly successful in the great Sacramento Valley, where warm days and cool nights were conducive to the growth and development of stone fruits such as peaches, apricots and almonds.

California's markets, indeed all aspects of life in the young state, changed dramatically when the Transcontinental Railway was completed in 1869. Irish women, scarce in early California, came to make up a third of the total Irish population. Sacramento Irish had shown a keen interest in Irish politics since the early 1850s. They were now brought closer to the news and events of their homeland, and of their fellow emigrants in the eastern United States.

For the California Irish, the local color and detail of their public life, of their sports, and of their celebrations expressed their close ties to Ireland. Display and pageant were especially popular in the Sacramento region: parades, grand balls, guest speakers, political gatherings, Gaelic sports and patriotic exercises were frequent and well attended. The promoters hoped these bright spectacles in the capitol of California would contribute politically to Irish independence from British rule. As one leading orator in Sacramento put it, the English "begin to believe that one Irishman in America is as much to be feared as a dozen in Ireland."

Local theater often alluded to Irish politics. At the height of the Fenian Movement, the Metropolitan Theater in Sacramento presented many dramas replete with Irish nationalist sentiment. In one performance, the concluding scene depicted Ireland as a Republic and a slovenly John Bull writhing in fear and guilt. At curtain time it was customary for the performers to come on stage and the audience to stand and together sing that old patriotic refrain, "A Nation Once Again."

Nostalgia for the Irish homeland and a keen interest in Irish culture and art brought the Irish into the Metropolitan Theater in Sacramento. That house staged, among other plays, Dion Boucicault's "Arrah-na-Pogue" (the first stage play this writer ever saw, at age twelve), "Kathleen Mavourneen," and "The Irish Mother."

St. Patrick's Day Parades

THE SAINT PATRICK'S DAY parades in Sacramento were alive with color, display, and enthusiasm. Like the local theater, they were a mixture of fierce nationalism and sweet sentiment. Brisk spring weather with occasional showers recalled, to Irish memories, the climate of the Old Sod. So, too, the pageantry and symbolism of the parade reminded them of their allegiance to the age-old struggle for freedom taking place on Irish soil. Saint Patrick's Day was a time to manifest strength in numbers, to be seen among one's own, to affirm the importance of being Irish, and to declare solidarity with the Irish at home.

Sacramento was not the only California city to put on a Saint Patrick's Day parade: in 1859, the day was celebrated throughout the Gold Rush region—in Placerville, Downieville, Nevada City, Yankee Jim's and Stockton. But the Sacramento parades were particularly elaborate, politically charged, and drew favorable notices from the state government and the California press.

Rituals enacted along the line of march showed the extent of Irish-American organizational life in early Sacramento. There were four hundred entries in the 1875 parade, including two divisions of the Ancient Order of Hibernians, the Sarsfield Grenadier Guards, the Father Matthew Total Abstinence Association, and the Hibernian Benevolent Association. The spectators were treated to a "Triumphal Coach" carrying the "Goddess of Liberty" flanked by the newly crowned "Maid of Erin" and the comely "Maid of Honor." Next came a lengthy caravan, trimmed in green and gold, bearing a delegation of charming young ladies, all dressed in white, representing the 32 counties of Ireland.

A purely American touch was provided by the popular Eagle and Modoc baseball teams, togged out in their respective uniforms, carrying bats and baseballs and banners associated with the national pastime. The Fenians, three hundred strong, came from such far-away places as Virginia City and Gold Hill in the mining region.

The State of California, recognizing the influence of its Irish population and the importance of their culture, contributed to the festivities. The Superintendent of Public Schools, Mr. Hickson, excused Catholic boys from public school attendance so that they might take part in the festivities. The California Department of Agriculture made the Agricultural Pavilion on the state fairgrounds available for the festivities following the parade. The spacious, airy structure was ideally suited for such a large gathering, which was in an ecstatic mood to celebrate following the Grand Parade. In appreciation of the Fenians, who turned out en masse, the orchestra, to the delight of the exuberant gathering, struck up one of their favorite ditties:

The Green Above the Red
And tis for this we think and toil
  and knowledge strive to glean—
That we may pull the English Red
  below the Irish Green.
And leave her sons sweet liberty,
  and smiling plenty spread
Above the land once dark with blood—
  the Green above the Red.

The display of historic symbols was as stirring as the sound of patriotic song. In the parade, the visual pageantry was headed by a banner depicting, on its face, the eloquent Daniel O'Connell pleading Ireland's cause in parliament; the gallant soldier Patrick Sarsfield at the Siege of Limerick was depicted on the reverse. Then came something out of the past—a twelve-foot-high Round Tower, borne aloft, as men filed past in the guise of Galloglasses, a throwback to the Milesian warriors. The Galloglasses dressed resplendently, sporting "a shirt of mail and flesh-colored tights; they wore mantles of yellow cloth with long hair floated over their shoulders."

These were potent cultural symbols, not just gaudy displays of antiquity. To the Irish, the parade provided emotional reminders central to the Irish sense of identity—that their forebears, the Galloglasses, were an ancient people possessed of a rich civilization; that theirs was a land of learning, preserved in the Round Towers and monasteries; that they were one people, drawn together from thirty-two counties; that against the oppressor they had brought forth heroes both in parliament (Daniel O'Connell) and on the battle-field (Patrick Sarsfield). The review encouraged the Sacramento Irish to advance with new vigor the cause they had heard about as youngsters—perhaps from a grandfather who charged the redcoats with pick in hand in '98.

THE SACRAMENTO IRISH celebrated the spirit of 1798 when the good ladies presented Captain John Foley, the prominent local Fenian, and his comrades of the Emmet Guard with a flag, six feet to a side, emblazoned with four symbols of the Fenian Banner—harp, shamrock, wolfhound and sunburst. The weighty flagstaff was topped with a "Pyke," the bloody and potent symbol of the '98 uprising.

The patriotic ladies looked forward to the day when their men of the Emmet Guards might go into battle for the cause of Ireland. "Whenever the time for which we all pray shall come—that time when the flag of Saint Patrick shall again flaunt the standard of the 'Sassenagh,' let neither this banner nor the men in whose trust we now deposit it, be absent from the fray." Captain Foley promptly assured the ladies that when the time arrived, "Not a member of the Emmet Guard will fall with his back to the foe," and added that the Emmet Guard to a man would follow the high example of the notable Irish Officers Corcoran, Sheridan and Meagher in the American Civil War.

Invoking the names of three Irish officers in the Union Army, Captain Foley reminded the Sacramento Irish that the Union Army and the Irish had a common enemy—England, which had supported the Confederacy. Captain Barney Ryan, the guest speaker at Sacramento's 1865 Saint Patrick's Day festivities, put it bluntly: "Have we not witnessed her (England's) bastard Lordlings in plots and councils with arch traitors in arms to assist in the work of demolition and dismemberment of this Republic?" For years after 1865, the issue of England's perfidy was kept alive for Irish-American audiences. Fenian spokesmen pointed again and again to England's unexplained delay in settling the Alabama claims—United States grievances against England during and after the American Civil War.

A local festival was like a looking-glass reflecting world affairs throughout the last decades of 19th-century Sacramento. The Irish, who saw Saint Patrick's Day parades as occasions to recognize international friends as well as enemies, welcomed the participation of the French and German communities.

A special committee of French and Irish was formed in 1871 to facilitate arrangements for the Saint Patrick's Day festivities. In attendance at the official Mass in old Saint Rose's Church was the French Vice Consul, Mr. Berton, who presented a French flag to be hung alongside the altar during the ceremony. The French entry in the parade was magnificent. Five gaily decorated carriages were drawn by prize Norman horses provided by Martin Murphy—the pioneering farmer who had become one of the most prominent Irishmen in Sacramento.

In the leading carriage was the honorable French Vice Consul in his robes of office; in four accompanying carriages rode leading French citizens from the Sacramento area. An Irish delegation escorted the bearers of the French flag to the California Agricultural Pavilion for the evening ceremonies following the parade. Alongside it in the pavilion stood the flag one Jeremiah Day had held aloft in the procession— an Irish flag, 93 years old, which had been brought to the United States in 1801. It was considerably faded, but its fine workmanship drew favorable comment.

IN 1871, FRANCE was a Catholic nation at war with mostly Lutheran Prussia. Germans, however, did participate in the 1871 Sacramento Saint Patrick's Day parade. Irish Catholics had been building friendships with German Catholics in the Sacramento area. When the Right Reverend Patrick Manogue was installed as the first Bishop of the newly formed Diocese of Sacramento, he invited German-speaking Franciscans to serve in the second Catholic parish. Bishop Alemany, in 1871, was planning the construction of a Christian Brothers school to serve the needs of both German and Irish Catholics: this provided a special impetus for the Germans to participate in the parade and its subsequent festivities. As part of the festivities in the Agricultural Pavilion that evening in 1871, German musical performers played, among other selections, a quartet from the local Turn Verein.

Not all participants were Catholic, as one local reporter noted: "Saint Patrick's Day is becoming quite a cosmopolitan and national

This very early view of J Street from the Levee, shows buildings that have been restored as a part of Sacramento's Old Town district.
Courtesy Sacramento Archives and Museum, Eleanor McClatchy Collection

day. In this city, on Sunday night the Methodist minister delivered a sermon, highly eulogistic of Ireland's patron saint; the colored soldiers here joined heartily in the procession together with scores of people who were neither of the Catholic religion nor of the Irish race."

Irish Nationalism

IRISH NATIONALISM seemed to have an international following when Saint Patrick's Day came around. The parade in 1879 was headed by William Irwin, the Governor of California, riding in a gaily decorated coach drawn by four prize horses in shiny harnesses. Next in the line of march came the Mayor of Sacramento, Jabez Turner. And a surprise entry from the newly formed Robert Emmet Club—showing a blend of nationalities sporting green berets—left no room for doubt that everyone was Irish, at least for a day, in Sacramento.

A roll call of Irish nationalist groups in Sacramento in 1879 would include the Fenian Movement, the John Dillon Branch of the Land League, the Sacramento Irish Sufferers' Relief Committee, the Emmet Guards, the Sarsfield Grenadier Guards of the State Militia, and the Ad Hoc Committee for the release of Fenians in British prisons. Both the Emmet and Sarsfield Guards were militia units named for leading Irish patriots. Robert Emmet was an early 19th-century martyr to the cause of Irish nationalism whose patriotic idealism transcended religious difference; Patrick Sarsfield initiated the Irish Catholic Resistance Movement in Munster.

The Irish Sufferers' Relief Association raised funds for the Famine victims in the late 1840s. At its meetings, speaker after speaker blamed English misrule in Ireland for the catastrophe. Memories were long, and resentment against Great Britain was rife in Irish California. Later in the 19th Century, an Irish cleric recalled the 1847 famine alongside the 1798 uprising. Brother Justin of the Christian Brothers Order exhorted his audience to keep faith with their Irish heritage: "But why go back to `98? Have we not in our own day examples of England's cruelty to Ireland? Have not some among you witnessed the effects of the famine of 47? Will we, in a word, forget our faith and Fatherland? Never!"

IN 1880 SACRAMENTO became home to the local John Dillon Branch of the Irish Land League, named in honor of John Blake Dillon, a leader of the Young Ireland Movement and the father of John Dillon of the Irish Parliament. The League organized resistance to the greedy landlords in Ireland, and tried to get lower rent and eventual ownership rights for Irish tenant farmers. The League defended farmers in legal trouble and supported their families. In Ireland, the Land League enforced its code and its edicts by imposing a "boycott"—named after Captain Charles Boycott, a notorious landlord in County Mayo who had defied a League edict. British troops and Orange sympathizers, who came between the Captain and a mob of angry farmers, prevented them from inflicting serious bodily harm on Boycott, but not from leaving a permanent mark on the English language. The Sacramento branch of the Land League contributed from afar to the cause of the "Land War United" in Ireland.

Irish nationalism came again to Sacramento in 1882 when the Honorable T. P. O'Connor, a shrewd Irish Parliamentarian, gave a public speech in order to raise funds for Irish nationalist activity. O'Connor's speech was one part of a great fund-raising tour which brought other leading Irish political figures to the United States, men such as Charles Stuart Parnell, Michael David, John Redmond and Eamonn DeValera. It was a time of patriotic awareness among the Sacramento Irish, who were asked to provide funds for Irish nationalist activity in the homeland. Sacramento Irish had a long history of answering the homeland's calls for assistance.

Thomas Francis Meagher

IN 1854, the fiery rebel Thomas Francis Meagher, famous for his 1852 escape from the penal colony of Van Dieman's Land in Australia, arrived in California's capitol. Meagher, whose militant tactics earned him the epithet "Meagher of the Sword," personified the Young Ireland Movement, which had risen in rebellion at Ballingary, County Tipperary in 1848.

To Irish audiences in Northern California, Meagher stressed two recurring themes—Ireland as the land of rebellion, and as the land of suffering. He lectured on three occasions in Sacramento in the spring of 1854. One of these lectures, at the local Congregational Church, was given at the behest of Reverend Joseph Benton, an outstanding Protestant religious figure in early-day Sacramento. Meagher also spoke at various mining camps in Marysville, Grass Valley and Nevada City.

Meagher and the Young Ireland Movement, though not successful on the field of battle, had been willing to fight and to die for Irish freedom. They served as models for later Irish nationalists. Until the tumultuous Easter Week of 1916 their courageous personal sacrifice inspired Irish nationalists to die for their cause. By the 1860s, their tactic of physical force was emulated in the Fenian groups that appeared in Ireland, California, and elsewhere.

The Fenian Organization

THE IRISH FENIANS, who adopted military organization and levels of command, were composed of separate Circles under the direction of a Head Center. As a precaution against informers, individual Fenians had limited contact with their comrades; no one member could be certain who else, or how many, had joined the society. The Fenians were papally denounced and condemned by the Catholic hierarchy in Ireland, because they were organized as a secret society. Cardinal Paul Cullen, of Dublin, saw in the Fenians a modern counterpart of the anti-clerical Risorgimento. Father Moriarty, a County Kerry Priest, declared that "Hell was not hot enough for the Fenians." But Bishop Keane of Cloyne, who had done a study which showed the inadequacy of English land reform in Ireland, disagreed with the papal condemnation of the Fenians and declined to circulate the proclamation in his Diocese.

Most American bishops were unhappy with the papal manifesto denouncing the Fenians, and made no effort to extend the ban to this

This exceptionally early photo shows the sidewheeler steamboat New World, *docked at Sacramento in the summer of 1850.*
Courtesy Sacramento Archives and Museum, M. Kibbey Collection

country. They knew that it would strain the loyalties of their Irish parishioners. Even the eminent Archbishop John McCloskey of New York was said to be particularly dismayed at the Papal action.

The American branch of the Fenian Society did not emphasize secrecy, and even marched openly at public functions. American Fenians pledged total support to the society, but were not bound to the same degree as their Irish brethren. In California, and Sacramento in particular, the society conducted its everyday affairs in the open. It permitted the *Sacramento Union* newspaper to list the Fenian Brotherhood among other local organizations, and named presiding officers, as well as the time and place of meetings.

Colonel Walsh, the Inspector General of the Fenians, addressed a rally in Benicia, the erstwhile capitol of California, in 1866, and traveled to a remote community in La Porte, Plumas County, a month later to address the local Shamrock Circle of the Society. A newspaper article early in 1867 surrounded the local Fenians with a mysterious glamour: "There is a circle of this Order in Sacramento numbering 210 members. We are not informed as to its workings, but presume that friendliness to British Rule in any part of the world is not one of its characteristics."

But the Sacramento Fenians actually went about their work publicly. They conducted a vigorous campaign for the release of prisoners held in Canadian gaols, helped form a Sacramento Irish Sufferers' Relief Committee, and worked for a Sacramento branch of the Land League.

Patriotic feelings ran high among the Sacramento Irish, as did resentment against England. Members of the Irish community met on February 8, 1872, at Dolan's grocery store on Sixth Street, to prepare for war in case of armed conflict between England and America. It was reported that the meeting place was filled with young Irishmen eager to serve their adopted country at the call of duty. According to one local journalist, "All that the Irishers needed to know was that England was the aggressor."

At the annual Saint Patrick's Day Parade in 1876, the guest speaker of the day, Adjutant General P. F. Walsh, spoke for the cause of Irish freedom:

> In adverse times a nation's armies may be routed, its fields wasted, its freedom crushed and the flag of a hated despotism unfurled above it as a badge of foreign conquest. But if love of country remains, freedom will reassert itself, liberty will burst its fetters and the Angel of a Righteous God will descend, and rolling away the stone from the sepulcher in which her foe would entomb her, the tyrant-wronged but Heaven-righted will walk forth clad in the radiant raiment of a glorious resurrection.

The Fenians were a strong presence at public festivals in Sacramento. At the 1866 Saint Patrick's Day parade, 250 stalwart rebels marched with all the flamboyance of West Point cadets. On June 8, 1866, the influential *Daily Bee,* published by Irish-born James McClatchy, warned its readers not to laugh off the Fenians. "In this state and in Oregon alone there are hundreds of places where branches of the Society maintain a flourishing existence. All over the coast, Fenian festivals are among the common occurrences of the day.

A Favorable Press in Sacramento

THE SACRAMENTO IRISH could always count on a favorable press. The *Sacramento Bee,* brainchild of James McClatchy, an immigrant from County Antrim, gave extensive coverage to Irish news from

California and from Ireland. The *Sacramento Daily Union* also reported these events. There were frequent editorials on the Fenian
Movement, the importance of the Land League in Irish affairs, and the
execution of the Manchester Martyrs.

McClatchy had an adventurous life before founding the
Sacramento Bee. His hazardous journey to California is one of the most
fascinating stories of the Gold Rush era. The ship he took passage on,
which had successfully rounded Cape Horn, was wrecked on the
rugged California coast, in a remote area with no sign of life in any
direction. The stranded party set out on foot and were near the point
of exhaustion when they met a Mexican farmer, who took them into his
shanty and shared what little food he had with the forlorn travelers.

Rested and refreshed, McClatchy's party trekked north until they
reached the Franciscan Mission at Santa Clara. Their clothing, when
they reached the Mission, was in tatters, and they had no shoes on
their blistered feet. The kindly Padres took in the lost sheep and cared
for them. When the men were physically fit they set out on the final
leg of their journey to the mines. But no pot of gold lay at the end of
their long journey; their hopes of striking it rich in the mines were dis-
appointed. Undaunted, McClatchy decided to remain in Sacramento
and found a newspaper.

Under McClatchy's guidance the *Bee* consistently championed
Ireland's rights and liberties. In 1888 the newspaper ran a series of
articles on Ireland's right to freedom and independence. Patrick Ford,
the influential editor and publisher of the *Irish World* in New York
City, co-ordinated his efforts with McClatchy's series. Although the
two powerful newsmen did not always see eye to eye on matters pertaining to Irish affairs, each was in his own way an avid promoter of
everything Irish.

MCCLATCHY'S TWO SONS, Valentine and C.K., wrote editorials and
held similar views on Irish affairs. They became co-owners of the
newspaper, with C.K. serving as editor. Their editorials and articles
showed a subtle understanding of the complex relations between the
politics of Irish nationalism and the conservative views of the clergy.

In May 1888, the *Bee,* in an editorial titled "The Same Old
Story," disputed in detail Lord Carnarvon's call for continued English
supremacy in Irish affairs. This proposal, argued the paper, spelled
slavery for Irish nationals. The *Bee* alleged that England's proposal to
"satisfy the people of Ulster means that the English Government shall
grind the Catholics of that province beneath the heels of the relentless
Orangemen."

In a follow-up editorial, McClatchy's paper described the recent imprisonment of the Irish leaders William O'Brien and John Dillon as "a holy martyrdom as sacred as the sacrifices of old, when brave men died for opinion's sake." Thomas Davis, the outspoken editor of the *Nation,* could not have put it in more abrasive terms.

Valentine McClatchy wrote a third editorial, "Davitt's Protest," taking strong exception to a recent Papal Bull which had condemned the Plan of Campaign and boycotting. The editorial described the edict as "diabolical" and applauded Michael Davitt for sounding "the first notes of rebellion against the interference of Rome in the political struggles of Ireland." The editorial went on to point out that the Pope is not infallible in matters other than faith and morals. McClatchy criticized Patrick Ford, editor of the *Irish World* and a staunch supporter of the Pope, for attacking injustices in Ireland, when the Pope had condemned rebellion against those very injustices. All three editorials appeared in later issues of the weekly *Bee.*

David Lubin, a Jewish merchant from Sacramento, was also involved. While living in Paris he got a copy of the three editorials. He then wrote to McClatchy, praising the editorials and enclosing a check for a hundred dollars to support the Irish cause. He asked only that the gift be identified as "from a Jew," because he did not want to be accused of self-advertisement. McClatchy forwarded the check to Patrick Ford in New York, for use as Ford saw fit.

Two weeks later Ford returned the check, giving as his reason that he objected to the criticism of the Pope in the editorial, and would have nothing to do with it. In Ford's words, "Those who would serve Ireland ought to find motive enough in the intrinsic justice of her cause, and not spite the Pope and incite the Irish to schism."

Unable to agree on how best to bolster Ireland's cause, and not wanting to continue the debate by letter, McClatchy concluded the matter with a conciliatory note, "expressing the highest respect for your personal integrity," and stating that the issue between them, "which you and I both honestly regret," resulted from different views as to whether the Pope was above criticism.

In Sacramento, festivals arranged by Irish clubs and reported by Irish editors kept the nation of Ireland alive, both as a cultural heritage and as a political ideal. In any capitol city cultural life will be heavily influenced by politics. Sometimes the burden is too heavy, but this was not the case in old Sacramento. In their parades, concerts, speeches, their newspapers and drama, the political pageantry of the Sacramento Irish remained bright, colorful, and distinctively Irish.

This view, looking west at 9th and M Streets in Sacramento,
was taken from the top of a very high building.
Courtesy Sacramento Archives and Museum, Eleanor McClatchy Collection

Other Prominent Irish Settlers in Sacramento

THOMAS DWYER was born in County Wexford in 1831 and immigrated to Toronto, Canada, in 1848. Subsequently he removed to Ohio and later on to Illinois, where he worked as a lumberman and farmer. In 1859 he traveled to California and settled in Colusa County where he operated a threshing machine during harvest time. With the intent of going into business for himself, he purchased a big spread of timberland, which he intended to harvest and sell to prospective builders and others in need of housing.

In the meantime, he hired local workers to assist him in cutting the timber and floating it on barges down the Sacramento River to San Francisco, which was in the midst of a building boom. Dwyer's river business, which was named the Sacramento Wood Company in 1866, was vastly expanded by 1879 and was renamed the Sacramento Transportation Company. This latter company bought out the California Navigation Company and became the leading shipper on the Sacramento River.

In 1891 Dwyer invested in riverfront property at Knight's Landing and Colusa, and constructed a brick factory on Riverside Road. The advent of the brickworks could not have come at a more appropriate time, during the construction of the State Capitol and the Blessed Sacrament Cathedral nearby. According to family records and diaries, the Dwyer factory provided the bricks for both institutions.

Dwyer was an intimate friend of Bishop Manogue and helped him acquire the site he had picked out at 11th and K Streets for the building of the Cathedral in the 1880s. As the Bishop wanted the Cathedral near the Capitol, the land was purchased in Dwyer's name. A stained glass window in the Cathedral bears the family name.

When Thomas Dwyer lost his life in a San Francisco ferryboat accident in 1890, his wife Mary Ellen carried forward his philanthropic ideals. She would invariably vouch for immigrant Irish girls and arrange for their passage to the United States, take them into her home in Sacramento and help them get started in their new environment. The Dwyer children were all well educated and became leaders in their respective communities. One of his sons took over control of Dwyer operation, which was so prosperous that it allowed some of his boys to live lavishly, as gentlemen. One of his daughters, Mary Ellen Devlin, was a patron of the arts.

WILLIAM F. GORMLEY was another successful businessman in Sacramento. Born in 1862 in County Fermanagh, he came to El Dorado County at the age of ten with his mother and siblings to join his father, Thomas Gormley, who was engaged in mining there. Two years later, the family removed to Sacramento, where William found work in the State Printing Office and where he eventually became assistant foreman.

While there he met Minnie Fogarty, who was born of Irish parents in Moore's Flat in the mining region. Having lost both of her parents when she was twelve, she had been raised by her uncle, Father Patrick Manogue, a priest in Virginia City. She became his faithful housekeeper and stayed with him when he became the first Bishop of the Sacramento Diocese in 1886.

Following Manogue's death in 1895, she married William Gormley and lived in Sacramento. About that same time, Gormley became a funeral director at the urging of Manogue's successor, Bishop Thomas Grace. The original Gormley undertaking establishment was located at 907 J Street, whence it moved to other locations, and eventually to its present address, 2015 Capitol Avenue. The Gormley Funeral Home, still doing business under the name of W. F. Gormley & Sons, celebrated its hundredth anniversary in 1987.

Over the years Gormley held a number of important offices. In 1902 he was elected to the office of Coroner, a position he held for thirteen years, until he became sheriff in 1915. This latter office he held until 1919.

Although a devout Catholic, Gormley downplayed his church connections when he ran for public office, saying that "if religion was his only qualification, he was a poor candidate." He was long an active member of the Sacramento chapter of the Ancient Order of Hibernians and served as its president from 1900 to 1902. Although the church in Sacramento has had an Irish presence and has championed certain aspects of Irish culture and tradition, its members have also been proudly American. The Irish in Sacramento and elsewhere in California have become as American as anyone.

William Gormley was an exemplar of the many Irish-Americans who looked on public life as an extension of their professional and personal connections with the local community. The Irish in Sacramento have been city councilmen, sheriffs, high-ranking policemen, fire chiefs, city managers and superintendents of schools. Many others have served in political office in Sacramento's capitol building.

I RISH BARS and saloons have long been a part of the Sacramento scene. One of the most prominent of the many 19th Century bars was Pat Kelly's place, near the Old Courthouse at 605 I Street. Born in County Limerick in 1839, Kelly emigrated to America and settled in Sacramento, where he worked as a barman at the Golden Eagle Hotel. In 1867 he married an Irish woman and purchased property on 4th Street between J and K Streets, where he opened a saloon and lived in an upstairs flat with his wife and family. Some years later he moved to another part of the city, frequented by businessmen, politicians and attorneys. By the 1890s Kelly's place, on the busy courthouse block, included a saloon, restaurant and boarding house, whose occupants were mostly Irish-Americans. About the same time he constructed a substantial home for his growing family. Pat Kelly died in 1913, just two years before his wife. Four of their children preceded them in death. The Kellys are all interred in St. Joseph's Cemetery.

T IMOTHY AND MARY SWEENEY were owners of the Hibernian Hotel at 1025 Front Street in Sacramento. It was patronized for the most part by railroad workers, deck hands on the Sacramento River and other boarding-house tenants who were mostly Irish. The Hibernian Hotel and Saloon was but one of the many such businesses in Sacramento's west end.

One of the most noted of the Irish bars of that period was Ryle's Irish Tavern, which closely resembled the unpretentious public houses

in the old country. The interior was a long, narrow room with a matching bar and mirror, sporting colorful decorations above. There was also a "snug" for women, separated by a curtain. Sometimes there was music by an accordion or concertina player, and patrons would sing and dance to their hearts' content during the evening.

There are still quite a number of Irish bars in Sacramento, most of which now cater to a diverse clientele. One is Malarkey's place on Broadway, established by Pat Malarkey, a prominent Irish-American and former Sacramento County Supervisor.

The late John Delury, whose thesis about the Irish in Sacramento was the source of much material in this chapter.

The Irish in early Sacramento had a sympathetic press, which was even more pronounced in the 20th Century, when Thomas Connolly founded the *Irish Herald* in March 1908. Connolly, a staunch Irish-American, came to Sacramento at the urging of Bishop Thomas Grace to start a Catholic newspaper in the diocese.

In the first issue Connolly criticized the offensive humor which often stigmatized the Irish. Most issues included an article on Irish history and culture, or on such Irish patriots as Robert Emmet, Daniel O'Connel and Father William Ellis. Connolly often dwelt on John Redmond's Home Rule bill in 1913, The Easter Week Rising, the Irish Relief movement by Cardinal Gibbons of New York, and the subsequent San Francisco rally, which drew over 12,000 people. He wrote glowingly of Eamon DeValera's visit to the United States in 1919-1920, trying to gain recognition of the newly declared Republic of Ireland

During that period the *Herald* repeatedly carried articles and advertisements about Irish Bond drives and came out strongly in support of the Irish Republican movement. In 1918 Connolly lauded the

United Irish Societies of Sacramento, who pledged anew their loyalty to the United States and to its ideals of freedom and democracy. Like many of the Sacramento Irish, Connolly sought to identify Ireland with the United States in the latter's struggle for national independence. Lest there be any doubt as to where he stood in related matters, Connolly in 1920 described how the American Flag had been "insulted by British minions."

Thomas Connolly directed the *Herald* in a momentous period and thus provided the Irish community with a rallying point. Although the *Herald* did not cover exclusively Irish doings, its tenacious focus on them was quite evident, and in retrospect it was a manifestation of the glory days of the Irish in Sacramento.

The majority of the millions of Irish-Americans identify themselves as Irish only on the occasion of St. Patrick's Day. Many American-born Irish have become involved in the Irish community out of cultural nostalgia, religious affiliation or politics. This same holds true for the Irish in Sacramento.

Michael Maurice O'Shaughnessy
Courtesy Beth O'Shaughnessy

– 7 –

MICHAEL MAURICE O'SHAUGHNESSY

SAN FRANCISCO WATER BARON

1864 - 1934

When San Francisco residents turn on their taps at any hour of the day or night, they can thank the prescient Irish-born engineer Michael O'Shaughnessy for their having the purest and tastiest water of any city in these United States. When California's census in 1920 totaled only slightly over three million inhabitants, O'Shaughnessy planned and executed a water system to meet the needs of six million in the future Bay Area. "My dam will stand for a thousand years," he once told an eager City Hall reporter. And it stands as a modern Parthenon of Utility, fused with an aggregate of cement, sand and reinforced steel. The marshaling of men and materials, and then transporting them over uncharted terrain to the construction site in the great Yosemite basin, vied with the building of the Panama Canal for national attention. It also caught the attention of the writer Jack London, who highlighted the dramatic story in his intriguing novel "Cruise of the Shark."

Although the Hetch Hetchy Dam is his crowning achievement, O'Shaughnessy's record in lesser engineering works was equally outstanding. He could well be called the founding father of Mill Valley, the lovely town at the foot of Mount Tamalpais. It was he who laid out the city and planned its water supply. Although the need for an adequate supply of water has plagued most of California for years, water is no problem for San Francisco and its neighbors, thanks to the foresight and persistence of Michael O'Shaughnessy.

The O'Shaughnessy Roots

MICHAEL O'SHAUGHNESSY, the son of Patrick and Margaret O'Donnell O'Shaughnessy, was born on May 28, 1864, in the Townland of Jointer, which lies between the villages of Loughill and

A family portrait taken at Loughill shows Michael O'Shaughnessy's mother and his sister Ellie with nephew Patrick, in front row, and his sister-in-law Anna with Michael's brother Patrick at the rear. Courtesy Helen Gilbourne

Glin, about nineteen miles southwest of Limerick City. His mother was a native of Pallaskenry. His father, a well-to-do farmer, was a Poor Law Guardian in the old Glin Union, the forerunner of the Irish County Councils. The family became known as the "Jointer O'Shaughnessys," in order to distinguish them from other branches of the numerous clan. The family farm where Michael was born and reared lies in a picturesque setting overlooking the River Shannon, famed in song and story. The area was made famous by Gerald Griffith, Irish Poet Laureate of "Fairy Lawn," which lies alongside the O'Shaughnessy homestead in Loughill. The "White River" of which Griffith speaks so endearingly flows through the O'Shaughnessy farm.

The Jointer O'Shaughnessys were a highly respected family in West Limerick, where they have lived and prospered for generations.

The eminent engineer, like his father and grandfather before him, was a man of splendid physique and engaging personality, a conspicuous figure in any gathering. As a youngster he lived for a period at

A view of the large farmhouse at Loughill, where Michael O'Shaughnessy was born and where he spent his early life. This photograph was taken at the same time as the picture opposite. Courtesy Helen Gilbourne

Pallaskenry, the ancestral home of his mother's family the O'Donnels, in one of the most productive agricultural regions in County Limerick. He attended school there for two years, whence he returned home to Loughill and became a pupil at the Mount Trenchard National School nearby. At age seventeen he became a student at Rockwell College in County Tipperary. He later studied at University College, Cork and the University of Galway, winning scholarships at both institutions. In 1884 he graduated with honors from the Royal University in Dublin (now the National University) with a degree in engineering.

With his leaving certificate in hand he went over to London in the hope of finding employment in his chosen field. Finding nothing, he decided to go to the United States, the land of opportunity. In high spirits he set sail from the Cove of Cork on the steamship *Wisconsin*, arriving in New York on March 18, missing by one day the spectacular Saint Patrick's Day Parade. From there he set out for

San Francisco, where he arrived on March 30, 1885.

Like many of his countrymen who immigrated to America, Michael had little money and no influential friends to help him get started. What he did have was a classic education and professional training, coupled with an optimistic spirit and an ardent desire to succeed.

One of his first assignments was that of assistant engineer for the Sierra Valley and Mohawk Railroad in 1885. This was followed by a more extensive project for the Southern Pacific Railway, where he worked for a period of two years, 1886-1888. Then he was called upon to do surveying and mapping in the surrounding Bay Area counties, and to draw up the plans and specifications for the development of the towns of Mill Valley and Sausalito.

In 1890, at age 26, O'Shaughnessy opened an office in San Francisco and began the practice of general engineering. The timing was just right, with plans already underway for the proposed California Midwinter International Exposition in Golden Gate Park. In 1892 he was appointed chief engineer, with full authority to plan that ambitious project and to carry it through to completion. The colorful exposition was thrown open to the public in 1893, luring visitors from far and near, and San Francisco's fame as the host city made headlines all over America.

During 1895 O'Shaughnessy drew up the plans for a twelve-mile stretch of narrow-gauge railroad for the pioneer Mountain Copper Company. This project, along with one for the Spring Valley Water Company, occupied most of his time through 1898.

Hawaiian Projects

IN EARLY 1899 Michael O'Shaughnessy was called to the Hawaiian Islands to design and oversee construction of a water supply for twenty or more sugar plantations. The colossal project included the Olokele Aqueduct on Kauai, ten miles in length, with many tunnels, and The Koolan Aqueduct of equal length, and a per day capacity of 90 million gallons, as well as the Kohola Aqueduct in Hawaii. When the work in the Islands was completed, the engineer returned to the mainland in 1906 and took up where he had left off in California.

At about that time Southern California was experiencing a period of tremendous growth, similar to that of Northern California half a century earlier. The San Diego city fathers engaged O'Shaughnessy to design the proposed Morena Rock Fill Dam, capable of supplying 44 million gallons a day, a project that took over four years to complete. From there he went on to central California, where he designed and supervised the building of a masonry dam on the Merced River for the Crocker Land and Development Company. This was followed by an assignment in Port Costa to design and oversee the construction of a waterworks for that city.

San Francisco Waterworks, an Engineering Masterpiece

ON SEPTEMBER 1, 1912, he was chosen by Mayor "Sunny Jim" Rolph as city engineer of San Francisco, a position he held until his death on October 12, 1934. In that capacity he designed and carried forward the construction of projects costing almost $42 million. Thousands of citizens use these facilities every day, without a thought of the man who built them: the Twin Peaks Reservoir at a cost of $5,750,000, a sewer system at $7,575,000, the Stockton Street tunnel at $656,000, the Twin Peaks tunnel at $4,250,000, the Ocean Beach esplanade at $270,000, the Municipal Railway system at $6,700,000, the city's leading boulevards, one bearing his name, at $1,700,000, and city streets and sidewalks at $15,000,000. It is hard to imagine what San Francisco would be like without these vital amenities.

However, it was in the planning and construction of the Hetch Hetchy Dam and Aqueduct in the Sierra Nevada Mountains, and transporting the sparkling waters through an intricate system of tunnels, pumping stations and pipelines all the way to San Francisco, a distance of more than 150 miles, that the name M.M. O'Shaughnessy will be forever associated. It is difficult for the ordinary citizen to comprehend the magnitude of this project, which alone cost in excess of $45 million and took more than twenty years to complete. The American Society of Engineers gives this account:

> From its source in the High Sierra Mountains, water is carried through 37.7 miles of mountain tunnels and pipes to the border of the broad San Joaquin Valley, thence in a steel pipeline 47.5 miles across the valley, then by tunnels through the Coast Mountain Range, 29.1 miles long, then through pipes skirting the flatlands and underneath the lower arm of San Francisco Bay, 21.2 miles, and finally through a tunnel 19.6 miles long to Crystal Springs Reservoir [Spring Valley Lakes].

The *News-Call* of November 28, 1934, said of Michael O'Shaughnessy: "He acquired and deserved not only a national but an international reputation as one of the foremost engineers of the time."

In 1913, during the administration of President Woodrow Wilson, Congress approved the necessary land grants, without which the project could not get underway. Residents of San Francisco and their neighbors could breathe a sigh of relief when work finally commenced. In addition to the massive Hetch Hetchy dam and its subsidiaries, the work called for the building of a standard-gauge railroad, 68 miles long, and a power plant of 3,300-KVA capacity to operate the machinery and provide light where needed.

This project was followed by a storage dam at Lake Eleanor, a multiple-arch concrete structure, 1,200 feet long with a holding capacity of over eight billion gallons. This latter addition brought the expenditures for the entire project to a total of $86 million, exclusive of interest.

The successful conclusion of the gigantic Hetch Hetchy Dam could as well be attributed to O'Shaughnessy's courage and tenacity, as to his engineering capabilities. In fact, throughout the period of construction, he had to resist the tactics of those who opposed the project for political or self-serving reasons, people who sought to hamper the progress of the work at every opportunity. Financial problems sometimes threatened to shut down the entire operation. But O'Shaughnessy's stout Irish heart, congenial personality and optimistic spirit enabled him to overcome the many obstacles he encountered from start to finish.

His most outstanding characteristic, however, was his undeviating trustworthiness in all of his undertakings, coupled with an Irish temperament, so that when the chips were down, he was prepared to fight vigorously for what he deemed right and worthwhile. There was no evasion or trickery when he was challenged by his critics.

When and Where it Began

IN AUGUST 1912 Mayor Rolph wired O'Shaughnessy in San Diego, inquiring if he would accept a position as city engineer of San Francisco. His previous experience with the city in 1891 had been none too encouraging, when he was engaged as surveyor for the proposed Market Street extension over Twin Peaks Mountain to the Pacific Ocean. Through political intrigue by the Democratic Board of Supervisors, he had been cheated out of his fee for the work. The same thing happened in 1892, when their Republican counterparts retained the talented engineer to extend Potrero Avenue and Bayshore Boulevard all the way to San Mateo County. No wonder he advised the Mayor that he would need at least a week to think over his offer.

In the meantime the thought of thousands of people who had lost their homes in the disastrous 1906 Earthquake and fire and the need to reconstruct public utilities as soon as possible played heavily on his mind. This, plus the influence of his good wife, the former Mary Spottiswood, a native of San Francisco, persuaded him to accept Mayor Rolph's proposal.

On August 31, 1912, O'Shaughnessy had his first official interview with the Mayor in the Whitcomb Hotel, which had become the seat of government during the reconstruction of City Hall. After a long discussion, they agreed that O'Shaughnessy would take over as city engineer at a yearly salary of $15,000.

The following day the Mayor, overjoyed, issued a press release in which he outlined the enormity of the project to be launched, and expressed his confidence in O'Shaughnessy:

> In addition to this system [Hetch Hetchy], if the city purchases the Spring Valley Waterworks he will take charge of the engineering department of that system and carry to completion the development of the Spring Valley sources of supply and the much-needed extensions of the distributing plant. This would include all the work heretofore done by Mr. Hermann Schussler, who for many years received a salary of $25,000 per annum as chief engineer of the company and is at present time receiving $12,000 per annum from them as Consulting Engineer. [O'Shaughnessy] must also take charge of the construction and completion of the Geary Street Railway and the contemplated extension thereof. In addition he will have charge of the sewer system, the auxiliary high pressure water system for fire protection, the construction of proposed tunnels and all the ordinary work of the city engineer.
>
> I venture to say that no corporation in the world, public or private, has a more extensive or varied program of immediate construction, involving a larger sum of money, than the City of San Francisco. I deem this salary of $15,000 a year not exorbitant in view of the experience and prestige of Mr. O'Shaughnessy and of the magnitude and cost of the work, and in view of the salary paid to other engineers of other enterprises. . . I am confident he will be able, with many suggestions directed by his experience, to save the city many times the amount of his salary.

Then Rolph called O'Shaughnessy to his office and said:

> Chief, you're in the saddle, you're it, you are in charge. Go to it, it's up to you. You must look on the city as your best girl and

treat her well. Do what you think is best for her interests.
Where reorganization is necessary, reorganize. We look to you
with all confidence.

Letters of support and encouragement poured in from all over
the city; the following excerpt is typical:

Dear Sir: This is what the people want. If you can do things—
we don't care how—you are worth twice the price, but if you
can't do things, you are dear at any price. We want things done.
Good luck to you, don't mind the red tape or a few dollars, but
get things done.

The media, too, were enthusiastic. A newspaper clipping from
September 27, 1912, was full of praise:

BLUE PRINTS ARE FOR OFFICE FORCE
NEW CITY ENGINEER A MAN OF ACTION
THEORETICAL FOLLOWS THE PRACTICAL IN CITY'S
MANY IMPORTANT ENGINEERING PROBLEMS

The Mayor wears a self-satisfied smile these days when any mention is made of the office of Chief Engineer. His trouble with
important bureaucrats is at an end, and if mention is made that
there is some engineering defect that needs attention, his answer
is, 'O'Shaughnessy has already taken the matter under consideration.' Judging from what has been done in the short time that
the new City Engineer has been in charge, many intricate engineering problems which the city has in hand have been reme-
died. He has proven the confidence reposed in him by the
Mayor and took hold of things personally and straightened out
matters which tended to impede City progress and embarrass the
administration, nor has he waited for the reports of his subordi-
nates, sat in his cozy office and studied blue prints and then
compiled an elaborate and technical report without personal
knowledge of the subject matter. Nothing of the kind for this
virile man. He investigates first personally; visits the spot where a
correction is needed; makes a hasty, though no less accurate survey, arrives at his conclusions, tells what should be done and
then gets his accurate measurements and the blue prints later;
and the practical and theoretical are combined with good results.
O'Shaughnessy had not been in office a day, before he was deep
in the study of the Twin Peaks Tunnel project, and there is
going to be a straight-from-the-shoulder and original report on
this important matter in a short time. The Polk Street regrade
has hung fire for months; O'Shaughnessy will soon have that
straightened out. There are many other matters: the San Bruno

Grade, Butchertown sanitation and other municipal problems which have been on the calendar for a long time. Watch O'Shaughnessy wipe them off the slate.

Construction of the Hetch Hetchy Dam

IN KEEPING with his easy manner and low profile, Michael O'Shaughnessy made no official announcement as to when he would tackle the massive Hetch Hetchy project. However, at the break of dawn on Saturday, September 14, he set out on the tedious journey to Yosemite by way of Oakdale, and from there took a stage-coach over the old wagon road to Groveland, where he spent the night in the historic Baird's Hotel. On Sunday he reached Hamilton and from there climbed over the ridge past South Fork and arrived safe and sound at the city's Log Cabin Ranch.

On the following morning he set out on horseback along the trail led by a pioneer mountain guide named Hank Williams, with two horses and a mule pack. By coincidence O'Shaughnessy met face to face with Secretary of War Henry Lewis Stimson, who provided him with a military escort through the park, shook hands with him and wished him Godspeed on his journey. At Hetch Hetchy cabin he met two city employees named Hill and Koppitz who accompanied him as he explored the breathtaking valley on foot, sizing up the bluffs and massive walls of granite that lined it on either side.

While there he discovered that Lake Eleanor, at an elevation of 4,600 feet, one of his primary interests, was created by turbulent glacial action in ages past when the granite rock was ground out by pressure from massive mountains of ice. The residue from the melting glacier was deposited in a gravel mass over a wide area below the lake, forming a natural mound of clear sand, excellent material for making concrete on the spot. All in all O'Shaughnessy made a number of discoveries that eventually proved beneficial. He also collected samples of rock and took many photographs from both the Hetch Hetchy and Lake Eleanor dam sites.

On September 19, he left Groveland and traveled by stagecoach to the nearest railroad depot, where he caught the Southern Pacific train bound for San Francisco.

September 20th, the very next day, he gave an interview to the San Francisco newspapers in which he stated:

> The country, while rough, was not as forbidding as portions of the Hawaiian Islands were where I completed thirty two miles of tunnels in about four years, but I was much impressed with

the great valley of the Hetch Hetchy dam site from a structural point of view, as it was very narrow, possessing excellent bedrock, furnishing every encouragement to rapid and successful dam construction, and its possession and use was indispensable to the interests of the present half million and the future four million in San Francisco.

He paused momentarily and in a more intimate manner, intended to disarm critics of the project, added:

The construction of a dam would add to the scenic features of the country . . . all objections of alleged nature lovers should be overruled, and the necessary permits should be issued by the Department of the Interior, with instructions to proceed. The City Engineer could not conceive why the City of San Francisco, with all its tribulations, should be subjected to the antagonism of the Washington Departments in endeavoring to acquire a watershed. The only exception was the Forest Service, which thus far has been fair and friendly.

Controversy and Connivance, the Order of the Day

ALTHOUGH Michael O'Shaughnessy had powerful backers in Mayor Jim Rolph, John Freeman, consulting engineer, and former Mayor James D. Phelan, he was beset by equally powerful detractors: landowners, speculators, real estate developers, environmentalists and politicians. One of the very first to object was the Spring Valley Water Company, under the leadership of General H. H. Chittenden, who blatantly predicted that Spring Valley was capable of producing in excess of 219 million gallons of water daily, when in actual fact that company's maximum output was less than 60 million gallons a day.

A more powerful opponent was the Sierra Club, who filed a brief in opposition to granting the Hetch Hetchy site to San Francisco for sanitary and other reasons. They pointed out that the question of sanitation would have to be considered in light of the enormously increasing numbers of people who would surely visit the region in the years to come. They pointed out that from 13,000 to 15,000 people had annually visited the park during the past few years, and that a large number had frequented the Tuolumne River watershed, the source of the proposed waterworks. In conclusion, they noted:

For many persons the climate of California, from the Sacramento Valley southward, demands for its complete salubriousness of the stimulus the ready access to snow altitudes.

Therefore, the number of those who in summer visit the National Park for the scenery will in winter be increased by those that go for their health, for the sports, and for the novelty of those winter scenes that never visit a sea-level Californian among his ever-blooming roses.

Judging by the trend of outdoor sports in other parts of the world this winter use of the Park will in the near future reinforce the summer use as surely as morning succeeds night. Even the present rate of increase in winter visitors indicates that from thirty to fifty thousand people will knock at the portals of Yosemite National Park in the winter of 1930, if facilities of access are provided.

> Respectfully submitted,
> John Muir, President
> Wm. E. Colby, Secretary, Sierra Club

John Muir was the guardian angel of preservationists, and as such his stand against the Hetch Hetchy development was bound to have a significant impact on the proceedings. Muir, a naturalist supreme, traversed the earth in search of nature as the Creator had endowed it. Having found it in an unexplored California hinterland, he invented a contraption to "trip" his cot, and thereby wake up at the stroke of dawn, not to miss out on Nature's Orchestra—wild beasts, birds and bees—that flourish in the serene woodlands. John Muir vowed to preserve for prosperity all that he had seen and heard.

While this opposition might have deterred a man of lesser courage and tenacity, O'Shaughnessy took it all in stride. In speaking of the matter in later years, O'Shaughnessy commented, "I never thought that the monumental Hetch Hetchy project would come so easily, and that the task of placating the many antagonists would prove so difficult."

The Washington Agenda

UNDETERRED by powerful opponents, O'Shaughnessy accompanied a shrewd Irishman named John Dunnigan, San Francisco city clerk, to Washington to seek congressional approval for development of the Hetch Hetchy water project. About that same time Woodrow Wilson became President, succeeding William H. Taft. One of the President's first acts was the appointment of Franklin K. Lane, former city attorney of San Francisco, as attorney general. The San Francisco delegation breathed a sigh of relief at having one of their own in that important position. The hearings by the House Committee on Lands, chaired by the Honorable Scott Ferris of

Oklahoma, got under way June 25, 1913. The committee included such renowned legislators as Carl Hayden of Arizona, Edward Taylor, Colorado, Nick Sinnot, Oregon, Tom Stout, Montana, many of whom looked on San Francisco as the pinnacle of Western America. O'Shaughnessy could also count on such stalwarts as Senator James D. Phelan and Congressman John Nolan of San Francisco.

In fact, it fell to the lot of Senator Phelan, a man who had a way with catchy words and bardic lore, to woo the opposition. After explaining San Francisco's needs and aspirations, he quoted from a John Hayes poem, "Little Breeches," which portrayed an old fellow who believed in nothing of a religious nature, and on being told that his child had wandered away in the woods and was to be restored by the angels, said:

> To restore the life of a little child,
> And to bring him back to his home,
> Is a darn sight better business
> Than loafing around the throne.

THUS the Irish involvement in every aspect of life in California was evident, even in relation to such monumental undertakings as the Hetch Hetchy project. This was particularly true in San Francisco, with such leaders as Supervisors Andrew Gallagher, Harrigan, Coffey, Duffey, Kelly, Lonegran and Walsh. But the opposition included P. H. McCarthy, former mayor of San Francisco, who opposed the purchase of the Spring Valley Water Company, on which the completion of Hetch Hetchy system depended, and Eugene Sullivan and Edward Cahill, two attorneys who represented the Blue Lakes Mokelumne River Scheme.

Finally, after lengthy hearings, the San Francisco delegation succeeded in getting the approval of the Senate Committee for the acquisition of Public Lands, partly thanks to the endorsement of the acting Secretary of the Interior A. W. Jones, as well as that of Secretary of Agriculture David Houston, one of the most distinguished members of President Wilson's Cabinet. Another ardent proponent was Congressman William Kent of Illinois, who had developed a kinship with California and settled in Marin County the following year.

All the San Francisco daily newspapers, including the *Call, Examiner, Post, News* and *Bulletin,* with the notable exception of the *Chronicle,* edited by John de Young, went all out in support of the Hetch Hetchy project, and were loud in their praise of the men who made it possible.

According to all accounts, however, it was the progressive engineer himself who won the day, not merely by his meticulously documented charts and specifications pertaining to every aspect of the project and the estimated cost, but more particularly by his engaging personality and powers of persuasion demonstrated at every stage of the proceedings.

Early on the morning on December 7, 1913, O'Shaughnessy, tired but enthusiastic, wired his wife, VICTORY AT MIDNIGHT—SAN FRANCISCO KNOWS HOW.- LOVE TO ALL, MICHAEL.

President Woodrow Wilson signed the bill on December 19, 1913, in his first year as President, issuing the following statement:

> I have signed this bill because it seemed to serve the pressing public needs of the region concerned better than they could be served in any other way and yet did not impair the usefulness or materially detract from the beauty of public domain.
> I take the liberty of thinking that their fears and objections were not well-founded. I believe the bill to be, on the whole, in the public interest, and I am the less uncertain in that judgment because I find it concurred in by men whose energies have been devoted to conservation and the safeguarding of people's interests, and many of whom, besides, had a long experience in public service which has made them circumspect in forming an opinion on such matters.

On their return to San Francisco the exuberant delegates gathered for an impromptu luncheon at the Saint Francis Hotel, where friends and supporters gathered to celebrate their accomplishments. It had taken almost a year of painstaking effort to secure the right to build the proposed water system. The delegates came home for Christmas, bearing the most stupendous present in the history of San Francisco. It was a time to celebrate, and celebrate they did, in the time-honored San Francisco tradition, led by Mayor "Sunny Jim" Rolph, who had no equal when it came to throwing a party.

Construction of the Hetch Hetchy Dam began in 1914; the entire project took nine years to build. A contract was awarded to the Utah Construction Company, with plans and specifications set forth by Chief O'Shaughnessy. The timing was right. By 1918 everything was in readiness: the railroad was operating, a plentiful supply of power was available, camps for the workers were built and an abundance of labor resulted as the first World War came to a close. It took almost four more years to build the dam alone, which was classed as the largest structure of its kind in the West.

Michael O'Shaughnessy addresses the dignitaries assembled for the
opening of Hetch Hetchy Dam on July 7, 1923.
Courtesy Beth O'Shaughnessy

The dedication of the Hetch Hetchy Dam took place on July 7, 1923. In addition to the planners, the workers and their families, two hundred and fifty or more guests attended the ceremony, most of whom came by an excursion train from San Francisco. O'Shaughnessy Dam was christened in honor of the Chief Engineer, whom Mayor Rolph described as "One of the great souls of our generation."

Fortunately, the photograph has been preserved for posterity by the City of San Francisco, and by his daughter, Beth O'Shaughnessy, the only surviving member of that renowned San Francisco family.

The Coast Range Pipeline

THE CONSTRUCTION of the pipeline and tunnels to carry the water to its destination in San Francisco proved an almost unimaginably formidable task. An article by the Old Mission Portland Cement Company of San Juan Bautista, which played an important part in the construction of the tunnels, proclaimed: "World Record broken by Construction Company of North America in the building of The Longest Tunnel in the World."

The tunnel, which ran through the coastal range from Tesla Portal, near Tracy in San Joaquin County, to Mission San Jose in Alameda, was over 28 miles long and took four years to build. O'Shaughnessy planned everything well and always with an eye to the future. He insisted on a gravity tunnel, which overall cost twice as much as an ordinary pipeline. But the pipeline would have been inadequate as the demand for water increased. He could well have agreed to use a pipeline and make himself look good, leaving future additional costs for someone else to grapple with. Once again his vision reflected the progressive spirit so characteristic of San Francisco.

O'Shaughnessy's high principles endeared him to his engineering staff, who vowed to stand behind him and produce only high quality work. They kept their word despite the criticism leveled at them by newspapers, politicians and others.

The final link in the Hetch Hetchy Aqueduct carried water from Irvington in Alameda County across the Bay to the Crystal Springs Dam and Reservoir, a distance of 23 miles. From the experience gained during the construction of the Coastal Range Tunnel, the planners were better prepared to meet the challenges that lay ahead. An improved pipeline carried the water across the south end of San Francisco Bay in a five-foot diameter steel pipe running underground

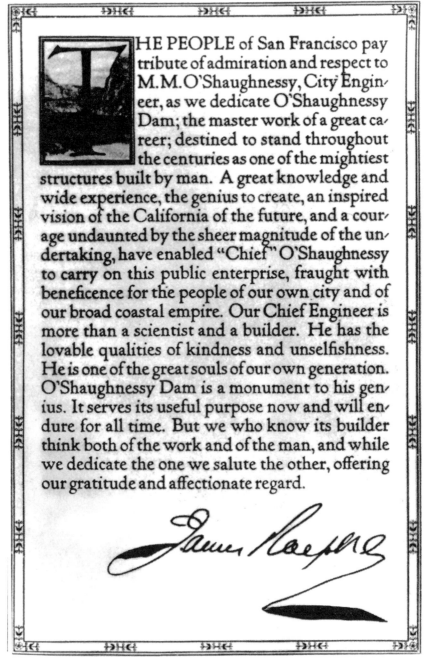

THE PEOPLE of San Francisco pay tribute of admiration and respect to M.M.O'Shaughnessy, City Engineer, as we dedicate O'Shaughnessy Dam; the master work of a great career; destined to stand throughout the centuries as one of the mightiest structures built by man. A great knowledge and wide experience, the genius to create, an inspired vision of the California of the future, and a courage undaunted by the sheer magnitude of the undertaking, have enabled "Chief" O'Shaughnessy to carry on this public enterprise, fraught with beneficence for the people of our own city and of our broad coastal empire. Our Chief Engineer is more than a scientist and a builder. He has the lovable qualities of kindness and unselfishness. He is one of the great souls of our own generation. O'Shaughnessy Dam is a monument to his genius. It serves its useful purpose now and will endure for all time. But we who know its builder think both of the work and of the man, and while we dedicate the one we salute the other, offering our gratitude and affectionate regard.

The program for the dedication of O'Shaughnessy Dam contained this proclamation, signed by Mayor James Rolph. Courtesy Beth O'Shaughnessy from Irvington Portal and then on a raised timber trestle over the salt marshes towards the Bay.

From there the pipeline, encased in solid concrete, ran to Dumbarton Strait and thence across the Bay on a specially designed steel bridge to the Pulgas Pumping Station near Redwood City, where it joined Pulgas Tunnel and carried the sparkling precious liquid to its destination at Crystal Springs Reservoir.

Over the years other pipelines have been built as demand for water increased. But old-time San Franciscans fondly remember the opening, when the water first flowed through Pulgas Tunnel and into Crystal Springs, on October 28, 1934. With the completion of the Hetch Hetchy project, the brainchild of Michael Maurice O'Shaughnessy, the danger of water shortages was eliminated for a century or more.

Unfortunately O'Shaughnessy did not live to see his dream become a reality. Just sixteen days before for the grand celebration, he complained of a pain over his heart and died before his doctor arrived. After his death his many accomplishments became more fully known and appreciated.

His successor, Lloyd McAfee, expressed his reverence for the Old Master: "The great genius and mastermind who alone was responsible for the prosecution of the work, who fought for it during the period of his employment by the city as Chief Engineer, has passed away. Let every San Franciscan honor him and revere him as we do who worked so long with him." Some of the very politicians who had been foremost in shoving him brutally to the side two years before were now quoted by the press as eulogizing him to the heavens.

Construction and Dedication of the Twin Peaks Tunnel

THE TWIN PEAKS TUNNEL, completed in 1918, was one of the outstanding developments designed and constructed under the watchful eye of Michael O'Shaughnessy. It linked the city east to west, and opened up the lands in the western half of the city for development in the sand dunes of the Sunset and Parkside districts and in the more inviting areas such as Ingleside Terrace, Saint Francis Wood and Forest Hills. The opening of the Twin Peaks tunnel was a cause for celebration.

No one loved a party more than "Sunny Jim" Rolph, the flamboyant mayor of San Francisco. The dedication of the Twin Peaks Tunnel gave vent, not to one but to three elaborate parties in succession, the likes of which had never been staged in the city.

*The O'Shaughnessy home at 60 Summit Avenue in Mill Valley was a
comfortable but unpretentious house for a family of seven.
At the top, mother Mary ("Mamie") O'Shaughnessy stands behind
her husband. At left are daughters Helen and Margaret. At right are
daughters Mary and Elizabeth ("Beth"), the baby of the family.
The handsome boy at center is son John, who died young.
Courtesy Beth O'Shaughnessy*

FOR NINETEEN MEMORABLE YEARS Sunny Jim presided over San Francisco, with "There Are Smiles That Make You Happy" as his theme song. During his term as Mayor the Irish ran the city, and nothing pleased Sunny Jim more than having his boyhood pals, the legendary "South of Market Boys," at every public event.

Poetess Kathleen Coffey eulogized "Sunny Jim" in bardic terms:

> We all liked to think of him.
> As smiling, friendly neighbor Jim.
> For such we found Mayor Rolph to be:
> The essence of sincerity.
>
> He always had the human touch.
> That seemed to us to matter much;
> The smile, the handshake warm and kind,
> The little acts that charm and bind.
>
> The ties of gentle fellowship
> That hold the heart with steady grip,
> The unremembered acts that last,
> When greater glories shall have passed.
>
> Those graces all and many more,
> Adorned him in abundant store.
> That's why we love to think of him
> As smiling, friendly neighbor "Jim.

His felicitations for the Irish remained constant through the years. When there was a job opening in City Hall, Mayor Rolph would first call on Archbishop Hanna, to see if he had someone in mind for the position. And on festive occasions, when well-fortified with brown ale from Noonan's Hibernian Brewery, Sunny Jim would sing the praises of his Irish friends and make known his pleasure in their company. When election time rolled around every Irish saloon in town became a "Rolph For Mayor" Campaign Head-quarters.

The first party celebrating the building of the Twin Peaks Tunnel was the Eureka Valley Carnival, a ritzy affair ruled over by a Valley Queen, Miss Tillie Muller, who led a week of dances, parties and parades for the Twin Peaks Property Owners Association. As work on the Tunnel proceeded, a second celebration, known as the "Holed Through Party," was staged. Michael O'Shaughnessy, Chief Engineer, met halfway in the "Bore" with Mayor Rolph and then walked to the East Portal, where they were serenaded by a spirited gathering and photographed profusely.

The third party was the actual Grand Opening of the Tunnel which took place on February 3, 1918. The K Trolley Car, with His Honor the Mayor at the controls, left City Hall at 2:45 P.M. and arrived at the eastern entrance of the tunnel where passengers were greeted by Joseph Leonard, developer of the Ingleside Terrace, and Ferdinand Nelson, the developer of West Portal Park and vicinity, along with an overflow crowd of well-wishers, with Papa and Mama and all the kids. Proper speeches were the order of the day and a lot of hugging and handshaking ensued.

The first five-cent fare was paid by O'Shaughnessy's daughter, Elizabeth, only eight years old at the time. Politicians and city officials tried to board the trolley car for the opening ride by paying with just their smiles, but O'Shaughnessy barred their way and wouldn't let them on board until they had paid their nickel fare.

Beth O'Shaughnessy, who made history over eighty years ago, is still with us, hale and hearty; she can describe the event as if it occurred but a couple of weeks ago. She takes delight in reminiscing about the Glory Days of Old San Francisco and of the accomplishments, trials and tribulations of her illustrious father.

More than sixty years later, another great ceremony took place at the re-dedication of the sparkling new West Portal Station on April 2, 1979, with bands and banners, a parade, speeches and parties that went on all day long and into the night. Nonetheless it could not compare with that day long ago when "Sunny Jim" and "The Chief" came on stage to greet the spirited crowd who roared their approval.

The Emerald Isle Beckons

A S AN IRISH SAYING GOES, "You can take the man out of the country, but you can't take the country out of the man." By 1920, with the San Francisco water project well on its way to completion, O'Shaughnessy decided it was time to return to the land of his birth, where he was eagerly awaited by his aged mother and favorite sister, Ellie. On the way to Ireland he stopped at the old Belmont Hotel in New York City, and while there penned a brief note on the hotel stationery to his sister Ellie.

July 2, 1920

My Dear Ellie,
You will be surprised to hear that I sail from here on the 8th with *"White Star Majestic,"* which lands at Southampton on the 15th & should be with you a couple of days later. I was due to

sail on the *Neobith* the 10th but she is 5 days overdue and by good luck I secured passage 7 days sooner, but as time is limited this is a great advantage. I will reserve all the news till I see you. In the meantime with love to everyone—

Your affectionate brother, Michael

Alas, that longed-for meeting with his dear old mother was not to be. She was so overjoyed at the thought of seeing her son for the first time since he left home almost forty years earlier, that she had a heart attack and died before he arrived.

The old homestead had changed very little in the intervening years, and a leisurely stroll through the green fields and along the Shannon rekindled fond memories of Michael's carefree days on the farm. The adjoining lands known as Fairy Lawn, which he took for granted as a youth, became an instant object of endearment and inspiration.

Gerald Griffith's "Aileen Aroon" and "I Love My Love in the Morning" are famous examples of his poetry set at Fairy Lawn; however, it is in his "Oh, Sweet Adair" that he bares his very soul.

> Oh, sweet Adair, oh lovely vale,
> Oh, soft retreat of sylvan splendour,
> No summer sun nor morning gale,
> E'er hailed a scene more softly tender.
>
> How shall I tell the thousand charms,
> Within thy verdant bosom dwelling,
> When lulled in Nature's fost'ring arms,
> Soft peace abides and joy excelling.

MICHAEL O'SHAUGHNESSY reflected on all that had transpired since he set out for America in 1885. His return visit in 1920, however brief, proved to be more than just a family get-together. It brought him not only a greater appreciation of his Irish upbringing, but also an inspiration for the work that lay ahead in his adopted homeland America. He returned to California and took up his work where he had left off, with renewed vigor and commitment.

In 1929 California was hard hit by the Great Depression, which put a crimp in the construction of Hetch Hetchy, pending the sale of bonds to finance the work. The project's most ardent foes again tried their level best to lay blame for the delay on the Chief himself. They continued their tirade against him, alluding to the number of lives lost, to engineering problems which cropped up, though he solved them promptly, and whatever else they could concoct to embarrass him, not foregoing quicksand nor ground swelling.

O'Shaughnessy alienated some bigwigs by publicly challenging members of the Board of Supervisors. At one point he showed some newsmen out the door of his office. His true friend Mayor Rolph was elected Governor of California in 1932, and was no longer available to support the embattled Chief Engineer.

O'Shaughnessy's days were numbered when the new city charter went into effect in 1932, forming the Public Utilities Commission, with jurisdiction over the Hetch Hetchy Water Department and Municipal Railway. Edward Cahill was appointed as head of the public utilities commission, and Lloyd McAfee, O'Shaughnessy's assistant, was appointed manager and chief engineer, replacing the aging master. O'Shaughnessy was given an office in the water department with the title of "consulting engineer." And to make matters worse, he was given no work and consultation with him was discouraged.

When the time for the final holing-through of the giant tunnel was about to take place, the old Chief didn't want to miss out on the event, but in his new position he had no way of knowing about it, and for whatever reason, those in charge never told him. Had it not been for his Irish friend Buddy Ryan he would have never known until it was over and done. When the date was finally set, Ryan had O'Shaughnessy meet him in Livermore. From there they drove out to the bore and along the tunnel without anyone knowing.

The bigwigs were already on hand, according to Ryan, but evidently unaware of the drama taking place behind the scenes. The tunnel boss, Pete Peterson, a long-time friend of the old Chief, was in on the plot, and held back on the last twelve inches of the bore, knowing O'Shaughnessy was on his way. Into the light came the motor "with only the Chief and me on, to the surprise of the wide-eyed officials and others. Ryan helped old Mike up onto the platform, and Pete punched the hole through from the other side, leaned through and shook hands with the Old Man.."

In appreciation of his many accomplishments as chief engineer, Michael Maurice O'Shaughnessy became more affectionately known by his initials M.M. Over the years, as taxpayers were called on time after time for more and more money to pay for his costly projects, he became known as "More Money O'Shaughnessy."

Alas, O'Shaughnessy is gone, but his great work lives on. One of his last official acts was in selecting the pipe used to carry water across the lower end of San Francisco Bay. It was tragic that he did not live to celebrate the completion of Hetch Hetchy and see the first flow of pure mountain water into the city's reservoirs. A grand celebration was planned in advance for October 28, with Michael O'Shaughnessy slated to be the honored guest. Everyone from the President of the United States on down wanted to pay him tribute.

Webster Nolan of the International News Service, wrote:

> President Franklin Roosevelt delegated Harold Ickes, Secretary of the Interior, to represent him at the colorful ceremonies scheduled for October 28, and to say to Michael O'Shaughnessy 'Well Done.' Not only San Francisco will heap honors posthumously upon the great constructor, for his fame is far flung. Detroit and Hawaii, Seattle, San Diego and Portland have massive monuments in granite reservoirs, mighty bridges or mountain-piercing tunnels whereby to remember the genius of the Royal University of Dublin. But the greatest of all the monuments that speckle the American terrain is his stupendous creation in the high Sierras of California, on the fringe of the beautiful Yosemite valley, the third largest water impounding project in the world, rivaled only in size by the great aqueducts of New York and Boston.

His Untimely Death

THE END CAME rather suddenly on October 12, 1934, with his wife and family gathered at his bedside. He died, as one newspaper put it, with "the fulfillment of the dream and goal of his twenty-two years as city engineer and consulting engineer for San Francisco almost within his grasp." On October 28th, when the waters of Hetch Hetchy came flowing through the 170 miles of pipeline, aqueduct and tunnel his wizardry had driven, and reached San Francisco, the great man was dead and buried.

The wake, in the age-old Irish tradition, was held at his residence on Vallejo Street. All day long and into the night they came to say farewell: state and city officials, business associates, the clergy and members of religious orders, longtime friends and neighbors, and men and women from every walk of life. Some knelt by the bier and offered a silent prayer while others stopped for a moment, bowed their heads in reverence and passed on.

Over the years M.M. had acquired a host of friends and not a few enemies, such as Alfred Cleary, the City Administrator, who would ordinarily be considered as a blood relative. Beth O'Shaughnessy said that he was not considered a friend of the family and that she would not accept his condolences. On the other hand she welcomed Supervisor Jesse Coleman, whom she spoke of as a true friend and perfect gentleman.

The funeral procession led from the family residence at 3753 Vallejo Street to Saint Vincent de Paul's for the funeral mass. In the line of march were two battalions of police and firemen, resplendent in their official garb. They formed a guard of honor outside the church and stood at attention as the remains were placed in the hearse for the final journey to Holy Cross Cemetery.

A reporter for the San Francisco *Examiner* noted:

> A sorrowing throng bowed before the altar of Saint Vincent de Paul's Church to hear the solemn requiem mass celebrated by Father Nicholas Connolly and the eulogy of Archbishop Hanna, who also gave the final absolution. In the sanctuary were many Monsignors, Priests, Christian Brothers and Sisters of the various religious orders. The church was filled to capacity with State and City officials and grieving friends and an overflow crowd stood silently on the street outside.

A T THE TIME of his death Michael O'Shaughnessy left four daughters and a son to mourn his passing. His youngest daughter, Elizabeth, (Beth) is the only surviving member of the San Francisco O'Shaughnessys; this writer is indebted to her for the story of her illustrious sire.

After his death O'Shaughnessy's many talents and accomplishments became more fully known, understood and appreciated. To quote the stirring words of the noble John Boyle O'Reilly,

> What shall we do nobler than mark their passage with kindly hearts, mayhap for kinfolk to follow? What shall we do wiser than pile a cairn with stones from the wayside that their tracks and name be not blown from the hills like sand, and their story be lost forever.

Michael O'Shaughnessy's memory is perpetuated in the names of the O'Shaughnessy Dam (which most people now call the Hetch Hetchy Dam), and in O'Shaughnessy Boulevard, which winds down from Portola Drive beside Glen Park.

Senator Thomas A. Maloney
President, South of Market Boys

– 8 –

THE MALONEY BROTHERS

THE SENATOR AND THE SAGE

THE IRISH, exiled from their native land, forced to seek refuge and asylum throughout the world, have brought with them a love of truth, liberty, fraternity, literature, music, art and religion. In their own country the Irish were oppressed, impoverished and maligned, but no force could destroy their character. In every land where human foot has trod they have left a lasting impression, despite the efforts of their enemies to degrade and stifle their mental energies. They have lighted the darkened areas of the world with the torch of civilization.

Wherever and whenever the human voice is raised in praise of God and his earthly kingdom, there you will find Irish poetry and song and sweet music to charm every heart and enrich every soul. Many a fireside is cheered by their writers and story tellers. Despite poverty and degradation, their light shines brightly in the history of all nations, and none more so than right here in our own U.S.A.

In the hallowed halls of the United States Congress the Irish have ever stood against the oppressor, and have protected the less fortunate by initiating laws for the betterment of humanity. Their gifted orators have raised their voices for the advancement of learning and the inalienable right of liberty and justice for all. No two men were better examples of the Irish influence in America, and California in particular, than the indomitable Maloney brothers, Tommy and Pete—the Senator and the Sage.

Tommy Maloney began life at the very bottom of the ladder, not by choice but by necessity. At the age of ten he was compelled to peddle newspapers on the San Francisco waterfront, before and after school, to support the family when his father was injured and unable to work. It was the beginning of a long and fruitful life that ended with his death at age 96.

His brother Pete had an equally meritorious career; among other things he founded the "South of Market Boys" in old San Francisco, one of the most renowned hometown organizations in the nation.

Their Irish Roots

THE MALONEYS in Ireland were a tenacious clan who suffered much for their unrelenting resistance to the persecution of their fellow Catholics at the hands of English mercenaries. In fact, one of their number, Father Donagh Maloney, Vicar General of Diocese of Killaloe, resisted so intently that he was arrested, thrown into prison, tortured at the whim of his captors and then beaten to death in the year 1601. Hence the name in Gaelic, "O'Maoldhombnaigh," which signifies a servant of the church.

The ancestral home of the Maloneys is located in the picturesque village of Rathangan, County Kildare, where John Maloney, the patriarch of the California Maloneys, was born. John's wife, Julia, was a native of Conshocken, Pennsylvania. They first met in San Francisco, and were married in the little town of Mountain View on the San Francisco Peninsula. Tommy was the second oldest in a family of nine children, six boys and three girls.

His mother died in 1899, when he was only ten years of age, leaving him and five other sons living at home in the care of their father. Six sons survived Julia Smith Maloney: James, the oldest, Thomas A. and Peter R., the subjects of this narrative; John J.; Joseph, who died in his teens; and William. Strange as it seems, there is no record of what happened to the three girls.

Having to care for so many youngsters proved quite a burden for John Maloney, a man working long hours at meager pay on the waterfront. There were times when John himself had to do without in order to feed and clothe his growing family

Some eight years after Julia's death John married an Irish lass, Marie Conroy, and of this union nine more children were born. Of these, the names of only six were supplied by Tommy's son, John Maloney: Nellie Maloney Crawford, Katherine Maloney Bolard, Esther Maloney Ferguson, Mike Maloney, Marcella Maloney Boyle and Edward Maloney. One can only assume that the others died in infancy.

For Tommy Maloney it all began South of Market, where he was born on May, 22, 1889. When young Tommy went to work selling newspapers on the San Francisco waterfront, his day started at 3:30 a.m. He went to the Ferry Building to purchase his papers, two bundles for fifty cents, and sold them at five cents per paper.

Being on the job so early was necessary in those days when the watches aboard ship were four hours each, starting midnight to 4 a.m., and so on around the clock. Watches in those days required more men in the engine room, because steam was kept up by burning coal, which was fed into the boilers by hand. In the so-called "black gang" were oilers, coal passers and firemen, good customers for the young vendors who came aboard.

Tommy sold papers until 8:30 in the morning and then returned to his home on Potrero Hill to prepare for a day at school. After classes were finished he would have his dinner at the Old Alameda Cafe on the Embarcadero, the meal consisting of

John Maloney

baked beans, a thousand to the plate, with a slab of sugary Napoleon and a cup of coffee, all for 20¢.

After his meal it was back to the waterfront, selling the evening papers, the *Call* and the *Bulletin*. There was little time in his busy life to develop any tendency toward juvenile delinquency. There were no playgrounds then, and for the youngsters with a liking for baseball the sandlots were the only place to practice. Bedtime at eight o'clock was mandatory for Tommy, who had to be back on the job at 3:30 in the morning.

Misfortune befell the Maloney family again when John Maloney, the breadwinner, was involved in an accident while working as a stevedore on the waterfront. Because there was no workmen's compensation or accident insurance at the time, his only recourse was to sue the employer, the Oregon Navigation Company, for personal injury. This turn of events made it necessary for young Tommy to quit school and find work to support the family.

In early 1900 the elder Maloney was awarded a judgment for the injuries he sustained in the ship accident. With the proceeds from the claim he purchased a saloon, the Cuckoo's Nest, at First and Brannan Streets. Tommy quit his work on the waterfront and took over as manager of the saloon., at the age of eleven. In his capacity as head barkeeper Tommy acquired the reputation of keeping and drawing the best steam beer in San Francisco. At times he presided over the free lunch counter in the manner of a qualified head waiter, dishing out ham and cabbage, boiled mutton and green beans, and Irish stew.

He also settled the problem of saloon brawls, not uncommon in those days, by constructing a ring in the back yard and demanding that all disputes be settled there. As an added inducement he provided boxing gloves that had been worn by such leading pugilists as Eddie Hanlon and Finny Britt.

Then a stroke of bad luck came to the Maloneys. The Cuckoo's Nest was caught in the whirlwind of the 1901 strike called by the Teamsters Union. The strike led to violent encounters and damage to buildings and businesses running into thousands of dollars. It escalated to the point that, when an outbreak began on the waterfront, the merchants had to close their doors until order was restored. Tommy Maloney was so distraught that he closed the doors of the Cuckoo's Nest for good. Tommy was then twelve years old.

However he could not break the habit of getting up early in the morning. Tommy bought a pair of greyhounds, and early every morning he and his dad headed out to the sand dunes to train the dogs by chasing jackrabbits that abounded in the area at the time.

Alas, the earthquake and fire of April 18, 1906, put an end to one of the most delightful periods in Tommy's Maloney's life, when he was ordered to kill his prize greyhounds by drowning them in the Bay. The military authorities in control of the city considered such pets a nuisance at a time when there was not enough food for the people in distress.

The Maloneys lost everything in the conflagration and were forced to take refuge on the steamer *Mariposa,* which was anchored at the mail dock at First and Brannan Streets. There they lived for a month, eating mostly rice and fish until they could find housing ashore.

To make ends meet, Tommy went to work helping soldiers remove the bodies of the victims from the debris of fallen buildings. His father John worked for the local authorities, cleaning bricks for use in the reconstruction work, which was getting underway.

When the emergency came to a close, Tommy went to work in a box factory at a meager $1.25 a day. He eventually found a better paying job as a ship scaler, although the work was quite strenuous for one of his age. At times he had to go down into the fireboxes of the big steamships that were used to transport American servicemen to and from the Philippine Islands. From the waterfront he went on to work in the lumber yards, where he remained until 1914.

World War I ushered in a period of prosperity, with work for every willing hand, and a big increase in wages to boot. The demand for ships to transport food and clothing and medical supplies to the Allies increased a hundred fold

So it was back again to his old haunts, this time as a longshoreman and eventually a labor leader. Tommy won election as president of the Riggers' Union. While serving in that position he represented the men in meetings and conferences in Washington, D.C., Brooklyn, Seattle, Vancouver and Victoria.

Tommy Maloney was the first labor leader to proclaim that there was more to be gained by cooperation between employers and employees than any other way. When this writer interviewed him in the Carlmont convalescent home in Belmont shortly before his death at the age of 96, he said, "My aim always was to preserve and maintain peace and harmony between the employer and the employed. At the same time, I tried to secure decent working conditions and good wages." The political editor of the *San Francisco Chronicle*, Earl Behrens, dubbed Maloney "The Great Compromiser," noting his knack for bringing opposing parties together in common agreement, especially in aggravated cases which pitted the employers against the workers.

Tommy Maloney's early education was limited to two schools: old St. Brendan's on Rincon Hill and the `School of Hard Knocks' on the San Francisco waterfront. But he made a little go a long way, rising through his own efforts from a lowly paper boy to a renowned California legislator.

At the age of 21, on November 23, 1910, Thomas Maloney and Helen Toomey were united in marriage before the altar of old St. Rosa's church at Fourth and Brannan Streets. By coincidence, on that same day Tommy lost his job as a lumber clerk; that cut short their honeymoon to a one day ferry boat trip to Oakland and Alameda. And for the next ten years jobs were where he could find them.

Maloney's Political Career

TOMMY MALONEY, a blue-collar worker with little money, decided the time was ripe for his entry into the political arena. And in the year 1919, at the age of thirty, he became a candidate for the office of State Senator. He barely lost that first election, but won every election from that time until 1956, when he retired from public service. Beginning in 1924 Maloney served two terms as State Senator and 24 years as an Assemblyman. As a member of the State Senate he was one of seven men who represented San Francisco in the Upper House of the

Julia Maloney
Mother of Thomas and Peter Maloney

Legislature. With the re-organization of that body in 1932, San Francisco lost all but one of its seats.

At that time the erstwhile Senator ran for the Assembly from the twentieth district in San Francisco and won election by a comfortable majority.

During his term as assemblyman, Maloney sponsored legislation that was progressive and beneficial not only to the working class but to his constituents in general. He initiated a bill for the establishment of the World Trade Center, which is housed in the landmark Ferry Building. Senator Maloney also championed the Foreign Trade Zone,

still in active operation on the San Francisco waterfront. He supported legislation for sick and disabled employees not covered by State
Workmen's Compensation, which allowed them to spend a maximum
of twelve days in hospital at $8 per day.

He cosponsored legislation providing for a State Capital Reserve
of $235,000, without the imposition of new taxes. The fund was used
where needed for schools, colleges, hospitals, correctional institutions
and other vital services. He also sponsored legislation freezing $75
million in state funds for use in the event of a decrease in state rev-
enues without imposition of new taxes.

He introduced a bill repealing the fifty-year-old law prohibiting
the sale of pre-colored margarine, and saw it through to completion.

He sponsored amendments which reduced the interest on small
loans to less affluent citizens.

He sponsored a measure which exempted ship construction and
repair from the California state sales tax, in order to encourage shipping companies to locate in California, especially in San Francisco.

He supported legislation to provide old age pensions, workmen's
compensation and a series of measures that led the construction of the
San Francisco-Oakland Bay Bridge and the Golden Gate Bridge.

In all those activities Tommy Maloney acquired a knowledge and
understanding of what made good politics and good sense. He held a
sincere belief that legislation ought to be for the greatest benefit for
the greatest number. He enjoyed tremendous success with virtually all
the legislation he introduced, especially bills affecting his San Francisco precinct. He was so admired and respected in the assembly that he
was elected Speaker Pro-Tem (presiding officer in the absence of the
speaker), for fourteen consecutive years. He served his native city and
state under seven governors: Governor Richardson, C.C. Young,
Frank Merriam, James Rolph, Culbert Olson, Earl Warren and Goodwin Knight.

On his eightieth birthday, Tommy was given the highest honor
his colleagues could confer upon him; the opportunity to address a
joint session of the legislature.

Despite his many accomplishments, the affable politico has been
given but scant mention in our history books. To make amends for
this oversight, and to set the record straight, I sought a personal interview with the old gentleman. On the appointed day I was accompanied by retired San Francisco Police Chief Tom Cahill, a longtime
friend of the aging Senator. We all sat around a table in the manner of
a fireside chat. Tommy seemed to relish the opportunity to relive his

childhood days on the San Francisco waterfront, and reminisce about the trials and tribulations of his adolescence and the challenges he encountered as a member of the California Legislature.

Among the more solemn events of his career in the State Legislature, Tommy counted the moment when as Speaker Pro Tempore he announced the death of President Franklin Delano Roosevelt on April 12, 1945.

The twinkle in his blue Irish eyes belied his years; his voice was forceful and distinct as he related the happenings of days long gone as if they were yesterday. At times he took over completely, talking and gesturing, joking and laughing as he trotted out story after story with the gusto of a man half his age.

Irish to the Core

THE IRISH COMMUNITY rightly claimed the beloved Senator as one of their very own. He lived up to his Irish heritage and prided himself in his Irish ancestry and in Irish-oriented community projects that he generously and enthusiastically supported. The dapper statesman was a familiar sight whenever the Irish were involved. He participated in every St. Patrick's Day Parade for half a century or more. As the parade's Grand Marshal in 1960, he led the troops up Market Street to the cheers of over a quarter million spectators lining the streets, all the way to city hall. And there to greet him on the grandstand were a number of his former associates in the State Assembly, city officials and Irish community leaders, including Police Chief Tom Cahill, resplendent in his gold braid.

The United Irish Societies and Ancient Order of Hibernians staged a grand affair in honor of Tommy Maloney's fifty years of governmental and civic service. An elaborate banquet held in the Garden Court of the Palace Hotel on October 26, 1974, included music and entertainment. The guest of honor wooed the gathering with his beguiling anecdotes and youthful gestures. He brought the audience to its feet by dancing an Irish Jig.

One of Maloney's last public appearances, at the age of 84, was at a fund-raising party for the proposed Irish Cultural Center which took place at Lowell High School in late 1973. He was almost in tears when he was introduced as "Mr. San Francisco," which he truly was in every sense of the word. In quieter moments he let it be known that this event was one of the highlights of his life.

Following a long and fruitful life Tommy Maloney passed away in the Carlmont Retirement home in Belmont on January 15, 1986.

The Requiem Mass was said at St. Theresa's Church on Potrero Hill, where the family worshipped for many years. He was preceded in death by his wife, Helen, and two children, Thomas and Alice. He is survived by his son, John Robert, of Belmont, and his daughter, Barbara Davis, and grandchildren and great grandchildren, for a total of 33 descendants. John, like his illustrious father, had a distinguished career in the business world, which led to his appointment as State Insurance Commissioner by Governor Earl Warren.

Barbara married Jim "Lefty" Davis, a professional baseball player in the Pacific Coast League with the Seattle Rainiers and Sacramento Solons. He went on to the Major Leagues as a relief pitcher for the Chicago Cubs, and then to the Saint Louis Cardinals. Lefty Davis is remembered in baseball annals as having pitched four strike-outs in a single inning.

The Sage of Tar Flat

PETER R. MALONEY, or "Pete," as he was more affectionately known to his friends, was born in San Francisco, September 21, 1891, the third oldest of John's eighteen children by two wives. After three years' schooling at St. Brendan's, at Fremont and Harrison Streets, at age nine he left and went to work to support the family. He found work on the waterfront as a ship scaler, being lowered down the stacks to clean them and the big steam boilers below.

At the age of twelve, while rolling a hoop for fun on the waterfront, he was run over by a runaway horse and wagon, and as a result both his arms and both legs were broken; he suffered internal injuries as well. His stay in the hospital lasted for weeks and weeks, but with youth in

Peter Maloney, age 10. Courtesy Warren Maloney

his favor, his broken limbs mended well, and eventually he was released, scarred only by the memory of the accident.

When he regained his former agility Pete found work as a conductor on the old Market Street Railway, keeping that position until he entered the San Francisco Police Department.

Pete's first assignment as a rookie policeman was in the Potrero Station at Third and Twentieth Streets, near Butchertown, with its notorious gang of hoodlums who called themselves "The Forty Thieves." Some of this gang had jumped Pete's predecessor on the beat; they hog-tied him, tore off his pants, and pinned his police badge to his rear end. Knowing this, Pete walked into the pool hall where they hung out and introduced himself as the new cop on the beat. He told them that as long as they behaved themselves he would leave them alone, but if they didn't he would not hesitate to arrest them all. At this point some of them made a move in his direction. Pete grabbed a pool cue, beat the hell out of the lot, and called for the paddy wagon. They all ended up in jail, and that was the end of the Forty Thieves.

Having proved his worth on the beat, Pete was transferred to the Hall of Justice in the office of Police Chief Daniel O'Brien. He became the Chief's front man, screening all comers and appointments. About that same time a novel idea came into being: training officers in the art of self-defense. To get the program underway, Pete was appointed athletic director of the Police Department. In preparation, the brass sent him to a Japanese man to learn Judo. The training sessions were held in a playground in North Beach. The ultimate aim was to prepare cops for any physical encounter that might arise in the line of duty.

A short time later the Police Department installed the first two-way radio in a police car. Pete and his partner, officer Nat Mascarrelli, were chosen to man the "Radio Car."

The South of Market Boys, a San Francisco Institution

PETE MALONEY is best remembered as the founder of the South of Market Boys, a unique social fraternity. The object of the association was "To promote friendship, maintain character, repute and mutual respect and ever a helpful influence for everything good and worthwhile among the Boys born and raised South of Market and their descendants; to perpetuate the memories, traditions and associations of boyhood days. To inspire among the young manhood of San Francisco proper respect and appreciation of days gone by; and instill among all an eternal desire and striving to make the lives and conditions of their sons a source of pride and satisfaction to the city of their birth. In brief, by deeds and example, to merit the esteem and confidence of their fellow men, and make the life, character and spirit of

Peter Maloney
Courtesy Warren Maloney

South of Market memorable and worthy of remembrance in the history of San Francisco."

The idea came to Pete in 1924, one day on the job in the office of Police Chief Daniel O'Brien. Pete didn't want the good old days to die. To him the flame of San Francisco's pioneer spirit was worthy of perpetuation, perhaps because of his own memories of more carefree days down South o' the Slot. Born on Rincon Hill, a place of reverence, he lamented the demise of the Market Street cable cars and with them the "Slot" in which the cable moved. He worked slowly and quietly until he gained the confidence of Chief O'Brien. When the Chief found out what Pete had in mind he became as enthusiastic about the proposal as his young subordinate, with the result that the first three members of the yet unborn organization all bore the name of O'Brien: the chief and his two sons, George, who became a motion picture star performing he-man roles, and Daniel Jr., who became a San Francisco attorney.

Pete then suggested that other men interested in the proposal get together and talk it over. As a result the following gentlemen attended a meeting in the Knights of Columbus Hall on Golden Gate Avenue, September 25, 1924: John Quinn, John J. Whelan, Michael Doyle, Albert Samuels, Thomas Maloney and his brother Pete. Temporary officers were elected and the South of Market Boys started to function.

At a second meeting it was decided to call a general meeting for November 11, to be held at the assembly room in the Call Building. At this meeting attended by 125 men, Thomas P. Garrity was elected president of the organization; Albert Samuels, first vice-president; Thomas A. Maloney, second vice-president; John Quinn, treasurer; Peter R Maloney, financial secretary; William Granfield, recording secretary, and Perry Goldstein, sergeant-at-arms.

The organization is immortalized in a stirring ballad by Miles Overholt:

South of the Slot

Whether you know your location or not,
The heart of the city is South o' the Slot!
That is the spot,
True to the dot!
The heart of the city is South o'the Slot.

Let Memory lead you with time withered hand
Out where the shanties once made their last stand;
Only a block away,
Imprints of yesterday—
Shanties! But once they were palaces grand.

Over on Mission Street, Memories tell
Stories of people who came there to dwell;
Homes of Olden Days;

Tears dim the golden haze;
Threnodies up from the heart seem to well.

Here lived the women and men of the town;
Who builded a city and never looked down;
    Fame beckoned some,
    The world bade them come.
And others were happy without the renown.

So this the reason each Mission Street lot
Can tell you the story and plot.
    And whether or not
    Geography's rot,
The heart of the city is South o' the slot!

At a meeting held on December 4, 1924, six hundred new members were initiated. The seeds were planted in virgin soil and became a stately tree spreading its mantle over city and state. The South of Market Boys stands as a friendly, protective institution, commemorating the "city that was" and keeping pace with the "city that is"—SAN FRANCISCO—serene and indifferent to fate. There is no organization like it, and I doubt there ever will be.

Pete Maloney was truly a man of vision. The small coterie to whom he revealed his plans and from whom he got inspiration and encouragement deserve to be classed as honored members of the South of Market Boys. Their influence spread through the land. Members became outstanding leaders in business, finance and art; their names are known not only in San Francisco but throughout America.

One in particular is Thomas Hickey, one of the organizers of the South of Market Boys, who was chosen by New York Governor Al Smith to second his nomination for President of the United States at the Democratic Convention at Houston, Texas, June 26, 1928. Hickey received his primary education at Father Mulligan's famed school, St. Joseph's, which he deemed the greatest honor ever bestowed on him. He then enrolled in St. Ignatius College, when it was located on Van Ness Avenue and Hayes Street, and was graduated with honors. Following graduation, while studying law, he taught school in the old college and many of his former pupils remember him for his ability. Among the branches of learning whose wealth he imparted to the young minds of the day was the art of elocution.

A self-made man who during his early youth peddled newspapers like his buddies the Maloney brothers, Hickey was long associated with Gavin McNab in the Democratic Party, and was instrumental in electing the Honorable James Phelan as United States Senator from California. He cared little for the limelight and never held political office. In consequence, his aims and accomplishments have remained practically unknown to the present generation.

There is no other organization like the South of Market Boys, founded on sentiment pure and simple, and holding out no material wealth or political benefits to anyone. Pete Maloney, the founder, was a visionary. His life was a full and happy one, and he enjoyed every minute of it. He organized the Sunrise Breakfast Club, the Mother's Day Breakfast, St. Patrick's Day Luncheon, Father's Day Luncheon, The San Francisco Shut-In Association, and was the prime mover in the Widows and Orphans Association of the San Francisco Police Department.

The South of Market Boys were celebrated in song by one J. Westhall:

Song of the South of Market Boys

Now back have rolled the years of old,
Of youth and dreams long past;
And scenes unfold in memories told
And raise their strains to last;
The mint walls speak the tales of yore—
The School and Temple night;
While horses race and engines roar—
And flames the bonfire high!
Now roll the drums of bygone days—
The streets awake to thrill;
The sand-lots gleam in golden rays;
And speak the drama still!.
And each and all—the gang is here—
The South of Market Boys;
He comes in scenes and echoes clear—
In strains of memories joy;
And many a one his name has blazed
On honor's roll of fame;
And Freedoms banner still has raised
Courageous in its name!
Now roll the drums of bygone years—
The streets awake to thrill;
The drama stirs to love and tears—
To that which binds it still !
All glory then to what lives on—

To scenes of storied pride;
To templed forms of wood and stone
Where cherished lights abide;
The South of Market's loyal heart
That's kindly, staunch and true;
To every deed and work of art
That speak its praises due!
Now roll the drums that hail the past—
The streets awake to thrill;
The drama drives its spell to last—
To rapture moves it still!.

The Old Time Boxers' Luncheon, A Grand Affair

ONE OF THE MOST DELIGHTFUL celebrations in the long history of the South of Market Boys was the banquet honoring the members of the boxing fraternity. It came at the request of founder Pete Maloney, who contacted a number of longtime members of the club and told them of his plans. "It is my purpose to pay a public tribute to these gentlemen while they are still with us and to let them know that we, who have always appreciated good boxing bouts are more than anxious and willing to show them we appreciated all of their efforts. I have on my list in and around San Francisco about seventy-five former boxers whose names are here. Do you know any of them? This will be their chance to sit down and break bread with one another and relive the old days."

"If you think your praise is due them," Pete continued, "now is the time to give it to them, because they can't read their tombstones when they are dead. No definite date has been set, but I would appreciate it very much if you will attend the committee meeting on May 8, 1941, 8 p.m., South of Market Boys Clubrooms, 150 Golden Gate Avenue. If you know any former boxer I may have left off the list kindly let me know and bring the name and where he can be located to the next meeting."

At the general meeting it was agreed to hold the luncheon on June 21, 1941, and where else but at the Garden Court of the Palace Hotel? The response was overwhelming. Letters of acceptance came pouring in from the great and near great of the boxing fraternity: heavyweights Jack Dempsey, Tom Sharkey, Victor McLaglen, Jim Jeffries, and Willie Meehan: welterweights Jack O'Brien, Frank McConnell and Harry Riley, lightweights, Willie Ritchie, Dick Hyland, One-Round Hogan, Frank Burns, Pete McGee, Spider Roache, Jack

This remarkable photograph shows the popularity of boxing in San Francisco in 1918. Every seat in the Civic Auditorium is filled, with a huge crowd standing on the main floor. There isn't a single woman in the crowd, and all the men are wearing jackets and ties, except for the sailors in uniform. The bout was between Phat Willie Meehan and Fred Fulton. Courtesy Warren Maloney

Downey, Paddy Smith, Frankie Dolan, Smiling Joe Kane, Willie O'Neill, South Side Jack O'Brien and North Side Jack O'Brien— many of them Irish-Californians.

There were a number of interesting replies; Gene Tunney sent his best wishes and regrets, saying "Unfortunately, it is out of the question for me to attend as I am in the Navy for the duration of the war, subject to orders of the Department."

The Palace Hotel began preparations for the great event. The storied Garden Court seats 850 guests, and every seat was sold in advance. All four San Francisco daily newspapers carried articles weeks in advance, one catchy story after another. The hoopla was such that one could excuse talk-show hostess Biddy Bishop, who got so carried away that she exaggerated the whole affair on her radio program. "There will be more than two hundred fifty great stars of the past at the party and about one thousand other invited guests," she said.

"Judging from the great interest and many famous boxers of the past who will attend, this will prove one of the most outstanding events of the year and will attract the attention of the entire country." How right she was. The grand affair proved to be perhaps the largest gathering of former boxing champions ever assembled in one room.

St. Patrick's Cadets

IN EVERY ASPECT of life in old San Francisco, the Irish led the way. A case in point is the St. Patrick's Cadets, a para-military organization recruited from the sons of those sturdy Irish pioneers who settled south of Market Street. The Cadets were all reared in St. Patrick's Parish and served faithfully under their beloved Chaplain, Father Thomas Larkin. The organization, formed in 1873, became one of the best drilled military units in California, winning prize after prize in statewide competitions. When on parade, sporting their regulation blue uniform with Kelly green stripes, carrying rifles and drawing a shining brass cannon on wheels, these young men were the idols of all San Franciscans.

The summer encampment was a big event in the lives of the Cadets, who bivouacked at various locations such as Monterey, Santa Cruz, and Glen Ellen in the Valley of the Moon. The encampment was strictly military, and discipline was maintained at all times. All the young men attended Mass on Sundays, celebrated by their beloved mentor, Father Larkin.

In the evening around the campfire, the Cadets sang and told stories until taps were sounded and the lights went out. Sentries were posted and quiet reigned until reveille sounded next morning. At one of the most notable encampments in Monterey, the Cadets were present at the exhuming of the remains of Father Junipero Serra for reburial in the Mission Chapel at Carmel. Somehow a number of the boys came home with pieces of the coffin and fragments of the garb in which the saintly priest was buried.

Old time residents of South of Market spoke glowingly of the city parades of former years, when the St. Patrick's Cadets, led by their commander, Captain Bernard Hanlon, stole the show, winning ovations for their up-tempo and close-order marching.

With changing times, St. Patrick's Cadets were officially disbanded September 12, 1883. A banquet to note their passing, given at the Baldwin Hotel, closed a chapter on one of the most popular organizations in California, each member a credit to his South of Market birthplace.

The Maloney Legacy

THE MANTLE of the Maloney clan has been passed on to Warren Maloney, who has left his mark in law enforcement and more recently as proprietor of Maloney Security, Inc., a firm steeped in the Irish tradition of old San Francisco. A third-generation San Franciscan, Warren followed in his father's footsteps in the Police Department. In 1958, within four years of the day he joined the force he was named "Cop of the Year." He earned his District Captain's commendation for bravery that led to the apprehension of Galena Nicholson and three other suspects who were on the wanted list for a series of telephone booth burglaries.

Proud of his Irish heritage, Warren, with his wife Jeanie and son Robert, made a trip to his ancestral homeland in the picturesque village of Rathangan, County Kildare. While there he compiled a diary enhanced with photos of relatives and items pertaining to the origin of the Maloney Clan.

Although the Maloneys were among the largest Irish families in San Francisco, it was not in number alone that they excelled but in the principles they espoused and passed on to each succeeding generation: a firm faith, coupled with an abiding love of God and country and respect for every human being.

And one quality more: they understood the feelings evoked by a part of San Francisco where humble origins bred strength and pride and loyalty among those who shared a special time and place.

Another balladeer (identity unknown but worthy of coming to light) described South of the Slot this way:

> T'was an old rustic hut down South of the Slot.
>   Twas a broken down hovel they say,
> But I'd long to get back to the tumble-down shack
>   And live there forever and aye.
>
> Twas a hole in the wall, twas battered and small.
>   Just a room and an old cozy cot,
> But memory recalls that old scene that enthralls
>   My Dear Mother down South of the Slot.
>
> But to me there's a plain down Mission and Main
>   In that paradise never forgot,
> Where the upheaving sand built a mansion so grand
>   In the days down South of the Slot.
>
> Yes, I'll take off my hat to the boys of tar flat.
>   And to each little chattering tot,
> To my neighborhood pals and those beautiful gals
>   I once loved down South of the Slot.

Tommy and Peter Maloney, the senator and the sage, devoted their entire careers to the advancement their native city and state. Their lives' work is but another example of the Irish contribution to this remarkable state.

Father John Francis Quinn

– 9 –

JOHN FRANCIS QUINN
A LATTER-DAY ST. IGNATIUS
1847 - 1821

THE SUBJECT OF THIS NARRATIVE, John F. Quinn, had much in common with Ignatius of Loyola, a soldier turned priest who founded the Jesuit Order (Society of Jesus) as a result of a vision he had at the Shrine of La Storta while on his way to Rome. Ignatius instituted various covenants and rules of conduct, loyalty and obedience based on his vision. The newly-founded order was orally approved by Pope Paul III on September 3, 1539, and solemnly confirmed by him in a Papal Bull (*Regimini militantis acclitantis*) on September 27, 1540.

John Quinn was also a soldier who had latent thoughts of becoming a priest when he enlisted in the Union Army during the Civil War. In fact, Ignatius and Quinn had many traits in common, particularly in matters of higher learning and communication. They were both men of letters. While studying in Rome Ignatius developed an enormous correspondence, including six thousand letters which were eventually published and circulated. He also drafted the constitution which formed the basis of the Jesuit religious foundation. emphasizing Christian charity, humility and obedience.

In like manner, Father Quinn compiled three hundred volumes of church-related literary works which he donated to the Catholic Library in Omaha, Nebraska. Unfortunately, no one knows what became of this scholarly collection.

Ignatius and Quinn both had tremendous love for their fellows and their religion, and both left their marks on a grateful society.

The Quinn Family Tree

JOHN F. QUINN was born on January 24, 1847, of Irish immigrant parents who settled in Albany, New York, following their arrival in America. He spent his childhood in that city, where he was educated by the Irish Christian Brothers, who instilled in him an abiding love of God and country, which he cherished and championed all the days of his life. Little is known of the Quinn family during their stay in Albany. However, it was this writer's good fortune to discover biographical information on the life and times of Father Quinn during an extensive period of research on the man.

At the tender age of fourteen years he enlisted in the 25th New York Regiment of the Union Army. His army service was short-lived, however; when the military authorities discovered his correct age, Quinn was discharged forthwith. He took the disappointment in stride and returned home to his family, planning to use his time to gain weight and look more mature in his next attempt to enlist for military duty.

As luck would have it, the famed Black Horse Cavalry was on maneuvers in the Albany area, drumming up support for the Union cause. Their military dress and precision so impressed young John Quinn that he vowed to enlist in one of their colorful regiments. He was further encouraged on learning that Abraham Lincoln, whom he idolized, had once served in the Black Horse Cavalry during the protracted Indian wars.

Early one morning he set out in high spirits for the cavalry headquarters to seek enlistment for the duration of the Civil War. In this second attempt, he was rejected again as being too young for military service.

Undaunted in his efforts to join the Union Army, John Quinn vowed to serve his country in one way or another. He found work in the nearby Watervliet Arsenal, a Union munitions factory which was in need of workers and where age was not a barrier; a number of young people, both boys and girls, were already working in the factory.

Watervliet Arsenal: a Landmark Military Institution

WATERVLIET ARSENAL was established in 1813 in the wake of the War of 1812, which led to the burning of the White House in Washington by the British and the flight of President Madison to nearby Georgetown. The Arsenal provided badly needed arms and equipment for the American forces which were engaged in battle with British troops along the Canadian border.

The Arsenal was constructed on twelve acres of land the United States had purchased from an Irishman named James Gibbons for the sum of $2,585. It was ideally situated near the confluence of the Hudson and Mohawk Rivers at a time when waterways were the principal means of transportation in the United States. Watervliet had an added advantage; the Erie Canal then ran through the property.

Nearby was a thriving village called Gibbonsville, so-named for the pioneer Irish landowner who was already well established in the riverside community. Also close by was the little hamlet of West Troy, a suburb of the city of Troy, on the west bank of the Hudson River. In later years West Troy became Watervliet City, from which the Arsenal took its name. Leland Stanford, California's Civil War Governor and founder of Stanford University, was a native of Watervliet, where his father was a saloon keeper.

During the Civil War the Watervliet Arsenal was the principal source of military supplies for the Union Army, which required in excess of forty barrels of powder a day to meet its needs. Although the Lincoln administration was hard pressed financially, cheap labor was in abundant supply and people worked long hours in order to meet the ever-increasing demand for guns and ammunition.

An Awesome Explosion

THE AUTHORITIES entrusted with the operation of the munitions works were conscious of the danger created by so many unskilled hands working in the building. Fortunately however, a new Ordnance Commander, Major William Thornton, a pragmatic Irishman, had been appointed to take over from Major Mordecai, who resigned his commission when he became the target of diehard Unionists who discovered that he was a North Carolinian by birth.

Safety was Major Thornton's primary concern. No stranger to Watervliet Arsenal, he had been stationed there from 1833 to 1836, serving as temporary commander in the occasional absence of the officer in charge. Yet despite every precaution on his part, a major explosion occurred in the plant's most vulnerable section, where the ball cartridges were lubricated. The awesome blast killed countless workers and destroyed some of the principal buildings in the complex.

Call it fate, or The Luck of the Irish if you will; the blast struck with such force that it lifted John Quinn off the floor and blew him through an open window into the yard outside. Miraculously he sustained no injuries other than shock from the frightening experience. When he came to his senses and saw the destruction on every side he ran for his life, fearing the battered walls of the Arsenal would come tumbling down and crush him to death.

The catastrophe was one of the best kept secrets of the Civil War period, and little wonder, for if the extent of the damage had leaked out it would have been disastrous for Union morale, which was already at a low ebb. Worse yet, it would have given heart and encouragement to Confederate forces at a time when the outcome of the war was a toss-up. The full extent of the disaster has never been made public. One historian of the period quoted a figure (no doubt inflated) of ten thousand casualties in the wake of the explosion that was seen for miles around.

John Quinn, a Soldier in the Irish Brigade

IRISH REGIMENTS fought under their national banners in the American Civil War, like the expatriate Irish Brigades that served meritoriously in the armies of France and Spain. The brigades were forced out of Ireland following their ignominious defeat in the Battle of Kinsale in 1691. The "Wild Geese," as they became known, are eulogized in the following lines:

Far in foreign fields from Dunkirk to Belgrade
Lie the soldiers and chiefs of the Irish Brigade.

The Irish formed their own regiments, emblazoned with their "Banners of Green." They were led by the fearless Irish Revolutionary, Thomas Francis Meagher, who was captured following the disastrous "Young Ireland" rebellion of 1848; he was transported in chains to the penal colony in Australia. Four years later Meagher and his comrades escaped from prison and made their way to freedom and a new life in America.

Meagher settled in New York City, where it was said he became the darling of the Irish in the big city. Little wonder then that he was chosen as commander of one of the famous Irish Brigades in America, which won the hearts of every freedom-loving American by their courage and daring during the Civil War. For example, at the battle of Antietam in Maryland on September 17, 1862, the bloodiest day in American military history, the Irish brigade bore the brunt of the battle on the Union side. As the Irish Brigade approached "Bloody Lane," a sunken road in the middle of the battlefield, a column of Confederates moved into position on the crest of the hill. When Meagher's men came into view they were cut down by Confederate artillery on the high embankment. Yet despite heavy losses, the "Fighting Irish" came on and on and held their own even though they were at a distinct disadvantage in the line of battle.

The courageous Irishmen who fell in that ferocious encounter in 1862 were buried in a mass grave which has recently been discovered by George Rees of Ohio and his associates, who swept the field with metal detectors. Their findings were turned over to Stephen Potter, an archaeologist with the National Park Service, for further study. Based on artifacts found in the graves, Potter determined that those buried there were all members of the 63rd New York Regiment, part of the famed Irish Brigade. Fragments of bones unearthed proved to be those of a middle-aged soldier, James Gallagher, a stonemason from County Kilkenny; Martin McMahon, a laborer from County Clare; and one James McGarrigan, from somewhere in the West of Ireland. As further proof of their Irish background, fragments of rosary beads were found among their belongings.

Another one of the famed Irish Regiments which deserve a place in American history was the Corcoran Legion (Fifth New York Regiment), whose catchy logo, "A FEW GOOD MEN WANTED," was featured in an East Coast journal. The appeal caught the attention of young John Quinn, who had survived the Arsenal explosion and had been twice rejected for military service because he was under age. But age didn't matter to Captain William Monegan, the Company Commander, or to Colonel Corcoran himself. All they needed was "a few good men" to bring the regiment to full strength. John Quinn's third attempt to enlist in the Union Army succeeded, and he was accepted as a recruit in one of the Irish Regiments.

In later years Quinn himself revealed to friends that as a soldier in the Irish Brigade he took part in a number of battlefield engagements and rose through the ranks to become a Captain. His service record made him eligible to transfer to the Fenian Army which was being reorganized at the close of the American Civil War.

The Fenian Invasion

WHEN THE IRISH BRIGADES were mustered out at the close of hostilities they merely exchanged colors and called themselves "Fenians." They made no secret of their intent to take up where they had left off at the outbreak of the Civil War, setting up their principal headquarters in the stately Moffat Mansion off Union Square in New York City. A military council was formed with Major Tom Sweeny, a Civil War veteran, as Secretary of War; Captain Charles Tevis, a West Pointer, as Adjutant General; and Colonel John O'Neill as Army Commander. "Fearless John Quinn," as he came to be known, was commissioned a Captain, a rank he had held in the Union Army, and as such played a major role in the Fenian Invasion of Canada.

On June 1, 1866, a day that will live long in Irish-American annals, Colonel John O'Neill led his "Bold Fenian Men" across the

Niagara River into Canada, tore down the Union Jack and replaced it with the Green Banner of Erin. The heroic effort to establish a Fenian base in Canada and drive the British out was stymied by President Johnson's proclamation against the Fenian movement, which prevented reinforcements from crossing over to support O'Neill's initial attack on Fort Eire. As a result, O'Neill and his men were forced to retreat and give up their efforts for the time being.

Although the incursion was a failure from a military standpoint, it was a tremendous boost for the Fenian cause in both America and Ireland. It served notice on Great Britain that the Irish in America were a formidable force, capable of carrying the war to their age-old enemy.

The very thought of an Irish Army parading openly in England's former colony and with the apparent consent of the American government shook the very foundation of the British Empire. The London *Times* sarcastically expressed its concern: "No Irishman could have invented such a scheme, no Yankee would have believed in it, but put American exaggeration and Irish credibility together and you have Fenianism." *

In late 1867, when the Fenian movement petered out, John Quinn returned home to the scenes of his childhood and enrolled at Niagara University to further his education. A man who put heart into everything he did, Quinn devoted every moment to his studies from that day forward and graduated with honors in June 1870. During his studies there, he edited the *Albany Reflector*, a religious journal.

Following a brief respite with family and friends, Quinn enrolled in Albany Law School and after a period of intense study, passed the New York State Bar on March 11, 1875. He took up the practice of law as a partner in the firm of Quinn and Cohen, a business which flourished from its inception. In fact, John Quinn gained such a reputation as a lawyer that his name was placed in nomination as candidate for city judge of Albany. With apparently little interest in political office, he very graciously declined the offer.

A Higher Calling: the Priesthood

TO THE AMAZEMENT of his family and friends, who remembered him as a lanky kid playing ball with the neighborhood boys in the streets of Albany, John Quinn withdrew from public life and enrolled in Our Lady of Angels Seminary at Niagara University to study for the priesthood.

*For a more complete account of the Fenians in America read *California, The Irish Dream*, chapter 18, page 343.

The Seminary of Our Lady of Angels, a part of Niagara University, Suspension Bridge, New York, was founded by Irish clergy.

The pioneer Seminary was co-founded by Irish-born Father John Lynch of the Congregation of the Missions, the Vincentioans, and Bishop Timon of the Diocese of Toronto. Father Lynch, a native of Ireland's County Monaghan, served as first superior and president of Our Lady of Angels. In later years he was appointed Coadjutor Bishop of Toronto with the right of succession. Ultimately in 1870 Bishop Lynch became the first Archbishop of the newly-established Archdiocese of Toronto.

Niagara University could well boast of its scholarly faculty, which included the brilliant and beloved Father Abram Ryan, C.M., who became known as the "Poet Laureate of the South." Father Ryan was among the most renowned clergymen of the Civil War period, serving as a chaplain of the Confederate Army.

Father John Young, a member of the faculty at St. John's University in Jamaica, New York, has provided a copy of the Seminary Journal entitled *Trinity Ordinations, May 26, 1877*, which included the name of Father John F. Quinn. The ceremony was preceded by the conferring of minor orders on all the men about to be ordained to the priesthood in the time-honored Catholic tradition.

On May 24, 1877, the Order of Subdeacon was conferred on John F. Quinn, and on the following day, May 25, that of Deacon. On May 26, 1877, at Our Lady of Angels, John F. Quinn was ordained a priest by the Right Reverend S.V. Ryan, Bishop of Buffalo, for the Vicarate of Nebraska.

After a few days with family and friends in Albany, Father Quinn set out in high spirits for Omaha to begin his priestly labors. In due course he was appointed Pastor of Holy Trinity Church, Omaha, a thriving railroad town on the western frontier. He felt quite at home in Omaha with the many Irish who settled there during the construction of the trans-continental railway. During his stay in Omaha Father Quinn compiled three hundred volumes of prose and poetry relating to Catholicism and the Church, which he donated to the Catholic Library in Omaha. After more than three years of ministering to the flock in Nebraska he moved to Denver, Colorado, in 1881. Two years later he was appointed Pastor of that city's Cathedral Parish. During his stay in Denver Father Quinn pioneered and edited the *Colorado Catholic*, a diocesan journal of such prestige that it inspired others throughout western America.

In 1886, the ninth year of his ministry, Father Quinn's health began to deteriorate, a condition that the medical authorities attributed to the high altitude in the Rocky Mountain city. After much consideration he set his sights on sunny California, which he perceived would not only be conducive to better health but would afford him a more extensive field for his priestly labors. At the behest of Bishop Patrick Manogue, who was already aware of Quinn's power of oratory, Father Quinn came to Sacramento in the fall of 1866. While awaiting an assignment he preached a mission at old Saint Rose's Church, assisted by Father Patrick Henneberry from Ohio.

Pastor of Red Bluff

FATHER QUINN'S first assignment in California was Pastor of Sacred Heart parish in Red Bluff, the hub of a fast-developing area of farms, orchards and vineyards. It was Father Quinn's custom to announce his coming in advance and invite everyone, regardless of creed, to attend. He won the friendship of the settlers by his genial personality, by his powers of oratory and his inspiring evocation of Catholicism's traditional faith. On occasion he visited Dunsmuir, which had no church of its own and celebrated Mass in the home of an Irishman named John McCann. The worshipers were predominantly Irish: Tim Ryan, Charley Hill, Patrick Furlong, George McInerny and their families, and a goodly number of Irish-born railroad workers who resided in the vicinity.

Father Quinn served as pastor of Red Bluff from 1887 to 1893, and his health improved with each passing day. In appreciation of the work of Father James Hunt, his predecessor and founding pastor, he inserted in the church directory the following:

> Entering upon my duties as pastor of Red Bluff I found, besides
> a very commodious brick church in the town, frame churches in
> Tehama, Redding and Shasta. The convent had twelve boarders
> and sixty-six day pupils. Red Bluff and neighborhood had about
> fifty Catholic families, and the whole debt was only $725.

On the trip to California Father Quinn had been accompanied
by two close friends, Fathers James Carr and Theodore Van Schie,
who had also served for a period in the Denver parish. When Father
Quinn became pastor of Yreka in 1894, it was Father Carr who
replaced him as Pastor of Red Bluff. As testimony of their lifelong
affection, Father Quinn delivered the eulogy at the funeral Mass for
Father Van Schie in Sacramento on September 20, 1921.

Father Quinn next moved to Sacramento, where he became pastor of the Blessed Sacrament Cathedral Parish, the hub of Catholicism
in the progressive city. It proved to be a strenuous assignment for
Father Quinn, who had to travel far and wide to minister to his scattered flock. It was then that he conceived the idea of a priests' retreat
in a secluded area for the over-worked clergy to rest and recuperate.

Fathers James Carr, Reynolds of Willows and McGrath of Yreka
pooled their resources with those of Father Quinn to purchase a prop-
erty suitable to their needs in Dunsmuir. They called it "The Ranch."
During his term as pastor in Sacramento, Father Quinn visited The
Ranch on occasion to rest in the tranquil woodlands of his beloved El
Dorado.

Quinn's Silver Jubilee

ONE OF THE MOST noteworthy celebrations in the history of the
California State Legislature was the celebration in 1902 of Father
Quinn's Silver Jubilee as a priest. Every chair was occupied, the lobby
crowded and the galleries filled. The decorations in the legislative
chamber were minimal but appropriate: a huge American flag behind
the speaker's stand and two potted palms at either end.

William Gormley, President of the Y.M.I., complimented Father
Quinn on his silver jubilee in the priesthood. He spoke of the many
benefits received by the congregation at the hands of the good pastor
and expressed the hope that the recollection of the day might prove
one of the high points in his life.

Gormley then introduced Judge Hart, who spoke of Father
Quinn's many years of labor for the good of mankind, and said that a

Father John Quinn during his years as pastor of Red Bluff.
Courtesy Betty Coman

life given to religious work was of the highest order. Whether a man was a Catholic, Protestant or Orthodox, his labors for Christianity were ever laudable, and all were working to the same end, the betterment of mankind.

After a selection by the Christian Brothers College Orchestra, Richard Cohn sang a solo and for an encore gave "The Banner of the Free." This was followed by a baritone solo by William Genshlea who for an encore sang "The Harp That Once Thro' Tara's Hall."

The Reverend C. M. Miel, a Protestant clergyman, was introduced, adding a touch of ecumenism to the celebration. He quickly put his audience in good humor by telling of a countryman who once took him for Father Quinn and gave him a cigar. He subsequently told the story to Father Quinn, who advised him that whenever he could get a good cigar by passing himself off as one of the Cathedral staff he should do so.

Rev. Miel noted that it was a wonderful and glorious day when clergymen of the Catholic and Protestant faiths meet on the same platform, address the same audience, and are able to congratulate one another on their good work done for the Master. He extended to Father Quinn his heartiest congratulations, and told him he should "continue to pray for the cause of the church and Christianity," and he hoped that when God saw fit to recall them, they would be found in the same place.

The Honorable Frank Ryan presented Father Quinn with a set of handsome silver on behalf of the Ladies' Sodality of the Cathedral Parish. He congratulated Father Quinn on having successfully passed through 25 years as a priest, after beginning life as a lawyer in his native city.

PROLONGED applause and a standing ovation greeted the good Father as he stepped to the podium to respond. He said that the day had been the most wonderful one of his life, and that he felt happier than ever before. He was particularly happy to find that so many people outside his congregation were eager to extend to him the hand of fellowship and bid him godspeed. They had offered him the best gifts God gave to man—song, eloquence and fraternity—and he felt they had come to him because for twenty-five years he had served God.

"He prayeth best who loveth best," Father Quinn declared, adding that he had ever been a true patriot. When he first started to school, his mother taught him that if asked if he were a "Paddy" or a Catholic he should reply, "No. I am an American." The lesson had never been forgotten.

At this point the Right Reverend Bishop Moreland of the protestant Episcopal Church entered the hall. Father Quinn remarked he knew of no more beautiful picture than to see an Episcopal Bishop attending a reception for a Catholic priest. The scene was an allegory, teaching him that there was no Protestant, no Catholic, no Jew, but all were Americans.

Father Quinn could hardly find words to express his gratitude for the kindness shown him. He thanked the members of his church, the members of the bar, the clergy, the representatives of the press, the members of creeds other than his for their kindness to him, and assured them that the spring of his love was more than ample to fill every heart in the big hall. He felt that he was honored not as a man, but as a priest who had humbly worked for the betterment of humanity and for Christianity.

Then Bishop Moreland took the podium to address the assemblage. He said that he was not officially on the program and had been taken by surprise, but that it gave him pleasure to reflect on the general feeling toward the honored Father Quinn. On arrival in Sacramento he recalled how a son of Erin told him that "there are some 'imoighty foine' clergymen at the Cathedral. Bishop Grace can't be bate, and Father Quinn, he's a peach." In his travels throughout the state, he had heard the name of John F. Quinn mentioned with deep affection. He had worked in the same field that Father Quinn had tilled. They had both been engaged in doing the work of the Master and building up His kingdom.

The celebration ended on a patriotic note. Bishop Moreland and Father Quinn engaged in a vigorous handshake, the audience arose, sang "America," and the reception came to a close.

Pastor of Winters, 1913 to 1921

WHEN BISHOP KEANE made his diocesan appointments for the year 1913, Father Quinn was chosen to become pastor in Winters, one of the remote regions in the far-flung Diocese of Sacramento. The announcement caused quite an uproar in the capital, where Father Quinn had endeared himself not only to Catholics but to men and women of every creed whose lives he touched in one way or another. According to Father Casey, a Diocesan chronicler in the early 1900s, Father Quinn was given a leave of absence during which he retired to the Ranch north of Dunsmuir to rest and recuperate.

Conjecture had it that there was a lack of rapport between the urbane, progressive priest and the Bishop, reputedly a conservative, if

The Catholic Church at Winters, California. Courtesy Betty Coman

not a reactionary. It was evident that they didn't see eye to eye in church affairs, and Bishop Keane surmised that by sending Father Quinn to the outer rim of the diocese he could avoid future confrontations. His fellow priests viewed the removal to such an isolated parish as a banishment, which in religious circles was referred to as "Felled by the Crosier."

In Ireland there were precedents for what happened to Father Quinn. To interrupt his story for a moment, here's an example: Two young clergymen, Fathers Mathew O'Keefe and Thomas O'Shea, were banished by Bishop Edward Walsh of Ossory to a remote area in the diocese as a result of their efforts in forming the Callan Tenant Protective Society, forerunner of the Irish Land League.

Ireland was in a sorry state in 1849, the Young Ireland revolution a pathetic failure, its leaders imprisoned and deported as felons, hunger still rampant and poorhouses overflowing. Evictions by ruthless landlords were numerous, and houses were felled every day by battering rams employed by the sheriff and his crew. The deplorable conditions of the tenant farmers caught the attention of the two curates, assistant pastors who vowed to alleviate the awful distress. At their instigation the tenant society was founded.

The Callan curates' ideas appealed to people who were in similar circumstances all over Ireland, and parish after parish followed suit by establishing like societies. They urged the members of their local society to band together and restrain the landlords' evictions.

Both curates were fine speakers, and goaded by the constant injustices their neighbors faced, their forceful eloquence was much sought after. Alas, their great work led to their undoing, and they were banished from Callan to parishes miles apart from each other. Father O'Keefe was sent to Dunnamagg in the south side of the diocese, and Father O'Shea to Cullohill, away to the north. The Callan curates came together again only when Father O'Keefe was made Pastor of Aghaboe (site of a 6th century monastery) and Father O'Shea was assigned to Camross, where he served as Pastor until his death at the age of 74.

Father O'Shea was affectionately known as the "Farmer's Friend" as pastor of Camross, and gained renown as Canon Theologian of Ossory in 1873, following the death of Doctor Walsh.

Father O'Shea is buried in Camross, the parish he served for 24 years, beneath a plaque on the weathered wall of the church:

Ecce Sacerdos Magnus

Sacred to the memory of very Rev. Thos O'Shea, Canon Theologian of Ossory and pastor of Camross for 24 years, in testimony of his untiring zeal in the cause of religion, education and charity, his enthusiastic love of country and deep affection for the oppressed, manifested in a life-long powerful advocacy of the people's rights and liberties, his endearing social qualities and surpassing priestly worth. Born 1813 at Cappaheaden, Co. Kilkenny. Died 30th March, 1887, aged 74 years. Pray for the repose of the soul of one who during life was affectionately called The Farmer's Friend.

LIKE THE CALLAN CURATES, Father Quinn held firm to his priestly vows despite his banishment to Winters. Three longtime Yolo County residents who knew Father Quinn have provided information about him. Mrs. Betty Coman had more than a passing interest in the work of Father Quinn, who she said had endeared himself to her parents over many years. They sometimes spent their vacations at the priests' retreat on the Ranch in Dunsmuir. "Father Quinn married my parents and baptized my two older brothers," Mrs. Coman said. Her aunt in Marysville, in her hundredth year and still hale and hearty, knew Father Quinn for years and spoke of him in endearing terms.

"Father Quinn was a marvelous person who liberated me from the frightening things about my religion. He told me to kneel in church and talk to God in my own way. I loved him very much." She often drove him to say Mass in Guinda, which had no priest of its own. "I would take up the collection, and we counted ourselves lucky if we got enough to pay for the gas."

A previous priest must have put a great fear into the hearts of all those who he ministered to. "I well recall my mother saying that she would go to confession quite often, far too often according to Father Quinn, who advised her not to come again until she had committed murder. Father Quinn gave my mother something that she passed on to her children. She taught us to love God rather than fear God. She also taught us that it is more important to be a good person every day than to sow your wild oats all week long and then think you can make it right by going to confession on Saturday and to Mass on Sunday."

When Father Quinn became pastor in 1913, he constructed a parochial house which cost over $4000, a considerable sum in those days. There were only about seventy practicing Catholics in Winters, a far cry from the bustling Cathedral Parish in Sacramento, where he had spent the previous eight years.

John DeVilbiss, Mrs. Coman's great grandfather, was one of the most active Catholics in the small community. An early settler in Winters, he had invested in land upon which he built the landmark Winters Hotel. DeVilbiss married an Irish lass, Esther Cunningham, who became a convert, and in recognition of her good deeds was given the honor of choosing a patron for the Winters church.

Her choice was Saint Anthony of Padua, to whom all frantic searchers appeal for help in finding items lost or misplaced (and many there are who feel that their requests have been granted). The DeVilbiss children and grandchildren were the principal supporters of Saint Anthony's church, along with the Sparks, Graf, Brison, Williams, and Sandborn families. There were also a number of Irish families: the Griffins, Murrays, McCarthys, McGarrs, Collins, Lowrys, Dunnigans, Bradys and Vaseys, who settled in Winters when Father Quinn became pastor. Were the Vaseys Irish? You bet they were! As Betty Coman tells it:

> My grandfather, Thomas Michael Vasey, was born in Tubbercurry, County Sligo, December 21, 1852, and lived in England for a short period before he came to California in 1884. His wife Annie (Coppinger) Vasey joined him two years later. Their first child was born in Winters in 1887. Although my grandmother was born in England, she claimed to be Irish. Both her parents, however, were born in Ireland, according to the census of 1900.

Father Quinn's first entry as pastor of Winters was a baptism recorded on January 31, 1913, and on that same day he performed his first marriage ceremony, for William Paul and Dolores Walters.

It was said that any couple married by Father Quinn could never forget their marriage vows, "until death do us part." Nor was it ever known that any couple married by him sought a divorce.

John Brinley, a business executive in Davis, where Father Quinn also ministered, offered information handed down by Brinley's parents. Mr. Brinley spoke glowingly of Father Quinn's tolerance and Christian attitude. The priest had married Brinley's parents even though his father was a Mason and his mother a Catholic, in days when mixed marriages were frowned on by the hierarchy. The wedding ceremony took place at the Parish House in June 1914. It was a happy marriage, inspired by Father Quinn's kindly ways and enlightened point of view.

During his eight years as pastor in Winters, Father Quinn made frequent trips to Sacramento to reminisce with old friends and parishioners whom he had served as Pastor of the Cathedral parish. He was held in high esteem by the Knights of Columbus, the most active lay association in the city at the time. Year after year he traveled all the way to Sacramento to attend the meetings of the Knights while serving as Pastor of Winters.

Customarily, the chairman would call on the congenial chaplain to address the gathering, and when he did so the members could look forward to a lively session. Father Quinn was an eloquent speaker, a man of words which seemed to come to him at will; he needed no preparation to deliver an inspiring address.

To Father Quinn a friend was always a friend regardless of his religious beliefs or station in life. When the Ranch at Dunsmuir was purchased by a family named Weirheim, who were of the Lutheran faith, Father Quinn and his associates continued to visit their former enclave and camped in the orchard as guests of the new owners. The Weirheims were so taken by this gesture of brotherly love that they saved newspaper articles, photographs and various mementos of the gatherings, and would display them with pleasure for their Lutheran friends.

In September 1921, Father Quinn preached at the funeral of one of his longtime friends, Father Theodore Van Schie, a native of Holland, little knowing that his own would be next. On the way home he was struck by a train in Davis and sustained serious injuries from which he never recovered. He entered the Sisters of Mercy Hospital in Sacramento, where he died on December 6, 1921.

This faded old photograph shows Father Quinn with two of his young parishioners at the Ranch retreat. Courtesy Betty Coman

Following a Requiem Mass in the Cathedral, he was laid to rest in the Priests' Plot in Saint Joseph's cemetery.

A tremendous crowd of mourners thronged his funeral on December 9, including a number of his fellow priests, religious orders, city and state officials, and men and women from every walk of life. In keeping with his priestly vow of obedience, Father Quinn deferred to Bishop Keane the right to select the place he would be laid to rest.

John Francis Quinn's varied and remarkable career as soldier and priest spanned a period of some fifty years.

Myles Poore O'Connor
Courtesy O'Connor Hospital

– 10 –

MYLES POORE O'CONNOR

1823 - 1909

"**H**is name will never be forgotten while God and nobility are remembered, for he has planted the seeds of better things in hearts without number," commented the San Francisco *Monitor* in summing up the life and times of Myles Poore O'Connor.

Living in abject poverty and subjugation in Ireland, the O'Connors were forced to emigrate, first to England, and eventually to America. The family settled in New York City and then removed to Saint Louis, Missouri, where Myles's Uncle Jeremiah was already a man of wealth and influence. Myles O'Connor continued his education in the public schools of that city until such time as he enrolled in the University of Saint Louis to take up the study of law. On July 27, 1844, he became a naturalized citizen of the United States. Two years later, he passed the bar and began the practice of law in St. Louis.

In 1849, when news of the California Gold Rush made headlines in newspapers all over America, O'Connor gathered up his law books and headed west at the first opportunity. Unlike so many others, he came not to dig for gold but to build a law practice in the new country. There being little demand for his legal services as yet, and running low on funds, he decided to try his luck in the diggings. O'Connor moved aimlessly about the gold country in search of the precious metal, and finding none, was about to give up.

However, an incident of a wandering animal focused many a prospector's attention on Grass Valley, and this event proved to be the turning point in O'Connor's life. A man named George Knight had lost a cow in Boston Ravine, below the town, and was chasing the animal when he stumbled over a protruding white rock. He glanced at the boulder and discovered that it was veined with shiny yellow streaks. It proved to be gold quartz. Although quartz mining had been attempted in certain areas by then, Knight's discovery suggested that the mineral ran deep in the white rocks. The mysterious source of the metal—the Mother Lode—had been found.

As a result of that discovery, on June 6, 1850, Myles O'Connor's fortune was in the making, and he decided to make Grass Valley his permanent home. Fascinated by the challenge of extracting gold from the quartz, he kept a close watch on the Grass Valley terrain for signs of a rich deposit. And on August 2, 1852, O'Connor and four other prospectors, the Doyle Brothers, L. Rudolph and H. Fuller, filed an extensive claim. Grass Valley, with its more stable quartz mining operations, began taking on an aura of permanence, while other mining camps gradually disintegrated into ghost towns.

O'Connor, encouraged by his good fortune, filed claim after claim in quest of a big strike. As his mining enterprises began to show a profit he was able to spend more time at his law practice.

The O'Connor Roots in Ireland

MYLES O'CONNOR was born on May 8, 1823 in the picturesque village of Abbeyleix, County Laois (formerly Queen's County). Abbeyleix, lying in the very heartland of the Emerald Isle on the main road from Dublin, the capital, to Cork City, derives its name from an Abbey founded by the clan O'Moore in the year 600 A.D., when Ireland was known as "The land of Saints and Scholars." After being plundered again and again by marauding Vikings and English mercenaries, the monastery declined as a religious and educational institution. The O'Moores, a tenacious clan, continued the struggle for repossession and eventually regained control of the acclaimed institution in the latter part of the twelfth century. The monastery was restored to much of its former glory by Connor O'Moore and continued to function as a Gaelic institution of learning until the reign of Queen Elizabeth in the sixteenth century.

The English conquest, which began in A.D. 1169, led to the subjection of the Gaelic Irish; consequently little Ireland, region by region, came under British rule. Ironically, this fertile territory which O'Connor called home was the very first land to be confiscated in a plot known as the "English Plantation." The rightful owners like the O'Connors, the O'Moores, the O'Dunnes, the O'Dowlings, the O'Kellys and others were evicted and replaced by English and lowland Scottish settlers.

Abbeyleix was the scene of the brutal murder of three Franciscan priests by marauding English mercenaries. The three clergymen sought refuge in the remote Slieve Bloom mountains, where they were eventually apprehended by a cavalry patrol and brought back to the military garrison in Abbeyleix. Here they were stretched on the rack and flogged unmercifully by the soldiers. The so-called "Papists" were then strangled, drawn and quartered.

In sheer desperation, the O'Connors packed their meager belongings and emigrated to England in 1825. The family settled in Manchester, which already boasted a sizable Irish population and where the elder O'Connor found work in a local factory. They made their home in the big industrial city for a period of thirteen years, by which time they had acquired sufficient capital to pay their fare to America. They were further encouraged to make the journey by Myles' Uncle Jeremiah.

Jeremiah O'Connor was one of St. Louis' earliest settlers, and in the ensuing years acquired considerable wealth by investing in land and property. A civic-minded man who took pride in his adopted city, Jeremiah O'Connor donated a large tract of land as the future site of St. Louis University, a prominent Jesuit institution.

Myles was a quiet, studious young man who found ready employment in the office of Major Wright, a notable Saint Louis jurist. He had three older brothers, Matthew, Jerome and James, living in that city at the time.

Matthew, who was already employed there, recognized Myles' aptitude for law and decided to help finance his younger brother through the University of Saint Louis. Myles, a diligent student, pursued his studies at the prestigious Jesuit institution and became a naturalized citizen on July 27, 1844. Two years later he graduated with honors and began the practice of law in his new home.

Matthew took part in the war with Mexico and died sometime later in Sacramento from wounds incurred at the battle of Buena Vista. Myles never forgot his brother's assistance during his law school days. In later years he built the O'Connor Sanitarium in San Jose and erected a beautiful chapel therein, which he named Saint Matthew's Memorial Chapel, in memory of his benevolent brother.

In 1848 tall tales of gold in California reached the east, and Gold Fever swept the nation. Pamphlets and guide books exaggerated the true situation, and gold-seekers flooded the emigrant centers in the eastern states. They were in a gullible mood. The clamor for gold caught the attention of Myles O'Connor, who was only twenty-five at the time. His interest was not, however, the pursuit of gold, but rather in the practice of law in the booming new country. Success in his chosen profession was his primary goal, and having once made up his mind to migrate to California, all he could think about was the quickest and the most economical way to get there.

California Bound

O'CONNOR CHOSE the overland route as the cheapest and the most promising way to the new country. In early April 1849 he packed his belongings and went to Saint Joseph, Missouri, the meeting ground for the argonauts on the trek to California. Quick-witted peddlers made a killing selling gadgets called "goldometers" as indispensable aids for locating the precious metal in the hills. Local merchants made huge profits by charging outrageous prices for goods and accommodations for those waiting to join a wagon train.

However there were forewarnings by returning scouts: "Yaas, and every day—rain, hail, cholera, breakdowns, lame mules, sick cows, washouts, prairie fires, flooded coulees, lost horses, dust storms, alkali water. Seventeen miles a day—or you land in the snow and eat each other like the Donner Party in '46."

Despite the warnings of the hazards that lay ahead, some 20,000 persons were poised on the Missouri River the morning of April 16 when O'Connor was lucky enough to secure a place as a mule skinner on one of the wagons. A captain was chosen for each wagon train with the authority to make assignments for every member of the company. By necessity rather than choice, O'Connor was given a new assignment as a cook in the camp kitchen. Sow-belly (bacon) and biscuits (hot bread) baked in a Dutch oven were the staples on the wagon trains. Pancakes called "Slamjohns" and pickles that were doled out to protect against scurvy were served on the trail. Dried fruit pies were an occasional luxury, prepared by the women folk who rolled the dough on the leather wagon seats and baked the pies over campfires in the evening.

In later years O'Connor took delight in relating the hardships encountered on the 2,000 mile trek and his tribulations as cook when the party made camp on the prairie at sunset. Despite the drawbacks, he lamented in his diary on November 25, 1877, "If I had to make the trip over again, having made known to me what I would endure and suffer and what I would enjoy, I would undertake it with alacrity and pleasurable anticipation."

The challenging trek from Missouri to California took 122 days, averaging fifteen plus miles a day. The graves of men, women and children and the skeletons of the fallen animals on the trail were grim reminders of those who came in search of their pot of gold and of their charges who died along the way. Historian Valeska Bari speaks of California as having seduced the cream of American manhood: "The strongest pushed on to their goal, the weaklings died on the trail and the cowards never left home."

Grass Valley was an exciting town in those days, following the arrival of Lola Montez, the captivating brunette for whom the Bavarian King Ludwig was willing to give up his throne. Montez nonchalantly moved into a house in town with a pet bear on a leash. Her appearance disturbed the good ladies of town no end.

In 1854 Myles O'Connor developed a romantic interest. A woman in the gold country, especially one so pretty and gracious as Amanda Butler Young, merited attention. Mrs. Young was already a widow who had moved to Grass Valley to be near her brother, John Butler. She had alienated her parents, having eloped at the age of sixteen. Her husband and two-year-old son had been killed by lightning in Ohio. Her brother John being the only one who stood by her, she decided to join him in California following the tragic loss of her own family.

At the time women were a scarce commodity in the mining country being vastly out-numbered by men. Any woman who came along brought admirers on the run. Some men took advantage of the situation to serve their own immediate needs. One miner was so hard-pressed to pay for his wedding that he conjured up the idea of charging admission to the ceremony. The miners were so eager to see the new bride in all her finery that they willingly paid five dollars a head to witness the marriage. The proceeds enabled the happy bridegroom to start housekeeping in a grand manner.

Miles and Amanda were united in marriage on December 7, 1862, by the Reverend Thomas Dalton, Pastor of Saint Patrick's Church in Grass Valley. It was a remarkable union that lasted for 47 years. Father Dalton and O'Connor, both Irish born, found they had much in common and worked hand-in-hand for more than nineteen years to foster the church's growth in the mining region.

Father Dalton, a graduate of All Hallows College in Dublin, came to California in 1855 and was given an assignment in the mining region by Bishop Alemany. His massive frame and energetic personality made him a conspicuous figure as he made his rounds by muleback with his kit in hand. In association with Myles O'Connor, Father Dalton was instrumental in bringing five Sisters of Mercy to Grass Valley in 1863 to teach school and operate an orphanage.

Amanda Butler Young O'Connor
Courtesy O'Connor Hospital

The Luck of the Irish

ALTHOUGH he had been doing quite well in his law practice and mining interests, it was May 1863, in partnership with the Coleman brothers, Ed and John, that O'Connor struck it rich, and surprisingly within walking distance of his home in Grass Valley. Their discovery of gold-laden quartz proved to be a veritable bonanza, which became known in mining annals as the Idaho Mine. From 1868 to 1877, the Idaho Mine produced over $4.5 million worth of the precious metal, which made O'Connor a rich man.

O'Connor had come to California to practice law and found gold instead. Countless others came for the gold, and finding little or none, stayed on as farmers or workmen, or returned home if they could afford the passage. One disgruntled miner tells of his plight:

> I dug and picked and picked and dug.
> And everything else I tried on.
> Until at last I was forced to eat
> The mule I used to ride on.

Other men struck it rich in the gold fields and went on to fame and fortune on the national scene: John M. Studebaker, the pioneer automobile maker, Philip Armour, who established the prodigious Armour Meat Packing Company, George Hearst of the newspaper clan, and the Irish Bonanza Kings, Flood, Fair, Mackay and O'Brien.

Myles O'Connor's Political Career

HIS QUIET CHARM and inherent honesty made O'Connor a popular figure in Grass Valley, which had grown from a mining camp to a spirited city of five thousand on the strength of solid mining and allied interests. In 1859, at the age of 36, he decided to embark on a third career - politics. Although a staunch Democrat in a Republican enclave, he ran for State Assemblyman and was elected by a comfortable majority. In that post, he served with distinction for the 1859-1860 term. In 1860 he was elected Grass Valley's Justice of the Peace, and the voters returned him to that honored position nine times in succession.

In the meantime, he developed a yearning for a more active role in the California legislature, and in 1869 he ran for the office of state senator on the Democratic ticket and won election over his Republican opponent. During the twenty-first session of that body (1874-75), Senator O'Connor reached the zenith of his political

career. Besides looking after the welfare of his constituents, he introduced eleven bills and served on thirteen influential committees.
When party officials sought to make plans for the newly-elected
Governor's inauguration, they chose O'Connor as master of ceremonies. Myles O'Connor's forceful bearing in the courts of law and
state office contributed greatly to bridging the chasm between the
hectic days of the forty-niners and the tranquil era of California's
domestication.

The European Safari

IN 1874 the O'Connors set out on an extended tour that took them
all over Europe. In Ireland, Myles eagerly sought out the scenes of
his childhood. Leaving his good wife in Dublin, he journeyed by
train to Abbeyleix, where he first saw the light of day. The visit was
somewhat disappointing. He commented, "I saw not a soul who
knew me or my family—save one man, a Carroll, who knew my
father and showed me the house in which I was born."

The O'Connors were particularly touched by the plight of
Ireland's working class and the sordid state of their hand-to-mouth
existence. On one occasion, after viewing the sumptuous estate of a
wealthy landlord, Amanda commented, "While that lord is entertaining his gay friends as they chase deer around the grounds, millions of
poor wretches are idle and half-starved."

From Ireland it was on to Rome, the heart of Christendom,
which won them over completely. Following a ride to Villa Borghese,
O'Connor wrote, "The whole panorama of the Eternal City is before
us. How wonderful to gaze for the first time upon the mighty spot
which filled the world for twenty two centuries with its life and
deeds." The couple toured other areas in Europe, sipping Bohemian
beer in Prague, climbing 292 steps up the leaning Tower of Pisa, tasting Italian wines and reveling in moonlit trips to the Roman
Colosseum. The O'Connors were so enthralled by the splendor of
the Eternal City that they were back again three years later, in 1877,
to spend the winter months.

Having had their fill of travel, they returned to Grass Valley to
plan for the future. It was then that they discussed the possibility of
moving to a more agreeable climate. Their favor fell on San Jose,
where Mrs. O'Connor had previously been entertained by Mrs. Anne
Murphy, whose husband Bernard had served two terms as state senator and three times as mayor of San Jose. The visit completely convinced Mrs. O'Connor. "San Jose is a delightful place with charming

drives in every direction." She further noted, "I trust one day to have a home there. I am sure Mr. O'Connor will like it as well as I do."

On November 1, 1879, the O'Connors moved to San Jose to begin a new and gratifying life in the Garden City. They felt quite at home among so many of their old Grass Valley friends like Edward McLaughlin, Myles's former neighbor and longtime business associate, and Judge Ryland, who had also resettled in San Jose.

McLaughlin, who had come to San Jose in 1868 and built a home at Seventh and Reed Streets, pointed out a choice location on Second Street which O'Connor purchased as the site for his future home. There he constructed a stately three-story residence at a cost of $40,000, a lot of money in those days, when a sturdy, middle-class residence could be built for less than $5,000.

The O'Connors resumed traveling, this time to Baltimore, Maryland, the cradle of American Catholicism, where a close friendship developed between them and Archbishop James Gibbons, who in 1866 had become America's second cardinal of the church. In several meetings, they discussed the Archbishop's support of the rising labor movement and his opposition to plans for setting up Catholic parishes on the basis of racial grouping.

The O'Connors also met Bishop John Keane, who pioneered in the founding of the Catholic University of America in Washington, D.C. Mrs. O'Connor decided to become a Catholic, perhaps as a result of these associations. Her conversion took place on May 11, 1884, in Baltimore. Following the conversion ceremony, the O'Connors went on a trip to Rome, where they met Pope Leo XIII and were permitted to attend mass celebrated by the Holy Father in his private chapel. This occurred just at the time when His Holiness was celebrating the golden jubilee of his ordination to the priesthood. Every ruler in Europe save King Humbert of Italy was in attendance. President Grover Cleveland, through Cardinal Gibbons, presented the pontiff with a bound copy of the United States Constitution, a gift which greatly pleased him.

Afterwards the O'Connors were introduced to the pontiff. "He seemed to have heard of us," Mrs. O'Connor noted in her diary. "When our name was told him, he said 'from San Jose?' He asked a few questions, then in giving us his blessings, he placed his hands upon Mr. O'Connor's head a second time and said 'A special blessing for you.' He placed his hand upon my cheek as he finished his remarks . . . I asked him to bless the hospital and chapel we were building and he blessed them, and gave us a bright, pleased smile. We thought this the greatest event of our lives."

The O'Connors' final trip to Europe took place in 1899-1900, when they again spent most of their time in Rome. "It would seem to me that life would have no charm after you have seen Rome for the last time," Amanda stated emphatically. But life and charm have many facets, the O'Connors were to discover, amidst the harvest of their bounteous benefactions.

They returned in high spirits to San Jose to continue their philanthropic endeavors. Santa Clara County could boast of its growth in population to 50,000 by the year 1884, and its four million fruit trees, seven thousand cattle, five thousand sheep and almost as many Angora goats roaming the hills. The county was spoken of as the prune capital of the world and the primary source of garden seed in America. Its principal claim to fame, however, was its unique blossom festival, which lured people from all over the west to celebrate in this veritable Garden of Eden, glistening in the land of perpetual sunshine.

Judge O'Connor's compassion for the less fortunate, the aged, the poor and the infirm induced him to build a sanitarium to meet their pressing needs. He chose a building site comprising 8.395 acres in the vicinity of Stevens Creek and Meridian Road, which in those days was well out in the country. Prussian-born Theodore Lenzen was the O'Connors' choice as architect for the sanitarium. Lenzen had proven his ability, having designed the City Hall, the Vendome Hotel, the vast Fredericksburg Brewery and Saint Ignatius College in San Francisco.

When the building was nearing completion in 1889, the O'Connors chose the Daughters of Charity of Saint Vincent de Paul to run the institution. The order founded in France in 1663 had a lengthy and reputable record of service. In America, the order was established by Elizabeth Bayley Seton in Emmitsburg, Maryland. Born in 1774 on the eve of the American Revolution, Mrs. Seton came from a sophisticated, well-to-do New York family and grew up to marry into wealth and society and bear five children. Then her world fell apart when within five years she lost her father, her husband, her sister and her money.

Mrs. Seton became a convert to Catholicism during those tragic years and in 1809 founded the religious community. The sisters operated schools, hospitals, orphanages, infant shelters, sanitariums and homes for the aged and the infirm throughout America. They even administered the United States National Leprosarium in Carville,

Louisiana, the only federal institution in the country operated by a religious order.

The Daughters of Charity came to California at the behest of Bishop Joseph Sodoc Alemany, who stopped at Emmits- burg in 1850. Two years later, in 1852, seven Sisters left the Mother House for San Francisco. Two caught the dreaded yellow fever while crossing the Panama jungles, and died; the other five survived the ordeal, and in time the order became firmly established in California.

Sister Francis McEnnis, leader of the first group of Sisters to arrive in San Francisco, August 18, 1852. Courtesy Seton Medical Center

The Daughters of Charity were conspicuous by their habit, resplendent in their old-time cornets with wide wings. They caught the attention of the *San Jose Daily Herald,* which described the habit: "They wear a distinctive dress. Their broad white head-dress is unlike anything worn by members of other orders. It has wings on the side more than a foot wide. It was adopted so that wounded soldiers might easily distinguish the sisters in the smoke of the battle-field. They wear plain gray serge habits with heavy sleeves. A wide white cape is worn over the shoulder and its ends extend nearly to the waist."

Their strange garb caught the attention of this writer in San Francisco as the good Sisters strode along Guerrero Street from the hospital to the convent chapel for daily prayer. For their neighbors it was a show almost equal to the changing of the guard at Buckingham Palace.

THE O'CONNOR SANITARIUM was self-sufficient for the most part. It had an artesian well on the site to provide water and a pump house operated by a windmill to carry the flow throughout the building. It could count on a plentiful supply of fresh vegetables and fruits that were grown on the grounds. C.T. Ryland and Bernard Murphy, Mayor of San Jose, donated a horse and harness, the McLaughlins

The original O'Connor Sanitarium, built in 1889, was built in the
open country, near Stevens Creek and Meridian Road.
Courtesy O'Connor Hospital

gave a carriage, and other well-to-do friends gave milking cows, pigs
and chickens—a cooperative before its time. Judge O'Connor put up
$100,000 to get the operation started and agreed to pay the salaries
of the hired help, plus $15 a month for each sister for the first year or
until the sanitarium was able to pay its way.

The two-story edifice was built of brick with sandstone facings in
a handsome style. White columns supported the portico over the
main entrance, harking back to colonial days. The north wing
housed the men's ward, a kitchen and storerooms. The south wing
was the women's ward and the upper story the sisters' residence. The
basement contained the engine room, furnace and laundry. The well-
constructed building was heated by steam and lighted by gas manufactured on the premises.

In 1892, when the sanitarium was well established, the
O'Connors built a home on the property in order to keep in touch
with future developments.

The sanitarium had no surgery, no maternity, no emergency and
no laboratory in its formative years, and yet it won the admiration

and respect of the entire community because of the tender care of the Daughters of Charity. An article in the San Francisco *Monitor* on April 2, 1893, tells it so:

A deputy at the San Jose City Hall was taken ill, and after much persuasion, consented to be treated at the magnificent home provided through Myles O'Connor. He regained his health in time and said, "I have been a rabid anti-Catholic for thirty-five years, but five weeks at the hospital has wrought a wonderful change in me. I never knew there were such ministering angels on earth as the sisters I found there. I see life in a new light. Now, and hereafter, my voice will be raised in praise of those blessed women."

As a further gesture of their philanthropy, the O'Connors gave over their palatial home to the sisters to be used as a girls' orphanage. On Saint Patrick's day, 1894, O'Connor ceremoniously named the new facility Notre Dame Institute. As a fitting tribute to the worthy institution, Sister Mary Theresa of Jesus, a niece of General Mariano Vallejo and the great-great-granddaughter of California explorer Don Gaspar de Portola, was installed as Mother Superior.

IN SAN FRANCISCO the Daughters of Charity are well remembered for their noble work during the cholera epidemic which swept the city in the 1850s. Weathered headstones in Mission Dolores cemetery are grim reminders of men and women in the prime of their lives who contracted the dreaded plague and died within a week or less. There were no doctors around to care for them, for most all of them had stashed away their medical books and headed for the mines in search of gold.

The Sisters' first medical institution in San Francisco was Mary's Help Hospital, located in the heart of the city on Guerrero Street. In later years, they removed to larger quarters in Daly City and changed the name to Seton Medical Center in honor of Mother Elizabeth Seton, who founded the order in America.

The Irish influence in Santa Clara County was particularly noticeable during the latter part of the 19th century. Men like Irish-born Martin Murphy and Mike Cahalan were among the first settlers who cleared the land and planted crops in the virgin soil. Others included the eminent physician Doctor A. B. Caldwell and the legendary frontiersman Charles (Mountain Charley) McKiernan, who lost part of his skull in a fight with a bear in the Santa Cruz Mountains. Left for dead, McKiernan made a miraculous recovery and lived to a ripe old age. He took up farming on a large scale and became a respected San Jose businessman, dividing his time between his hay and grain establishment and his productive vineyard.

Influenza in Santa Clara County

THE 1918 FLU EPIDEMIC resulted in the deaths of over twenty million people world-wide and close to a million in the United States. The Spanish influenza epidemic, so-called in America, was brought home by the troops after the first World War.

San Jose and the vicinity were hard hit, with over two hundred cases and seven deaths in a single 24-hour period. Worse yet, there were few doctors on hand to care for the sick, for the vast majority were already in uniform caring for the troops here and in Europe. It seemed almost providential that the O'Connor Sanitarium was ready to care for countless victims when the flu hit Santa Clara County. Fortunately the O'Connor School of Nursing, housed in the sanitarium, turned out a goodly number of trained nurses, who worked hand in hand with the sisters during the epidemic.

Doctor Willard Bailey, San Jose's health director, ordered all schools and libraries closed. Everyone was instructed to wear masks to help prevent the germs from spreading. Every precaution was taken, including washing down the streets and fumigating articles of contact, but the influenza virus proved to be far more formidable than the most pessimistic observers could contemplate. By the war's end, the dreaded malady had run its course and the world breathed a sigh of relief.

A Supreme Philanthropist

DURING THEIR TRAVELS in Europe, the O'Connors acquired a fabulous art collection, which they had crated and shipped home to San Jose to be housed in the sanitarium. As cargo after cargo arrived, it was evident that the building would not accommodate the entire collection. After much deliberation, in 1898, they decided to make a gift of the prized collection to their adopted city of San Jose. The inventory listed 425 pieces with an estimated value of $250,000 or more. Through their attorney, the O'Connors informed city officials that the collection was theirs, provided it could be adequately housed in a gallery on the Normal School campus.

Civic-minded residents, obviously overjoyed, made plans to raise the money by subscription. When asked, Governor James Budd said he foresaw no objection to the gallery's location on state property:

"I consider the state very lucky to be proffered so magnificent a gift. I congratulate the City of San Jose on its good fortune."

The *San Jose Mercury* shared the Governor's feelings, declaring, "San Jose cannot afford to ignore so splendid an offer. Such an elegant art building would give San Jose a prestige such as no other city on the Pacific Coast except San Francisco enjoys. The money will be subscribed. The project is chiefly in the hands of the ladies of San Jose, and with them there can be no such thing as failure."

The San Jose Art Association organized a "Committee of One Hundred" to promote the project. Yet, despite the enthusiasm, the citizens were loathe to contribute to a cultural venture of this enormity. Unlike San Francisco, San Jose was not culturally minded in that early period. The turn of the century did little to arouse the community's sense of history and culture, to the utter disappointment of the O'Connors. Although the residents of San Jose had pledged more than $7,000 towards the art gallery, only $3,600 had been deposited in the bank.

Some years previous, Myles and Amanda had become friends with Sister Julia McGroarty, Mother Superior of all the Sisters of Notre Dame de Namur in the United States. When they learned that Sister Julia was founding a new institution, Trinity College, in Washington, D.C., they offered her the collection for safekeeping and exhibition. She accepted without a moment's hesitation. San Jose's loss was the capital's gain.

Since they were eager to contribute to the construction of the new school, the O'Connors decided also to erect a gallery at their own expense to house the art collection. They also agreed to finance the central wing of the main building, which was appropriately called O'Connor Hall.

By coincidence, the affable President William McKinley visited the Garden City in May 1901, staying at the Vendome Hotel, the first modern structure of its kind in central California, with big bay windows and such amenities as electric lights and running hot water. During his stay, the President won over his hosts completely while parades and receptions toasted the historic occasion. The news of his assassination in Buffalo, New York, four months later stunned the residents of Santa Clara County. As a token of their bereavement, San Joseans, at the behest of Reverend Robert Kenna, president of Santa Clara College, decided to build a worthy monument, using the $3,600 left over from the abortive O'Connor art gallery drive to launch the fund.

The local art association approved the idea wholeheartedly, and the drive got underway. When the building fund reached a total of $13,728, the project's success was assured. The monument was erected and unveiled in Saint James Park on the exact spot where the President had addressed an enthusiastic gathering the previous May. An impassioned oration by Father Kenna highlighted the unveiling ceremony. It was said that Mrs. O'Connor never passed the monument without feeling that somehow she and her husband had unwittingly played a part in its creation.

About that time, the grand opening of the O'Connor Art Gallery was held in abeyance to coincide with the college's first commencement exercises in June. The judge, by this time almost blind, feeble but uncomplaining, waited patiently for two months while Mrs. O'Connor assisted with the arrangements in Washington.

The trip to Washington in 1904 was the O'Connors' last outing together; from then on, Myles rarely left the sanitarium. Sightless and aging, the judge spent most of his last seven years strolling in the sun-latticed garden, guiding himself by means of a white rope strung along the pathway. Nurses read to him from his favorite works in the O'Connor library, and on special occasions a young violinist stopped by to play the tunes he loved so well. On Sunday afternoons, the St. Joseph's School Band and Bugle Corps, which he personally outfitted, gave concerts on the lawn for his special enjoyment.

In the judge's decline, Amanda, his wife for 47 fruitful years, was ever at his side, ministering to him night and day. The *San Jose Mercury* noted, "Her devotion was most sublime, and of a depth and intensity seldom witnessed."

Myles Poore O'Connor died on June 9, 1909, at the age of 86. Edward McLaughlin, a lifelong associate, spoke of his friend in endearing terms.

> He was kind, courteous, considerate, and possessed a noble and refined character. He was particularly interested in orphans, and was always planning on their behalf. His greatest pleasure was in visiting them and looking after their welfare. Not only did he give money freely to help the needy and suffering, but he did noble deeds as well. He was always genial, always thoughtful of others even under grievous affliction. His patience was truly marvelous. He never complained and his mind was calm, serene and unclouded to the last. He was a wonderful mind; he was a man of great depths, possessed a vast fund of information and he took pride in his fine library. He leaves ample funds for his

widow to complete any charitable undertakings which he may have planned. He was an honor to his state and a worthy example of a large-hearted, unselfish, benevolent citizen who was actuated solely by the desire to benefit humanity. This county and state may well be proud of the record of Judge Myles P. O'Connor.

Myles O'Connor's funeral cortege was one of the most impressive in Santa Clara County's history. Mourners came from all over California to pay their last respects. The Chancery office, led by Archbishop Patrick Riordan, attended en masse, as did the Daughters of Charity from the O'Connor Sanitarium. His burial was in a marble crypt in Santa Clara's Catholic Cemetery. Sometime later his widow, Amanda, built the stately O'Connor Memorial Arch that graces the cemetery entrance.

O'Connor's Last Will and Testament

With the exception of Mrs. O'Connor, the largest individual stipulation in Myles's will was $50,000 bequeathed to a brother, Jerome, of Peipers Fork, Tennessee. He left $10,000 each to the Los Gatos Novitiate and the Notre Dame Institute, and $5,000 to the Daughters of Charity of O'Connor Sanitarium.

As the decades passed, the tremendous increase in population and the advancement of medicine made obvious the need for an up-to-date facility at the sanitarium. O'Connor's chief of staff, Doctor Leon Fox, and Sister Stella decided that the institution would have to expand to meet the challenge. On March 23, 1947, at the behest of Archbishop John Mitty, a fund drive was undertaken. The goal in public subscription was $1 million, with matching funds by the sisters. The effort brought together the entire community, with Protestants, Jews and Catholics alike giving of their time and financial help. The ecumenical spirit was already a way of life, judging from the O'Connor Hospital's sixty-year history, which showed that 54 percent of the patients had been non-Catholics. During all that time, the sanitarium had never approached the community for financial aid. Within a period of four months, the drive had gone over the top, with $1,046,997 in the coffers. The Irish led the way, with Patrick Peabody as director and Frank O'Connell, a Gilroy cattleman, capping individual subscribers with a $30,000 gift. A matching federal grant in excess of a million dollars was the largest ever made to a hospital on the Pacific Coast.

*The modern O'Connor Hospital, built in 1953 and expanded in the 1960s,
is today a fully equipped facility serving the entire San Jose community,
a testament to the generosity of Myles and Amanda O'Connor.
Courtesy O'Connor Hospital*

There were recurring problems along the way, but finally, on July 19, 1951, the San Francisco firm of Barrett and Hilp broke ground and the construction work got underway. The building was completed and the cornerstone laid on June 12, 1953. The O'Connor Hospital's average of one thousand admissions a year during pre-World War I years increased to over nineteen thousand in 1957. The facility had registered more patients in comparison to its capacity than any other hospital in the United States or Canada.

Since the early years, when Myles O'Connor arranged for Bishop Keane, the first president of the Catholic University, to spend summer rests at the sanitarium, the institution welcomed many well-known figures. Famed violinist Yehudi Menuhin gave a 30-minute performance of Bach for 125 hospital staff members in 1955 as an expression of his gratitude for the very professional treatment his wife had received as a patient. Edgar Bergen, the ventriloquist, along with

Charlie McCarthy, Ward Bond and June Haver, all performed for patients and nurses.

THE O'CONNOR master plan was completed in December 1965, with the opening of the hospital's chapel, a $250,000 investment, with seating for one hundred people. The demand for the most modern facilities has grown in tandem with the advancements in medical science. And in order to maintain the O'Connor as one of California's leading medical institutions, the staff, led by administrator Sister Roberta, planned a $3 million expansion program. The project, which called for an up-to-date X-ray, laboratory and physical medicine facilities, recovery rooms, an intensive care unit and a new administrative office, took eighteen months to complete.

Born in the horse and buggy era, the magnificent O'Connor Hospital entered the Space Age with the same vision and high ideals that characterized its founder, who struck out for California and an uncertain future on that spring morning in 1849.

The never-ending quest for new means to lessen the suffering of humankind carries on in the spirit of compassion and philanthropy inherent in the life of Myles Poore O'Connor, an impoverished Irish immigrant from old Abbeyleix.

Frank McCoppin
Courtesy Society of California Pioneers

- 11 -

FRANK MCCOPPIN

FIRST IRISH-BORN MAYOR OF SAN FRANCISCO

1834 - 1897

The election of Irish-born Frank McCoppin as Mayor of San Francisco in 1867 rolled out the green carpet on which the Irish marched to political power, and which they maintained for well over a century. There would be other Irish mayors, councilmen and political bosses in the intervening years, but none whose self-advancement would bring such heartfelt satisfaction to a deeply ambitious and volatile race.

At that time the Irish were the most numerous of all the diverse inhabitants in Northern California. San Francisco, the leading city on the Pacific coast, had already a larger number of Irish than any other major city of the Western Hemisphere. In the wake of the Gold Rush more San Franciscans had come from Ireland than from any other country or any state of the Union. Out of a total population of 149,000 the Irish numbered some 41,000, or approximately 29 per cent of the city's inhabitants. But even more significant was the fact that the San Francisco Irish wielded far more political power and influence than any other national group in proportion to their number. The only thing they lacked was a leader, a spokesman to give them a voice in matters that affected their present and future welfare.

The election of one of their very own, Frank "Faultless Physique" McCoppin, made all of that possible. From that day forward no political office in California was beyond the reach of the Irish. There were others who said that the seeds of Irish influence were planted way back in 1850, when John White Geary, who was Irish on both sides of his family, became the first duly elected Mayor of San Francisco. All told, six stalwart Irishmen: John Geary, Frank McCoppin, James D. Phelan, Patrick McCarthy, John Shelley and

Frank Jordan have served as Mayor of San Francisco from 1850 to 1995. It's a record unmatched by any major city in the United States.

McCoppin's Irish Roots

FRANK MCCOPPIN was born July 4, 1834, in Longford, the principal town in County Longford, in the heart of the beloved Isle. According to the parish register of Templemichael and Ballymacormack (Longford), his parents were Richard and Elizabeth Duffy McCoppin, and at his baptism on July 8, 1834, he was christened Francis McCoppin, his sponsors being Michael McCoppin and Elizabeth Heanden. The Penal laws, which were being enforced at the time, may account for the fact that the officiating clergyman did not sign the Baptismal Certificate for fear of being apprehended and put to the sword for his disobedience.

Longford, known as "Annaly" in ancient times, was the ancestral home of the O'Farrells, a tenacious clan, one of whom proved his valor under the leadership of King Brian Boru at the historic battle of Clontarf in 1014. Three brothers by the name of O'Farrell served as officers of the Irish Brigade in the French Army during that period. However, the O'Farrell best remembered by Californians was Jasper O'Farrell, the Dublin-born engineer who laid out the streets of San Francisco way back in 1846. Coincidentally, Longford is also the birthplace of the Honorable Albert Reynolds, the scholarly Prime Minister of Ireland, who was instrumental in bringing peace to Northern Ireland.

A lanky survivor of the potato famine at the age of eighteen, McCoppin immigrated to the New World with his parents, who settled in New York City. From there he removed to Illinois, where he resided until he came to California in 1857. During his stay in Illinois he studied engineering, which paid off when he eventually settled in San Francisco.

When Tom Hayes, founder of Hayes Valley, formed a company to build a public transportation system on Market Street, McCoppin was appointed construction foreman. The rail line ran from the vicinity of Donahue's Iron Works on First Street, out through the sand dunes to Fifteenth and Valencia Streets. The roadbed became a mass of soggy mud when the rains came, and caused the tracks to sink in the streets. The locals humorously referred to the line as McCoppin's Canal.

McCoppin took it all in stride and despite the damned canal, he was elected supervisor from the 26th district a mere two years after his arrival in the city. He had everything going for him, with a winsome Irish smile to match his splendid physique. He also had the right connections: bankers, brokers. saloon-keepers and party-givers. His wife was the daughter of James Van Ness, who had served earlier as mayor for twelve years and had succeeded in settling the vexing question of land titles which had plagued San Francisco since the American acquisition of California.

The Early St. Patrick's Day Celebrations

EVERY SAINT PATRICK'S DAY since 1853, when the San Francisco Irish gathered in Hayes Park, the city's pioneer public playground, to celebrate the grand occasion, the Irish would literally take over the city as if it were their very own. There was no parade in that early period, as there were no paved streets to parade on. Kearney Street, the principle thoroughfare, was like the "Old Bog Road," dusty in summer and muddy in winter when the rains came. San Francisco's priorities were evidently different from those of other American cities. San Franciscans had Grand Opera before they had paved streets and sidewalks.

1866 was a banner year for the San Francisco Irish. On Saint Patrick's Day, the paraders gathered in Happy Valley and set out along Kearney Street and up California Street to the brow of the hill, where they were serenaded by the bells of Old Saint Mary's Cathedral and the ringing cheers of a pent-up gathering. Leading the grand parade were the proud McMahon Guards, followed by a fife and drum band, its members arrayed in green and gold; then the Fenian Brotherhood, three hundred strong, the Montgomery Guards, the Saint Patrick's Brotherhood, the Wolfe Tone Guards, the Saint Joseph Benevolent Society, the Robert Emmets and the Sons of the Emerald Isle. Everyone was in a mood to celebrate; the spectators roared themselves hoarse as each entry sought to outperform the other. The celebration was so boisterous the sober and somber Anglos, Prussians and Asians closed their doors, pulled down the shades and stayed put until it was all over.

A lone piper stood on the steps of the Cathedral and played appropriate Irish airs. The mass was celebrated by Reverend Peter Grey, Pastor of Saint Patrick's Church and Chancellor of the Diocese of San Francosco.

Following the services the huge gathering marched to Platt's Hall on Montgomery Street, the only building big enough to hold them. When all were well fortified with lager beer and porter from

Noonan's Hibernian Brewery on Folsom Street, McEwand's pale ale and Hotaling's whiskey, the celebration began in earnest. Speaker after speaker paid tribute to the good Saint Patrick, who brought the faith to Ireland, and thence to America and the whole wide world through Ireland's sons and daughters. The highest balconies resounded with the names of Robert Emmet, Earl Fitzgerald and Terence Bellew MacManus. On hand was the celebrated thespian, Lawrence Barrett, who was performing in the stirring moral drama called "The Apostate" at the Opera House on Mission Street. His recital of "Seamus O'Brien" brought the audience to their feet. There were Irish musicians by the score, and dancers who danced as never before. The grand affair came to a close, as the massive doors of the great hall were thrown open so that the huge outdoor gathering could join in the rousing chorus:

> Glorio, Glorio to the Bold Fenian Men,
> Glorio, Glorio to the Bold Fenian Men.

The revelers recessed until later in the evening, when they reassembled at the fashionable Metropolitan Theater for the grand finale. The Honorable Thomas Mooney addressed an assemblage of Phelans, Foleys and Flanagans, Donahues, Dunnes, Donovans, Dowlings, Doolans, Doolings and Dalys, O'Connells and O'Donnells, O'Briens by the score, and Murphys galore.

It was, Mooney said, a day that marked an epoch in the history of the whole existing Earth when the Apostolic Labors of Saint Patrick, under the guidance of the Omnipotent, brought the Christian Faith to Ireland, a day to be remembered until time be no more.

And right up front, seated at the head table were such Irish luminaries as United States Senator Eugene Casserly, the Pride of old Mullingar; the Silver Kings, James Flood and Billy O'Brien; and Ireland's favorite son and candidate for Mayor of San Francisco, the personable supervisor of the 11th Ward, the Honorable Frank McCoppin.

Like many of their countrymen, the McCoppin family first settled in New York, where they resided for a period of seven years. During their stay in the big city, Frank studied engineering, which he put to good use following his arrival in San Francisco.

Fortune smiled on Frank McCoppin from the day he first set foot in the booming Gold Rush city. By chance he met up with a fellow countryman, Tom Hayes, of Hayes Valley fame, who was by then a man of means, and his lesser-known brother Michael. The Hayes brothers were already planning to provide a system of transportation for their adopted city.

A committee was formed with Thomas Hayes as president, and S.C. Simmons as secretary; Directors, Tom Hayes, Peter Donahue the industrialist, Michael Hayes, J.P. Haven, H. Cobb and the newcomer Frank McCoppin. They were all men of stature and accomplishment with the exception of McCoppin, who had as yet little to commend him, but who eventually proved his worth as the project's engineer and went on to become Mayor of San Francisco.

The road, which ran from Third and Market to Mission Dolores, was incorporated in early 1859. The laying of the rails commenced on June 7th of that year and was completed the following year, July 4th, 1860, when it was named the Market Street Railroad. Shortly thereafter McCoppin was appointed Superintendent.

McCoppin's Political Career

A rising star on the San Francisco political scene, McCoppin, a Democrat, was elected to the Board of Supervisors by a sizable majority, a mere two years following his arrival in the city. As a member of that body he lost no time in making known, among other things, his belief in the system of private enterprise as opposed to public ownership. He went even further by declaring his willingness to sponsor any measure that favored private control.

During the Civil War, with Abraham Lincoln as President and Leland Stanford as Governor of California (both Republicans), the Republican Party had most everything going its way. During the reconstruction period that followed, California was politically in a state of flux, as evidenced by an on-going dissatisfaction with the party or parties in power. The San Francisco Democrats, in particular, felt that the time was right for them to reassert their leadership and to put forward a strong candidate for Mayor. They settled on the dapper supervisor, Frank McCoppin, who they believed would garner the all-important Irish vote. In the minds of the Democrats, the personable, quick-witted Irishman was the only one who could possibly win election at that time.

Frank McCoppin, in addition to his good looks, was without a doubt the smartest, most articulate and most popular supervisor San Francisco ever had. For the disgruntled citizenry who sought change, Frank McCoppin was their man. He had the wherewithal to win higher office at the city or state level if he could only resolve the question of the Outside Lands, a problem that would vex a saint. The disputed lands were taken over by squatters who laid claim to them by virtue of their having resided thereon for many years, an off-shoot of the Homestead Act.

The ownership of this 17,000-acre spread had been in dispute for nigh on twenty years and involved the city, state and federal governments. Some years earlier the city had laid claim to four square leagues of the disputed lands, basing its case on city rights as successor to the Pueblo of Yerba Buena. The Federal Government disagreed on the grounds that these Outside Lands while within the boundaries of the city as established in 1856, never had been part of the Mexican pueblo and therefore were public domain. As for the squatters themselves, they asserted their traditional rights under the Homestead Act which entitled each of them to a quarter section (160 Acres) of uninhabited public land.

The United States Lands Commission upheld the city's claim to 10,000 of the original 17,000-acre parcel. Neither party, however, was satisfied, and eventually they both appealed the decision. The case dragged on until 1864, when an appeals court confirmed San Francisco's right and title to all 17,000 acres "in trust for the use and benefit of the inhabitants of the city."

The Founding of Carville

MANY YEARS LATER a small portion of the land near the southwest corner of Golden Gate Park became known as "Carville," a collection of old trolley cars which were converted to homes. The story of Carville forms a bizarre chapter in the history of Old San Francisco. Emmitt O'Brien, a columnist for the *San Francisco Chronicle,* describes it as "the odd city on Ocean Beach." And no mortal could have given it a more appropriate title.

The Market Street Railway placed an ad in the newspapers offering horse-drawn trolley cars for sale at $20 with seats, and $10 without. To make it more attractive the company transported the cars along the rails to a diversion on Lincoln Way. One enterprising merchant bought one and set it up as a food stand. Other were positioned in the sand dunes and used as rental cottages at a very reasonable rate—affordable housing before that catchy word was ever coined. Carville was San Francisco's first Bohemia.

The trolleys were grouped together in a street pattern at right angles, or U shaped, like a cul-de sac, or set on top of each other to create two story abodes. The Falcon Club, an organization of lady cyclists, used one as their clubhouse. It was beautifully decorated with a dining table capable of seating 28 people when lowered from the ceiling. As the good ladies were of a literary bent, well known writers, editors and orators were invited to dine and enjoy the lively conversation. It was said that if the inner sanctum was too crowded one could easily run around the outside and enter by the back platform.

By the late 1890s most of the trolleys were taken over by the "Fuzzies" or early day "Hippies." They were mostly artists, musicians and dreamers who found the quaint habitat perfect for their creative aspirations. They were no doubt encouraged by ardent patrons who supplied the picnic car, stocking it with drinks and eatables to encourage the artists in their various endeavors. Hilarious high jinks ensued when a group of musicians christened their trolley car "La Boheme" and entertained the entire New York Metropolitan Orchestra when they came to town in 1908.

Some of the cars had modern amenities, such as sunken bathtubs under the floorboards, secluded compartments with Victorian embellishments, fancy birdcages and potted tropical potted palms. Fremont Older, editor of the *San Francisco Bulletin,* and his wife Cora moved into Carville after the 1906 Earthquake and Fire destroyed their home. Their progressive-minded housekeeper Mary Gunn had three cars set together nearby and turned them into a tea room; it remained in business until 1923.

At one time more than two thousand people called Carville home. They could boast of a church and a school as well as an Improvement Club, which they christened Oceanside. The quaint village had paved roads, gas streetlights and cement walkways.

Alas, Carville's glory days were coming to an end. The Oceanside Improvement Club, its most ardent proponent, had a change of heart and voted to improve Carville by burning it. And on July 4, 1913, a number of cars were ceremoniously burned in keeping with the motto, "Make clean today by sweeping and burning up the debris of yesterday." The city donated the trifling sum of $10 worth of fireworks. Despite the hullabaloo the rest of Carville hung on for another fifteen years or more until the last of the old relics were removed to make way for the development of the Sunset district.

But way back in 1867 the Congress and the California state legislature had passed bills which provided for the squatters in the Outside Lands to keep what was not set aside for a specific public purpose. The San Francisco Board of Supervisors agreed in principle, but decided to keep for public use the ocean front and three hundred acres for a much needed recreation park. At the time most everyone knew that the squatters' domain was mostly sand dunes spotted with tall grass and scrimpy lupine, but none would hazard a guess about what it might be worth in the future.

Carville was eulogized in a movie called "Sandlot City," produced by the History Department of Lowell High School, and written and directed by Thomas Harrison, a leading San Francisco historian and educator. It was a big hit with San Franciscans of every age and drew excellent reviews from film critics and historians alike.

THE COMING of the transcontinental railroad linking East and West, some two years later in 1869, provided California with the means for future development of its vast resources, and guaranteed San Francisco's future as the Queen City of the West.

By 1870 the gold and silver mines were disgorging their treasures at an amazing rate, bringing wealth in abundance to San Franciscans, who were now in a buying mood. The price of city lots was skyrocketing. A newly arrived steam paddy, manned by a brawny Irishman named Cunningham, was at work grading the sand hills in Happy Valley to make way for the city's main thoroughfare, Market Street. It was an opportune time to purchase land that trebled in value almost overnight. It was also a good time to enter politics.

About that time a local political party was organized, which called itself the "Equal Distributionists." Their plan was to reverse the Supervisor's ordinance favoring the squatters, strip them of their property, subdivide the Outside Lands, and distribute the acreage in equal amounts to the public. The Equal Distributionists went even further by making known that every citizen subscribing to Party principles would be entitled to a fifty-vara lot (approximately 150 x 150 feet). If the party didn't need the land they could sell it at a good profit and take a vacation at Calistoga Hot Springs.

Supervisor McCoppin was at the cutting edge of the dispute. A less courageous man would have conceded defeat. McCoppin was the leading proponent of the "Clement Ordinance," giving squatters title to their claims and keeping only the ocean front and 300 acres for public use. How could he now refute the argument that it had been grossly unfair and short-sighted to give a few opportunists a property that could be sold for millions of dollars or doled out to poor San Franciscans who needed homes? How could he counteract the logical appeal of J. B. Roberts, the People's Independent Party candidate for Mayor, who vehemently opposed the Clement Ordinance as a sham?

The *Bulletin's* fiery editor took up the attack on McCoppin. "Never let it be forgotten that Frank McCoppin voted for Order No. 734, giving the Outside Lands of San Francisco to the land-grabbers."

But McCoppin had one particular advantage at a time when being Irish and a Democrat was tantamount to election in San Francisco. Dignified and stately, with a mane of wavy hair, and graced with a melting Irish smile, he could have sailed through most elections in grinning silence.

With the election a few weeks hence, the Distributionists called for a public rally at Platt's Hall on Montgomery Street. Most of the candidates, with the exception of Frank McCoppin, vowed to air their contempt for the Clement Ordinance. "The people are decidedly against deeding the Outside Lands to squatters," said the honorable speaker of the evening, Judge Turner. "That would be putting the more than four hundred claimants above the one hundred twenty thousand inhabitants of the city." The emotional crowd roared its approval. But outside the hall a stalwart group of Irish loyalists raised three cheers and a tiger for McCoppin. And that was all he needed.

The very next day, in a burst of enthusiasm nurtured by necessity, McCoppin announced his well conceived plan: to create an enormous park with one thousand acres or more of public playgrounds, lawns, lakes and dells, gardens and forests. Not a mere 300 acres, as his critics had earlier proposed. There was no denying that the Clement Ordinance, the brainchild of supervisor Frank McCoppin, would make it all come true. In an upbeat mood, McCoppin stated further, "As soon as these claims are quieted and settled, confidence will be restored, values will increase largely, improvements will follow, and the revenue of both city and county will be immensely increased."

On that premise Golden Gate Park was born, and Frank McCoppin could rightfully claim to be its founding father. This was the turning point in McCoppin's political career. Voters crowded around him and slapped him on the back. The erstwhile villain was now their hero. The Equal Distributionists were momentarily confounded, and had nothing to offer as a rebuttal to McCoppin's visionary plan. History was made, and from that day forward all went well for the Irish.

Irish Power in San Francisco

THE INAUGURATION of Frank McCoppin as Mayor of San Francisco on December 2, 1867, set in motion an Irish political surge in California that lasted for well over a century. His election as the first Irish-born mayor of any major American city predated by seventeen years that of Hugh O'Brien, who became mayor of New York City in 1884. McCoppin's election in the western metropolis was an inspiration to every Irishman aspiring to public office. From that day forward no political office in California was beyond the reach of the Irish.

One of McCoppin's first official functions as Mayor took place at the grand opening of Hunter's Point Drydock, which at the time was the largest shipbuilding and repair facility on the West Coast. The historic occasion, which brought together businessmen, bankers and public officials from all over Northern California, did much to enhance his political career.

The Transcontinental Railroad

AN EVEN GREATER honor awaited the mayor with the advent of the transcontinental railway. The meeting of the rails linking east and west was heralded with great anxiety and expectation. At Promontory, Utah, an animated throng stood shoulder to shoulder, eagerly awaiting the driving of the "Golden Spike," which joined the two portions of the railroad. Mayor Frank McCoppin of San Francisco opened the program by introducing the celebrated Irish songster, O. P. Kennedy, who rendered the "Star Spangled Banner" with such power that he was called back for a repeat performance.

In the background, standing tall, were the Irish railroad workers who could feel justly proud of having laid the rails across the desolate desert and over the snow-capped mountains all the way to this very spot. In a prominent place were the Irish Bonanza Kings, James Fair, John Mackey, James Flood, and Billy O'Brien. There, too, were such Irish stalwarts as James Phelan, pioneer builder and banker; ex-governor John Downey, Senators John Conness and Eugene Casserly. The whole affair appeared like a victory celebration for San Franciscans. The *Alta California* voiced the prevailing sentiments: "No brighter day ever dawned upon San Francisco than yesterday. It seems as if all nature joined in the Grand Jubilee of San Francisco upon the completion of the great work in which so much interest had been felt upon both sides of the continent."

There too, were the railway barons, Charles Crocker, Collis Huntington, Leland Stanford and Mark Hopkins, as well as other well-known men, such as William Ralston, James Lick and James Baldwin.

Governor Leland Stanford stepped forward to drive the "Golden

Spike" as the roar of the enormous gathering reverberated over the landscape. A great nation which had been joined politically by the Declaration of Independence on July 4, 1776, was now joined physically by the coming of the Transcontinental Railway on May 8, 1869.

It was a great day for San Francisco, for California and the nation, and a great day for the Irish as well. The renowned poet laureate and historian John McGroarty called it "One of California's Five Miracles." What the other four were he didn't say.

McCoppin returned in high spirits to his beloved city, where a huge celebration in his honor was already underway. Buildings were draped in patriotic buntings, bands played appropriate numbers while people danced on the streets and strangers hugged each other. A torchlight parade was formed to meet the Mayor at the waterfront and escort him all the way to City Hall, where thousands waited to greet him.

McCoppin served for only one term as Mayor, but in that short space of time he did more for San Francisco than most others have done in a lifetime. When the demand for a public recreation ground in San Francisco arose in the 1860s, Mayor Frank McCoppin led a delegation to the State Capitol to demand that a sizable area of the Outside Lands be saved for a park. A settlement was finally agreed on by all parties in 1868. The state agreed to put up $801,593 for the desired 1,017 acres for Golden Gate Park, which today draws visitors from all over the world.

In 1878 California Governor Henry Haight appointed the first San Francisco Park Commission. The following year, when the park was surveyed and mapped, William Hammond Hall was appointed park superintendent and authorized to proceed with its development. It was not until 1887, when John McLaren, a Scottish landscape gardener, became superintendent, that the work began in earnest. The commissioners told McLaren, "We want you to make Golden Gate Park one of the beauty spots of the world. Can you do it?" Young Scotty replied, "With your aid, gentlemen, and God be willing, that I shall do." And that he did and more.

However, when all is said and done, Frank McCoppin was truly the founding father of Golden Gate Park. Thanks to his foresight and determination, San Franciscans can boast of having one the most unique year round playgrounds anywhere in the world.

In 1874, McCoppin ran for state senator on the Democratic ticket and was elected by a sizable majority. Like his Irish cohorts, Senators John Conness and Eugene Casserly, he proved to be an able and trustworthy legislator. One of the first measures he sponsored was to set streetcar fares at five cents for cities having a population of more than 100,000. It was little wonder that longtime San Franciscans reminisce about the Good Old Days—about McCoppin's five-cent carfare, the five-cent cigar and the five-cent beer with a free lunch to boot. The seven-mile trolley car ride from the Ferry Building to Ocean Beach was given as the finest and cheapest in the city.

A fiscal conservative, McCoppin introduced a bill which, when passed, became known as the McCoppin Act, specifying "that no greater amount of liability against San Francisco treasury should be authorized, contracted or paid in any one month than one-twelfth of the total amount allowed by law to be expended within the fiscal year." In other words, no deficit spending was allowed, and the rule would be enforced monthly, rather than once a year.

Two years later McCoppin was re-elected to the State Senate for a second term. From then on he took a more active role in the senate hearings on various proposals having to do with the growth and development of the state as a whole. He was said to be one of the handsomest men in the California Legislature at the time. In a journal called *Pen Portraits*, he is pictured as "Tall, straight and handsome, a gentleman of commanding appearance, with a lively step and greying hair. Very refined, although not born of the higher classes of Ireland."

Following a successful career in business and politics, McCoppin passed away at the age of 63 on May 26, 1897, in his home on the southwest corner of Valencia and 17th Streets. He was a longtime friend and neighbor of the pioneer builder and banker, James Phelan, who preceded him in death by seven years.

As Shakespeare remarked, "The evil that men do lives after them, the good is oft interred with their bones." The same can be said of Frank McCoppin. Here's a man who served his adopted city and state with honor and dignity for well over half a century, and is now almost forgotten. McCoppin Street, a short street connecting Mission, Valencia and Market Streets, is the only reminder that he ever existed.

Eugene Casserly
Courtesy California State Library #5818

EUGENE CASSERLY

THE PATRICK HENRY OF CALIFORNIA

1822 - 1883

A S CALIFORNIA CELEBRATES a century and a half of its illustrious public servants, Senator Eugene Casserly deserves special mention as one of the most personable and scholarly pioneers of early California. In various positions of public and private trust, he never failed in the honest, faithful and satisfactory discharge of his duties.

Eugene Casserly contributed to the legal and political development of California during its formative years of statehood following the war with Mexico. During the Civil War Casserly stood firm for Abraham Lincoln and the Union. In later years he played a leading role during the revision of the original California Constitution at the Sacramento Constitutional Convention in 1878. The constitution under which the State of California is still governed was largely the work of Irish scholars, assembled at Monterey in 1849, where the document was devised by Philip Augustus Roache, from County Cork, and William Shannon, of County Mayo, and recorded and printed in both English and Spanish by John Roos Browne, from Dublin. It was revised in Sacramento in 1878, to meet changed conditions, under the supervision of Eugene Casserly, from County Westmeath.

As a staunch Democrat in a Republican-dominated Congress, Senator Casserly steadfastly upheld constitutional principles, regardless of party politics, and advocated a tempered, rational, conciliatory attitude toward the Confederate States. Although the Democratic Party was in the minority in the Senate so far as numbers were concerned, his influence was felt at every level and his oratory was listened to with rapt attention. His contributions are practically unknown to the present generation because he lacked the glamour that would have made him a popular figure in his day. And, although he is not in a class with such notables as Leland Stanford, Senators David Broderick or John Conness, he well deserves a place in history as one of California's most respected and trustworthy legislators. In the corrupt politics of that period, he would not submit principle to expediency, or sacrifice moral issues to advance his political career.

Casserly's Early Life and Times

EUGENE CASSERLY was born in Mullingar, County Westmeath, a town revered in song and story, in the year 1822. His father, Patrick Sarsfield Casserly, was a renowned Irish schoolmaster, well versed in the literature of Gaelic Ireland, as well as that of Greece and Rome. As one of the participants of the Irish Rebellion of 1798, like his father before him, Patrick Casserly was a marked man in his native land. It was then that he set his sights on America the "land of the free and the home of the brave." Under threat of death the Casserly family made their escape to America and settled in New York City which was already a hotbed of Irish nationalism.

On the day of his arrival in the bustling city he went straight from the ship to the nearest courthouse and declared his intention to become a citizen of the United States, leaving the matter of lodgings to be taken care of afterward.

Ireland's loss was America's gain. Patrick Sarsfield Casserly was a classical scholar whose intellect was truly remarkable and of the highest order. It was little wonder that he was appointed associate editor of the *New York Weekly Register* shortly after his arrival in America.

The following year he opened the Chrestomatic Institute, a classical school, in New York City, the only institution of its kind in America. As a student in that school young Eugene acquired a thorough training in Greek and Latin and in classical literature. His father felt that this knowledge was so important that he commenced to instill the rudiments of Greek and Latin languages into the minds of his children at an early age. Eugene began his studies of the classics at five years of age, and became deeply involved in reading, writing and study. In later years this abiding interest proved invaluable, not only during his brief term as a journalist but also in his long career as a lawyer.

Eugene grew to manhood in this combined home and school. A diligent student, he found the Greek and Roman heroes more entertaining than friends of his own age. The Casserly children attended Saint Joseph's Church on Barrow Street, where their father was one of the parish trustees.

At the age of nineteen Eugene helped his father in compiling and editing *Jacob's Greek Reader*, which became a standard textbook. In addition to the school, the Casserlys operated a well-stocked bookstore on Nassau Street, the English, Classical and Catholic Bookstore, which carried standard works for schools and libraries, and specialized in foreign books and Catholic literature. They were also the first literary agents to make the *Dublin Review* available to American readers.

Apparently Patrick Sarsfield Casserly, schoolmaster, was a strong-willed person, prepared to stand up for his rights, even though he might draw the ire of the Catholic hierarchy. The trouble started when Bishop John Dubois transferred the Reverend James Quinn to an out-of-the-way parish in Troy, in upper New York State. A committee from the board of trustees headed by Patrick Casserly and Richard Hogan wrote letters to the Bishop, objecting to the removal of Father Quinn and to the appointment of Father Constantine Pisa. Father Pisa resigned as a result of the controversy, and Father John McCloskey, later the Cardinal Archbishop of New York, was appointed.

Patrick Casserly and Father McCloskey also had their differences as time went on. Nevertheless, the religious education of the Casserly children was not neglected. Patrick continued sending his children to church, and even insisted on Father McCloskey preparing them for their First Holy Communion. The significance of that memorable occasion was still fresh in Eugene's mind some thirty years later, on the occasion of his election as United States Senator from California, when he sent a telegram to Archbishop McCloskey in New York: "One whom you prepared for First Communion has today been elected United States Senator."

Apparently Eugene received his classical education only in his father's school, as no records exist of his attendance elsewhere. However it appears he had a close association with Georgetown University, for that renowned educational institution conferred on him a Master of Arts degree in 1856, when he was living in California. And again in 1872, when Eugene was in the Senate, Georgetown conferred an honorary LL.D. upon Eugene Casserly, Senator from California.

Despite his rise to fame in America, Casserly retained a vital interest in his native land. He took an active role in Irish organizations like the Irish Emigrant Association, formed in New York to assist Irish immigrants to obtain housing and employment. He was also a charter member of the Young Men's Appeal Association, and in the following years served as a worthy officer. Casserly's stirring address on the Repeal Movement, championed by Daniel O'Connel, was published in the February 1842 issue of *Freeman's Journal* in New York City. The *Journal*, edited by an Irishman named James White, was first launched on July 4, 1840, and became a powerful advocate of everything Irish in the ensuing years.

At the age of twenty, Eugene Casserly set out to seek an independent career. His first choice was in the field of journalism. His friendship with Bishop John Hughes of New York led to his appointment as editor of the struggling *Irish Catholic Weekly*, which was only in its second year of publication. He also contributed articles to similar journals in Boston, New York and Washington.

About that same time Casserly took up the study of law in the office of an eminent New York Lawyer, John Doyle. A diligent student, he was admitted to the bar two years later, in 1846, and shortly thereafter began the practice of law in partnership with John Bigelow. The partnership, however, was short-lived, because William Cullen Bryant offered Bigelow an editorial position on the *New York Evening Post*.

Life has its mysteries; of that there is no doubt. Why did Eugene Casserly set aside a well-established law practice in the big, vibrant city of New York to try his fortune in California, which at that time had few inhabitants and little to offer in the way of business activity?

Casserly's Career in California, 1850 -1869

IN 1850, Casserly set out for San Francisco by way of Panama, rather than the more tedious route around the Horn, or the more treacherous wagon trail across the prairies and over the mountains. His arrival in the Golden Gate city could not have come at a more appropriate time. The unprecedented increase in population transformed the insignificant pueblo of Yerba Buena, numbering 196 inhabitants in 1842, into a rowdy, crowded city almost overnight. Irish, German, Russian, Danish, Swedish, Asian and French immigrants mingled with Yankees and Hispanics, all in pursuit of their Pot of Gold.

Coincidentally, Eugene Casserly arrived about the same time as the newly-appointed Bishop Joseph Sodoc Alemany, who devoted many years to building up the Catholic Church in California, and with whom Casserly was later associated in the Pious Fund case and other religious matters.

By a stroke of Irish luck Casserly became acquainted with Benjamin Buckelew, a New Yorker who had come overland to

California some two years earlier. Soon after his arrival Buckelew opened a jewelry and watchmaking shop close by the waterfront, at Sansome and Pacific Streets. He purchased the *Californian,* the state's first newspaper, from Doctor Robert Semple, the proprietor and founding partner.

As a result of a dispute with the daily *Alta California* newspaper, Buckelew decided to start a newspaper of his own. He hired an Irishman named Michael O'Connor to travel to the east coast to purchase a printing press for him, "first class in every respect." While this elegant equipment was being installed in Buckelew's building on Gold Street, beneath Clark's Point, he and O'Connor quarreled, and O'Connor withdrew from the venture.

Eugene Casserly, newly arrived in San Francisco, succeeded O'Connor as editor of the new newspaper. For whatever reason, the firm was named Eugene Casserly & Company, although it was Buckelew who provided the capital and equipment.

The first issue of the journal, the *Public Balance,* came out in December 1850 from an office at 276 Montgomery Street. The price of five cents an issue was less than half the cost of the other six dailies in a city of only thirty thousand people.

The Buckelew-Casserly honeymoon was short-lived, however. When a difference of opinion arose over the layout and the editorial policy of the paper, Casserly moved the publication office to the old Plaza and continued to issue the *Public Balance.* Buckelew took up the challenge, claiming the newspaper as his property, and then began to publish the *California Public Balance.* He was quite disturbed when the locals referred to his paper as *Public Balance No 2.* San Franciscans reveled in the hilarious feud while at the same time they bought and read both newspapers.

To further complicate the issue, Casserly announced that he had sold his interest in the business to Casserly, Callender and Company, consisting of Miles Callender, B. F. Foster, H. V. Toomey and Eugene Casserly as consulting editor. The change took effect on March 3, 1851, and the *Public Balance* became the *True Standard.*

San Francisco caught the attention of the men and women nationwide, who dubbed it as the bizarre capital of America, where the unusual was an everyday occurrence. "Doc" Robinson, the poet laureate of Montgomery Gulch, wrote:

> San Francisco has forever something new,
> There's leisure for the working man
> And pleasure for the blue.

Casserly's printing establishment was destroyed in the fire of 1851, but he somehow managed to save his well-stocked law library. In the conflagration every newspaper in the city except the *Alta California* was destroyed. For two days in May 1851 the *Alta* was the only newspaper on the streets of San Francisco. In the May 5 issue Casserly and Company inserted a notice announcing that, notwithstanding the total destruction of their establishment, "we are rapidly completing arrangements which will enable us in a day or two to continue the paper. Notice change of address at the store of Messrs. Cook Brothers, California Street, or at the office of Burgess, Gilbert and Still, on the Plaza."

Despite the optimistic announcement, the *True Standard* never made a comeback. The disaster put an end to Casserly's publishing career, and he left the field of journalism to resume the practice of law.

On May 1, 1851, the California Legislature, meeting in the State Capitol at San Jose, elected Eugene Casserly to the office of State Printer. However, Governor John McDougal considered the Senate action irregular, and during adjournment of that body appointed George Fitch, a Republican, to the office. As a result the Secretary of State ignored Casserly and delivered the state journals to Fitch. Casserly filed suit, and followed up by presenting one of the ablest briefs ever set before the state tribunal. As a result the California Supreme Court declared that Casserly was the legal printer and that the appointment of Fitch was null and void.

Casserly Takes a Wife

IN 1853, at age 31, Eugene married Theresa Doyle, the daughter of John Doyle, a prominent New York attorney who had migrated to San Francisco with his family. The Casserlys and the Doyles had been family friends in New York, where Eugene had studied law in the office of John Doyle, Jr. The marriage united two of the most notable Irish-American families of New York. Young John Doyle and Casserly formed a law partnership in San Francisco and worked together or separately according to their needs.

Casserly drew the wrath of James King of William, the fiery editor of the *San Francisco Bulletin* and self-appointed champion of the rights of the people. As a lawyer, Casserly had vowed to uphold the law at all times. He was well aware of prevalent political corruption, and yet he deplored any extra-legal methods, which he thought would eventually lead to violence. How right he was.

On May 14, 1856, James King of William was gunned down by

James Casey, a city supervisor, whose past imprisonment had been publicized by the militant editor. Casey surrendered to police and was jailed while the authorities made plans for his trial. The task of guarding the prisoner fell to the lot of Sheriff David Scannell, who issued a summons to the citizens to help defend the jail against the marauding Vigilantes. Eugene Casserly was among the men who volunteered to assist the sheriff in protecting Casey from the Vigilante mob. Although he had no sympathy with the prisoner, he firmly believed that justice should be meted out by properly constituted courts, and that the offender should have a fair trial.

The Vigilante mob overpowered the defenders of the jail and subsequently hanged Casey and another prisoner, Charles Cora, in the old Plaza.

The Pious Fund

THE PROVEN REPUTATION of Casserly and Doyle as legal counselors at the State Bar caught the attention of the Very Reverend Joseph Alemany, Archbishop of San Francisco, who entrusted to them the solution of the Pious Fund case involving the Church in California. The successful arbitration of the claims during the hearings before the Mexican-American Claims Commission in 1876, and a quarter of a century later at the Hague in 1902 as the first case to be presented to the International Court of Arbitration, bore testimony to the skill and tenacity of the two lawyers.

The Pious Fund had its roots in early Mexican history at a time when both Baja and Alta California were still Spanish territory. The fund was made up of donations contributed by members of the Catholic Church for the founding and maintenance of the Missions. The Jesuits who were given charge of the work presciently invested the principle only, which they held in trust, and used the accrued interest to finance the missions. When the Jesuits were expelled from Mexico in 1768, the work of conversion in Baja California was given over to the Dominicans, and in Alta California to the Franciscans. When Mexico gained its independence from Spain in 1821, she succeeded as administrator of the fund. There were other changes as time went on, too numerous to include here.

Eugene Casserly, who was serving his first term in Congress at the time, filed a claim on March 30, 1870, with Hamilton Fish, Secretary of State. In 1872 Casserly and Doyle engaged a qualified associate, Philip Philips, to assist them at this important stage of the proceedings. Together they sought to prove that Mexico, by promising to pay the interest on the Fund, had thus acknowledged that the money was held in trust down to the secession of Alta California. The attorneys demanded that Mexico fulfill its promise to pay the interest to the church in California. This was the turning point in the belated proceedings.

The Claims Commission announced its decision on May 19, 1875. Mexican commissioner Manuel Zamacona moved to dismiss the case; the American commissioner, William Wadsworth, demanded payment by Mexico. Since the commissioners differed, Sir Edward Thornton, British Ambassador to the United States, was selected as an umpire to review the case. Casserly, Doyle, and Associates presented briefs, each one of which contained a summary of the case as presented to the Claims Commission.

On November 11, 1875, Thornton handed down his decision: "The umpire, consequently, awards that there be paid by the Mexican Government, on account of the above mentioned claim, the sum of nine hundred and four thousand, seven hundred Mexican gold dollars and seventy nine cents." This sum represented the six per cent interest on the Pious Fund from 1848 to 1869. Mexico paid the award as directed by Sir Edward Thornton.

Casserly earned a reputation for honesty and integrity in the field of law, for he worked diligently and conscientiously for his clients. His thorough investigation of his cases, as well as the clear and logical reasoning evident in his presentation at the bar, brought him recognition as an able and skilled attorney, and a leading member of the California bar in pioneer San Francisco.

The Civil War Period

WHEN EUGENE CASSERLY arrived in California he became an active and influential member of the Democratic Party. In the Presidential election of 1860, the question of secession had a disastrous effect on the unity of the party. When the committees met to select delegates to the national convention in Charleston, the Lecompton and anti-Lecompton delegates were irreconcilable. Separate conventions were then held at Richmond, where John Breckenridge won the nomination, and at Baltimore, where Stephen Douglas was chosen as the candidate.

Casserly threw his support to Douglas, but when Civil War threatened he became first and foremost a Unionist. He saw it as a question of loyalty or disloyalty, not a party issue. "I was for peace while peace was possible and for full concession and guarantee to the

States of the South while they allowed them to be offered. I take my stand without rancor but without hesitation, with my own government and country. There is no other place for the patriot."

Casserly was determined to have California declare herself definitely and enthusiastically for the Union. He saw only disaster in the prospect of California's seceding. "It will blast all her fair prospects at a stroke, destroy her credit, arrest the flow of wealth and population and paralyze all the elements of her posterity and power."

He was convinced that the majority of the people of California wished to remain with the Union, and therefore it was imperative that the voters should elect the officials who would follow the true sentiments of the people of the state. His pronouncements worked to the advantage of Leland Stanford, the Republican candidate, who won election for Governor in 1862 over John McConnell, a Breckenridge Democrat, since many Douglass Democrats had voted the Republican ticket in order to insure the election of a Union candidate.

Casserly, the Savior of the Democratic Party

ALTHOUGH he wholeheartedly supported President Abraham Lincoln, a Republican, during the Civil War, Casserly nonetheless remained a leading proponent of the Democratic party. Toward the close of the Civil War, the Democrats, faced with constant defeat, seemed doomed to extinction as an organization, had it not been for Casserly, who vowed to keep the party afloat. Though the California Democrats failed to elect their gubernatorial candidate in 1864, the next three years saw changes in the political balance so that the party achieved a complete triumph in 1867 with the election of Governor Henry Haight.

This was the first time in many years that the Democrats were in the majority in the California Legislature, with seventy Democrats and only ten Republicans. In that same year Frank McCoppin was swept into office as Mayor of San Francisco, beating out John Roberts of the Peoples Independent Party, who had the backing of the influential *Evening Bulletin.*

A rising star on the political scene, Casserly was elected Senator from California to serve in the Forty-first Congress in March 1869, replacing the retiring Irish-born Senator John Coness. At that same time the Republican party had swept General Ulysses Grant into the White House and had also captured the majority in both houses of Congress. As a result Casserly found he was one of only ten Democrats in a Senate dominated by war-triumphant Republicans.

Casserly, Co-founder of the U. S. Sanitary Commission

A PROVEN EXPERT in planning and organizing, Eugene Casserly took the lead in the formation of the United States Sanitary Commission, the forerunner of the Red Cross. His colleagues were M. C. Blake, D. C. McRuer, R. G. Sneath, and E. H. Washburn. This humanitarian program was initiated in New England and gradually took hold across the nation. Californians contributed over a million dollars to the fund, or a quarter of the total amount received by the commission. Their generosity can be attributed in no small measure to the unswerving patriotism of the Pro-Unionists led by Eugene Casserly, Governor John Downey, Senator David Broderick and others. The Commission jubilantly reported that "just at this crisis, when the Commission's plans were embarrassed by an inadequate supply of money, the Mayor of San Francisco, Maurice Carey Blake, telegraphed that a hundred thousand dollars had been raised in that city for the benefit of sick and wounded soldiers."

The saying "Once a Democrat always a Democrat" had a special meaning for Eugene Casserly. While he vigorously supported the Unionists in their war campaign, he was constantly at odds with the well-entrenched Republicans during the Reconstruction era after the war's end. He opposed the Radical Reconstruction Policy, as he termed it, with its financial burden on the Northern States and its political demands on the south.

In financial affairs he was committed to a strong currency and the continuance of the Gold Standard. He berated the Republicans for allowing the rapid growth of the national debt. He claimed that, "The men in power have not practiced economy, they have not reduced taxes, they have not brought the currency of the Government any nearer to par than they found it at the close of the war."

United States Senator, 1867-1869

A S A CONSEQUENCE of his unswerving loyalty to the Democratic Party, Casserly was elected United States Senator when the Party regained control in California in 1867. The political imbalance in Congress did not discourage him as he set out to meet the challenges that lay ahead. There were troublesome issues to be dealt with, not the least of which was the Fenian invasion of Canada, which added to the already strained relations between the United States and Great Britain.*

*The Fenians, precursors to Sinn Fein, were Irish nationalists determined to free Ireland from British rule.

Senator Casserly served on the Foreign Relations Committee with such stalwart legislators as Senators Charles Sumner of Massachusetts, William Fessenden and Hannibal Hamlin of Maine, Oliver Norton of Indiana, John Sherman of Ohio, and William Steward of Nevada. As an avowed Irish Nationalist like his father before him, his sympathy was with the Fenians. But he wisely perceived that this was not the time and place to make known his sentiments. And as it turned out he didn't have to; his peers, mostly Northern Senators, did nothing to deter the Fenians' efforts or to downplay their achievements. In fact, Senator Sumner attended Fenians gatherings on occasion, and left no doubt that he was in sympathy with their cause. Coming from such an important figure in the United States Congress, his actions infuriated the British authorities.

Anti-British feelings had reached an all-time high in the U.S. when it became known that the British were in sympathy with Confederates and had connived with them to sabotage the Union war effort on land and sea. By contrast, Americans felt indebted to the Irish, many of whom were Fenians, who had formed their own regiments and fought courageously on the side of the Union Army during the Civil War. Their bravery and fidelity on many a battlefield forms one the most heartwarming chapters in American history. President Ulysses Grant was well aware that had it not been for the Irish the Union Army might never have achieved victory over the Confederates.

Although the the war between the states had settled the question of the federal union, other serious problems, such as the legal status of the Southern States and the rights of Negroes, had to be worked out by Congress. There was also the vexing problem of Reconstruction, which involved questions of justice, expediency and above all party politics. In all these matters Senator Casserly was deeply and consistently involved. He served as a minority member of the Foreign Relations committee, on the Public Lands Committee, and on Printing with the firm of Anthony and Harris of the *Congressional Globe*.

The evolution of Reconstruction policy into law aroused constant resistance from minority Democrats, led by the indomitable Eugene Casserly. With his nine colleagues he vigorously attacked the proposed Reconstruction measures, which seemed to him planned to antagonize the southern states rather than ease their return to the Union. His speeches on important measures debated during President Grant's first administration show precisely where his interests lay. He made his presence felt time after time by his courage and tenacity in defense of the democratic principles which he believed were just, and by his efforts in the cause of peace.

He was also a powerful advocate for the repeal of the Tenure of Office Act, which would give the Senate the power to nominate appointive offices, and had been manipulated by radicals to curb the powers of Andrew Johnson, who assumed the office of President following the assassination of Abraham Lincoln. Casserly chided the Republicans, who were at odds amongst themselves on the advantages which the party might gain by repeal. Casserly argued that repeal of the law should stand on constitutional principles, not on party politics. "Where is the power of removal of certain officers of this government vested? It is a cardinal feature in our form of government, that where the executive and legislative powers are united in one man, there can be no liberty."

He concluded that if the Constitution gave the President the power to execute the laws, then he had the power to remove unacceptable officers in his department; moreover, it was "a notable fact that the leaders of the party which carried through the measure are not agreed among themselves as to the ground upon which to rest it under the Constitution."

To the suggestion that the law be suspended for a few months, Senator Casserly arose and lambasted the Republicans: "If it's a good law, maintain it; if bad, do away with it. I am for repeal of the Law, because I believe the Tenure of Office Act to have endangered some of the most important balances of the Constitution."

Consequently Congress passed a modified act which allowed an officer to be removed either by consent of the Senate or by appointment of a successor accepted by Congress. During Senate recess, the President could suspend an officer and nominate a successor within thirty days of the next Senate session. Complete repeal came under the Cleveland administration.

Casserly and the Railroad

CASSERLY'S INTEREST in the Transcontinental Railroad was akin to his concern over Reconstruction legislation. The unprecedented venture was very much an Irish affair. The Central Pacific tracks leading west from Omaha, Nebraska, were laid by brawny Irishmen, while the Union Pacific, working eastward from Sacramento, employed mostly Chinese workmen under the supervision of Irish-American foremen. The United States Government provided generous subsidies to both construction companies, as well as lavish land grants and the right to sell bonds to finance the work.

Despite such generosity the companies informed the authorities that they might not be able to complete the railroads under the terms of the contract. Senator Casserly and other legislators could not believe that the railroads would default on their bonds, since the Union Pacific had already paid big dividends to its stockholders and the company was under obligation to return a government grant of some $28 million when the road was in operation. An alarmed Congress passed a law empowering the Attorney General to ascertain whether or not the franchise of both companies had been forfeited by illegal dividends on stock. If so, legal proceedings against the companies would be instituted forthwith. Casserly regarded the issue in a broader sense:

> The real question is how best to secure the completion of this great transcontinental railroad. This was the object for which the government bestowed upon these companies, monies and lands with a munificence unknown in history. This bill is directed to the specific point of compelling the giving of security by these companies, to secure the completion of the roads. The Government has made a contract by statute with these companies for the building of these roads.

As Casserly saw it, the transcontinental railroad was a responsibility of the legislature to the American people.

> We should not go home to our constituents unless we are able to say 'We have done what we should for you; we have provided that these roads should be completed according to law as first class roads; we have enabled the chief magistrate to demand security . . . that these roads be completed, and we have enabled him to go to court in the name of the United States . . . to compel it.

Suffice to say that the railroads in the end fulfilled their contracts and completed the last section at Promontory, Utah, in May 1869.

However it was not until President Grant's second term that the scandal came out following a congressional inquiry. It showed that the Credit Mobilier for the Union Pacific received $73 million for work that cost them less than $50 million, and involved men such as James Blaine.

Eugene Casserly, who served on three of the most important

committees, was ever the voice of reason and reconciliation. In the debates on expenditures Casserly, a fiscal conservative, proposed putting a limit on indebtedness unless a specific law was passed to authorize a special expenditure. "The Legislature shall not create any debt which shall exceed the sum of three hundred dollars, except in case of war to repel invasion, unless the same shall be authorized by law for some single project".

In order that citizens could be informed about any public work submitted to the people at a general election, Casserly demanded that the particulars of the proposed project "shall be published in at least one newspaper throughout the state for three months preceding the election at which it is submitted to the people." Casserly's masterful proposition was incorporated in the Constitution as part of article XVI on State and City Indebtedness.

In California the memory lingers of the railroad barons— Stanford, Huntington, Crocker and Hopkins—who became the biggest land owners and employers in the state, with phenomenal influence on state government. They could manipulate freight rates at will and could make or break almost any merchant, industrialist or agriculturist in the state. Their exploits drew the wrath of Senator Hiram Johnson in later years. But that's another story.

Governor's Pardoning Power

THE SUGGESTION that the pardoning powers of the Governor be allotted to a special board was ably refuted by Eugene Casserly, who could see no advantage in divisive responsibility. "What we want in our government is concentrated responsibility in the executive, not a divided or watered responsibility. With a concentrated responsibility you are surer to have your work well done; without it you have something which is neither one thing nor the other." Casserly's proposal was unanimously adopted and the Governor continued to exercise his authority under the original California Constitution adopted in 1849.

Judges' Salaries

A NUMBER of the legislators evidently had little regard for the judicial branch of government and advocated leaner salaries as a measure of economy. Casserly cautioned his fellow members against such a move. Generally speaking, he claimed, "An economical government is an honest and pure government, and if the people of California desired capable men in the judiciary, they must be willing to pay a satisfactory salary." He hesitated for a moment and then said:

I am one of those who do not believe that the most important thing in the administration of justice is that it should be cheap. The really important thing is that it should be right, sensible, conscientious, and speedy. . . . As a mere question of economy, it would be a very serious mistake, in my opinion, for us to reduce the salary of judges. One incompetent judge costs the State more than five judges that are honest and capable, as a judge should be.

With the support of other lawyers at the convention, his argument swayed the legislators, and became the law of the land under Article VI of the State Constitution.

On other important matters, such as freedom of the press, Senator Casserly left no doubt as to where he stood. "The people of this country have always classed freedom of the press among their fundamental rights." He reminded the assemblage that the First American Congress in 1774, as well as the California State Convention in 1849, specified "that liberty of the press is essential to freedom and ought to be inviolate." Casserly firmly believed that the framers could not have spoken so explicitly if they intended nothing more than "that restricted and slavish press which may not publish anything, true or false, that reflects on the character and administration of public men."

However, he opposed the idea that the press should claim such unlimited freedom that it would with impunity publish falsehood. Such an abuse of power would be incompatible with the good order of society.

The Supreme Court

As a lawyer Casserly had an abiding interest in legal questions during his term in the Senate. The Supreme Court underwent attack during Grant's first administration. In order to prevent President Johnson from making appointments, Congress reduced the number of justices from ten to seven in 1866; then when Grant came into office it restored the number to nine. Because the Supreme Court members were overburdened, the appointment of eighteen justices was proposed, with the idea that many of them would discharge Circuit Court duties. Casserly vehemently opposed the plan, saying "There is a very serious objection to such a large court set to work in the manner proposed. The smaller the court of review is, the better for efficient and rapid discharge of business." He could not see in the division of the Court anything but "constitutional questions of a very grave character," and he did not believe it wise "to leave a fundamental question of constitutional power to be a trouble and obstruction to the members of that court and to the validity of its decisions for all times."

The final bill as proposed by Senator Casserly provided for a Chief Justice and eight Associate Justices for the Supreme Court, and for a separate set of judges named to Circuit Courts under the supervision of assigned members of the Supreme Court.

Casserly, an Advocate of Human Rights

ONE OF HIS final acts in the Senate involved the suspension of the Habeas Corpus and an Amnesty Act in 1872. President Abraham Lincoln had suspended the privilege of Habeas Corpus as a necessity during the Civil War. Congress authorized this suspension by the acts of 1863 and 1867.

In May 1872 the new Habeas Corpus and Amnesty Acts became the focal point of a political confrontation in Congress. The Radicals tried to rush through a bill extending the President's suspending power in time to have it voted on together with the Amnesty Act, which the liberal Republicans and the Democrats strongly favored. The Democrats, led by Senator Casserly, were equally determined to defeat the scheme by forcing the Republican majority to pass the Amnesty Act without amendment or political bargaining.

Casserly spoke forcefully on Amnesty: "There is nobody standing in the way of amnesty except the majority who vow and declare their determination that amnesty shall not pass until something else is passed before it." The Democrats worked together to secure public pledges from the radicals that Amnesty would be passed. The end result was more than the outnumbered Democrats could have expected, for Amnesty did in fact become law when the Senate adopted the House Amnesty bill as it was presented to them.

Senator Casserly's years in the Senate were marked by his tempered oratory and sincerity of purpose at all times. He served faithfully and honorably in the Congress of the United States during one of the most trying and distressful periods in the nation's history. With prejudice directing public policy at the time, the burden of responsibility became doubly difficult for men of such high principle as Eugene Casserly.

The constant and overpowering demands of political life aggravated Casserly's ill health, and with but two-thirds of his term completed, he announced his resignation in November 1873. The

Governor appointed John Hager to complete his term in the Senate. Following his return to San Francisco in that same year Casserly resumed the practice of law on a limited basis, while spending most of his time quietly at home with his dear wife and their three children.

In both his public and private lives, Casserly never failed in the honest, faithful and satisfactory discharge of his duties. In domestic relations he was singularly happy. In religious convictions he was a steadfast adherent of the Catholic faith, and much esteemed by the higher ecclesiastics in the Archdiocese of California.

His earthly career is closed, but his influence, like that of other ingenious and trustworthy Irish-Californians, is of perennial duration. In the outer world, the lowest whisper that is breathed, nay, the slightest motion that is made is recorded in the realm of nature, though no trace of it is visible to us. So too, in the moral world every act or utterance, though we cannot define its scope, is a permanent contribution, a mixed blessing which constantly descends as a lasting heritage to future generations.

> We men who, in our morn of youth, defied
> The elements, must vanish. Be it so!
> Enough, if something from our hands have power
> To live, and act, and serve the future hour,
> And if, as toward the silent tomb we go,
> Thro love, thro hope and faith's transcendent dower,
> We feel we are greater than we know.

LITTLE IS KNOWN of Eugene Casserly during the last years of his very active and fruitful life. He spent his last few days quietly with his wife Theresa and family, and died in his home on Van Ness Avenue in San Francisco on June 14, 1883.

Casserly was buried from Saint Mary's Cathedral, where Archbishop Alemany celebrated a solemn requiem mass. The Bar Association attended in a body, as did a number of religious orders who were recipients of his generosity. His pallbearers included men prominent in San Francisco public life: General Scofield, Justice Field, Judge McKinstry, Judge Coffee, Hall McAllister, A. H. Longborough, William Norris, D. J. Oliver, Richard Tobin and John Deane.

Dr. Hugh Toland
Courtesy Jim Toland

– 13 –

DR. HUGH TOLAND

PIONEER SAN FRANCISCO PHYSICIAN

18?? - 1880

LEGENDARY PHYSICIAN, Doctor Hugh Toland, from Columbia, South Carolina, arrived in San Francisco in 1852 and pioneered the development of a medical institution that would become world renowned. Here was a man who kept his deceased wife in a glass coffin in his office for twenty-five years— merely an eerie sidelight in a life of medical eminence. A brilliant young man, Hugh had learned to read at the age of four, and graduated at the head of his class in medical school. Hugh Toland's Medical Institute on Stockton Street, founded in 1864, was the forerunner of today's University of California Medical Center on Parnassus Heights.

San Francisco was not the homey Old South, where Doctor Toland had grown up, but was a rather primitive society in search of stability and an identity of its own. There was no public health service or a county hospital to care for the indigent sick and dying, and nowhere to bury a man but in a pauper's cemetery in the sand dunes.

Doctor Toland began the practice of medicine on the second floor of a flimsy wood frame building on Montgomery Street by the water's edge. It appeared so forlorn that a writer for the *Alta* newspaper said it reminded him of the plaster houses of Paris during the reign of King Louis Philippe.

Some years later a large brick building, the American Theatre, on Sansome Street near Sacramento, was constructed. As a result of the building's foundation being laid in mud into which sand had been deposited, the weight of the audience, on opening night, caused the building to sink two inches. Fortunately, the locals took it all in stride as if it were a part of the performance. Flimsy construction quickly became a thing of the past when the first wave of gold diggers struck it rich in the mines and returned to San Francisco to invest their earnings in land development and construction. Doctor Toland belonged to the Old South Park set, the majority of whom were either Irish immigrants or their descendants.

The Toland Family

THE SURNAME TOLAND was O'Tuathalain in Gaelic, later changed to O'Toolan(d), and O'Tolan(d) and finally the O was dropped. O'Tuathalain (pronounced Dwath-leen) were members of the Hy-Naull (Ui Neill tribes of Ulster, Meath and Connaught). The family and its tribes can be traced back to the first century A.D.

Most Irish names were Anglicized in the latter part of the sixteenth century and thus the name became O'Tuathal, and O'Tuathalain, meaning grandson of. In time these names became Towlane, O'Tolane, O'Toolane, O'Toolan, Toolan, Toland, Tolan and Toolis. The very common Irish name of O'Toole is also derived from Tuathal.

In Ireland all people bearing the same last name are entitled to the same coat of arms. This rule could include different surnames derived from one common family name. In the case of the Tolands the original name was Tuathal and all derivatives of this name would be entitled to use this coat of arms. The Toland family takes its name from Tuathal Techmar, High-King of Tara in the first century A.D. the ancestor of the Ui Neill, while the O'Toole family, Ui Tuathail took their name from Tuathal Ui Nuiredaig, High-King of Leinster in the tenth century A.D.

A branch of the O'Tauthal clan migrated with the O'Donnells in the seventeenth century to County Mayo, where their Anglicized names became Tolan and Toolis. From the latter clan came one Patrick Toolis to San Francisco in the 1920s, where he became active in Irish affairs as co-founder of the Mayo Men's Association.

Another branch of the Tualthals (O'Tooles) of Wicklow were driven to Connaught ("To Hell or to Connaught" was the cry) in the wake of the Cromwellian wars. They became quite numerous in both Galway and Mayo. The name is mentioned in connection with the Sept Hy-Niall, descendants of King Niall of the Nine Hostages.

The ancestral home of the O'Tolands is in Cardonagh, County Donegal, which lies on the most northerly point of the Emerald Isle near Malin Head. A lone survivor of the clan, Mickey Toland, in his seventies, lives in a 300-year-old thatched cottage, one of only five left in the village.

In America the Toland name lives on in the world-renowned University of California Medical Center on the slope of Mount Sutro, from the rootstock of Toland Medical College, founded by the intrepid Doctor Hugh Toland.

It began its rise as one of the world's greatest institutions of medical learning and research under its first dean, Doctor Herbert Moffitt. The hospital features a rigorous residency program, under which many of the West's outstanding specialists were trained. It now has schools of dentistry, veterinary medicine and pharmacy, a radiological laboratory with a 70-million-volt synchrotron for cancer treatment, a Metabolic Research Laboratory and a Radioactivity Research Center. This renowned medical institution is committed to the future, but a future tied gratefully to the past, and to one man in particular: Doctor Hugh Toland, whose foresight, medical acumen and persistence made it all possible.

Doctor Toland was a successful physician and a widower in Columbia, South Carolina. A sedate man, Toland stood well over six feet, with jet black hair, piercing blue eyes and a jutting, determined jaw. When he met the winsome beauty, 21-year-old Mary America Avery, at her debut ball in Columbia, it was love at first sight for the solemn medico, who was taken by the girl's striking beauty. Despite the disparity in their ages, they married after a whirlwind courtship.

The newlyweds settled down in Columbia, where Doctor Toland had a well-established medical practice. However, the discovery of gold in California and the threat of war between the Northern and Southern states led to a change in their plans.

Knowing that his young bride was as delicate as she was beautiful, Hugh Toland thought that California's salubrious climate would improve Mary's health.

California Bound

Knowing of Mary America's mother's concern about her daughter's health, the good doctor made a firm promise before leaving that should any ill befall her in California he would return her to her home to Columbia. He also invited Mary's brother, Doctor E.T. Avery, to accompany them on the hazardous journey west.

The newlyweds planned well for the long journey, sparing no expense in travel arrangements. The Toland caravan followed the trail blazed by earlier argonauts and arrived safely in California in the fall of 1852. The party set up camp on a warm September night a few miles north of San Francisco, unaware that area was infected with cholera. Mary America Toland caught the dreaded disease and suc-cumbed three days later. The weathered grave stones in Mission Dolores Cemetery are grim reminders of the frightening epidemic, which felled young men and women in the prime of life.

Doctor Toland's painful, wracking grief etched deeply into his stern face as he felt personally responsible for her untimely death. He was so heart-broken that he had her lifeless form embalmed, and kept it in a glass coffin in his San Francisco office for more than 25 years.

Eight years later he married another Mary, a poetess of consider-able acclaim. She too was a remarkable woman, presumably free from jealousy, for she apparently never objected to the continued presence of her predecessor, cold and still.

A short while before he died in 1880, Doctor Toland recalled the promise he had made to Mary America's mother, and took her back to Columbia, where she was laid to rest near her home in Ebenezer cemetery. His third wife, Mary Bertha Toland, graciously accompa-nied him on the long and tiresome journey to South Carolina and participated in the obsequies.

The epitaph on her grave was said to have been composed by Doctor Toland himself.

> No one so beautiful as she,
> Fair of form and face.
> A queenly mien with modesty,
> Crowned in every grace.

Toland Medical College

FOLLOWING A BRIEF local practice in Newberry, South Carolina, Dr. Toland traveled to Paris for surgical training at the Hotel Die, mother house of the Sisters of Charity, founded by St. Vincent de Paul. When his term in Paris came to a close he returned home to South Carolina and took up where he left off with renewed vigor and inner confidence. Little wonder that he had mixed feelings about coming West in 1852, thereby forfeiting a thriving practice in South Carolina.

Doctor Toland became San Francisco's most popular and wealthi-est early medical practitioner. A family doctor in every sense of the word, he was known to have treated one hundred patients a day, and provided his home-brewed medicines according to their needs. His curatives he concocted himself and stored in used beer kegs. He also bottled, packaged and shipped them by mail all over the west. Little

Toland Hall is shown here in 1873, at the time when the Toland Medical
College became associated with the University of California. The building
was located at Stockton and Chestnut Streets in San Francisco.
Courtesy Jim Toland

Hugo Toland, only son of Dr. Hugh Toland, became a star of Broadway musicals in New York.
Courtesy Jim Toland

wonder he died leaving an estate in excess of $2 million.

With little fanfare he opened his pioneer medical institution, the first of its kind in California, on Stockton Street. No one remembers the original name, Toland Medical College. There were only eight students when its doors opened in 1864. This did not deter Doctor Toland, a brilliant man who knew the value of an education.

In San Francisco Doctor Toland's success was truly remarkable. He had the foresight to open up an office in the city's business district on Montgomery Street, to meet the demands of an ever increasing population, many of whom were miners in dire need of medical attention. In addition to his lucrative medical practice, he was obliged to spend considerable tine at the Toland Medical Center.

By coincidence it was Toland's meeting with a fellow medic, Dr. Richard "King" Cole, that led to the development of the institution we know today. Doctor Toland had been one of the many physicians who attended James King of William, the newspaper editor who was gunned down by James Casey in May 1856. As King lay wounded in an upstairs room on Montgomery Street, some twenty doctors probed, examined and argued amongst themselves about how to save his life. While all this debate was going on the patient succumbed to his injuries.

Doctor Toland drew the wrath of his peers, including his close associate Doctor Cole, by maintaining that the publisher's death was the result of bungling rather than the assassin's bullet.

San Franciscans mourned the death of James King of William as the funeral cortege wended its way through a city in distress. Casey paid with his life on the scaffold at the hands of the notorious Vigilantes, a self-appointed organization whose members took the law in their own hands and meted out mob justice.

In the meantime the two leading physicians, Doctors Toland and Cole, reconciled their differences and pooled their knowledge in the development of a medical school that would be forever worthy of their calling. The school was financed for the most part by Doctor Toland, the only man in a position to do so at that time. In due course Doctor Cole was elected president of the American Medical Association and became dean of the medical school as well.

In 1873 the University of California regents agreed to incorporate Toland's school as a medical department. As a condition of the transfer, the regents further agreed to name one of the school's amphitheaters Toland Hall, a name it retains to this very day.

The development of the world-renowned medical center began during Adolph Sutro's term as Mayor of San Francisco. A civic-minded philanthropist, Sutro donated a thirteen-acre tract as the site of the proposed Medical Center. Other acquisitions brought it up to its present boundary lines on the panoramic hillside. It was Doctor Cole who perceived the idea of an affiliated professional college system to house the various schools on one campus. The School of Medicine, established in 1873, was the first of the University's affiliates, followed by the schools of Pharmacy, Law, Dentistry, and Veterinary Science.

Under the leadership of Doctor Herbert Miff and his peers, George Whipple (Nobel Prize winner), Karl Meyer, internationally acclaimed epidemiologist, and Howard Naffziger, famous brain surgeon, the University of California, San Francisco (UCSF) became eminent in the fields of medical research and clinical accomplishments.

The towering building complex, visible for miles around, stands as a beacon of hope for the sick and injured who come from all over the world to avail themselves of the most up-to-date facilities the medical profession has to offer.

*A gathering of one branch of the Toland family
in San Francisco, April 1904. Courtesy Jim Toland*

Doctor Toland's Lone Mountain

THE HISTORY of Lone Mountain brings to light the lives and times of two of San Francisco's most illustrious pioneers, Archbishop Joseph Sodoc Alemany and Doctor Hugh Toland. Both men came on different missions, the former to minister to people's spiritual needs and the latter to care for their health and physical well-being. Over the years they became inseparable friends, working hand in hand for the welfare of those early settlers.

The old Spanish trail that led from Mission Dolores to the Presidio of San Francisco ran along the ridge known to old-timers as the Divisadero, the memory of which is kept alive in a street by that name. On the brow of the hill in the Presidio, facing north, was the famed El Polen Spring, whose water was said to make men virile and women fruitful.

Everything west of Divisadero Street was known as the "Outside Lands." It was not until 1866 that the settlers acquired clear title to their properties, subsequent to an Act of Congress on March 8 of that year. Thereupon the San Francisco Board of Supervisors passed its famous Ordinance number 800, "For the settlement and quieting titles to the land in the City and County of San Francisco, situated above the high water mark of the Bay of San Francisco and the Pacific Ocean and within the corporate limits of the city of San Francisco." This order was ratified by the California State Legislature on March 27, 1869. As of that date all residents of the Outside Lands, squatters or otherwise, having quietly claimed their holdings to the city, were given clear title forthwith.

This put an end to the vexing question of squatters rights that had plagued the city fathers for years on end. The man most responsible for this act of fair play was Mayor Frank McCoppin, who fol-

Mary Bertha Toland, third wife of Dr. Hugh Toland. Courtesy Jim Toland

lowed up by having the city reserve for itself 1,000 acres for Golden Gate Park and various parcels of land for public squares and playgrounds.

Under this provision the City of San Francisco granted clear title to the large rural cemeteries which were then opening up. The old public cemetery in North Beach (bounded by Powell, Stockton, Lombard and Chestnut streets) had been closed, and the bodies reinterred at Yerba Buena cemetery in Hayes Valley, where the Civic Center is now located. The city's first cemetery at Mission Dolores served the needs of Catholics from the founding of the Mission until some twenty years after California came under American rule in 1846. Laurel Hill had been opened for burials as early as 1854.

The Bishop had long had his eye on Lone Mountain for a Catholic Cemetery. With the tremendous growth of the population, he saw the necessity of providing larger burial places for the dead. In this, the Irish played a leading role, as they have done in everything for the early development of California and of the Catholic Church as well. None was more noteworthy than Doctor Hugh Toland, who sold and deeded to the Archbishop his prized holdings of 43 acres, which had within its limits the solitary peak known as Lone Mountain.

*Three members of an
illustrious family:
Top left: Charles Daniel Toland,
Featherweight pro boxer and founder
of Teamsters Union Local 85,
San Francisco.
Center: Dr. Clarence G. Toland, Los
Angeles, president of the California
Medical Association, 1934.
Bottom, left: John Toland
Courtesy Jim Toland*

Bishop Alemany then got a commitment from the owners of the surrounding properties, which were mostly in Irish hands; a 50-acre parcel owned by Michael Cook, a pioneer farmer, 59 acres of the property belonging to Edward Martin of the Hibernia Bank, and lesser acreage from John Williams, James Creigh and John Sullivan. The first recorded interment in Calvary cemetery was that of Joseph Soultier, a native of Canada, on October 14, 1860.

Just as the early Spanish explorers had raised the Cross on the heights above the Presidio, so too did Archbishop Alemany mark the pinnacle of Lone Mountain. When it came time to erect the huge cross, the work was entrusted to another Irishman, a building contractor named John J. Doyle. On August 1, 1862, the Bishop dedicated the gigantic cross, which could be seen for miles around. From 1862 onwards the Cross stretched its gaunt arms in benediction over the great city of St. Francis. For all these years the symbol of Christian faith has pointed heaven-ward, a constant reminder of our citizenship with God in heaven, man's eternal goal.

Fortunately, the building of the San Francisco College for Women in 1931 insures the Church's continuous presence on the high mountain. From that lofty position the College, now a part of the Jesuit University of San Francisco, and the world-renowned University of California Medical Center will face each across the valley as reminders of two great San Franciscans—the saintly Archbishop Joseph Sadoc Alemany and the indefatigable physician, Doctor Hugh Toland.

A Multi Family Tree

DOCTOR HUGH TOLAND JONES of Santa Ana sheds further light on his wide-spread physician-filled family, according to an article in the *San Francisco Chronicle* on March 25, 1970. According to Doctor Jones, Dr. Hugh Toland's father, John Toland, arrived in Charleston, South Carolina, in the 1800s. He left Ireland at the age of 18, after resisting the seizure of his father's wagon and team by the English constabulary.

John Toland's oldest son Joseph (also a doctor) was born in 1803, and Joseph's son, John Francis Toland, born 26 years later, was Doctor Hugh Jones's grandfather. Many Tolands, women as well as men, have been doctors. In past years there were seven in Southern California alone, and most likely all of them were descendants of the John Toland who was banished from Ireland like many of his countrymen following the Act of Union in 1801, making England and

Ireland one nation, under English rule.

The Toland family tree includes one Irene Toland, who practiced medicine in Saint Louis, Missouri. During the Spanish-American war she served on a hospital ship in Cuba and died at Santiago Bay in 1898. According to Professor James Robert Toland, a member of the faculty of San Francisco State University and former copy editor for the *San Francisco Chronicle*, the Tolands can trace their roots to County Donegal. The ancestral home of the clan is centered in the hamlet of Cardonagh, which lies some twenty miles south of Malin Head, the most northerly point in Ireland. During a visit to Donegal Jim Toland and his wife Laura of San Francisco were both surprised and elated to meet an aging Mickey Toland, the lone survivor of the once numerous clan in old Cardonagh, living in a thatched cottage erected in the 1600s.

Doctor Hugh Toland had an only son, Hugo, who was eleven years of age when his father died in 1880. Unlike his father, Hugo chose the stage for his career and eventually became an accomplished actor. He was a close friend of actress Lillian Russell and eventually became her leading man. Chief Justice Hugo Black, who was a distant cousin to Doctor Toland, as a young boy saw his namesake perform in Birmingham, Alabama.

Mary Bertha, third spouse of Dr. Hugh Toland and mother of Hugo, outlived her husband by fifteen years and died in the old Occidental Hotel on Montgomery Street in 1895.

The Tolands are buried in Cypress Lawn Cemetery in Colma, along with the ashes of their only son Hugo, who died in Philadelphia in 1908. Doctor Hugh Toland's memory lives on in the magnificent University of California Medical Center in San Francisco, of which he was a founder.

James Earl Cunningham
Courtesy Louise Cunningham

– 14 –

JAMES EARL CUNNINGHAM

SAN BERNARDINO'S BOY WONDER

1916 - 1992

JAMES EARL CUNNINGHAM combined three careers: civic, judicial and military. He rose to prominence in San Bernardino, the largest county in California, a massive empire of more than 20,000 square miles, which could swallow three or four eastern states. It was even larger when the boundary lines were drawn up in 1853, and was then the largest county in the world.

A native of Santa Barbara but a resident of San Bernardino since the age of two, "Jimmie," as he was affectionately known, was destined to be successful in every undertaking nurtured by his energy. He earned his spurs as an orator perched on a soap box on the sidewalk outside his home, giving passionate speeches about any subject that caught his attention.

Almost everywhere he went Jimmie was called upon to say a few words about the topic of the moment, and invariably he knew the right thing to say. This trait proved advantageous in later years when Cunningham ran for public office in Southern California.

If there had not been a Jimmie Cunningham, someone would have had to create one, for he was truly one of a kind: a loving husband and father, kindly brother and model uncle, a man ever faithful to the tenets of his church, God and country. For nigh on half a century he served his native state with honor and dignity as Mayor of San Bernardino, California State Senator and Superior Court judge.

When he was elected mayor in 1947, at age thirty, he was the youngest chief executive in the city's history and by all accounts the youngest in the nation. Few men have been so successful in so many fields of public service. An exemplar of the highest order and an inspiration to the youth of America, Cunningham was like the legendary

"Minstrel Boy." There was no way of stopping this fearless San Bernardino youth, who had been in the vanguard of the Normandy invasion at the age of 27.

Cunningham was born in 1916 of Irish-American parents. His father, Wilfred, was a traveling salesman for the Santa Fe Railway and often took one of the children on business trips, which could last for several days. More often than not it was Jimmie, the liveliest and most inquisitive of the boys.

The spirited youngster acquired his primary and secondary education in the schools of San Bernardino, and in 1935 enrolled in Loyola University in Los Angeles, earning a Bachelor of Science and Bachelor of Laws. As war clouds drew closer, he registered for military duty in 1941 and was drafted into the army as a private. Cunningham was admitted to the California State Bar in his soldier's uniform, setting aside any thought of practicing law for the duration of the war.

While stationed at Camp Haan near Riverside, Cunningham was granted special leave to go to Los Angeles, where he was admitted to federal court practice by Judge Harrison, a family friend and former San Bernardino attorney. Promoted to corporal, he applied immediately for officer training and was assigned to officer candidate school at Fort Lee, Virginia. In 1942 Cunningham was commissioned a second lieutenant. In 1944, he was on his way to Normandy with the U.S. First Army. Lieutenant Cunningham took part in the Normandy landing, winning five battle stars along the way.

A born leader, he rose to become a highly decorated captain by war's end. As a qualified lawyer he was given a special assignment as a military examiner to review in depth the cases of Jewish and other prisoners liberated by Allied forces from the infamous concentration camp at Buchenwald, Germany. Subsequently he served as military judge in the province of Leipzig, as well as legal counsel with the 21st Army Corps.

After his discharge on December 15, 1945, Captain Cunningham returned to San Bernardino and took a job as a deputy in the district attorney's office. Six months later he took up private practice under the firm name of Cunningham and Parry.

The Cunningham Roots

THE SURNAME Cunningham is quite numerous in Ireland and can be found in all four provinces. In the Ulster counties of Antrim and Down, Cunninghams are for the most part of Scottish origin. In the republic's western counties of Mayo, Galway and Roscommon, they are of pure Gaelic stock. Their ancestral homeland is located in a triangle where the three counties meet: Ballyhaunis in County Mayo, Dunmore in County Galway and Castlerea in County Roscommon. And from that lineage came the Cunninghams of San Bernardino.

The original forms of the name in the English language were O'Cunnigan and MacCunnigan. However the names were Anglicized during Britain's centuries of occupation and control in Ireland. The native Irish were forced to drop the O and the Mac and assume an English sounding name. Hence Cunnigan (O'Cunnigan) became Cunningham.

Despite the total destruction of the Gaelic Order in the early 1600s as mandated by the Act of Union, making England and Ireland one nation, the Cunninghams vehemently refused to accept English rule. This may account for the fact that no coat of arms is on record for either O'Cunnigan or MacCunnigan in Dublin Castle, which was for long under British control. What the records do reveal are the names of prominent Irishmen named Cunningham. Among them, Timothy Cunningham was the leading philanthropist of the Royal Irish Academy; Marquis Henry Conyngham, a man of considerable influence, was an Irish parliamentarian in the (English) House of Commons during the American Revolution. In association with Edmund Burke, the great Irish-born voice for political freedom, Cunningham manifested support for the American rebels led by George Washington.

In America and California in particular the name is prominent in pages of city telephone directories. In the 1949 San Bernardino City Directory, for instance, the list of Cunninghams is quite extensive, beginning with Arthur P. Cunningham, a miner, and ending with Wayne Cunningham, a city fireman.

The current San Francisco telephone directory bears the names of 127 Cunninghams, including those active in the business and professional world, from art galleries to a moving and storage firm, all too numerous to mention.

The Cunninghams of "Wild Geese" fame (Irishmen who fought in the 19th century armies of France and Spain) are noted among the Spanish nobility, along with such greats as Conde (Count) Alesandria O'Reilly, Generalissimo of the Spanish Armies and Ministero of the Spanish colonies in America, who joined Viceroy Bucarelli in planting the standard of Spain and taking possession of Alta California in the name of the king. There were others, like Conde de Lacy, Spanish ambassador to Russia and president of the War Council, and Felipe de Barry, who served as the second governor of Spanish California.

Wars of conquest and depredation drove the cream of Irish youth to the continent of Europe. More than 30,000 fighting men left Ireland in Cromwell's time. Many of the Cunninghams, who resisted English rule, were forced to leave their native land or take the consequences. In this case, Ireland's loss was California's gain.

The Cunninghams in America

JAMES CUNNINGHAM'S great-grandfather immigrated to America in the late 1840s and settled in New Jersey, where he stayed in a boarding house managed by a close friend of his mother. While there he fell in love with and married the landlady's daughter. Their son, James Valentine Cunningham, was born in 1882. With the exciting news of the Gold Rush in California and the fortunes that were being made, the family decided to try their luck in the new west.

On their journey west by way of Iowa, the mother became ill and was cared for by the close-knit Irish community in Davenport. The Cunninghams were so taken by the friendliness and hospitality of the people that they decided to settle there. James Valentine Cunningham grew up in Davenport, where he met and married an Irish colleen, Hannah Condon.

James V. was a railroad engineer who never tired of telling the story of how, when pulling the superintendent's private car, he was instructed to go as fast as he could so his boss could keep an appointment in Davenport. He got the big eight-wheel steam engine up to sixty miles an hour on the fifty-mile run. For this unheard-of feat he received a pat on the back and was told, "That was great work, Jimmie." The accolade became part of family lore.

In the Irish tradition the oldest son was named after his father's father, and hence the name given our subject follows in that order.

Louise Clark was born in Redlands, California, where her father was killed in an accident when she was an infant. Her mother eventually married a Canadian who owned a sheep ranch in the province of Alberta. Louise moved to the ranch when she was eight years old to be with her mother. At the close of World War II she returned to her former home in Redlands to live with her grandparents.

Louise was working in the district attorney's office in San Bernardino in 1946 when a handsome Army Officer, Captain James Cunningham, came home to San Bernardino at the end of the war.

When they met it was love at first sight. Following a brief courtship they were united in marriage in 1947. There's an old Irish saying that "wherever there is a good man there too you will find a good woman to cheer him on." Louise Cunningham put her husband's interests ahead of her own, stood by his side in the battle of life and cheered him on when the going got tough. Louise had much to offer in her own right.

Theirs was a happy marriage, blessed with six robust children. The union lasted 46 years, until Judge Cunningham's death at the age of 75, in June 1992. He left his wife, Louise; three sons, James E. Jr., Joseph P., and John M.; three daughters, Renee Daniels, Mary Pickett and Teresa Cunningham; a brother, Frank C. Cunningham; and nine grandchildren.

In all of California history where the Irish were involved, no one surpasses San Bernardino's illustrious son as both shaper and exemplar of the city and county whose interests he served.

Political novice to competent legislator

As A WAR VETERAN with countless friends, James Cunningham ran for Mayor of San Bernardino in 1947. Although opposed by veteran incumbent W. C. Seccombe, he won election by a comfortable majority. Captain Cunningham became Mayor Cunningham, and from then on it was onward and upward in the political arena all the way to State Senator and Superior Court Judge.

His mayoral administration was progressive and forward-looking in matters for the benefit of the community at large. Long before women's rights were a popular issue, Cunningham formed a council of the various women's organizations and worked with them for more effective legislation dealing with crimes against women and children.

Mayor Cunningham was instrumental in having his city cooperate with other cities and counties throughout Southern California in the state's battle against organized crime. He saw to it that San Bernardino would play a large part in the statewide anti-crime program, inasmuch as it was the first major city in the path of automobile and rail traffic entering Southern California from the east. He emphasized that an estimated 85 percent of the tourists arriving in California for the first time did so by way of San Bernardino. In this important undertaking there would be no halfway measures as far as he was concerned. To back it up, he promised that the police department would cooperate with other major cities by dispatching copies of offenses and arrest records to other police departments.

The Cunningham family enjoys a carousel ride.
Courtesy Louise Cunningham

The mayor, in response to the governor's commission, said that narcotic rings and bookmakers were the two major problems facing state law enforcement officers. He strongly backed a proposed measure to change two procedures then followed by officers, to eliminate the detail involved in minor cases and thus allow the officers to devote more time to major offenses.

The changes he suggested would (1) make it permissible for officers to issue citations in cases involving misdemeanors in place of taking someone into custody and police court trials; and (2) allow officers to place drunks in a state hospital instead of city jail. In all of this Mayor Cunningham, at the age of 31, proved that he possessed more logic than administrators twice his age.

He strongly endorsed the "red light" abatement proceedings filed by the vigilant district attorney, Jerome Kavanagh, against one of the city's leading hotels. Kavanagh said he had proof that prostitution was being practiced on the premises, and asked the court to allow him to padlock the hotel for one year. Mayor Cunningham declared,

> Prostitution is a social curse and will not be tolerated. I have ordered Chief Murdock to continue with diligence the stamping out of this demoralizing and crippling vice. Regardless of the nefarious interests of a small and vicious group of white slave dealers, San Bernardino will be a clean city. Persons interested in such illegal traffic must know that their presence in our community is unwanted. They will not be permitted to engage in such illicit gains.

THE FOLLOWING WEEK, on November 18, 1947, Mayor Cunningham announced the establishment of a police training school, a permanent academy for members of the San Bernardino Police Department. Enrollment would include a score or more San Bernardino County sheriff's deputies. The principal reason for inaugurating the classes, said Cunningham, was to increase police effectiveness, and therefore an attempt would be made to conduct the program year-round. By early January, instructors from the Federal Bureau of Investigation were set to lead classes in arrests, criminal investigations and other major facets of police work. In this, Mayor Cunningham set an example for every law enforcement agency in Southern California and eventually won the plaudits of his fellow San Bernardinians.

As a lover of homespun entertainment Cunningham was instrumental in bringing both comic and light opera to San Bernardino during his first term as mayor. The first presentation was Irish-born Victor Herbert's "Naughty Marietta," which played for three nights in the Senior High School auditorium. The delightful performance led to the founding of the Civic Opera Association, a community project enlisting the aid of talented young men and women in furthering the city's cultural interests. Mayor Cunningham served on its first board of directors.

San Bernardino's "Days of Gold"

ONE OF THE MOST spectacular celebrations ever staged in San Bernardino was the "Days of Gold" extravaganza and parade in October 1948, celebrating the area's covered wagon days. Mayor and Mrs. Cunningham lent an official air to the festivities. His Honor was radiant in handing out special prizes. A crowd estimated at well over 100,000 lined the downtown streets in brilliant sunshine to watch the Grand Parade, with the beautiful view of the mountains in the background. Fifteen bands and drum corps with high stepping majorettes led the way. There were fifty colorfully decorated floats and horses by the hundred, riders and mounts lavishly accoutered, all having their day in the sun. All the splendor of Sunny California was expressed in gold—golden oranges, that is—a historical float, depicting the planting of the first orange grove in San Bernardino Valley in 1856 and the fruit of that labor.

Reelection in 1949 provided James Cunningham with an opportunity to complete the progressive programs he initiated during his first term. He had the courage of his convictions and saw to it that any project he undertook for the benefit of his constituents was carried forward to a successful conclusion.

California State Senator

AFTER MUCH soul-searching Mayor Cunningham announced that he would be a candidate for state senator in the 1950 June primary election. A registered Republican, the mayor filed on both major party tickets, knowing that he would have to work both sides of the aisle. Cunningham had much going for him. He was young, dark and handsome, with a warm personality. In many ways he foreshadowed John F. Kennedy, who won the heart of young America and in so doing won election as President of the United States.

He made sure the voters understood his political goals:

> One of my prime objectives in seeking the office will be to provide for and encourage the location of new industry in the state and to make possible an increase in payrolls, which I consider to be of the first importance. A necessity involved in attracting new industry is to provide adequate schools and recreational facilities. Provisions should be made now for sound and fair legislation for both management and labor. The tax structure of the state of California should be studied and

every effort made to avoid an increase in real property taxes, with due regard for a person's ability to pay.

Strong logic coming from a young man of thirty-plus years. People took his timely message to heart. For far too long politicians had been speaking of management and labor as if they had nothing in common, when in fact they were partners in everything having to do with community development, as Cunningham pointed out. He received the endorsement of the State Labor League. The league delegates in attendance at the party convention represented some one million members affiliated with the American Federation of Labor in the State of California. Shortly thereafter Cunningham won endorsement from the Order of Railway Conductors of America.

As might be expected, Cunningham got unanimous endorsement of the United Veterans of the Republic in his campaign for State Senator from the San Bernardino County District, a gesture that carried considerable weight. As noted by Commander C. T. Johnson of Unit 29, San Bernardino, it was in fact the only endorsement from such a long established veterans' organization. All agreed that the former Army Captain was truly deserving of the honor and support.

Cunningham was elected state senator in the primary and continued to serve in that position until his appointment by Governor Goodwin Knight to the newly established San Bernardino Superior Court in 1957. During his term in Sacramento he served on a number of important committees from Public Works to Rules to one involved in reorganizing the state's municipal courts. He was a member of California's Earl Warren delegation to the Republican National Convention in 1952.

Judge of the Superior Court

IN LATE 1957 Governor Knight appointed Senator Cunningham as judge of the Superior Court, a post he held until he declined to seek re-election in 1976. During those nineteen years he served as presiding judge of the Superior Court and as presiding judge of its Appellate Court. In 1966-67 Judge Cunningham served as president of the Conference of California Judges, succeeding Superior Court Judge Charles McGoldrick of Santa Rosa.

As one who served in all three branches of government—legislative, executive and judicial—Judge Cunningham believed that the cure for America's ailing court system lay in the development of a professional judiciary. "I would have all judges start out in the lower courts. Judges should be appointed to the higher courts on the basis of merit," he said.

"I do not believe judicial offices should be handed out as political patronage plums. I do believe a judge should prove his ability before being elevated to higher office." When asked why a successful attorney would want to become a judge, he replied:

> There is no greater satisfaction than being an active participant in the administration of justice. The highest professional calling is probably that of a clergyman whose field of endeavor is that of the Creator and the created. The second highest is that of the attorney who deals in the area of service to the created. The judiciary is the most solemn level of the legal profession. This is the reason attorneys, at great financial sacrifice, will seek election or appointment to the bench.

Asked about courts being too lenient, he remarked:

> I think the courts are turning the other way. I believe public opinion is creating such political pressure on our government leaders that the pendulum of change for the sake of change is swinging the other way. Experimental change has caused chaos and confusion in the courts. The most notable factor is the rising of unrest on our campuses and other demonstrations for change without adequate thought and planning. I do not foresee the clock being turned all the way back, but modified to reflect moderate and lasting progress.

In the meantime the astute justice was commissioned a lieutenant colonel in the Air Force Reserve, and on October 16, 1962, he was sworn in for practice in the Court of Military Appeals and the United States Supreme Court. His duty was to act as legal advisor to the commanding general of the North American Air Defense Command. In 1966 he was promoted to colonel and sworn in by Major General Alfred Kuhfield, U.S.A.F.

San Bernardino's National Orange Show

ONE OF Judge Cunningham's pet projects was the annual Orange Show in San Bernardino. In the manner of a fellow Irish-American mayor, James Duval Phelan, who vowed to make San Francisco the "Paris of the West," Cunningham sought to make San Bernardino the hub of economic and cultural development of Southern California.

The region was nestled in a veritable Garden of Eden, surrounded by majestic snow-capped mountains that tower some ten thousand feet, casting their shadows over green foothills and verdant valleys. In the center, vast orchards produced millions of oranges glistening in the sun.

The first oranges were brought to California in the late 18th century by the Franciscan Mission Fathers, led by the saintly Fra Junipero Serra. In 1857 the seedless navel orange made its debut in the lush valley of San Bernardino.*

Shipped overland by the newly constructed railway to brighten winter tables across the nation, these glowing spheres of sunshine also symbolized California as an affluent Eden. One of the original trees was transplanted by the city of Riverside to its present location, where it thrives to this day under the watchful eye of the University of California's Citrus Experimental Station. There it stands, a living monument to California's citrus industry.

San Bernardino's first orange show was held in 1889, when that city was the county seat of the largest county in the world. Three years later the county was split up, along with San Diego County, to form Riverside County. This move made it possible for the city of Riverside to become a county seat.

According to statistics, the original 7,500 orange trees had grown to 1,347,900 by 1900; the 15,000 boxes of oranges shipped in 1881 became 1,560,000 by 1903. In cash value the crop leaped from $2,450 in 1860 to $1.6 million by the turn of the century. All this meant new money to the economy, evidenced by growth in rail car shipments from 4,000 in 1886-87 to 22,000 in 1902-03

It was a proud moment in Judge Cunningham's life when he was chosen president of San Bernardino's National Orange Show in 1960. Well aware that San Bernardino had something to call its own, something no other community in the southland had to offer, he went all out to make it bigger and better than ever before. His wife Louise was equally enthusiastic and committed. They traveled to Los

---

*That account however, does not jibe with the author's findings that the first trees to bear fruit were planted in nearby Riverside. To quote from an article in *Westway Magazine* by a writer named Jeff Book: "A Parent Navel Orange: The tree that launched the Inland Empire continues to bear fruit in Riverside. Behind an iron fence at Magnolia and Arlington Avenues grows one of California's two original navel orange trees sent to Eliza Tibbets in 1873 by the Department of Agriculture. Mrs. Tibbets soon had a booming business selling buds from her prize stock. In the ensuing years at least one hundred thousand acres in the state were planted with progeny of her trees, and the sale of navel oranges had reached two hundred million dollars."

Louise Cunningham

Angeles to invite its officials to participate in the Orange Show, underscoring their invitations by passing out oranges to Raymond Darby, chairman of the board of supervisors, Sheriff Eugene Biscailuz and other dignitaries. Judge Cunningham appeared with Supervisor Darby on the latter's weekly radio broadcast to the southland. All went so well that San Bernardino came away with a commitment: that the Angelenos would arrive in force on Los Angeles County's own day March 14. An official cavalcade of county and city officials would come from Los Angeles for the day, stopping at other cities en route to add their respective Mayors and civic leaders to the entourage.

The *San Bernardino Sun Telegram* went all out in its efforts to promote the 1960 National Orange Show, featuring the eighteen directors led by President James Cunningham, A. B. Drake, Vice-President, and G. Walter Glass, secretary-manager.

James Earl Cunningham was a man of many talents, not the least of which was gourmet cooking, an interest he acquired during a stint as a mess officer in the U.S. Army. He owned an extensive collection of cook books, and attended meetings of the American Society of Chefs and the California Academy of Chefs. He even admitted to making a systematic study of cooking the world over and the history of various dishes. His abiding interest in cooking led him to accompany the U.S. team to the Culinary Olympics in Germany in 1963.

A lively Gaelic spirit flourished in the Cunningham household. In the evenings the family gathered round to sing Irish folk songs and recite old Irish ballads. Every member of the family was expected to participate, including the three children Jay, Charlene and Wilfred Lemann, whose father died of polio and who were taken in and cared for by the Cunninghams. The Cunninghams were a very close-knit family. In the Irish tradition the home was the center of life.

The Cunninghams were members of Holy Rosary parish in San Bernardino. Jim served as an altar boy at first Mass every Sunday for a number of years. He assisted Bishop John Cantwell of Los Angeles, lugging the holy water vessel at the groundbreaking ceremony for St. Bernardine's Hospital. He was a friend, confidante and legal adviser for priests and religious over many years. Judge Cunningham interceded with the United States Minister to Ireland to expedite visas for the Presentation Sisters to come to the San Bernardino Diocese.

The Judge, like his father, loved being around the Irish and made them welcome whenever they paid him a call. Knowing that many were far from home, he would invariably have them telephone their families.

In all of California history where the Irish were involved, no one surpasses San Bernardino's illustrious son as both shaper and exemplar of the city and county whose interests he served.

John Murphy
for whom the town of Murphys was named.

— 15 —

THE MARTIN MURPHY FAMILY

1785 - 1865

ANY FAMILY WHICH HAS A TOWN named in its honor in the Golden Land of California has something to crow about. The Martin Murphy clan, with roots in County Wexford, is that family, and the town so named is Murphys in Calaveras County. Murphys was founded by John and Daniel Murphy following their discovery of gold in that locality in 1850. The brothers came over the mountains with the Murphy-Miller-Townsend party in 1844, in search of a better way of life. The prescient old patriarch, Martin Murphy, Sr., brought his family from Canada to Missouri in 1820 and from there to California 24 years later. Thus began one of the most fascinating stories in the history of Irish in America.

Martin Murphy Sr. settled in the fertile plains of Santa Clara and founded the town of San Martin, which he named in honor of his patron saint. His son, Martin Jr., followed in his father's footsteps and acquired more arable land in California than in all his native County Wexford.

James Murphy went to Corte Madera (the place of cut wood) and made his fortune supplying timber for the construction of the developing community of Yerba Buena (San Francisco). James, like his father, removed to Santa Clara Valley where he purchased land in the vicinity of San Jose and built a showplace known as "Ringwood Farm."

John and Daniel Murphy worked with their brother-in-law, Captain Charles Weber, who came west with John Bidwell in 1841, and who later founded the town of Stockton on the Sacramento River.

Margaret and Johanna Murphy came directly to California from Canada with their families. Margaret had married Thomas Kell and Johanna wed Patrick Fitzgerald during their stay in Quebec.

The name Murphy rings a bell in every land, wherever the wandering Gaels have set foot. It became a household word in California. As in Irish lore, "For in that name there is no shame/ It's an Irish name, me boy!" the name Murphy is as Irish as the Shamrock on Saint Patrick's Day, and yet is as American as apple pie or the Fourth of July.

Murphys: a California Landmark

MURPHYS (the town name has no apostrophe) is a place where time stands still and the memory of the good old days and ways lingers on. If you're looking for things as they used to be, Murphys is the place you will find them. Nostalgia is everywhere about. Every year the close-knit residents throw a party to celebrate their good fortune and go all out to share their feelings with everyone who comes their way. This family celebration is a part of Murphys' "Gold Rush Days."

The event turns back the clock to a time when people were less affluent but more appreciative of what life had to offer. Visitors are urged to come early and enjoy a delicious pancake breakfast with the home folks, starting at 7 a.m. Then comes a period costume parade that has been weeks and months in the making, with a flotilla of gift baskets for the lucky winners. There's something for everyone—a Dixieland jazz band, a silent auction, fine eats, winemaking displays and tasting tours provided by various wineries in Calaveras County.

A high point is the hilarious grape stomping contest, in which everyone is invited to participate. The contestants work in twos, a stomper and a swabber to collect the juice as it gushes forth from the vessel. Grape stompers can wear shoes, though most prefer to go it barefooted, an old world tradition. The stomping duo who collect the most juice in a given time are eligible for the grand stomping finale in the evening. Cash prizes are awarded to the winners.

The Founding Fathers

MURPHYS was founded in 1850 by the brothers, John and Daniel, after they struck gold in the area. Both men were born—John in 1825 and Daniel in 1826—in County Wexford, Ireland, and were brought by their parents to Canada, where the Wexford Murphys first settled.

According to Henry Walsh, S.J., in his book, *Hallowed Were the Gold Dust Trails,* John Murphy unearthed the largest vein of gold in California mining history. Before he quit the mines in late 1849,

"John Murphy took $2,000,000 in gold from the Murphy Diggings in about a year's time," enough to make him a millionaire for life at the age of twenty-three. He took out seventeen huge pouches of gold, all that a six-mule team could haul away from the mining camp.

Despite his wealth, John was no carouser or spendthrift. According to the Reverend Walter Coulton, the American Navy Chaplain at Monterey, John Murphy never allowed any liquor in his mining camp. When a trader brought in a barrel of rum for local consumption, John gave him exactly five minutes to leave the grounds or have the head of the barrel knocked in.

John, like his father, removed to San Jose in 1850 and invested his proceeds from the mines in various business projects. In that same year he married Virginia Reed, the daughter of James Reed, a survivor of the ill-fated Donner Party. Of that union eight children were born: John Jr., Virginia, Mary Margaret, Thomas, Daniel, Virginia, and Ada, making sure that the Murphy name would not die out. Over the years John, Sr., served in various capacities in Santa Clara County, as Sheriff, Recorder and County Treasurer, and as a member of the San Jose City Council.

John's older brother Bernard married Catherine O'Toole. He served two terms as mayor of San Jose before he died in an explosion on the steamer *Jenny Lind*.

On the hillside beneath Butte City in the Mother Lode country, a colony of Hibernian immigrants settled and took unto itself the title of "Irish Hill." Heading the list were the Murphys, with their relatives the McCarthys, Muldoons, Stewarts and Longs, as well as the Scullys, the Dooleys, the Mulliens and the Gannons. Those early settlers prospered from the gold deposits in the hills, and also from the fertile lands in the sheltered valley, where they raised crops and livestock.

John's daughter Margaret Murphy was born in Butte City in 1857. She grew up to become a teacher in the public schools in that region. She then enrolled in Notre Dame convent in San Jose, and took her final vows in religion as Sister Berchmans Joseph. In 1894 she was appointed Superior of the Order in Alameda, going from there to Marysville, where she served as Superior for eleven years. In 1910 Sister Joseph was given charge of Notre Dame Convent in San Francisco, where she became Mother Superior and served for ten years. Finally in appreciation of her long and faithful service to the Order she was elevated to the office of Provincial of the Notre Dame Order on the Pacific Coast.

Doctor Henry Parish, a practicing physician in Oakland in 1926 and a former pupil of Sister Joseph, had this to say:

I attended the first school Maggie established in Butte City. It was a private school in the old Catholic Church, which stood beside the road near John Murphy's home. I afterwards went to Washington District School, where she also presided. She was a born teacher, qualities highly essential in guiding the destinies of the wild bunch of youngsters in that neck of the woods. In attempting to discipline me on one occasion, I swore at her. That ended the punishment for the time being. Later on, in one of her social visits at my home in Big Bar, I well remember the dread I experienced on sight of her coming down the road. I was not held in suspense very long—there quickly followed a painful interview between my father and myself in the woodshed. Many years later, when [I was] called to attend professionally her brother, John, in Oakland, she remarked, on learning who the Doctor was, "Harry Parish! My, but he was a bad boy! But he had a nice mother."

Daniel Murphy, like his older brother, acquired enough gold bullion in a year's time to make him a rich man for life. Daniel then removed to San Martin, where his father, Martin Sr., had acquired a large tract of land known as the Las Llagas Rancho and which Daniel fell heir to after his father's death in 1865.

Daniel married Mary Fisher, who bore him five children, Julie, Mary, Diana, Daniel Jr., and Dianne. As time went on he acquired vast tracts of land and large herds of livestock in California, Arizona and Mexico. When he died at his favorite hacienda in Halleck, Nevada, in 1872, he was said to be the largest stock raiser in the world.

Murphys' first house of Worship

WHEN Father Daniel Slattery first arrived in Murphys there were quite a number of Catholics, most of whom were Irish Catholics working in the mines, but no church. They welcomed the priest into their midst. A committee comprised of Irish miners was formed, with the intent to build a church of their own. They built a little wood frame church on the rise of Irish Hill in 1855, where services were conducted by Father Slattery every Sunday.

That first church had a checkered history. Three years after it was finished, when mining operations reached the edge of the church property and the miners were convinced that there was a rich vein under the church, they spoke with Father Motter of San Andreas, the non-resident Pastor, and promised him they would build a fine brick

church in its place if he
would give them permis-
sion to remove the build-
ing and work the ground
where it stood. Father
Motter gave them per-
mission, while at the
same time reminding
them of their equal obligation.

True to their word,
the miners began con-
struction of the new
church almost immedi-
ately on land donated by
Doctor Jones, a surgeon
from Ireland who had
come to Murphys from
New York with a group
of prospectors. The
bricks used in its con-
struction were made
from a red clay deposit
in the nearby hills.

Although the church
was completed in 1859,

St. Patrick's church in Murphys
Courtesy Dick James, photographer

it was not dedicated until 1861, when Archbishop Alemany of San
Francisco visited Murphys to officiate. It appears that his Lordship
was not very fluent in English at the time of this entry in his calendar:
"Visited Murphys blessed new church to Saint Patrick November 3,
1861." As a result of the Bishop's long association with the Irish he
eventually learned to speak English, but with a faint Irish brogue.

According to the United States census of 1870, the Irish far out-
numbered all other nationals in the fifteen mining counties of
Northern California. In the six southern mining counties the Irish
formed 23.3% of the foreign born population, followed by the
Germans at 15.8%, the English at 14.1% and the Italians at 10.5%.
In the nine northern counties it was the Germans at 20%, the
English 16.7%, the Irish 15.6% and the Italians at 6.9%. However in
San Joaquin County the Irish were way on top with 34.3%, and in
Stanislaus County 30.2%.

Interior of St. Patrick's church
Courtesy Dick James, photographer

When Father Motter came to San Andreas he took over all of the pastoral work in Calaveras County. A successful church builder, he directed the construction of churches at San Andreas, Angels Camp, Albany Flat and Murphys. Having proved his ability in the mining country, he was recalled to San Francisco to serve as secretary to Archbishop Alemany.

Murphys' church has been administered from Angels Camp since 1900, when Father James Vaughn became pastor. He was followed by Father James O'Flannigan, who served for twenty years, and Father John McGuire, who served for nineteen. In 1948 Father James Kenny became pastor and it was during his time that Saint Patrick's celebrated its 100th year of active service to the Catholic community at Murphys. In 1862 the parish was transferred from the Sacramento Diocese to the Diocese of Stockton.

In 1965 Robert McCabe, a Sacramento architect who was writing a book on historical churches, visited Saint Patrick's in Murphys and commented, "I am very impressed with Saint Patrick's Church. It is probably one of the best examples of a small church in the Golden Chain. It is beautifully done. There are bigger churches that show the same things, but none is any better." A bronze plaque giving a brief history of the Church was placed in 1971.

There is presently no resident pastor at Saint Patrick's church in Murphys. However the parish is ably served by Father Henry Johnston, the pastor of Saint Patrick's Parish in nearby Angels Camp. An affable and ambitious clergyman, Irish-born Father Johnston brought new life to the Catholic community in that region.

The Irish influence remained constant in Murphys down through the years. When Father James Kenny became pastor in 1948, Saint Patrick's celebrated its one hundredth year of service to the Catholic community, During the historic celebration which took place on June 15, 1958, the Right Reverend Joseph T. McGucken, Bishop of Sacramento, presided. Father Kenny was the celebrant of a Pontifical Mass assisted by the choir from St. Andrew's church in San Andreas. Six years later Father Donahue became pastor to continue the Irish line until his removal in 1980. Two non-Irish priests, Father Gruber and Father Miani, served briefly in the interim until the arrival of Father Johnston in 1985.

Murphys Hotel

PART OF THE laisse-faire charm of Murphys is the weather-beaten Murphys Hotel, the show place of the Gold Rush country. Fear not, the welcome wheel is out and no hangman's ropes attached, as in the days of the Wild West. If the hallowed hallways and gingerbread verandas of the old landmark could only speak, what stories they could tell. Visitors can easily picture what the hotel was like in the days when Black Bart, the highwayman who plagued the Mother Lode country over a century ago, would ride through town.

The hotel was built in 1855, when Murphys became the gateway to Calaveras Big Tree country on the west flank of the Sierra Nevada range. Yankee travelers paid glowing tributes to the giant redwoods, taller than the masts of ships and as thick as New England hay barns.

The hotel, which caught the attention of Bret Harte in "A Night in Wingdam," remains much as it was well over a century ago, with old iron shutters guarding the windows. Bullet holes, reminders of old shootouts, are visible in the hotel's doorway. The horsehair sofas and red plush furniture may be faded but are true relics of the past. A guest register, showing the names of such illustrious visitors as Mark Twain, J. Pierpont Morgan, and Horatio Alger, is displayed in the lobby, along with a photograph purporting to show Charley Bolten (Black Bart) in the act of holding up a stage coach.

Hitching posts line the street in front. Stately locust trees with fragrant white blossoms line the main streets, setting off the faded

Murphys Hotel, on Main Street
Courtesy Henry P. Johnson

limestone buildings. Murphys was chosen as a setting for a Will
Rogers movie in 1934.

The Murphy Pedigree

A CCORDING TO Edward MacLysaght, the noted Irish Genealogist,
Murphy is the commonest surname in Ireland. Birth statistics
prove that the Murphy clan of Leinster, centered in County Wexford,
are the most noteworthy and the most numerous. The best known of
these were two priests, Reverend John Murphy, the Hero of
Boulavogue, and the lesser-known Reverend Michael Murphy. Both
men lost their lives in the Rebellion of 1798.

Many Murphy descendants of Irish emigrants distinguished
themselves in lands apart: Irish Brigades who served in the Armies of
France and Spain and in the various phases of life in Canada, the
United States and Australia. Irish-American Audie Murphy was the
most decorated hero of World War II, and became a movie star afterward. General Patrick Murphy of San Jose was California's first
Adjutant General. And last but not least, another Patrick Murphy
was remarkable for his height, standing eight feet tall. He was once

photographed with Ulysses Grant, Jr., who was three feet four at the age of twelve when the likeness was taken by Mathew Brady, the famed Civil War photographer.

WHEN AND WHEREVER the Murphys are involved, one finds poignancy, excitement and humor, as in the old song, "Who Threw the Overalls in Mrs. Murphy's Chowder?" The author's neighbor, Tom Hayes, has a repertoire of Irish ballads to charm every audience. His rendition of the Murphy-Cohen encounter always brings down the house:

> Sure I knew a man named Cohen,
> He was a very cagey little Jew.
> Who owned a great big brick hotel,
> And every brick in it was new.
> He called this hotel, Ireland,
> Said I, "Thanks—a very impressive name."
> But, listen and I'll tell you
> How this grand hotel came.
> Sure there was a man named Murphy,
> Who owned a fine brick yard one day,
> And this little guy named Cohen
> Lived in a house across the way.
> Now Cohen started calling Murphy
> A big old Irish Mick,
> Murphy, he got mad as hell,
> And started throwing all his bricks.
> Sure he threw the whole damn brickyard
> Trying to hit poor little Cohen.
> And Cohen said, "I thank you, Mr. Murphy,
> For all the bricks you've thrown."
> Then he took them and he placed them
> And built a hotel grand,
> And when he had it finished,
> Sure he called it Ireland.

To share in the Murphy lore is like kissing the Blarney Stone. An old rule of thumb: the next time you feel like hugging someone, make sure that person is a Murphy.

Captain Michael J. Wrin
Courtesy Tom Wrinn

– 16 –

CAPTAIN MICHAEL WRIN

1837 - 1903

ISTORIANS GENERALLY DESCRIBE THE IRISH arriving in New York and Boston from the old country during and after the potato famine as "huddled immigrant masses." While that may have been accurate for the East Coast, it was far less true of those arriving in San Francisco.

The Irish in San Francisco soon built a multi-layered society which filled their needs for social, protective, spiritual and material welfare. It also gave them practical outlets for their energies, directed toward charitable, benevolent, religious, social, patriotic, and Irish nationalistic purposes, among others. Dozens of Irish parishes, societies, associations, institutions, militias, organizations, leagues, orders and clubs took form in the booming city. Memberships in multiples of these entities provided financial, political and spiritual stability. The result was a secure, well-established, largely self-sufficient and mutually cooperative Irish-American community in San Francisco.

While a few of the San Francisco societies emulated similar organizations in the East, most seemed designed to meet the specific and unique needs of the large population of Irish adventurers in San Francisco. Once the chaos of the lawlessness and Vigilantism of the 1850s, and the uncertainties of a seemingly endless Civil War were past, it was time for San Francisco to change from a community of unattached young fortune seekers into a civilized city populated by family folks gifted with above-average initiative and adventurousness. All the Irish who crossed the Atlantic and then sailed around the Horn or crossed America did so to improve their own lot in life; but it seems that many were also inclined as a result of their Christian upbringing to care for the well-being of their fellow countrymen in time of need. A relatively small core of Irishmen with talent for organizing brought about the collective prosperity and vitality of the Irish in old San Francisco—and of a good many non-Irish as well.

Michael Wrin, a tinsmith who became a successful businessman in San Francisco, was one of those organizers. He was a founder and fund-raiser in turn for many of these developing societies. Following his arrival in San Francisco at the end of the Civil War, Michael first organized a successful business partnership, and then set about gathering his countrymen into organizations to ensure their future well being.

Wrin's experience living under the rule of English conquerors of Ireland caused him to see firsthand that a big government could well be the biggest problem people could have. There is not room to detail all the laws here. A quick summary of the Wrins' life in Ireland makes clear their attitude toward English rule and explains their opposition to governments and politicians later in America.

The ancient Celtic ancestors of the family were the O'Rinns of the Ui Macaille tribe, after which the Barony of Imokilly in County Cork got its name. The earliest reference to the family in recorded history is an account of the death of Ui Macaille chieftain Maelgorm Ua Rinn, at the hands of Thormond forces in 1135 A. D.

Rinn, in the Gaelic language, means "spear" or "point." The Penal Laws imposed by the English prohibited the use of Gaelic names in written records, so some of the Rinns complied with the law, when writing their name for land records, by substituting a W for O'. Since there is no W in the Gaelic alphabet, their name was thus anglicized by the spelling "Wrinn" without changing the pronunciation. Some dropped the last "n" simply to distinguish between immediate families. To add to the confusion, there was an English colonist with the very English name of Wren living in the English colony at Bandon, and the Roman Catholic clergy in the chapels near the intimidating government center at Bandon felt compelled by law to anglicize the Wrin and Wrinn names even further to that of Wren whenever making entries in the parish register. So some descendants of the O'Rinns used the spellings Wren and Wrenn thereafter. The consequent confusion down through the ages caused the family's name itself to be a constant reminder to Captain Wrin and his descendants of what happened when a distant government forced people to misspell their own names, a law which some refer to as the "Curse of Cromwell."

Michael was born in 1837 in Murragh Parish, County Cork, not far from the exclusively English Protestant stronghold of Bandon (at first called Bandon Bridge by the English). Before England had sent its first colonist to America, it had seized the lands of the Desmonds and O'Mahonys on the Bandon River and established there a "model" colony to be inhabited exclusively by English Protestants. The colonists proceeded so effectively to antagonize the displaced native Irish (whom they referred to as the "Bungling Paddies") that the newcomers soon felt it necessary to build a fortified wall around the town to protect themselves from the displaced Irish. By one account, the Bandon wall was said to have been 30 to 50 feet high and 9 feet thick, and to have incorporated 6 gun towers.

Over a gate in the wall was written:

A Turk, a Jew, or an Atheist
Is welcome here, but no Papist.

The Irish had had this aggravating, arrogant foreign presence to contend with at Bandon since before the year 1600. However, by 1689, they tired of looking at the wall and proceeded to dismantle it. The government's theory was that the Irish would imitate the English Protestants, and gradually become anglicized. But the theory backfired; it seems that the English Protestant citadel has tended to Hibernicize, as Bandon is now a charming, peaceful Irish town situated below the imposing edifice of Saint Patrick's Roman Catholic Church.

Injustices to the Irish in the vicinity did not stop with the seizing of the land, and the taking of the lives of the Desmonds and the O'Mahonys. The continuation of this suppression of the Irish Catholics by their English conquerors is detailed in *History of Bandon and the Principal Towns In The West Riding of County Cork* by George Bennett, Cork, 1869. In later years, to the Wrins, the Vigilante "justice" handed out in the Wild West seemed like enlightened jurisprudence when compared to the treatment meted out to the native Irish in Bandon.

America Bound

FROM THE environs of the hostile foreign enclave of Bandon, Michael's parents brought their family to Roxbury, Massachusetts about 1850. The Wrins had had a metal smith shop in Ireland, so Michael took employment as a sheet iron worker and tinsmith while finishing his education in Roxbury. The *Boston Pilot* reported that, at age 18, Michael was vice president of the Roxbury branch of the Young Catholic Friends Society, which raised funds to provide orphans in the Catholic school with clothing and tuition. He also helped raise money for the House of the Angel Guardian Home for boys in Roxbury. He had seen many children orphaned by hunger and poverty in Ireland, and as a teenager in America he worked to help parentless young people.

In 1861 Michael stood proudly before the altar of St. Joseph's Church in Roxbury, taking for his wife an Irish lass named Mary Broderick. It was a happy union that lasted until Michael's death in San Francisco at the age of 66. At the same time he was an active member of the Fenians and Hibernians.

By the year 1864 there were three generations of Wrins in Roxbury, and they were getting restless to improve their lot. Living near Boston was not the full realization of the Irish American dream. The "establishment" seemed to consist of early English settlers who considered the Irish to be an underclass, and this is not what the Wrins had come to America for.

The Wrin family had saved old 1847 copies of the *Alta Californian*, the first English-language newspaper published in Alta (upper) California. They particularly relished the slogan in the paper's masthead, "The world is governed too much," a sentiment established during a transition period between Mexican and American governance, when there was hardly any government at all.

California, and the amusing items in the *Californian*, intrigued Michael, his parents and his brothers and sisters. Other closely related Wrins had parted with them after landing at Boston in 1850 and had headed directly overland, arriving in California in 1852, just in time to dig for gold in the Sierra Nevada mountains. Their letters back to Roxbury confirmed that California was a land of opportunity, with a classless society, no English influence, very little government regulation or taxation, and unlimited chances for self-confident people.

ABOUT 1864, three generations of Michael's immediate family took the long voyage to California. Michael Wrin felt quite at home from the first moment he first set foot in San Francisco.

Michael's father, James, and his grandfather Michael, were tinsmiths by trade in Ireland. Their smithy was on land seized by England and ultimately vested in the Duke of Devonshire. They and other branches of the Wrin family leased larger plots and then sub-let buildings and smaller plots to individual tenants. That was as far as their entrepreneurial spirit could take them in Ireland, as there was no hope that there would ever be land reform, or sales of land in this area to Irish Catholics.

The situation in the boom town of early San Francisco was entirely different. Michael saw opportunities on all sides. There was no practical overland transportation of goods from the East before the railroad, so everything needed in the Bay Area, or in the gold fields, had to be manufactured locally to avoid many months of delay in placement of orders and in shipment around Cape Horn or trans-shipment via the Isthmus. There was plenty of demand for sheet metal products, so he and a German acquaintance, Jacob Freeman, established the partnership of Freeman & Wrin at 344 Third Street. The firm eventually out-lived both of its founders, but succumbed 41 years later when it collapsed into a brick pile in the '06 earth-quake.

The firm produced metal containers of all types, ductwork and any metal products customers wanted. There was also great demand for furnaces and stoves because of all the new construction, so Freeman & Wrin expanded down the street and became a stove and heating shop.

THE NEXT DEVELOPMENT was the availability of piped gas, which became the fuel of choice for both lighting and heating. Wood and coal stoves and furnaces were replaced with gas, which required plumbing, so Freeman & Wrin expanded down to 326 Third Street and became a plumbing and gas fitting shop. Rival gas utility compa-nies had parallel gas lines in the streets and waged rate wars with one another, offering big incentives to users to disconnect from their pre-sent supplier and connect up with the competitor. One of the com-petitors was the San Francisco Gas Company, owned by Irish American capitalist Peter Donahue. When the gas company agreed to pay for a potential customer's gas fitting, Freeman & Wrin received the business. Donahue was very generous in support of Irish causes. In one year when Michael Wrin mentioned to him that he had not yet been able to raise enough funds for the St. Patrick's Day celebra-tion, Donahue contributed the entire unfunded amount.

Jacob Freeman and Michael Wrin became fast friends. They worked side by side, and lived side by side. They acquired a big piece of hillside property far out in Bernal Heights, at the intersection of two unmarked roads which later became known as California Avenue and Fair Avenue. Freeman built a large place on the corner. Farther down the hill, at what is now a much-modified 47-49 Fair Avenue, Wrin built a big two-story plus basement and attic home topped with intricate artistic bird-deterrent metalwork, which identified the house as that of a descendant of ancient Celtic metal smiths.

Brodericks and other relatives of Michael's wife, Mary (Broderick) Wrin, came to California and located on Fair Avenue and one block over on what was then Powell Avenue. Several went to work for Freeman & Wrin as tinsmiths and plumbers.

Freeman & Wrin never advertised. The firm's success seemed to reflect the good will its partners had generated by their work in the public interest in the community, and not just by their well-conducted business. While very little has been learned about Captain Jacob Freeman, it is known that he was a prominent member of the German-American population. His military title probably came from the command of a German-American militia in the Sixth (German) Regiment of the California National Guard.

Freeman joined with Wrin in charitable work through their firm when it served as the best instrument of assistance to those in need. Such actions were confidential, but the St. Rose's Conference of the St. Vincent de Paul Society did reveal one such instance when it published a note of thanks in the *Monitor.* There had been one of those big fires for which San Francisco was known, this one in a residential area on Brannan Street. The displaced survivors had lost all their furnishings and were being re-established in other living quarters by the Vincentians. A notice in the paper thanked Freeman and Wrin for providing stoves to the Vincentians at considerably reduced prices.

As a result of Wrin's position as treasurer of the Ancient Order of Hibernians, as well as of other Irish Nationalist and charitable societies, his office at Freeman & Wrin functioned as a financial office for the distribution of benefits. Since the A.O.H. was the largest of the Irish societies and distributed disability and death benefits, his office at Freeman & Wrin was visited by many wives of disabled Hibernians and widows of newly-deceased members.

Widows coming to his office to see about death benefits complained to Captain Wrin about the cost of funerals. The quiet Captain was, above all else, a good listener and a problem-solver. He looked into the costs actually incurred by funeral undertakers. He already knew the cost of metal caskets, as his firm manufactured them. He concluded that he could reduce the widows' outlay for funerals by providing the funeral service himself. Michael and some of his trusted associates organized a new funeral undertaking business across the street from St. Patrick's Church, at 777 Mission Street. Pacific Undertakers did not advertise, notwithstanding the fact that the four other undertakers lined up in the same block regularly had display advertisements in the *Monitor.*

While the undertaking establishment was located at 777 Mission Street, the office of the president was listed in the City Directory as being around the corner and down the street, in the Freeman & Wrin office. When widows came about their husbands' death benefits, Captain Wrin was in position to detect whether the loss of the breadwinner was causing an immediate financial crisis for the widow. If such proved to be the case, he could help them out with financial assistance through one of the charitable societies in which he officiated.

When Michael died in 1903, his long-time associate in Irish society matters, Michael C. Gorham, took over Pacific Undertakers. By that time, Gorham had succeeded Wrin as treasurer of A.O.H. On April 18, 1906, Pacific Undertakers, Freeman & Wrin and St. Patrick's Church all collapsed into so many brick piles. Only St. Patrick's came back.

Michael the Organizer.

IT SEEMED that nearly half the people in San Francisco were self-motivated and action-oriented folks of Irish birth or Irish extraction who had brought their families to an unfamiliar, undeveloped country, all on the strength of their own self-confidence. They were already in agreement with one another in their Catholic faith, and in the values for which the Church stands. They were mostly bilingual in English and Gaelic, and had the strength of numbers to accomplish whatever they set out to do.

With all these favorable unifying factors present, there was no need for a spellbinding orator or a charismatic hero to convince the Irish that they should form organizations to better their lot. Instead of a motivator, the situation called for an organizer who quietly defined objectives. First and foremost, the organizer had to be a good listener, able to appraise people and determine who should be asked to help organize which society. He had to pick doers, not talkers, to get real results. He needed a wide circle of acquaintances in the Irish population, and he needed to be on good terms with everyone. Important for success in organizing was a reputation for success in his endeavors, particularly as an organizer and as a funder.

In addition to all of the above, the organizer had to be ideologically dedicated to the causes for which each society was to be founded, and had to be willing to work for them zealously without compensation. Real success in such work depended upon directing all attention toward the cause (and not toward the organizer, as sometimes happens with causes advocated by politicians). Michael's quiet, behind-the-scenes organizing style, and his aversion to politics and politicians in all matters, made him a naturally successful organizer among the Irish population. Since his businesses always seemed to be secondary considerations in Michael's life, we'll first take a look at his unpaid voluntary organizing.

The Fenian Brotherhood

THIS organization had for its purpose the freeing of Ireland from English occupation. Their arm in Ireland was the Irish Revolutionary Brotherhood, another of those groups of freedom fighters that kept constant pressure on the English to get out of Ireland during the entire time of its centuries of occupation. (An earlier O'Rinn had entered recorded history in County Cork as a Captain of the Rapparees on December 24, 1694, when he signed, with other officers, a proclamation posting a reward of 200 pounds for arrest of members of the Limerick Privy Council for their having issued certain unsatisfactory proclamations.)

Already a Fenian when he arrived in San Francisco, Michael found that there were only two groups, known as circles, here when he arrived. Thanks to his organizational talent, by 1870 there were six enthusiastic circles. That year, in a show of force for the Fenians' Chief Executive Officer, followers held a picnic in Redwood City. Special trains streamed into the small community from north and south, and a crowd of 12,000 swamped the little town. The *Redwood City Gazette* suggested that, if the Fenians had held their picnic in Canada instead, they would have captured it in one day and could have traded it back to Britain in return for Ireland's freedom.

Two enormous setbacks hit the Fenians in 1872. An effort by eastern Fenians to organize an invasion of Canada was an absolute failure, and the Catholic Church said further membership in the Fenians would result in excommunication, since the Order's oath required absolute obedience. Michael promptly ended his Fenian membership, as did his countrymen generally, and their San Francisco office and newspaper closed down. Instead of trying to wrest Ireland away from England by armed invasion, most former Fenians directed their future efforts at sending financial aid to those working for the liberation of Ireland by other means.

The Ancient Order of Hibernians

IN 1869 a few Irishmen met in San Francisco to start an Ancient Order of Hibernians organization in California. The local divisions would be guided and coordinated by a county-level board. A state-level board would be comprised of delegates from each of the county units. Within the first year Michael Wrin was chosen as the San Francisco County Delegate in the State organization. Subsequently, at one time or another, he held nearly every position in the order, including that of President of the California state organization. He was usually also treasurer of his local division, as well as county treasurer.

Membership in the A.O.H. required being of Irish birth or descent, and a practicing Roman Catholic. The organization sponsored a wide range of social, religious, patriotic, Irish Nationalist activities. It also offered all-important disability and life insurance to members. Membership mushroomed, quickly making it the largest Irish society in the West, with Michael representing the members in San Francisco County during much of the rest of his life. In 1896, his wife, Mary, served as the founding financial secretary when the first Ladies' Auxiliary was organized and named the Martha Washington Circle No. 1.

This tremendous surge of organizing of many thousands of Irishmen into the Fenians and the A.O.H. in the period around 1869 and 1870 coincided with the release of Bennett's *History of Bandon*. The work recorded centuries of suppression and maltreatment of the Irish by the English and even lauded Oliver Cromwell! Descendants of Michael Wrin are convinced that their practical forefather was thankful for the publication of this unpleasant book, because its many readers wanted to join the Fenians immediately.

Michael Wrin, Commander of the Shields Guard Irish Militia

BECAUSE OF the negligible government presence in the West at the time, the only large military force that the state or federal government could bring to bear in time of emergencies was the California National Guard, composed of private, permanent militias. The only reward the unpaid citizen-soldiers received was a certificate of lifetime exemption from all California state taxes after seven years of service. Because the militias represented the only bulwark against outbreaks of large-scale lawlessness or riots, or natural disasters, and because the militiamen served unselfishly without pay, their members were held in high esteem by fellow citizens. From the suppression of the Vigilantes after the Gold Rush up through police work in the disastrous 1906 earthquake and fire, the militiamen stepped out of their civilian lives at a moment's notice, like the Minutemen of the Revolutionary War, and put on their Army uniforms to serve as ordered.

LIFE IN THE MILITIAS was the very antithesis of life in Ireland. In Ireland, one could not bear arms, much less form militias for self-defense. Living in Ireland had meant paying Hearth Tax, Pane Tax, Knowledge Tax, tithes to the hated Protestant Church of Ireland, and other forms of taxation. California militiamen paid no taxes after seven years' service. Life in Ireland meant continuous insurrection and resistance against English rule. California's militias provided the patriotic thrill of laying one's life on the line in support of one's country. In Ireland, people had for ages been subjugated by the army of a foreign invader. In California, men could organize to protect themselves and their families from foreign invaders. Membership in the militia was another way of improving one's lot in life. Irish Americans flocked into the service of the Montgomery Guard, McMahon Guard, Shields Guard, Wolfe Tone Guard, Meagher Guard, Emmet Rifles (Petaluma), Benicia Guard, Emmet Life Guard, Sarsfield Guard and the Oakland Grenadiers. These Irish militias collectively comprised the Third (Irish) Infantry Regiment of the California National Guard.

Michael Wrin was not inclined to get involved in anything that did not need his help. He saw a situation in the Shields Guard Militia which seemed to call out for his assistance, and so, at age 37, he joined in May 1874 as a private. The members of this unit were intensely patriotic, but were malcontents as well. They were equipped with completely obsolete muskets with worn-out flintlocks, so they had to borrow another militia's weapons for target competition. They did not have enough uniforms to go around, so the troops had to take turns wearing the available uniforms for the twice-monthly drills. This caused high absenteeism. After each drill Captain Ryan would immediately request new uniforms and weapons from the state Adjutant General, who denied the requests.

Private Wrin explained to his commander, Captain Thomas O'Neil, that governments were there to take, not give, and that asking the state government for uniforms and rifles was a waste of time. Captain O'Neil then explained to the troops that Private Wrin had a plan to solve their problems. The troops quickly elected Private Wrin as treasurer of Shields Guard. Wrin then accepted a donation of a full complement of modern, specially-modified Springfield rifles for which the Fenians would no longer have any use. Next he obtained donations for uniforms; eventually every member of the Shields Guard had two full uniforms, including a sharp tweed of the unit's own design for non-military events.

Morale soared, and Treasurer Private Wrin was promoted to Captain and Commander of Shields Guard. When mustered by the State to maintain order in labor disputes, or to back up the police in the Chinese Laundry Riots of 1877, the Shields Guardsmen responded as would any well-disciplined military unit. The Captain excelled in marksmanship contests. The Shields Guard competed with the other militias in the Irish Regiment, and the Irish Regiment won the Brigade medal in marksmanship year after year.

In 1879, illness caused Michael to relinquish his command, and he could never again march on foot for any organization for the rest of his life. Nevertheless, old-timers and others alike continued to address him as Captain, in respect for his memorable leadership in the Shields Guard.

Organizing Defenders of the Faith

IN 1873 the *San Francisco Chronicle* revealed the existence of a secret organization opposed to "Papist candidates and Popish mercenaries" in general. This archaic language, last heard from the English foreigners in Bandon, got the immediate attention of Captain Wrin and friends. The bigots in Bandon got away with it because they were protected by the conqueror's superior military strength; not so in a free country.

The secret organization's actions soon had to withstand public scrutiny. A "nameless party" gave the *Catholic Monitor* a set of books of the offending secret organization, plus a list of its members, only 6% of whom were registered voters. The *Monitor's* readers were invited to draw the conclusion that the troublemakers, who fancied themselves as an "American Association," were actually non-citizens. They had also associated themselves with a particular religious denomination in the naming of their organization. Later disclaimers of responsibility from non-Catholic ministers indicated that the organization was in no way connected with the religion suggested in the group's name.

One of the secret oaths taken by the group's members was to refuse to discuss employment with Catholics, which meant refusing to hire Catholics. This anti-social behavior, coming from a small group, was not a serious matter at that stage. To keep the threat small and insignificant, Captain Wrin and his friends organized the Celtic Protective and Benevolent Society on August 23, 1873, with the stated objectives of extending aid to members in case of sickness or accident, and to bury the dead. They added, and "to offer mutual protection in business." Then, lightening it up a bit, "and, to elevate the character of its members." Captain Wrin served as president in 1877 and 1878.

The notice of the founding of the unfunded Celtic society served to advise the hate group that it had now attracted the attention of veteran Irish rebels with instinctive intelligence-gathering aptitudes, well-practiced during life under English rule. During the two periods in which the anti-Catholic group came on strong (once in the 1870s and once in the 1890s) it was beset by incidents in which the embarrassing details of its secret meetings found their way into the newspapers, as did embarrassing information from their records. Neither the Celtic Protective and Benevolent Society, nor anyone else, was mentioned as having a role in these revelations, which appeared to represent simply good investigative reporting.

At one point a bundle of the secret group's records became separated from one of its officers. The information promptly found its way to the front page of the *Monitor.* In the spirit of helpfulness, the paper published the records in their entirety to help the owner identify and claim his property, from secret oaths and financial data to membership roles. The *Monitor* added:

> For reasons unnecessary to mention just now, we take it for granted that the high and honorable position of the Recording Secretary, is at present without an occupant. When they set about appointing one it would be very wise of them to select an individual who can carry home at night his books and his Bourbon without losing either on the way, and who has more discretion than to make a temporary resting place of a sack of potatoes belonging to a "poor benighted papist."

The Irish (called "Popish mercenaries" in the group's preamble) who were the intended victims of this renewed Know Nothingism, removed the threat by simply exposing the facts in the aggressors' records. No oratory was needed. No need for court action, and certainly no legislative action. The worst way of handling it would have been to get the government involved. The intended victims of this bigotry handled the matter quietly and effectively themselves. The offending organization eventually altered its name somewhat and moved across the Bay.

The United Order of Friends

IN THE 1880s, Captain Wrin left the heroic goals of freeing Ireland and protecting America to those in better physical condition, although he still raised money for those causes. As more Irish came to

San Francisco from the old country, from the eastern states and back from the gold fields, Captain Wrin directed his attention to finding means by which those in distress could overcome their predicaments. Whereas the established Irish had protection from their own benevolent societies, the newcomers did not. And many were too proud to ask anyone for help, even when they and their families were in dire straits.

Captain Wrin and his fellow Irish businessmen in the then densely populated South of Market neighborhood often came in contact with such hardship cases and had the natural Irish impulse to help out, but lacked a practical way to be of real assistance. About 1883, Captain Wrin and Michael C. Gorham, with some like-minded men of the neighborhood, formed the United Order of Friends, a private Irish society with the sole purpose of helping unfortunates. The Friends singled out those who were known to be in real need, but were too self-respecting to ask for help. Other Irish businessmen in the neighborhood readily joined in this endeavor. Once in a while a *Monitor* reporter would learn of a gathering of Friends and would marvel at their enthusiasm and harmony. The two Michaels were usually the financial officers and/or on the relief committee. This group worked so well together that it subsequently started a second program to raise funds for humanitarian use in Ireland.

The Bay City Club

THE UNITED ORDER OF FRIENDS became such a popular idea that the businessmen in the neighborhood of Wrin's residence in the outer Mission District decided to form a charitable organization in their area. The Bay City Club was organized along the same lines for Irish business and professional men in the outer Mission and Bernal Heights. Little more is known since their activity was most confidential in nature. Michael Wrin, busy with his other activities, held an office that did not require his constant presence, namely, second vice president.

St. Vincent de Paul Society of St. Paul's Parish

IN 1887 St. Paul's parish organized a St. Vincent de Paul Society to help the needy. Michael Wrin, the president, arranged to have the names and home addresses of the officers on the Relief Committee printed regularly in the *Monitor* so that parishioners in need could easily know who could help them. It was an unusually aggressive move, inconvenient and disruptive to the families of the officers, whose homes then became relief stations of sorts. But it also saved the time of the parish clergy.

Vincentians all over the world collect funds for the needy by requesting alms at the church doors after Mass on fifth Sundays of the month. They also pass the hat among themselves. While these methods had worked for the Order since its founding in France in 1833, Wrin had a new idea. He invited prominent men of the parish to be subscribing members, thus setting up a sustained revenue flow from those most able to give, and making it unnecessary to embarrass anyone at the church door who might be unable to contribute. At various times, the parish conference had 80 to 120 subscribing members, with ten to twenty doing relief work. It was a genuinely popular way for men of the parish to exercise the virtue of charity.

While the A.O.H., of which Wrin was a top officer, was aiding native countrymen still under foreign dominion in Ireland, he independently organized other groups for the same purposes.

The Irish Land League

THE IRISH LAND LEAGUE was a nationwide movement by Irish Americans to send funds to the old country to assist Irishmen who were in danger of being dispossessed because of their inability to meet land obligations. The Wrins came from an area in County Cork where all the land was claimed by big English landlords through "forfeiture" from the original Irish owners. The various branches of the Wrin family tended to have master leases on somewhat larger parcels. Hence, they had been in the dual positions of sub-landlord and tenant and had experienced the binds in which both head tenants and sub-tenants found themselves because of being unable to own the confiscated land. The Irish Land League collected large sums to intervene in evictions and negotiate new leases in the common interests of the tenants, head tenants and landowners.

Michael Wrin joined one branch, comprised of businessmen in the Inner Mission District, and organized a second branch for his neighbors in the outer Mission, with meetings at Comerford Hall on 30th Street. Newspapers noted the special enthusiasm of this group's members.

The Irish National League

ANOTHER MEANS to help matters in the old country was the Irish National League. This organization collected funds to support Irish nationalists who were elected to the Irish Home Rule

Parliament in the time of Stewart Charles Parnell. No salaries were paid to Members of the Parliament, so only the affluent could afford to run for office, and they tended to be the Unionist English landlords. In addition to collecting funds for the Irish National League, Captain Wrin also collected funds for use by Parnell directly in his legislative efforts. Mary Wrin was a member of the Ladies League.

United Irishmen of California

THIS SOCIETY was organized in December 1886 as result of a meeting of 58 people who wanted to advance Irish Nationalist, patriotic and social aims without having to contend with the political turbulence in the big established societies. Members agreed to send money to Parnell, and to celebrate St. Patrick's Day and the Fourth of July. They wanted this to be a harmonious society, and did nothing to promote membership nor to publicize the society's activities. Members had the satisfaction of doing good, and of enjoying it, free of political considerations. Captain Michael Wrin was elected president of the new society at its first meeting.

The Youth Directory

IT SEEMED only a matter of time before this accomplished fund-raiser and dedicated organizer would connect with an Irish priest in San Francisco who fit the same description. Father Donald Crowley had started a shelter for homeless and troubled boys with the purpose of helping them to mature as good citizens. The institution grew very rapidly, and so did its need for buildings to house its wards. The benevolent society of St. Joseph's Union was the main support, but the Directory grew faster than the benevolent society could raise money.

Michael Wrin was treasurer of an "umbrella" organization in which all of the Irish societies participated. Wrin was responsible for funding the annual celebration. Father Crowley met Captain Wrin and explained the urgent need for a new building. He asked if the enormously popular St. Patrick's Day celebration, in which all the Irish in San Francisco participated, could somehow be turned into a fund-raiser for the Youth Directory.

All of the Irish in San Francisco had always attended the free parade; there was no facility in the city large enough to accommodate a paid-admission celebration. A Captain Wrin ally proposed that the delegates from all the Irish societies meet again after Lent to plan a special fund-raiser exclusively for the benefit of the Youth Directory.

Saint Patrick's Day Convention delegates and their respective Irish societies volunteered to assist as requested. In fund-raisers by Irish societies, Captain Wrin, usually designated treasurer, this time was assigned to the music committee, although he, his father, and his grandfather were tinsmiths, a far cry from those who had an ear for fine music.

This detail was irrelevant to Captain Wrin. The music committee promptly reported that it had lined up all the choirs of all the Catholic parishes in San Francisco to perform in a grand concert. Suddenly, the affair had the support of all parishes, and the assured attendance of the families and friends of all the singers, plus other parishioners who would attend for the pure enjoyment of it all. At the next meeting Wrin's name showed up on the finance committee roster.

There is no record of how Captain Wrin organized the concert in just a few days, and before the availability of telephones. A clue might be that Captain Wrin and James R. Kelly had helped raise money for the then-new Cathedral on Van Ness Avenue just three years earlier. These men, along with Father Crowley, exemplified that circle of noble Irishmen who seemed to get their fun from seeing who could do the most good, the most quickly.

St. Patrick's Day Celebrations

IN MID-MARCH of each year San Francisco was treated to a spectacular parade which demonstrated unmistakably that the Irish were not only the biggest, but also the best-organized, best-humored and most enthusiastic segment of the City's population. The parade was organized by a convention of Irish organizations in the city, with Michael Wrin playing a key role.

Over the years, participation in the parade has increased ten-fold. Many people who were not Irish wanted to be Irish, and vented their feelings by wearing of the green, claiming some Irish ancestry and trying to affect a bit of brogue. The parade has become a multi-cultural celebration; German, Italian, Hispanic, French, Chinese and Polynesian groups march along with the Irish. The San Francisco Saint Patrick's parade has been called the most colorful in all America.

In Michael Wrin's time, such Irish organizations as the Hibernians, Knights of the Red Branch, the Sons of the Emerald Isle, Irish Regiments Bands, various parochial schools and Irish-oriented institutions vied with each other to show off their strength and individuality in the gala parade. Wrin was a mediator in debates about the order of the march and other issues. He also raised money to pay the convention's expenses, since parades generate no revenue.

In the late 1800s it was decided to celebrate Saint Patrick's Day with big paid admission entertainments instead of a parade. This move forfeited the public relations value of a parade and ended for a time a very popular San Francisco tradition. The conventions themselves changed with the abandonment of the parades. They had been the means to get thousands of people organized in the spirit and excitement of parading.

At one such convention Captain Wrin and a few of his friends remained after adjournment. Then they pulled their chairs together and got organized. Tom Maguire, who owned the Opera House, made the building available for the celebration. Others in the group agreed to buy two-thirds of the boxes outright immediately, which they would re-sell at their own places of business. This put Sherman & Clay, and Captain Wrin's Pacific Undertakers and others, into the box office business for St. Patrick's Day. This scheme put a good portion of the proceeds into the bank before the celebration had even been planned. They then agreed on which musicians, singers and orators should perform, and on who would contact each. All of this was done in full confidence that none of those contacted would refuse to volunteer their talents.

AT THE FIRST CONVENTION at which the Youth Directory would be the beneficiary, an audacious decision made by the committee would set the tone for more to come. Since the Youth Directory had dire need for a new building, the show had to be a big financial success. The master of ceremonies would be James R. Kelly, the very popular president of Hibernia Bank, who was an excellent and most entertaining speaker. They did not ask Kelly to serve. They just named him master of ceremonies notwithstanding the fact that he was neither present nor asked. Captain Wrin agreed to advise Kelly of what he was going to be doing on Saint Patrick's Day.

When it came Father Crowley's turn to be chairman of the St. Patrick's Day Convention, he recalled how quickly the funds got into the bank when Captain Wrin and his cohorts got together. Father Crowley worked out with James R. Kelly a ploy to get the money into the bank even more quickly, and to give Kelly a good-natured opportunity to get even with Wrin for having stuck him with the master of ceremonies job.

At the opening of this convention, Father Crowley introduced Kelly, and Kelly made a few introductory and entertaining remarks. He then stated simply that this year the entire responsibility for the St. Patrick's Day celebration was given to Captain Wrin for him to conduct as he saw fit. Captain Wrin graciously accepted, making all appointments and arrangements with his customary economy of words. Turn about was fair play, or so it seemed, but the game was not over yet.

Captain Wrin's first appointment was to name James R. Kelly as master of ceremonies for the celebration. Kelly graciously accepted again. Wrin contacted 200 Irish leaders who each made a contribution in addition to the price of admission, and were named vice presidents of the event. The beneficiary was the General Phil Sheridan Monument fund. Captain Wrin named many army officers, along with city and state officials and Congressmen, to a Committee of One Hundred to raise the necessary funds. These supporters attended the St. Patrick's Day celebration. With an audience of 2,000, containing 200 Vice Presidents and 100 Generals, Colonels, Majors, Captains, Mayors, Governors and Legislators, all of whom had contributed extra money for the cause, the event could only be a financial success. All Irishmen still remembered and thrilled at how the 31-year old Irish-American General had turned an apparent defeat into a great Union victory at Cold Creek; so the event became a celebration of two Irish heroes, Saint Patrick and General Sheridan.

The Saint Patrick's Day celebrations were driven by three of the ways the Irish most like to express themselves: (1) by honoring the Apostle of Ireland, (2) by sentiments of Irish nationalism, and (3) by contributing to good Irish causes.

All three, plus many strong sentiments of American patriotism, made the success of the celebrations a sure thing.

The Cathedral

ABOUT 1880, Archbishop Riordan started a campaign to build a new Cathedral on Van Ness Avenue, far across town from Michael Wrin's residence and place of business. By 1887 the building was reaching completion, and money was badly needed to pay for it. The long arm of the Chancery Office reached out to get Wrin's help in putting on a giant public bazaar to raise funds. Captain Wrin was named to the general committee, along with Myles Sweeney and such prominent men as capitalists Peter J. Donahue and James D. Phelan.

James R. Kelly was also on the Executive Committee, and on the committee on invitations for the bazaar. Wrin was asked by his pastor, Father Lawrence Breslin, to take responsibility, along with Thomas McGrath, for the St. Paul's Parish Booth, which would be staffed by the ladies of the parish.

Mrs. Peter Donahue, wife of the tycoon who founded iron works, steamship lines, railroads and utility companies, decided to take a booth of her own. Each parish had its own booth, with each trying to outdo the others in its contribution to the cause. There were also booths for each nationality—a French Booth, an Italian Booth, a Spanish Booth, a German booth. In an age when ethnicity was politically correct and a reason for public expression of competitive pride, each nationality tried to outperform the others in raising funds for the cause. Then there was Mrs. Donahue's booth, which outperformed all the others.

Mrs. Donahue's booth was staffed by herself, James D. Phelan, Peter J. Donahue, and Mervyn J. Donahue, plus immediate members of the Phelan and Donahue families, and in-laws. The all-star line-up was a great attraction, as the famous investors competed with one another to draw in the visitors to their booth. The crowd enjoyed the opportunity to visit with the industrialists whose names were already a part of California history, while laying more of their money on the table for each spin of the wheel. Visitors would go to their own parish booth, then to their own nationality's booth, and then all would go over to hobnob with the nabobs while unloading their spending money. Mrs. Donahue's booth got nearly as much action as all others combined.

Inevitably, the competition led to a lot of good-natured humor, which made the fair all the more entertaining. The Cathedral bazaar was a great example of how the Irish in all strata enjoyed competing with one another to see who could do the most for good causes.

St. Paul's Parish

THE WRINS had already been established in Bernal Heights for eight years when the first Mass of St. Paul's Parish was celebrated by Father Breslin in temporary quarters in 1876. The parish got off to a fast start as a result of the pooled talent of many zealous parishioners. Captain Wrin apparently saw no need to participate in the initial work, which proceeded smoothly and rapidly. At that time, he was simultaneously the commander of Shields Guard, County Delegate of A.O.H., officer of the Celtic Protective and Benevolent

Society, and partner in Freeman & Wrin, all of which were headquartered downtown, far from St. Paul's. The Wrins attended Sunday Mass in the original wooden church (in Pew 77, when not already occupied), and helped run the annual bazaars and picnics.

All parishioners got involved in the annual bazaars because these events were run by the women of the parish who, naturally, drafted their husbands, sons and daughters to do much of the work. Instead of having one party win a big prize for a mere coin, and everyone else lose, the ladies had a straight auction, with Captain Wrin as the auctioneer. This way, nobody lost, and the parish revenue was more proportionate to the value of the substantial merchandise collected.

Family members and others competed in a variety of ways. Mrs. Wrin and Mrs. Broderick were contestants in the Most Popular Lady competition. Captain Wrin's youngest son, Bill, was a candidate for Most Popular Gent. Getting away from the Sacred Heart Booth for a few minutes between auctions, Captain Wrin competed with his friends and his sons' friends at the shooting gallery run by the League of the Cross Cadets. Competition was the yeast which made the dough rise.

This particular bazaar ran for 25 consecutive days, and produced a net profit of $10,178, a very considerable sum in those days. Saint Paul's was able to retire the debt on the original church, and start funding for a much-needed bigger and better church. This event shows how the Irish got their own institutions established so readily in old San Francisco, by energetically working at it, with every member of the family doing his or her share.

The most important work which Captain Wrin did in St. Paul's Parish was not visible to the public, or to anyone except those directly affected. This was his work as a founding member and officer of the St. Paul's Conference of the St. Vincent de Paul Society. This work took him into the homes of people who were without resources, most of whom needed food, better clothing, heat, and help with their rent.

Discovering families huddled together without food or heat, and in weak health, reminded Captain Wrin of the conditions of his countrymen during the potato famine in Ireland. Seeing the glow on the faces of people enjoying their first real meal in days was powerful motivation. Usually, first calls would find an immediate need for food, and often for wood and coal, and these would be bought and delivered immediately. On the later calls, the Vincentians would try to solve the underlying problem of the client's distress.

If the father was out of work, Captain Wrin would try to find a prospective employer among his many associates. Sometimes the solution would be to find work that could be done at home by various members of the family.

If the family included a troubled youth, the Vincentians could bring the good offices of the Youth Directory to bear on the problem. If signs pointed to alcoholism, the Vincentians would get someone from one of the Catholic abstinence or temperance groups to accompany them on their next visit. The client would be brought into the company of people who knew from experience how to assist one with that problem.

Vincentians fit the "practical man, and not a talker" description given to Captain Wrin by his eulogizers. They practice, not talk, their faith, and few know of their work because everything done is confidential.

Captain Wrin was a quiet man, a stocky genial redhead with a cheerful voice and a heartfelt handshake. He was not a speech-maker and did not accomplish his objectives by assertiveness or oratory. Instead of joining in an endless debate, he would distill his thoughts into a very concise question, and state the question tersely. One or two of the Captain's supporters might suggest the appropriate answer, also tersely. Concise syllogistic reasoning stated tersely and seconded instantaneously was the means for politely ending excess oratory.

CAPTAIN WRIN was intrinsically humble. When asked to state his occupation, he always answered "tinsmith." Mary Wrin referred to her husband as "Mike the Plumber." Not until after his death was anything about his accomplishments reported in the press. In most of the societies he organized, his permanent role was one of support, such as Treasurer or benefactor, rather than head officer. He never stood for public office; he avoided all contacts with, or dependence upon, politicians and government offices. He had so little use for politicians and governments that he did not even register to vote until 23 years after becoming a citizen. He believed that people did not rise to political office, but fell into it.

Captain Wrin applied a timeless physical law "for every action, there is an equal and opposite reaction," to the art of group behavior. Being assertive brings equal and opposite reactions, or conflict, whereas an unassertive but inquiring style brings assistance and agreement.

Why did Captain Wrin devote most of his time to providing

unpaid services to his fellow men? After all, the Wrins were just ordinary people who shared with all their fellow Irish Catholics the understanding that they had been given life to be of service to God and mankind, and were just doing what comes naturally. The special motivation behind Michael's drive to be of service started in Bandon, in County Cork, where he learned the rudiments of the Catholic faith, particularly the Commandments, Beatitudes and Virtues.

Michael was conditioned by his society to be motivated to get England out of Ireland. Then, when he was age nine, the potato famine struck. Michael observed famine, fever and death. He saw charity practiced many times daily, and saw that many people's lives depended entirely upon receipt of that charity. Michael's generation matured very quickly as a result of growing up in the abject disaster of the potato famine while under the oppression of foreign rule.

Michael formed a clear idea of "the problem of evil." He was an idealistic youngster who wanted to combat the evils he encountered. He saw people surviving by cooperating with one another, and he saw others surviving by the charity of strangers who were fortunate enough to be in position to give. He saw children survive because their parents gave them their own shares of food, only to become orphans as a consequence thereof.

As a young adult, the thought processes which motivated him were along the following lines. He considered the theological virtues of Faith and Hope to not only be good common-sense psychology, but to naturally make people successful in their endeavors. Keeping the faith and never despairing were the only ways to overcome any difficulty. The resulting success in endeavors enabled one to practice the virtue of Charity generously, and Michael did so quite naturally.

Like every well-ordered human being, Michael needed a set of guidelines to follow in his day-to-day life, and no other guidelines made more sense, or were more consistent, than the Commandments on which America's civil laws were largely based. To him it was just good common sense to avoid the so-called deadly sins of pride, avarice, envy, anger, lust, gluttony, despair and sloth. These were just behavior problems, which are simply ignored by strong people. He had already learned that when one practiced the virtues of prudence, justice, fortitude and temperance, one earned the respect and confidence of all.

When Michael Wrin died at home on June 19, 1903, he had every reason to feel that his fellow Irish Americans in the city could be sure of financial assistance and other help as needed from the benevolent and charitable services he and his friends had organized.

As Monsignor Connolly offered the Requiem Mass, Captain Wrin's four surviving adult children could contemplate the myriad good deeds of their father. All they had to do was to follow his examples, and they could not go wrong. His descendants are at a loss to explain how a man could do all of the things he did, and do them so well, in the horse-and-buggy days when transportation and communication were slow.

When the Requiem Mass ended, Captain Wrin's remains were transported to Holy Cross Cemetery under the auspices of a competing funeral parlor, for his employees at Pacific Undertakers were too personally involved and too much in mourning themselves to handle the matter properly. At that point the "Curse of Cromwell" had its last shot at the Captain when the newest resident of the cemetery was registered under the English-sounding name of Wren (since corrected). In a final passive act of permanent harmony in his relations with his in-laws, Michael's remains were laid to rest in the same plot with his second wife's first husband, Peter Broderick. (After Mary [Broderick] Wrin had died at age 46 in 1883, and Peter Broderick had died, Michael married the widowed Ellen Broderick in 1892. The Wrin family plot at Calvary Cemetery was already full, and the cemetery had closed.)

Then and Now

IN MICHAEL WRIN'S time San Franciscans' economic security came from people's accepting their personal responsibilities, of natural groupings of individuals (based on family ties, race, religion, gender, language and national origin) reinforcing their members' interests with strength of numbers. People then were virtually untaxed, and had all their income to dispose of as they saw fit. There was no federal income tax, no state income tax, no social security tax, no self-employment tax, no sales tax, no utility tax, no fuel tax, and public and personal charity met the needs of the vast majority of folks who required help to survive.

The Irish had a variety of ways to provide for themselves in their old age. Their first objective in California was to buy a house, however humble. They did this by continuing the same practice of thrift which had enabled them to buy passage to America, and on to California. It was simple common-sense thrift which gradually made the Irish a "landlord class" of residential San Francisco. Rather than buy in developed and established neighborhoods where prices were the highest, they bought property on or beyond the outer edges of development, where prices were lower and the chance for appreciation greater. The Hibernia Bank lent money for the purchase of homes and provided a trustworthy place to deposit savings for one's old age.

Some took in roomers or boarders, mostly Irish, to supplement their income or help to pay off the mortgage. It was an ideal situation for newly arrived immigrants, who felt quite at home living among their own. Men found work as carpenters and painters; the women did dressmaking and laundry work at home. In the Mission district, predominantly Irish, it was the custom to buy a pair of flats, live in one and rent out the other to help with the mortgage payments. Widows without property often did domestic work which provided living quarters.

Orphaned infants and youths, troubled boys and girls, single mothers, other single women, and the aged, poor and infirm were taken care of in institutions staffed by the Little Sisters of the Poor, the Sisters of Mercy, the Sisters of Charity, the Daughters of Charity of St. Vincent de Paul, the Sisters of St. Francis and Father Crowley's Youth Directory. Benefits were determined by needs, and provided through the generosity of fellow Catholics practicing the virtue of charity.

The profusion of Catholic charitable institutions was not attributable to just the natural generosity of their faith. The Irish and Irish-Americans in San Francisco were aware of their own superior well-being as compared with that of their counterparts still in Ireland, and even with some still climbing out of the "huddled immigrant masses" in eastern ports of entry. The sense of economic well-being was a great stimulus to contribute for the benefit of those less fortunate.

Captain Wrin's Descendents

MICHAEL AND MARY WRIN had four daughters and two sons. Their youngest, Susan, died in 1880 at age six. Their next youngest daughter, Gertrude Jane, had already died in 1872 at age 24 days and was registered in Mt. Calvary Cemetery as Wren. Michael's wife, Mary A. Wrin (nee Broderick), died in 1883 at age 46, and was registered in Mt. Calvary Cemetery as May A. Wren. The Curse of Cromwell, unable to disturb living Wrins, really went to work on the family's burial records. Their oldest daughter, Minnie (Mary), never married. Daughter Sarah at age 34 married contractor Michael Loftus when he was 54; their children were William and Mary Loftus. William Loftus was treasurer of Santa Clara University at the time of his death in 1965. The family lost touch with Mary after her marriage.

Michael's youngest son Bill (Michael William) was a plumber in the family business until the Spanish-American War, when he volunteered and fought in the same battles with his Uncle James Wrin in Cuba and in the Philippines. Both were in the charge up Cuba's San Juan Hill. Both Wrins took their discharges in Peking and came home to help with the family business, after which Michael Wrin and his oldest son, James Broderick Wrin, died in rapid sequence. After the family business was destroyed in the 1906 earthquake and fire, Bill had other jobs and business ventures. He married, but had no children.

Michael's oldest son, James Broderick Wrin, married Mollie McGuire, a native of Monterey. Her father, Henry, had arrived in Monterey from County Longford early enough in the Gold Rush to buy the 144-acre Rancho of Point Pinos for a sack of gold worth $900. In Monterey, he met Bridget Fitzpatrick from Belturbet in County Cavan, and they were married by Father Angelo Casanova, pastor of the then nearly century-old Mission church. By 1877, Henry and Bridget had three children of school age.

They also had a feeling of prosperity as their developed farm and ranch had appreciated in value, and they were homesick for "the auld sod." Within the next two years these restless "Irish rancheros" had sold their land (a bit south of the lighthouse) to Felipe Gomez, sailed to Ireland, sailed back to California, and established a grocery and liquor store two blocks from St. Paul's Church at Church and Duncan Streets in San Francisco. That is the roundabout way Mollie got from Monterey to San Francisco to meet James Broderick Wrin.

James and Mollie were married in St. Paul's Parish in San Francisco. They had two sons and two daughters. James had inherited the calm demeanor and the red hair of his father. He outlived his father by only six months. He met an untimely death before becoming a moving force in any of the Irish societies. At age 36, he received a minor cut at the metal shop and was dead of blood poisoning within a few days.

The widowed Mollie divested herself of the interests in the metals and undertaking businesses and started a coffee company, marketing coffee, tea and spices. Mollie, an Irish Nationalist, often addressed the meetings of the Irish societies, invoking the spirit of her father and brother James. Mollie died of a heart ailment in 1917 at age 46, while her youngest son was with the A.E.F. in France.

Michael Wrin's extended family includes 36 great-great grandchildren and 26 great-great-great grandchildren, all but one of whom are still living in California.

John Barry Curtin
Courtesy Tuolumne County Museum

– 17 –

JOHN BARRY CURTIN
1867 - 1925

ONE OF THE MOST RENOWNED of California legislators, John Barry Curtin, more affectionately known as Constitutional John, began his adult life as a teamster, studied law and became district attorney of Tuolumne County in 1892 at the age of 22. A lawyer of singular ability, he was elected State Senator from the Twelfth District in 1898 and re-elected in 1902. In all, Sonora's favorite son served in that honored position for sixteen years. He ran for Governor of California on the Democratic ticket in 1914. He lost to the Republican incumbent, Hiram Johnson, first elected in 1911, the most noteworthy politician in California at the time.

John Barry Curtin was born at Gold Spring, a mining camp in Tuolumne County, on May 5, 1867, and resided there until his family removed to Cloudman on the old Sonora Road. Here John Sr. purchased a ranch where he built a house for his growing family. Tuolumne County's first post office was opened in the Curtin front room, with Daniel Cloudman, for whom the town was named, as Postmaster. The first telephone exchange in that region was housed in the same room.

John B. took over as property manager in 1908 and added to the Curtin family holdings by purchasing a number of adjoining ranches. The Curtins planned well, keeping their livestock on the home place in winter and pasturing them on their high mountain range, known as "Gin Flat," in summer.

How Gin Flat got its name is a fine story of the Wild West. A freight wagon, bouncing on the rocky road across the flatlands, lost a barrel of gin along the way. A gang of thirsty road workers set their tools aside and promptly rolled it into the shrubbery. They tapped the barrel in short order by knocking a hole in the top where they inserted grass straws to sip the stimulating contents. Sheepherders tending their flocks in the high country heard the commotion in the valley, and they too joined the party and had their fill of gin. When the men had been missing for a day or so, a search party was dispatched to see if they had been attacked by bandits or wild animals. Some went so far as to suggest that a burial squad might be necessary, which was not far from the unfortunate truth. In this spot the Curtins built a log cabin, still standing to day as a sturdy ruin.

Parents John and Ann Cochrane Curtin, both natives of Ireland, immigrated to America in 1848, settling in Boston, Massachusetts. They stayed there until 1852, when John set out for California by way of the Isthmus of Panama. His wife planned to follow as time and circumstance permitted.

Following his arrival in San Francisco John went into the lumber business in Bodega, supplying timber for the construction of houses in San Francisco, which was growing rapidly at the time. His principal interest, however, was in mining; he soon moved to Columbia, in the heart of the gold country. Ann came by covered wagon across the plains to join him in Columbia in 1854. About that same time Curtin, in partnership with another Irishman, invested $18,000 in a ditching company, and lost everything when it failed.

It was a very dark and discouraging period for an ambitious man like John Curtin. He sought to immediately regain his lost fortune in mining, but no claim he worked proved profitable. He was forced to peddle fruit and vegetables to make a living. Eventually he found employment as a teamster, transporting freight from the Port of Stockton to various points in Northern California. As an independent contractor, he enlarged and extended the business, which prospered until the coming of the Sierra Railroad into Tuolumne County.

In 1870 he purchased a 1,280-acre ranch which he ran so successfully that he could boast of having in excess of seven hundred cattle on his range. After all the hardships along the way, he finally became a man of means.

The Curtin Family Tree

THE ELDER Curtins had seven children, two of whom died young. The other five were Michael J., Mary Hannah, Robert A., Margaret Ellen, and John Barry, the subject of this narrative, who settled in Sonora and became its most renowned resident.

John Jr. attended public schools in Columbia and then was instructed by a private tutor employed by his father at the ranch. He showed an early interest in legal matters and began the study of law under the supervision of a noted barrister, Colonel E. A. Rogers. In

1892, at age 25, he passed the California Bar examination, and was admitted to practice in all the courts of the fast developing state.

His legal acumen led to his nomination by the Democratic party for prosecuting attorney of Tuolumne County, a seat he won by a comfortable majority. As a public prosecutor he gained the respect of his peers throughout the state. He was recognized not only for his legal ability but also for powers of oratory that held audiences spellbound.

In November 1898 the affable attorney was elected to the State Senate by the largest majority on record up to that time, and the largest vote cast for any senator from that progressive district.

November 22, 1897, was the turning point in John's life when he married a local belle, Lucie Shaw, the accomplished daughter of John Shaw, a leading pharmacist. This happy marriage lasted until John died at his palatial residence in Sonora. The residence was described in an article in the *Tuolumne Independent* at the time: "The house is solidly built and gives one the idea of permanence and stability, with a handsome front door, a magnificent staircase, richly finished open fireplaces, large and very airy bed chambers and an upstairs bathroom with roll-rim porcelain and nickel-trimmed tub."

Curtin and his bride moved into their newly constructed residence in 1897, just in time to celebrate Christmas. The stately mansion was the center of life in Sonora and the scene of celebration of his many triumphs in state politics over sixteen productive years.

John Barry Curtin was so proud of his Irish heritage that he named his only son Barry Curtin, after his illustrious grand-uncle John Barry, the "Father of the American Navy." Tragedy struck the Curtin household in 1916 when young Barry died of appendicitis. This loss plagued the senator for the rest of his life.

Senator Curtin made his relationship to John Barry public in a speech before the California Legislature on January 8, 1913. He stated that he was a grand-nephew of Commodore John Barry, and that he had been christened John Barry Curtin in honor of the naval hero. The link was confirmed by Mrs. Mary Porter Herring of Needham, Massachusetts, a distant cousin of the naval hero through her grandmother, Margaret Barry Curtin.

Commodore John Barry

JOHN BARRY was born in Tacumshin, County Wexford, close by the ancestral home of President John F. Kennedy, in 1745. He was reared by the sea and developed a fondness for the tall ships that anchored at the old port town of Wexford.

The Curtin mansion in Sonora
Courtesy Tuolumne County Museum

At the age of fifteen, with his father's permission, Barry signed on as a deckhand on a ship bound for Philadelphia. A robust youth, he found immediate employment on merchant vessels plying the eastern seaboard. At the age of twenty he was appointed master of the brig *Barbadoes* (60 tons), and shortly thereafter as master of the prestigious 200-ton *Black Prince*.

Following the outbreak of the Revolutionary War he resigned that position, saying, "I am quitting the finest ship ever built, giving up my first employment in America to join in the service of my adopted country."

At the age of 31 Barry was given an assignment by the Congress to assemble the first American fleet, to sail from Philadelphia and to take part in the war at sea. In March 1776 John Barry was appointed commander of the lead ship *Lexington* and ordered "to clear the coast of enemy cruisers."

The infant American Navy, commanded by John Barry, set sail from Boston to challenge the mighty English Navy for freedom of the seas. Heading down the east coast to Charleston, South Carolina, they encountered their baptism of fire from British Naval guns. Barry and his men fought back with grit, and victory crowned their efforts. Barry's first dispatch to the congressional authorities tells the story:

Virginia Capes
April 7, 1776

Gentlemen:
I have the pleasure to inform you at 1 P.M. this day, I fell in with the sloop *Edward* belonging to the Liverpool Frigate. We shattered her in a terrible manner - (I will give a special account of the powder and arms captured).
I have the pleasure to inform you that all of our men behaved with courage -

I am, dear gentlemen—
John Barry.

Members of Congress lost no time in making known their delight and appreciation. Back came this terse reply:

WELL DONE.
—JOHN HANCOCK

Barry's next assignment was to guard the supply ship *Nancy,* bringing badly needed gunpowder and supplies from the Caribbean. He and his crew, assisted by another brig, fought off a number of British warships until the *Nancy* was safely anchored in port, with 274 barrels of gunpowder in her hold.

Captain Barry was then ordered to proceed to Philadelphia, to take command of the thirty-two-gun *Effington,* but found his way barred. The enemy had superior forces along the Delaware estuary, blocking the entrance to Philadelphia harbor.

Unable to do battle by sea, Barry joined the Revolutionary Army. He rose through the ranks and was given command of a group of newly enlisted men, whom he trained and later led in the crucial battle of Trenton, New Jersey.

In 1778 he was back in naval uniform as commander of the 36-gun ship *Alliance.* When he and his crew cleared harbor they were attacked by two well-armed British gunships, *Atlanta* and *Trepassy.* A fierce battle ensued in which a number of the *Alliance* crew were killed. Barry himself was badly wounded and had to be carried below deck. A junior officer came to him saying, "Our ship is badly damaged. Do you want to surrender?"

"No," he shouted. "If the ship can't be fought without me, carry me back on deck." His staunch courage so animated the crew that all able-bodied seamen took up positions and fought back with all they had. At that point a fair wind arose, favoring the *Alliance.* Despite the odds, Barry and his men not only won the day, but also captured both ships with their supplies and two hundred prisoners.

The *Alliance* was then put up for repairs. Captain Barry got a badly needed rest, which helped restore him to the good health and vigor of previous years.

In recognition of his long and faithful service; the First Commodore of the United States Navy received from President George Washington in a proclamation dated February 22, 1797, the rank of Captain in the U.S. Navy, and the assigned duty of commanding the frigate bearing our young nation's name.

> THE PRESIDENT OF THE UNITED STATES OF AMERICA
> To JOHN BARRY
> I, GEORGE WASHINGTON, President of the United States reposing special Trust and Confidence in your Valor, Fidelity and Abilities, have nominated and by and with the Advice and Consent of the SENATE appointed you Captain in the NAVY of the UNITED STATES, and Commander of the FRIGATE called *UNITED STATES*, to take RANK from the Fourth Day of June, one thousand seven hundred and ninety four. You are therefore carefully and diligently to discharge the duty of CAPTAIN and COMMANDER by doing and performing all manner of things thereunto belonging. And I strictly charge and require all Officers, Marines and Seamen under your command to be obedient to your Orders as Captain and Commander. And you are to observe and follow such orders and directions, from time to time as you shall receive from the PRESIDENT OF THE UNITED STATES or any superior OFFICER set over you according to the rules and discipline of WAR and the usage of the Sea. THIS COMMISSION to continue in force during the pleasure of the President of the United States.
> Given under my hand at Philadelphia the Twenty Second day of February in the year of our Lord one thousand seven hundred

and ninety seven and of the Sovereignty and Independence of the United States the Twenty first.

G Washington
(By the President)
James McHenry
(Secretary of War)

An imposing marble statue stands in Fairmount Park in Philadelphia, with the following inscription:

John Barry, 1st Commodore U S Navy
Born 1745 - Wexford, Ireland
Died Philadelphia, Sept. 13, 1803

A truer, braver man never lived; John Barry founded our Navy, fought its early battles and trained its most skillful officers, and died in quiet relief, knowing that the United States Navy was well ordered and in capable hands.

Commodore John Barry's epitaph is memorialized in the following ditty.

There are gallant hearts whose glory
Columbia loves to name,
Whose deeds shall live in story
And ever-lasting fame.
But never yet one braver
Our Starry banner bore,
Than saucy Old Jack Barry
THE IRISH COMMODORE.

The John Barry - John Barry Curtin Connection

JOHN BARRY CURTIN inherited his patriotic zeal and fidelity from his illustrious grand-uncle, Commodore John Barry. They were both men of singular ability, fearless in the right, who held firm to the principles of liberty and justice for all.

The Barrys were of Norman stock who settled in Ireland in the late twelfth century; won over by the natives, they became more Irish than the Irish themselves. That connection is important as Commodore Barry becomes part of the larger story.

Senator Curtin introduced the following resolution (No. 10) in the California State Senate on January 31, 1913. It gave vent to his feeling on matters relative to Irish freedom and the Irish contribution to American Independence and development:

WHEREAS, after years of adversity, work and hope, but never of despair, on the part of the Irish nation, the British House of Commons recently passed the Irish home rule bill, thereby recognizing the eternal truth that an intelligent people should be sovereign in governmental affairs which concern themselves; and Whereas, it is meant on the great occasion of the granting of Irish home rule that the fairest of all free states, California, should extend its hearty congratulations to the Irish people, and to the British House of Commons which granted the same: therefore, be it
RESOLVED, by the Assembly of the State of California and the Senate, jointly, constituting the Legislature of the State of California, that we hereby extend on behalf of the State, our hearty congratulations to the Irish people on their increased assumption of powers and responsibilities, and to the British nation for the act of frank justice rendered, and further
RESOLVED, that the Governor of California be hereby requested to transmit a certified copy of these resolutions to the Honorable John E. Redmond, leader of the Irish party, and to Premier Asquith of the British Parliament.

On the question, Senator Curtin made an address to the Senate, quoted here in full, as an outstanding example of eloquent Irish oratory, as follows:

"MR. PRESIDENT and fellow members: Might I ask the indulgence of this body for a short time, to give expression to a few words on the subject of this resolution, 'Relative to Irish Home Rule.'

"My friends, there is no country beneath the sun that has a better right to claim the attention of any legislature in the American Union than has dear old Ireland.

"It is not my purpose at this time to occupy your attention with a history of Ireland. That history is undoubtedly familiar to us all. By way of introduction of the two names I shall refer to, I may say that from early history until about the year 1800 Ireland had self-government, and she was a prosperous and happy land until England's complications with other nations brought about internal dissension in Ireland—dissensions that rent her in twain, dissensions that separated the North from the South and left Ireland indeed unhappy. Every attempt, even in civil life, made by any of Ireland's illustrious sons to emancipate his co-religionist of the Catholic faith and also the dissenting Protestants from the disabilities which attended and degraded them—every effort made to win religious liberty—every struggle made to again obtain legislative independence for that island, met with stubborn resistance, and it resulted in the execution of many an Irish patriot.

"While in that deplorable state, her lamentable condition was taken advantage of and her sovereignty destroyed, and her right of self-government was terminated about the year 1800 by acts of the British Parliament, and with unremitting energy she has ever since struggled to gain it back, and by this resolution we express our gratification that her struggles seem soon to be fruitful. In 1803, a young man, then but twenty-four years of age, wrote a declaration of principles for the future government of Ireland, should the efforts for her future government then being made be successful, and that declaration was called 'The Provisional Government for the People of Ireland,' and the man who wrote it was the immortal Robert Emmet. That declaration has been frequently referred to as 'Emmet's Manifesto.'

"For that 'offense,' as it was then called, Emmet was charged with treason and his tragic end is the blackest spot in all England's history. At that time Emmet was engaged to a beautiful and highly accomplished young lady, Sarah Curran, the daughter of John Philpot Curran, the most eloquent man who ever stood before a court or jury in any land at any time in all history. Because of her devotion to him and of her grief over his future, should he be captured, his manly impulses caused him to come out of the seclusion to which he had fled when he became aware that nothing but his life would appease the law. It was then administered by corrupt courts and packed juries in all cases where the life or liberty of an Irish subject was at issue. It was while offering consolation to the girl he loved that he was arrested, charged with treason, tried and convicted by a jury before Lord Norbury in Dublin, and was executed at Downpatrick, Ireland, on October 21, 1803.

"MR. PRESIDENT and fellow members, all history does not record any words so eloquent as those uttered by Robert Emmet on that fateful date when asked by Lord Norbury what had he to say why sentence should not be pronounced upon him according to law. The response given by Emmet stands today as the masterpiece in all our literature. Would that I could at this time read it all to you, but the hour does not permit it, and I therefore give you his concluding words as he stood in the shadow of death: 'I have but one request to ask at my departure from this world; it is, the charity of its silence.

Let no man write my epitaph; for, as no man who knows my motives dares now vindicate them, let not prejudice or ignorance asperse them. Let them and me rest in obscurity and peace, and my tomb remain uninscribed and my memory in oblivion, until other times and other men can do justice to my character. When my country takes her place among the nations of the earth, then, and not until then, let my epitaph be written. I have done.'

"Mr. President and fellow members, in carrying out that awful sentence of the law, it is recorded that the court directed that there be two men then confined in the prison in Dublin who would take that body out upon a lonely sidehill and in the ground unmarked, bury it for all time so that the grave of Robert Emmet would be unknown, and one of those men in carrying out that sentence, while carrying the body, broke from a weeping willow tree a couple of branches and planted them at the head of the grave. And when the work of burial was over these two were returned to prison and quickly transported to Van Diemans Land, where they remained until they became very old. One of the two men was allowed to return to Ireland some twenty-eight years afterward, and when he arrived he sought the grave of Robert Emmet and, my friends, from the inspiration thus furnished, the immortal Thomas Moore wrote these beautiful lines:

> Pray tell me, I said to an old man who strayed
> Drooping o'er the grave that his own hands had made;
> Pray tell me that name of the tenant that sleeps
> Under yon mossy slab where the lone willow weeps.
> Not a stone in the grave bears the name of the dead,
> And yonder black slab declares not whose spirit has fled.
> In silence he bowed and beckoned me nigh,
> Then stood on the grave and said with a sigh:
> He told them - commanded them, the lines o'er his grave
> Should never be traced by the hand of a slave.
> You see we obeyed him; 'tis now twenty-eight years,
> Yes we come here to moisten his grave with our tears.
> O breathe not his name - let it sleep in the shade
> Where cold and unhonored his relics are laid;
> Sad, silent, and dark be the tears that we shed,
> As the night dew that falls on the grass o'er his head.
> But the night dew that falls, though in silence it weeps,
> Shall brighten with verdure the grave where he sleeps;
> And the tear that we shed, though in secret it rolls,
> Shall long keep his memory green in our souls.

"Today, in Ireland, of all our patriots, the dearest and most revered name is that of Robert Emmet, and from his grave in words more potent than those of any living man, he is still appealing for her liberty. Let us bow in reverent commemoration of the ideal patriot of Ireland's heroic period. Let us join with her and rejoice that the prejudices and the hatred, that have kept obscure the grave of Robert Emmet, have long since died away and that patriot who, when facing the executioner, uttered that inspiring address, and begged in vain for the charity of silence and left his epitaph for other times and other men, has become the favorite hero of popular liberty, his name above the need of eulogy, and his motives beyond the reach of malice.

"And here, my friends, let me pay a tribute to that lovely girl, Emmet's sweetheart—Sarah Curran. History attests that she was the noblest type of womanhood, gentle, kind and affectionate; and because of her devotion to Emmet and because her loneliness during his seclusion was the cause of his return to offer her consolation, that her grief over his fate rendered her life truly sad. Her parents took her to France and to Italy, and all the crowned heads of Europe offered her consolation, but in vain. And why not in vain? No human plummet has ever sounded the depths of a woman's love. No surveyor's chain will ever mark the limits of a woman's patient devotion, and only the wings of the Archangel will ever transcend that pinnacle to which the sublime principle of self-sacrifice exalts a woman's soul. It was because of her noble attributes that the Bard of Ireland immortalized her in his beautiful poem, 'She is Far from the Land.'

"MY FRIENDS, in those stirring times around the years 1800 and 1803, there is another name that was brought forth - a name that shines bright on the pages of Ireland's history, a name that is heard on the 17th day of every March in every land in the civilized world, and that name is James Napper-Tandy, familiarly called Napper-Tandy. About that period there was formed in the city of Dublin a society called the United Irishmen. It had for its purpose the diffusion of education among all Irish subjects and to raise money and provide the means for restoration to Ireland of her right to self-government. Napper-Tandy was secretary of that society. About that time the British Parliament had passed an Act making it a death penalty to float the green flag of Erin or to wear the Irish emblem, the shamrock.

"For his part in that society, Napper-Tandy was arrested, charged with treason. He was defended by John Philpot Curran, and on May 19, 1800, was acquitted. He was again brought up on a similar charge, and seeing no justice to be had before a corrupt court and a packed jury, he pleaded guilty to the charge and in April, 1801, was sentenced to death; but his sentence was commuted and he was exiled to France, where he died on August 24, 1803.

"Fellow Senators, within the phraseology of our national anthem, 'The Star-Spangled Banner,' abides a sentiment that finds a responsive throb in the heart of every American wherever it is sung. It writes the history of our country as in the year 1812. Out of veneration to the Stars and Stripes we rise and do it homage. In Ireland's anthem, 'The Wearing of the Green,' abides a sentiment that strikes a responsive chord in the heart of every man, woman and child through whose veins flows even one drop of Irish blood. It writes Ireland's history as it was in 1800, and in it is a beautiful tribute to America. It is because of its beautiful sentiments that I shall crave your indulgence while I recite it:

The Wearing of the Green

O Paddy, dear, and did you hear the news that's going round?
The shamrock is forbid by law to grow on Irish ground;
St. Patrick's Day no more we'll keep; his colors can't be seen;
For there's a bloody law against the wearing of the green.
I met with Napper-Tandy, and he took me by the hand,
And he said, "How's poor old Ireland, and how does she stand?"
She's the most distressful country that ever yet was seen;
They are hanging men and women for the wearing of the green.
Oh, if the color we must wear is England's cruel red,
Sure Ireland's sons will ne'er forget the blood that they have shed,
You may take the shamrock from your hat and cast it on the sod,
But 'twill take root and flourish there, though under foot 'tis trod,
When law can stop the blades of grass from growing as they grow,
And when the leaves in summertime their verdure dare not show,
Then I will change the color I wear in my caubeen;
But till that day, please God, I'll stick to wearing of the green.
But if at last our color should be torn from Ireland's heart,
Her sons with shame and sorrow from the dear old isle will part;
I've heard a whisper of a country that lies beyond the sea,
Where rich and poor stand equal in the light of freedom's day.
O Erin, must we leave you, driven by a tyrant's hand?
Must we ask a mother's blessing from a strange and distant land?
Where the cruel cross of England shall nevermore be seen,
And where, please God, we'll live and die still wearing of the green.

"Mr. President and fellow members, who is there in all these United States who would raise a voice against an Irishman floating the green flag or wearing the green in our glorious land of the free? I apprehend there is no one who would do so.

"Ireland's contribution to the cause of freedom entitles her people to our everlasting gratitude, and we may well pause in our busy activities and voice our appreciation of her patient efforts for self-government.

"My friends, in those days of the early history of our country, Ireland furnished many of the men who paved the way for our present greatness. They drew the inspiration of this Republic from the spirit of resistance to unwarranted authority. They consecrated their lives and fortunes to the cause of human freedom.

"From Lexington to Yorktown, with sword and bayonet, they wrote an imperishable record on the tablets of American history. In every struggle in that memorable war, the Irish sword flashed in the van of victory. In every contest it was on the side of freedom, and though sometimes defeated, has never been sheathed with dishonor.

"Among those heroes, who, like Barry, fought the battles of freedom, were General John Stark, the hero of Bennington; General Anthony Wayne, the hero of Germantown; General Richard Montgomery, the hero of Cowpens; General Moylan, who was side by side with Washington on every field; Knox's artillery and Morgan's riflemen - all Irishmen - wrote the history of the battle of Monmouth.

"General Joseph Warren, the son of an Irishman, saw his 453 heroes wafted heavenward by the beat of the angels' wings from the summit of Bunker Hill, and he too, ere he left the battlefield, sacrificed his life in the cause of freedom.

"When we call the roll of honor of those who participated in that war, we find no names that shine brighter than those of the sons of Ireland and their descendants.

"If we turn to the constitution of our country, we find thereon the names of Ireland's descendants in the persons of the illustrious Thomas Fitzsimmons, Pierce Butler and Daniel Carroll. When the war of the Revolution was over and Benjamin Franklin was the first American minister to England, the British minister asked him this question, 'Please Sir Franklin, state the different nationalities in the American army in the war of the Revolution.' Think of his reply, which is a matter of record of today. His answer was: 'Fifty per cent Irish, thirty-three per cent other nationalities and seventeen per cent native born.' Think of it, it was fifty per cent Irishmen who raised the American flag in victory at the battle of Lexington and who went down in defeat at Bunker Hill. It was fifty per cent Irishmen who, without firing a gun, but with drawn swords, fought with the flag in glorious victory at Stony Point. It was fifty per cent Irishmen in the army who sent those bullets to victory at Camden and Eutaw Springs.

"It was fifty per cent Irishmen in that small army on the bleak cold night of December 25, 1776, that filled the boats and, with George Washington crossed the ice-blocked Delaware River and captured those hired Hessians in the battle of Trenton. It was fifty per cent Irish blood that crimsoned the snows that covered the grounds under the starless nights at Valley Forge. It was fifty per cent Irishmen that marched home with the Father of this Country after eight long years of weary battle to a glorious victory—a victory that established on this land the lasting union of these United States.

"MAY WE NOT well be proud of a people that rendered such valiant aid in establishing this land of freedom? May we not feel proud of our attachment for a people who began their struggles in 1800 to restore their government, by hanging in the banquet hall at Donegal Arms the portrait of Benjamin Franklin and beneath it the motto, 'Where liberty is, there is my country,' and ended with a toast to our country, 'Lasting freedom and prosperity to the United States of America.'

"That historical, friendly, national interest spoken of so feelingly by Washington, Jefferson and Monroe continued. Between 1800 and 1861 Ireland was sending her children to populate our country and we have never asked them to renounce their affection for their native land. In 1848, the star upon Ireland's horizon was growing brighter than before, since 1800, and efforts were again made to secure Ireland's freedom. A mass meeting was called in the city of Dublin, presided over by William Smith O'Brien. Thomas Francis Meagher addressed the meeting, urging all Ireland to strive for self-government, then an offense punishable by death.

"They were arrested, tried, convicted and sentenced to be hanged and drawn in quarters. Through the intercession of the Empress of Austria, their sentence was commuted and they were exiled to Australia for life. Long years afterward, William Smith O'Brien was allowed to come and remain in Italy, where he died. His remains were brought home and the longest funeral procession that ever followed a man to his grave through the city of Dublin followed

William Smith O'Brien to his. Thomas Francis Meagher escaped from Australia and came to New York in 1852 and began the publication of the *New York Freeman's Journal,* then one of the most ably edited papers in New York, out of which he amassed a considerable fortune.

"When the war with the South broke out—when misguided sons sought to disintegrate this Union and found an aristocracy on its ruins, and sent Mason and Slidel on the British ship *Trent,* which had run the blockade at the Port of Charleston, South Carolina, and which was pursued by the American ship, San Jacinto, there was imminent danger of a war with England as a result of their seizure. A mass meeting was called in the city of Dublin for the purpose of raising funds to defray the expense of sending every Irish soldier and sailor to America to fight for the preservation of the American Union. At that meeting, in an address, it was said: 'We must fight for the preservation of the American Union - we must save the American Union at all hazards; we must save it for our countrymen there - for their children and for ours—for with the American Union lost our doom is sealed.'

"FELLOW SENATORS, they did aid in saving the American Union. On every battle field in that war, Irish blood was shed in defense of our Union. You may call the roll of honor on all those battlefields and you will find that Erin's sons were at the forefront in every battle. The lamented Thomas Francis Meagher mustered the 69th New York regiment—every man of whom was a son of Erin and wore a uniform of green, and they carried the green flag. On the 21st day of July, 1861, in the battle of Bull Run, when the Union army was routed and beating a retreat, and was pursued by the Southern Black Horse cavalry, that 69th New York regiment, commanded then by Colonel Michael F. Corcoran, turned upon that cavalry and with drawn swords and 'like lions leaping at a foe, when mad with hunger's pang,' they charged and literally cut that cavalry to pieces. They saved the rear of the Union army from annihilation. In that battle, besides the 69th New York regiment, were the 1st, 2nd, 3rd, 4th and 5th New York regiments—all Irishmen.

"On December 13, 1862, in the battle of Fredericksburg, there were the 63rd, 69th and 88th New York regiments, all Irishmen, and they were there under the command of Colonel Thomas Francis Meagher. Their green flag was shot to pieces, and when the day was turning against the Union army, Meagher scaled the walls of Fredericksburg and shouted to his regiments: 'Boys, our green flag has been shot to pieces, but there is more green here yet. Let us wear the green in our hats and fight to victory.' And they tore sprigs of boxwood from the hedge, and put it in their hats and fought until the battle was over.

"Fellow Senators, of the battle of Fredericksburg, John Boyle O'Reilly wrote a poem in which this verse occurs:

'O GOD what a pity,' they cry in their cover,
As rifles are readied and bayonets made tight;
'Tis Meagher and his fellows, their caps have green clover;
'Tis Greek to Greek now for the rest of the fight.'
Twelve hundred the column, their rent flag before them,
With Meagher at their head, they have dashed at the hill.
Their foemen are proud of the country that bore them;
But, Irish in love, they are enemies still.
Out rings the fierce word, 'Let them have it..'
The rifles are emptied point-blank in the hearts of the foe;
It is green against green, but a principle stifles
The Irishman's love in the Georgian's blow.
The column has reeled, but it is not defeated;
In front of the guns they reform and attack;
Six times they have done it, and six times retreated;
Twelve hundred they came, and two hundred go back.
Two hundred go back with the chivalrous story;
The wild day is closed in the night's solemn shroud;
A thousand lie dead, but their death was a glory
That calls not for tears—the Green Badges are proud.

"Fellow Senators, was it not the son of an Irishman, that intrepid little Phil Sheridan, to whom Grant said with reference to Winchester, 'Go in,' and post haste didn't he ride that fifteen miles and 'go in'? And didn't he lead his division of the Union army to victory at Perrysville and Stone River?

"Was it not the son of an Irishman, Major General Edward O. Ord, who led his army to victory at Dransville, Vicksburg, Fort Harrison and Petersburg? There was General Joseph Mulligan, who commanded at the battle of Lexington and saved Missouri to the Union, and when wounded at Winchester, and being carried from the battlefield said: 'Let me down and save the flag.'

"It was the New York and Massachusetts regiments of all Irishmen that bore the brunt of the six days' battle at the Sunken Roads and Antietam. At Gettysburg, the Waterloo of the Confederacy, it was Col. O'Rourke and his Massachusetts regiment of all Irishmen that held Little Round Top in the fiercest of that fight. Why, sirs, you could call the roll of honor until the last name was reached, and around none would you place a laurel where it would shine brighter than on those of Irish blood.

"When the war was over, in appreciation of his splendid services, President Grant appointed Meagher the first Governor of Montana Territory. While coming down the Missouri River on the night of July 4, 1865, he accidentally fell overboard and with one splash of water his body passed from sight and that finished scholar, that brilliant orator, that brave soldier, Thomas Francis Meagher, was no more. Today, in the city of Butte, Montana, stands a heroic statue to his memory.

"Now, fellow Senators, if I have occupied too much of your time in these busy moments, I trust I may be pardoned. It is to me the proudest privilege in my years of service here. My great-grand-uncle, Commodore John Barry—an Irishman to the core, and for whom I was named, and for whom my only son is named—is the accredited founder of the American navy. He won the first and also the last naval victory in the War of the Revolution, and loving hands erected o'er his grave in Philadelphia a beautiful monument, and the congress of the United States, without a dissenting vote, appropriated sixty thousand dollars to erect, and did erect, in the grounds of the national capitol at Washington, a heroic statue to the memory of Commodore John Barry.

"I had another uncle, Andrew Corcoran, who was on a British battleship at Quebec when the call to aid the American Union was heard in the city of Dublin in 1861, and he responded to that call and was with Admiral Farragut when he cut the cable of hulls that misguided sons had stretched across the Mississippi River, and therefore I respond cheerfully to that sentiment:

> No matter where in any land the Irish race are seen,
> Their one and only thought is on that little isle so green.

"To dear old Ireland, I can with much feeling devote time to do her reverence. Although many of you may not be of her faith or descend from her people, yet you can join in a slight way towards expressing good will and a fond hope for her deliverance, and thus show that we are interested in her common welfare.

"On every field of American war their blood has been shed in our defense. There is no instance where an Irish sword has been drawn against the cause of freedom.

"IRELAND HAS GIVEN US the brightest lights that adorn our legal profession, and has given us those who are among the highest type of our citizenship, and the noblest mothers in our land.

"She has contributed unsparingly her children to enrich our literature.

"She has sent the ministers of her faith to spread among us the truth of the gospel and the precepts of her holy religion.

"She has helped watch through her distressful tears the splendid efforts of her children to maintain in this land the fair and equal chance for all, then and still denied them in the country that gave them birth.

"Let us unanimously adopt this resolution and join with the Irish people in a fervent prayer that their country will soon be given Home Rule, for which they have longed and patiently striven. I hope, therefore, there will not be one dissenting vote on this resolution."

The resolution was unanimously adopted.

SENATOR CURTIN'S stirring address is on file in the California congressional record, and forms an integral part of the history of this state.

John Barry Curtin had two brothers, Michael J. Curtin of Sonora and Robert A. Curtin of San Rafael, who also left their imprint on California.

Michael or "Mike," a native of Gold Springs, acquired his education in the public schools of nearby Columbia and while still a young man moved with his family to Cloudman. A teamster by occupation, he began life hauling freight as an independent contractor, from Oakdale to Sonora and later as superintendent of the old Sonora-Mona Road after it became a state highway. About that same time he was appointed steward of Tuolumne County Hospital, a position he held until his death at age 73. Besides his wife Mary, Mike left a daughter and three sons to mourn his passing, Mrs. Mercedes Burt of Alameda, and Lloyd, Emmet and Carlton Curtin of Martinez, Contra Costa County.

Robert A., a San Francisco policeman, lived in San Rafael. In his day Robert was one of the most admired officers on the police force. It was said that if the office of Police Chief had been an elective one, the affable cop, Robert Curtin, would have been the people's choice.

Robert, who grew up in Cloudman on the family ranch, knew the intricacies of mountain farming, stock raising and freighting from years of actual experience with cattle drives and jerk-line teams. In later years Robert, who had a way with words, delighted his listeners with hair-raising tales of bygone days.

JOHN BARRY CURTIN—Constitutional John to his constituents—was a man of many talents: successful rancher, district attorney, and California State Senator: so much wrapped up in three brilliant careers. Who but the Curtins could better characterize California's Irish heritage, wherein a salty hero of the American Revolution, John Barry, has his place?

Right Rev. Msgr. Thomas J. Fitzgerald, V. F.
Pastor of Sacred Heart Parish, Redlands, California
1857 - 1930

– 18 –

HARPS IN RIVERSIDE COUNTY
MISSIONARIES AND ENTREPRENEURS

IN ALL MISSIONARY ENDEAVORS, the need for religious service is determined by the number of inhabitants in a given region at a given time. There was little need, however, for such service or a house of worship when Father Thomas Fitzgerald arrived in Riverside County in 1893, for there were only a handful of Catholics in the area at the time. This did not deter the ambitious young clergyman who took delight in the landscape of Riverside County and declared it to be the most beautiful place he had ever seen. Despite the lack of prospects he vowed to build a church there.

Redlands' beautiful Sacred Heart Church stands as a memorial to Father Fitzgerald's foresight and tenacity. It all began in an old brick building, the site of the present Casa Loma Hotel, where the first Mass was celebrated. A zealous layman collected a little money, rented a store in the building, and had a temporary altar erected and some rude pews set up to accommodate the worshipers.

The arrangement was only temporary, as both priest and people wanted a church of their own, despite the many obstacles. The Catholic citizens were few and mostly poor, and a church of any dimension was a formidable undertaking. One forthright Catholic called on Father Fitzgerald with this admonition, "Father, you are very foolish to build a church in Redlands. You cannot do it."

That was too much for the priest, who replied, "If you are as sure of going to Heaven as I am to build a church in Redlands you are a lucky man." Father Fitzgerald made good his word, and on the day the roof was placed on the new church, he received a sizable donation from that same person.

On December 1, 1895, Father Fitzgerald celebrated the first mass in the newly constructed Sacred Heart Church, and on the first day of January, 1896, the church was formally dedicated by Archbishop Montgomery. A pontifical High Mass was sung by Father McCarthy of Pasadena, while the Archbishop preached the sermon. People came from surrounding parishes, from as far away as Los Angeles. Mrs. Lewis Grant of Los Angeles was the organist, and the choir was under the direction of Joseph Scott, a leading Catholic layman in Southern California. This dedication marked a new and inspiring epoch in the history of Redlands, and was a harbinger of good things to come. As Father Fitzgerald noted, "there was at least a little house in which Jesus would live."

The tenacious pastor can be regarded as one of the pioneers of Riverside County. He arrived when it was but a sunny wilderness, with few inhabitants to share his optimism. There he would spend the best years of his Apostleship; he remained at Sacred Heart until his death at the age of 73.

Born in County Kerry on October 25, 1857, Thomas Fitzgerald received his primary education in the parochial school and at a private school conducted by the Dominican Fathers. He then enrolled in Saint Brendan's Seminary in Killarney, where he spent the next four years in training for the priesthood. From there he entered the University of Maynooth, where he completed a seven-year postgraduate course.

Little is known of his studies at Maynooth because the records, according to present-day authorities, were destroyed by fire. He was ordained to the priesthood in 1883. His first assignment, in Scotland, lasted just one year. In 1887 he was called home to his native parish, but within a year's time his health began to deteriorate, which necessitated his removal to a more equitable climate. At that time tuberculosis was rampant in Ireland, and Father Fitzgerald was one of its victims.

Without further delay he immigrated to America and settled in Colorado, hoping that the altitude and clear air would prove beneficial for his respiration problems. While the brisk mountain air brought some immediate relief, it also was conducive to hemorrhages in his lungs. In 1893 he left Colorado and came to sunny California.

Father Fitzgerald settled first in Beaumont in Riverside County, where the air was clear and dry, ideal for his respiratory ailments. However, at the request of the venerable churchman Father Stockman, he decided to begin his labors in nearby Redlands, a small place with very few Catholics to support the undertaking. Yet he accepted the challenge wholeheartedly and began laying the foundation for a new parish.

Soon the population of Redlands had grown to the point where it was feasible to provide Catholic services on a regular basis. The first such religious service was held in a rented store where the Stater Brothers supermarket is now located. Father Stockman, a pioneer founder of churches in San Bernardino and Riverside counties, celebrated the first Mass in that building on Easter Sunday, March 25, 1894. He continued to provide religious service in Redlands until he was transferred to Santa Barbara the following year.

It was then that Father Fitzgerald took over, having regained his health to the extent that he was able to assume full parish-oriented duties. He traveled by horse and buggy from Beaumont to Redlands to say Mass and minister to the sick and dying when called upon. For over two years he came by freight train (courtesy of the Southern Pacific Railway) to serve the growing community. His Irish cohorts the Doyles, Mulvihills, Butlers and Carrolls, would take turns to meet the train and drive him to the rented church facility in Redlands. Following dinner with one of the families, they would then take him part way to El Casco, where other friends would meet him and drive him home to Beaumont.

March 27, 1897, was a memorable occasion, when services were conducted with more than one half non-Catholics in the congregation. Bishop George Montgomery spoke on the Transfiguration and held everyone's attention for an hour. Immediately thereafter the Sacrament of Confirmation was conferred on John and Margaret Mulvihill, Katie Murphy and Edna Harrington. After the ceremony Denis Mulvihill, one of the prime movers in the development of the new parish, presented a check for five hundred dollars in payment of one half of the church debt. The remaining amount of $1,000 was paid off within the year.

THE FIRST CATHOLIC FUNERAL in Redlands, for E. J. Waite, recorded on April 9, 1897, will also go down in history, as he was the man who planted the first orange orchard where the city of Redlands now stands. Father Fitzgerald conducted the funeral service and delivered the eulogy for the pioneer citrus grower. Another memorable day in the life of Sacred Heart parish arrived when Daniel Murphy, the first altar boy, was ordained a priest by the venerable Cardinal Gibbons of Baltimore. Some years later Bishop Montgomery appointed Father Murphy as an assistant rector of Saint

Vibian's Cathedral in Los Angeles. His next important assignment was to a parish in Hollywood. While serving in that active parish he fell sick and passed away in 1913. Daniel's brother Leo, the youngest of the Murphy family, studied for the priesthood and was ordained in 1919, six years after his brother's death.

In 1897 Father Fitzgerald purchased additional property for the construction of a rectory. When the building was completed the pastor moved from Beaumont to Redlands, in late October of that year, and made it his home from then on.

ONE OF Father Fitzgerald's pet projects was the establishment of a parochial day school for local Catholics who could not afford the cost of young students living away from home. In carefully chosen words he said, "No matter how grand and beautiful a church may be, how large and well-ordered the Sunday School it may have, how elegant the parochial mansion, a parish without a school is incomplete. A school is the nursery of the church." With this inspiring philosophy ringing in their ears, parishioners looked forward to the day when a fine school could be built for their children. Little did they dream that within a year's time their expectations would be fulfilled.

Two Ursuline sisters, after years of teaching, arrived in Riverside in 1896 in the hopes of regaining their former good health and vigor in sunny California. They were met by the affable pastor, who asked, with a twinkle in his Irish eyes, "Why not come to Redlands and start a school?" The offer, with no strings attached, commanded their immediate attention. The sisters toured the new city and were convinced that its glorious sunshine and entrancing beauty would lure more and more people as time went on.

In November 1897 the good sisters took possession of the two-story structure adjoining the church property on Eureka Street. The following year they opened a school in a corner of Sacred Heart Church, with an initial enrollment of twelve children. From this humble beginning the school went on to become the first truly parochial facility in Riverside County. It is still flourishing at 215 South Eureka Street, With plans in the making to celebrate its hundredth anniversary.

In 1908 Father Fitzgerald brought five Sisters of Mercy from Los Angeles to Redlands, following the Ursulines' return to the Mother house in Pittsburgh, Pennsylvania. The five Sisters were all of Irish extraction, as their names would indicate: Rev. Mother M. Joachim McBrinn, Sister M. Dolores Dunn, Sister M. Vincent Needham, Sister M. Benedict Rooney, and Sister M. Frances de Sales.

One of the Sisters who came to Riverside in 1896 and started the first Catholic school in the county, with Father Fitzgerald's help.

One of Sacred Heart's most renowned parish organizations, "Lovers of the Poor," was credited with distributing more benefits than any other charitable association in Redlands. The first Knights of Columbus chapter was founded on April 3, 1910, at the behest of John Reilly and Father M.P. Scanlon. The Council, like the Lovers of the Poor, took an active interest in charity work in the developing community.

Father Fitzgerald, who had suffered from tuberculosis as a youth, made a bold attempt in 1911 to establish a Tuberculosis Sanitarium in Mentone, where a former hotel stood on a seven-acre parcel and only needed remodeling for the new purpose. He requested additional Sisters of Mercy to run the proposed medical institution, with the promise of erecting a building on the grounds large enough to serve as a convent. The new medical facility opened in November 1911, and was filled to capacity almost immediately.

DURING WORLD WAR I, the U.S. Army used the new hospital to treat its soldier patients. However, at war's end, the civilian patients could not afford even the moderate charges, and as a result the good sisters had no choice but to close Saint Thomas Sanitarium and sell the property. This was the only setback for Father Fitzgerald during his eventful years as pastor of Sacred Heart Parish in Redlands.

However, the disappointment was overshadowed by all the honors which were about to be bestowed on him. On the twenty-fifth anniversary of his ordination to the priesthood, the citizens presented him with a silver loving cup inscribed "A token of the appreciation for his life, his character and his services to this community." In November 1918 Father Fitzgerald was appointed Vicar Forane of the San Bernardino deanery, which encompassed the eastern portion of the Diocese of Los Angeles.

Two years later, in 1920, the Right Reverend John J. Cantwell, Bishop of Monterey-Los Angeles, officiated at the investiture of Father Fitzgerald as a Domestic Prelate with the title of Monsignor. Following the religious ceremony a banquet was held in his honor by the Knights of Columbus. This was another city-wide celebration that showed the esteem in which he was held.

In 1921 Sacred Heart Parish was said to have a membership of some 1,200 adherents, a far cry from the handful of Catholics who greeted Father Fitzgerald when he arrived in Redlands back in 1894. About that time the Church was completely renovated at a cost of several thousand dollars, which the parishioners could well afford, according to a historical review of San Bernardino and Riverside Counties published by *The Tidings* in July 1922. The report said the district was considered the largest orange shipping center in the world; in a single year more than six thousand carloads of "sun-kissed" oranges had been shipped from Redlands.

Redlands was also touted as the "Flyless Town," famed for its health-giving, insect-free climate. To this, Father Fitzgerald could well say "Amen." He had arrived in Redlands a very sick man and was now hale and hearty at the age of 66.

FOR ALMOST THIRTY YEARS Father Fitzgerald had cared for his flock and befriended others who were not members of his congregation. His contributions were endless. He founded the Holy Name Society, open to all men of the parish, as well as the Altar Society, which helped the Sisters, decorated the altar with home-grown flowers, and kept the altar linens, albs and the altar boys' robes clean and mended. They also sang in the choir and reached out to the community as a whole in the spirit of ecumenis, visited the sick, hosted a World Day of Prayer, and took part in meetings of Church Women United.

Father Fitzgerald founded the Legion of Mary, which served the various needs of the community in ensuing years. The members, working in pairs, made sick calls, took the congregation census and assisted at baptisms and other important functions. Sacred Heart Church was filled twice on Sundays, and services were held every weekday, mornings and evenings. All this betokened a thriving, active parish.

In 1929 the aging pastor's health began to fail, and his superiors prevailed upon him to accept an assistant pastor, Father John Rudden, a zealous fellow Irishman. Over the years Father Fitzgerald had been offered more important assignments, but he refused them, determined to keep to the little place he loved so dearly.

On January 15, 1930, the beloved pastor died at the age of 73. His funeral was the largest ever witnessed in the Inland Empire up to that time. The mourners included nearly three hundred of his fellow priests in the sanctuary and an overflow crowd of friends and parishioners who came to say a last farewell.

The local branch of the American Legion provided a uniformed escort for his cortege as it passed through Redlands on the way to the cemetery. The words of Bishop Thomas Conahy at the 1908 school celebration were quoted in an obituary notice on January 16, 1930 by the *Redlands Daily Facts*:

> He has in both word and truth been a priest of God, who has never thought of himself, but of others. I cannot recount his many works of Christlike goodness, but if we could but hear, many of the voices from graves and from far-off lands would raise themselves in words of love and praise for his goodness to them.

The Ecumenical Spirit in Redlands

THE ARRIVAL of Reverend John B. Toomey, a Congregational minister, led to more cordial relationships between the various religious denominations and paved the way for the ecumenical movement in Riverside County. Father Fitzgerald and the Reverend Mr. Toomey, although of different religious persuasions, had much in common. They were both Irish—the former was Irish born, and the latter's father, Edward, was a native of County Cork who came to America and settled in Missouri.

As a young man Edward Toomey enlisted in the Union Army and served for the duration of the Civil War. His mother, Martha, belonged to a pioneer Missouri family who had relocated from Tennessee some time previously.

Reverend Toomey was born in Ray County, Missouri, in 1868, and following his ordination spent some fifteen years laboring in his native state as a church builder and preacher of considerable merit. Like his father, Reverend Toomey was imbued with the spirit of patriotism and served as chaplain at Fort Kearny.

A graduate of Otterbein University, Ohio, he subsequently enrolled in Yale University where he earned a Bachelor of Divinity degree. Reverend Toomey brought years of experience to his pastoral duties in Redlands. He had traveled widely and took an extensive tour of the Mediterranean region, where he visited the great cities of Rome, Athens and Constantinople, as well as Egypt and the Holy Land.

Following his arrival in California, Reverend Toomey was made pastor of the Congregational Church in Ontario, where he ministered for a number of years and built up his congregation. During that time he built a house and brought his parents, both of whom were over eighty, to live with him. He was an active member of the El Camino Club, which was made up of local educators and philosophers.

In 1891 he married Miss Minnie Bender, a daughter of Daniel Bender in Westerville, Ohio. Mrs. Toomey died young in Ontario in 1919. Their only daughter, Helen Toomey, was a student at Pomona College at the time. Some years later Mr. Toomey married Inez Crawford, a retired missionary from Japan, whose father John Crawford was a pioneer resident of Ontario.

Reverend Toomey and Father Fitzgerald sought to serve their respective congregations in an ecumenical manner by bringing together people of different beliefs and customs. Although California was unique among the states in having no "Sunday Laws," church attendance and morality were as good or better than in states which did have them.

The ecumenical aspect caught the attention of other congregations: Baptists, Episcopalians, Methodists and Presbyterians, who saw in it a way to increase their flocks. The results were truly phenomenal. However it was not until 1957 that the extent of the pioneer ecumenical movement was made known when the *Redlands Daily Facts* published the religious census in Redlands.

Sacred Heart	567 Families
Saint Mary	541 Families
First Baptist	527 Families
First Presbyterian	509 Families
First Methodist	457 Families
Episcopal	389 Families
Congregational	362 Families

The ecumenical movement begun by Father Fitzgerald and Reverend Toomey paved the way for the rise in church attendance by the various Christian denominations in the vicinity of Redlands.

Michael Murphy, Pioneer Community Builder

MICHAEL MURPHY was another Harp who played a leading role in the development of San Bernardino and Riverside Counties. From his arrival in 1875 he was concerned with various enterprises of importance to the community, and in the civic and material development of the state as a whole. There are many incidents in his long and vigorous career that pay him tribute as a man of vision and action, a citizen of sterling worth and a construction genius of singular ability.

Michael Murphy was born in Waukeegan, Illinois, on April 15, 1847, a son of John and Bridget (Rogers) Murphy, both natives of Ireland. John Murphy, Michael's father who arrived there in 1829, was one of its early pioneers at a time when the future city was little more than a frontier trading-post.

A farmer at heart, John had the prescience to purchase a tract of land a short distance from the booming city of Chicago. It was there that his children were born and reared in the Irish tradition, with the home as the center of life and learning. Michael was seventh in line of birth.

Michael A. Murphy
from an early History of San Bernardino and Riverside Counties

John Murphy was an exemplar of high principles and religious fervor which he dutifully passed on to his children. Both he and his wife, Bridget, were devout communicants who lived and died in the bosom of Mother Church.

Michael acquired his primary education in the public schools, whence he enrolled in the College of Saint Mary's of the Lake in Chicago. Following graduation he took a course in business administration at Poughkeepsie, New York. At the completion of his studies there he returned home to Waukeegan and continued to live with his parents. Shortly thereafter he found employment as a bookkeeper with John McEwen, one of the leading building contractors in Chicago. He held that position until the great Chicago fire that swept the city in 1871.

During the reconstruction period he formed a partnership with Owen Lauback in the lumber business in Chicago, which venture lasted for a little over two years. In 1873, Murphy sold his interest in the business and went to Silver City in New Mexico where he became a pioneer in the silver mining industry by creating the first revolutionary smelting works established in that state. The only drawback was that he had to use native sandstone instead of brick in the construction of the big smelting furnaces. Sandstone was unable to withstand the heat the furnaces generated. As a result the company was unable to continue its smelting operations and eventually went broke. Murphy lost his hard-earned investment in the project and had to start all over again.

Michael headed for San Diego and from there to Los Angeles where he found employment as a salesman in the lumber firm of Perry, Woodworth and Company. In October of 1875 he was given a position of trust and sent by the company to Colton, San Bernardino County, with the authority to establish the first redwood and pine lumber yards in that county. This venture proved financially successful, and when the firm incorporated, Murphy became one of the principal stockholders.

In 1886 Murphy was engaged to organize and incorporate the Pioneer Lumber and Mill Company and went on to become company president and general manager. Under his guidance the company conducted substantial operations in both San Bernardino and Riverside counties and also had a branch in Los Angeles County. Murphy continued as chief executive of this company until its charter of incorporation ran out.

During that progressive period Murphy became involved in real estate and agricultural operations in both San Bernardino and Riverside Counties, and in so doing made a large and valuable contribution to the civic and industrial advancement in that part of the state.

In 1896 he purchased a substantial block of shares in the California Portland Cement Company at Colton, reorganized the company and assumed charge of its far-flung business operations. Murphy was the first man in California to manufacture Portland

Cement and market it in a commercial way. To do so, he initiated a vigorous and well-ordered campaign to make the product available to users all over Southern California.

Four years later, in 1900, he sold his interest in this lucrative business and set his sights on Northern California. Shortly after his arrival in San Francisco he became allied with the California Safe Deposit and Trust Company with the prospect of erecting a large cement manufacturing plant on the Telsa Coal Company's land in Alameda County. Following a thorough survey of the property Murphy discovered that the required materials were not of sufficient volume to justify the needs of a cement plant of such magnitude.

During the survey he discovered abundant deposits of red clay and kaolin, well suited for the manufacture of terra cotta, fire-brick and sewer-pipe, which were in big demand at the time. On the strength of this discovery the Carnegie Brick and Pottery Company was formed and incorporated, with a capital of $2,500 000, and with the indomitable Michael Murphy as its first president and general manager. It was a successful venture from the beginning, with an increase in production year after year.

A BOUT THAT TIME San Francisco was devastated by the earthquake and fire on April 18, 1906. During the reconstruction period which followed, the Carnegie Company, the largest on the Pacific Coast, did a land-office business in excess of $1,250,000 a year.

However, while the city was still burning, Murphy was called upon by the Relief Committee to construct housing for the unfortunate victims who had lost everything in the catastrophe. He proceeded as ordered and was given full authority by General Funston to commandeer all the lumber be needed and to round up immediately as many tradesmen as he deemed necessary to get the job done as quickly as possible.

With five thousand carpenters, teamsters and laborers at his disposal Murphy supervised the construction of a row of barracks, enough to accommodate twenty thousand or more homeless refugees in Golden Gate Park. This massive housing project was completed in record time, and Murphy won the plaudits of General Funston, his aide Major McIvor, and leading city officials.

The combined industries, the Carnegie Brick and Pottery Company and the California Safe Deposit and Trust Company, both of which were organized by Murphy, were successful in bringing the Western Pacific to the coast. The acquisition of the San Joaquin

Railroad's rails and terminals gave the Western Pacific entrance to the Oakland estuary, and thence to San Francisco.

Unfortunately, Murphy was one of the largest stockholders in the trust company when it failed in 1907, as a result of manipulations which form a dark chapter in California financial history, entailing a gigantic personal loss of some $16 million—a tragic blow for a man who had contributed so much to San Francisco in its darkest hour. Since banks were not then insured by the federal government, there was no way for Murphy or other investors to recoup their losses.

Broken in wealth but not in spirit, Murphy returned to Los Angeles in 1911, where he maintained a fine residence on Figueroa Street, which was in the heart of the city in those days. He stayed there for the next five years, and then he returned to his lovely Orange Grove estate in Riverside County, which he pioneered and developed in that sun-drenched fertile enclave.

ON APRIL 15, 1879, Michael Murphy married Elizabeth Young, the charming daughter of Doctor Edmond Young, a leading physician in the City of Oakland. As a young man he served as a lieutenant in a San Bernardino Cavalry regiment attached to the California National Guard, and was later commissioned to the rank of Major by Governor Stoneman.

In politics Murphy was an active member of the Democratic Party and served as a member of county and state committees, and as a delegate to county and state conventions, until the election of Grover Cleveland, a Democrat, as president in 1885, when he transferred his allegiance to the Republican party.

One can only assume that the reason for Murphy's abandonment of the Democratic party was the nationwide bank panic, during President Cleveland's second term, when Murphy lost most of his life savings. Michael was one of the many who switched party affiliations in that period of financial depression. As a result the Republican party regained control with the election of Benjamin Harrison as President in 1889.

As elsewhere in California, the Irish influence was particularly noticeable in Riverside County and Redlands, the pride of the Inland Empire.

Abigail Meagher Parrott
Courtesy San Mateo County Historical Museum

– 19 –

ABIGAIL MEAGHER PARROTT

1829 - 1917

No history of California would be complete that did not include Abigail Parrott and her husband John, who were in the forefront of every movement for the betterment of their adopted state.

The long and fruitful life of Abigail (Abby) Parrott began in Whitefield, Maine, where she was born on June 7, 1829. Her parents were James Meagher, of Rathcash, County Kilkenny, and Susan Landers Millay, the daughter of a Revolutionary patriot of the Eastman family line.

The Meaghers came from a long line of Irish nobility who suffered much at the hands of English mercenaries. James's father, Thiege (Timothy) O'Meagher was a noted scholar who took delight in speaking of his father, one of the so-called Wild Geese that served in the Army of Spain, and also of his equally illustrious grandfather, who held a seat in the Parliament of King James.

James himself refused to accept a commission in the British Army, with the admonishment that none of his family ever did or ever would wear a Red Coat. Instead he set out secretly on his uncle's ship bound for America, where freedom was already a way of life. He settled in Whitefield, where he met and married Susan Millay. In time he became a successful farmer and on occasion worked at his trade as a stone mason to supplement his income from the land. While building the Catholic Church in Whitefield, he was badly injured and lost a leg, and as a result he died a young man in 1867.

The children of that union were James M., Timothy, William T., Mary, Patrick Byrnes, John Cheverus, Dennis Ryan, and Abigail, the subject of this narrative. Speaking of her family in later years, Abigail reminisced to her son John:

My maternal ancestors were of Flemish descent, a colony of whom
came to America and settled on the coast of Maine. My great-
grandmother, Abigail Eastman, married James Millay, a native of
Kilkenny City. In Boston he met James Meagher, and on learning
that he was from the same place in Ireland, took him to Maine,
where he met and married Susan, Millay's eldest daughter, who
lived with her family in Bowdoinham, Maine.

After their marriage James and Susan spent several years in Boston,
where she was received into the Catholic Church by Bishop
Cheverus, later Archbishop of Bordeaux, France. They later bought
a farm in Whitefield, where they lived out their lives.

One of Abby Parrott's grand-uncles (an Eastman) was a member
of the rebel party who threw the tea overboard in Boston, in protest
of the Stamp Act.

In 1826 Timothy Meagher migrated to Mobile, Alabama, and
began his career on the Alabama River. There his older brother,
James, joined him and together they engaged in shipbuilding. In
1842, they constructed their first steamboat, the *William Bradstreet*,
and shortly thereafter the *William G. Jones*. Their next was a sidewheeler, the *Southern Republic*, the largest steamboat to ply the
Alabama River.

I N DUE COURSE the brothers constructed a number of fast schooners
for overseas service, including the *Sarah E. Meagher*, so-named in
honor of their mother. Their prized schooner was seized in an international incident during the Crimean War, in addition to the slave
ship *Clotilde*, built by Captain Timothy Meagher (Maher) in Mobile
in the fall of 1858. During the war between the States, the Meaghers
constructed three blockade runners, including the highly celebrated
Gray Jacket, the first twin-screw boat of this type.

The Meagher brothers, having prospered in shipbuilding, were
now in a position to send their youngest sister Abigail to the prestigious Saint Joseph's Academy in Emmitsburg, Maryland. There she
first met Magdalena Parrott, who had been sent by her father from
Mexico to be educated in the United States. Their meeting was the
beginning of a life-long friendship between the two ambitious young
women.

On graduation day, Abigail was chosen as valedictorian, reciting
the Academy theme song, "Farewell to Saint Joseph's." What a thrill
it must have been 32 years later in 1880, when Abbey's younger
daughter Regina May, at the same school, recited in her turn
"Farewell to Saint Joseph's," and Isabelle, May's sister, won a Medal of

Honor in music and premiums in art and ornamental needle work. When Abigail completed her studies at Emmitsburg she returned to Mobile and lived with her brothers until her marriage to John Parrott, Magdalena's father, who was 18 years her senior. Magdalena and her brother Tiburcio had been born out of wedlock; John Parrott had always provided for them.

The Parrotts in California

AFTER COMING to California in 1853, Abigail seemed quite lonely, a continent apart from her family back in Alabama. In a letter to her sister-in-law Helen Meagher, April 4, 1857, she tells of her delight in having received her recent letter. She speaks of the problem of the Southern mails to and from California. She says that her many acquaintances here from Mobile have been distressed, not having received any tidings from home, and that she assumed her letters to Helen and her brother Byrnes were mislaid with the rest.

Despite the foregoing complaints, Abby had good things to say about her new home, a beautiful mansion on Rincon Hill in San Francisco:

> I wish I could take you around my garden just now. I have such superb roses bending under countless blossoms, making the whole atmosphere fragrant with their rich perfume. March, April and May are the best months for flowers in San Francisco, though no day in the past year has found me without fresh flowers on my table gathered in the open air in my garden. So much for the great outdoors.
> I have a Sewing Machine—and it works like a charm—both in its perfection of stitching and rapidity of execution. Have you seen them? They are a great invention, converting the burden that makes a house a veritable jail into a mere pastime. Now that I have learned to use mine, I have no patience with the old fashioned needle, and turn the work over in disgust for the seamstress to finish off.

Abigail's husband John was one of the most unique men ever to grace the California scene. In 1829, at the age of eighteen, he left his native Tennessee to join his brother William in Mexico City. William, who was John's role model, having served with distinction in the War of 1812, and later at the crucial battle of New Orleans, led by Andrew Jackson. When Jackson, the "hero of New Orleans," was elected President, he appointed William Parrott as U.S. Consul of Mexico City, a post he maintained for two years, when he resigned and returned to the United States.

John Parrott
Courtesy San Mateo County Historical Museum

In the meantime John Parrott moved to Mazatlan, Mexico, where he became a leading merchant. Four years later, in 1839, like his brother before him, he was given a consular appointment in Mexico. A flamboyant individual, John reveled in his role as United States Consul, and even purchased an elegant uniform to wear on special occasions. Attired in cream-colored silk knee pants, gold-braided blue military jacket and ostrich fringed hat, he made a striking figure on the Mexican scene. As Consul, John Parrott played a major role in the American acquisition of Alta California.

As a consequence of the Parrott brothers' experience and knowledge of old Mexico, they were able to help diminish the animosity between the two nations before the Mexican-American war, 1846-1848. When hostilities broke out, Parrott pressured Commander John Sloat, whose Naval Squadron was stationed at Matazlan, to seize California. Then he gathered his belongings and fled Mexico forthwith. While residing in Cuba during the conflict, John Parrott reported directly to Secretary of State James Buchanan regarding the course of the war. When the American forces landed at Vera Cruz in 1847, Parrott returned to Mexico and reported on the battlefield situation to the Secretary of War. At war's end in 1848 he was restored to his consulate in Mazatlan.

Although he was already a wealthy man, when the word got around that gold had been discovered in California, John Parrott resigned his consular position and headed for San Francisco.

A Timely Venture in Old San Francisco

IN SAN FRANCISCO the prescient cavalier invested his Mexican fortune in real estate and building development. Like a latter-day Arthur Brisbane, he firmly believed that land would never depreciate. Parrott's granite building on Montgomery Street was the first substantial structure to be constructed during the Gold Rush. Rock for its foundation was quarried on Goat Island (Yerba Buena) by Thomas Henry Dowling and floated across the bay on barges. Granite blocks for the building itself were meticulously cut in China, carefully inscribed with Chinese characters, and shipped to San Francisco, along with a score of coolies and a qualified Chinese architect to supervise the construction. With heavy iron shutters attached, the building was said to be completely fireproof. This massive structure, known as the Parrott Block, survived a violent explosion in 1866, and two devastating earthquakes in 1886 and 1906. It was finally demolished in 1926.

By the 1870s Parrott owned, besides the four-story Parrott Block, another three-story brick building on Montgomery Street, as well as other buildings in the area. In total wealth his closest rival was said to be William Ralston, who built the world-renowned Palace Hotel, completed in 1875. John Parrott owned and operated merchant ships and transported wheat and other commodities grown on his property in the Sacramento Valley to England, for distribution in the British Isles and beyond.

Back in 1859 Parrott had acquired the old Macondray property, a 377-acre spread west of El Camino Real, in the town of San Mateo. The house, one of the first to be built in the area, was a sturdy "cottage" surrounded by inviting verandas. In 1868 Parrott enlarged it into an ornate mansion, the earliest of many great houses to be constructed on the Peninsula. Parrott christened his splendid house "Baywood." And thus began one of the most unusual family stories in California history.

THE PARROTTS were a well-matched couple, although Abby was a whole generation younger than her husband. In matters of charity and benevolence they were of like mind. When the Parrotts moved into Baywood, John decreed that no one hungry should ever be turned away from his home. His equally charitable wife Abby took this rule to heart and held it as a sacred trust; she continued to honor it long after her husband's death in 1884.

*The "Cottage" which John Parrott bought for his family and renamed
"Baywood" was the earliest mansion in San Mateo.
Courtesy San Mateo County Historical Museum*

The charitable matriarch budgeted a hefty sum for her household
expenses for this avowed purpose, and even hired a capable cook to
prepare meals for an ever-increasing number of transient "guests."
She kept a close watch to insure that the food was of the same quality
and abundance as that which was set before her own family.

Through periods of prosperity and depression, one hundred or
more homeless wanderers might sit down to a well-appointed table.
The itinerants were even allowed to camp overnight if they chose to,
in a specified area of the estate. In the evening, when all were fed, the
wanderers would often gather around a bonfire to sing and swap tales
of life in the open. Although many of them were perennial drifters
and panhandlers, others were professional men down on their luck
who were deeply grateful for the timely help afforded by the Parrotts
in such a welcome place.

One of Abby Parrott's most benevolent projects after her husband's death was to convey to the Archbishop of San Francisco a portion of the Baywood estate for a burial ground, known as Saint John's
Cemetery, with the provision that a private section would be reserved

for her family. The cemetery, fenced and landscaped, is said to be the most beautiful burial ground anywhere in Northern California. There is a feeling of peace in the secluded, sun-dappled hillside, which affords an unobstructed view of the wooded terrain and the broad expanse of the coastal range.

The massive monument of Florentine Renaissance stone commemorating the Parrotts is a work of art. The inscription on the back of the huge Parrott vault reads as follows:

St. John's Cemetery
Given to The Catholic Church of San Mateo
In Memory of John Parrott
Born in Virginia, April 16, 1811
Died in California, March 29, 1884

Abby is buried with her husband in that section of Saint John's cemetery devoted entirely to her family, including such illustrious names as de Guigne, de Lande and Hayne.

The Parrotts were blessed with eight children. Josephine (Parrott) Burgess, who died on September 21, 1980, at the age of 89, brought to a close the long and involved history of one of the Peninsula's best known families. Three of her brothers died in their youth: Joseph, at home; Edward, who at age 22 lost his life in an air battle during World War I (he is interred in St. Michael's Cemetery, Thiau Court, France); and Francis, killed in an auto collision in Burlingame in 1917. William, the oldest, died in 1965 in Florence, Italy, where he made his home for many years. John is buried in the family plot in Saint John's Cemetery. Josephine had two other sisters, Emily and Abby.

Saint Matthew's Church in San Mateo

ONE OF Abby's pet projects was Saint Matthew's Church in San Mateo, to which she subscribed the sum of $50,000 towards its construction. The work was begun by Father Denis Dempsey, a native of Dublin, who established the first parish in San Mateo County. Father Dempsey studied for the priesthood at St. Patrick's College in Carlow, where he was ordained in May 1861 for the Diocese of San Francisco. Following his arrival that same year he was assigned to the Cathedral of Old Saint Mary's on California Street. Two years later he was sent by Bishop Alemany to seek out the best location for a parish church in San Mateo county. The place that seemed ideal was San Mateo, and in 1863, during the height of the Civil War, he took up permanent residence there, a pastor without a

This side view of Baywood shows the extensive addition John Parrott made to the original small cottage.
Courtesy San Mateo County Historical Museum

Church or a home. He began his ministry by celebrating Mass on Sundays in a one-room schoolhouse close by the Parrott estate, off El Camino Real.

In order to provide for his scattered flock, he put a notice in the *Redwood City Gazette* in September, 1863, that Divine Service would be held at the following places:

At San Mateo - September 6th
At St. Denis Church* - September 13th.
At Redwood City - September 20th
At Spanishtown** - September 27th
Mass at 11 A.M. Sermon immediately after the 1st Gospel.

Father Dempsey didn't have long to wait for a larger congregation in the new parish with the coming of the San Francisco-San Jose Railroad, completed on October 17, 1863. The first train, with Governor Leland Stanford and four hundred guests aboard, left the depot at 18th and Valencia Streets in San Francisco at 10:30 A.M. and roared into San Mateo 37 minutes later. The San Mateo railroad station became the hub of the original town from San Mateo Creek to 5th Avenue, between South Ellsworth and Delaware Streets.

---

*St Denis was at Searsville Lake
**Spanishtown is now Half-Moon Bay

In those days Father Dempsey made his home with a fellow Irishman, Peter Casey, at his ranch in Beresford. The inevitable need of funds for a new church and parish house became the concern of Father Dempsey and his host, who rode on horseback around the countryside soliciting donations. C.B. Polhemus, who owned considerable property, donated land at the southwest corner of Third and Ellsworth for a Catholic Church and a parish house. In a relatively short time the funds were at hand and the work was begun on the building, a modest wood-frame church with a high steeple and bell tower typical of that period.

On Sunday February 7, 1864, Archbishop Alemany traveled by train to bless the new church under the title of Saint Matthew. His excellency was thrilled to see the steeple towering over the town like a diamond in a perfect setting. Saint Matthew's was indeed the Mother of Parishes in San Mateo County.

Father Dempsey was so inspired by the benevolence of the settlers that while Saint Matthew's was still under construction he began collecting money for a church in Redwood City. In his eighteen years of pastoral work Father Dempsey founded six churches, all of which grew to multiply the fruits of his labor.

FOLLOWING his death on April 5, 1881, Father Dempsey was interred temporarily in a private vault in Lone Mountain Cemetery in San Francisco. At the time it was agreed that he be returned to his beloved San Mateo when a consecrated burial place was made ready. And so it came to be. Father William Bowman, who had been Father Dempsey's assistant for a number of years, became the second pastor. His term as pastor was short-lived, just seven months. In that time he did manage to build a vault beneath the church to house the remains of his good friend, Father Dempsey. Together in life and in death, Father Dempsey and Father Bowman were laid to rest in the same vault beneath Saint Matthew's where both men had served as pastor.

Father Peter Birmingham, born in Coxtown, near Ballinasloe in County Galway, on April 5, 1839, became the third pastor of Saint Matthew's. He had come to the United States when very young and entered the Seminary of Saint Thomas Aquinas at Mission Dolores to study for the priesthood. Father Birmingham was ordained in December 1865, and served at Saint Vincent De Paul's in Petaluma, at Sutter Creek, at Saint Vincent's Orphanage in San Rafael, at San Bernardino, and at Old Saint Patrick's in San Francisco before coming to San Mateo. Father Birmingham remained as Pastor of San

The original St. Matthew's Church in San Mateo
Courtesy San Mateo County Historical Museum

Mateo for just three years.

IN LATE 1884 Father Timothy Callaghan was transferred to Saint Matthew's as pastor, and Father Birmingham replaced him as Pastor of Saint Brigid's in San Francisco. By coincidence both Saint Matthew's and Saint Brigid's were established as parishes in the same year, 1863.

No history of the church in San Mateo County would be complete that did not include Father Callaghan. This kind and gentle priest was almost forty years old when he arrived; he served the San Mateo community for more than half a century, until his death on March 31, 1937. During that time he officiated at countless weddings, baptized hundreds of children and celebrated the last Requiem Mass for many of his parishioners.

Timothy Callaghan was born in Balleydonane, Donoughmore, County Cork, on October 16, 1845. He received his primary education in the Nation School and at Saint Coleman's College in Fermoy. After studying for the priesthood at All Hallows Seminary he was ordained there on June 24, 1869, and was assigned to serve in the Diocese of San Francisco. He traveled by ship to New York, where he boarded a train on the newly completed transcontinental railroad, arriving at his destination in the fall of that year.

His first assignment was at Mission Dolores, beginning on December 9, 1869. He served at Old Saint Mary's and at Saint Rose's in Sacramento until his appointment as pastor of Saint Brigid's in 1875. In 1884 Father Callaghan was transferred to San Mateo, where he remained for the rest of his long and fruitful life.

In the next decade there were changes in the quiet suburban village, which was incorporated on September 4, 1894. The population quickly soared from just a few hundred to a thriving town of over 1,800. Saint Matthew's was growing too, and Father Dempsey's little church was fast becoming too small to accommodate the overflow congregation.

When it was decided a new and larger church should be built, Abigail Parrott donated her property fronting on Ellsworth between Second and Third Avenues in exchange for the site of the old church and rectory. Father Callaghan launched a fund-raising campaign, and the people responded very generously, pledging $6,000, a very handsome sum in those days. In her usual quiet way Abby Parrott informed the pastor that her donation would be $50,000.

September 23, 1900, was both a sad and happy day as Father Callaghan celebrated the last Mass in the old church and preached a farewell sermon that touched the hearts of many longtime worshipers. He spoke sadly of how difficult it was to leave a building that had been home for decades. But in God's way the sorrow at leaving the old blended with the joy of entering the new.

THE ORIGINAL LITTLE CHURCH with its high steeple towering above the forest is long gone. The site was occupied for a number of years by the town's first dime store, the Ben Franklin. Fortunately one memento remains intact: the original black iron bell, cast in Peter Donahue's Union Iron Works in San Francisco in 1861. The bell, which tolled for forty long years calling the early settlers to Mass, can be seen in the San Mateo County Historical Museum.

Father Callaghan was widely known and highly respected. Almost every day he traveled around his parish greeting all he met, eager to chat with friend or stranger. He made a point of walking along the railroad to meet the incoming hoboes in order to give them a helping hand. He followed up by asking local merchants to help when his transient friends came to town. His name was a household word among the "Knights of the Road." When he died they came in a body to his wake, viewed his remains and went away with tears trickling down their furrowed cheeks.

Time was running out for the white-haired pastor, who was now in his 85th year and his 45th as pastor of Saint Matthew's. At the time of his death on March 31, 1937, Father Callaghan was the oldest priest in the Archdiocese of San Francisco, having been ordained for almost 68 years.

Following a solemn Requiem Mass he was laid to rest in Saint John's Cemetery. A poem written for the occasion by Clarence Anderson, a non-Catholic, appeared in the April 2, 1937, issue of the *San Mateo Times:*

Hail Mary, Hail

Oh, not of his faith, or communion
No whit of our sorrow shall fail.
We grieve with the flock in their grieving—
Hail Mary, hail.

We kneel as the mass is resounding—
Oh love of the virgin avail,
For rest through the aeons eternal.
Hail Mary, hail.

A glory is gone from the township;
A dimness o'er the city and dale.
The flame of his presence has vanished.
Hail Mary, hail.

On April 1, 1937, the *Examiner* said of Father Callaghan: "He was famed for his charity in San Mateo. On his daily walks he gave money and comfort to anyone who asked, regardless of creed or color."

For more than forty years Abigail Parrott and Father Callaghan had worked hand in hand for the betterment of the community as a whole and Saint Matthew's parish in particular. With their combined principles of Faith, Brotherly Love and Benevolence, they set an example for every community in California. They were together in life and are together in death. Both are buried in Saint John's Cemetery, Abby in the Parrott Mausoleum and Father Callaghan in the Priests' plot a short distance away.

In 1903 Orville Wright made history in a contraption called an airplane. But the conservative residents of San Mateo were more interested in a proven form of transportation. On New Year's day of that year the electric streetcar line connecting San Francisco with the Peninsula went into operation. For 25¢ people could take a trolley to the city, with transfer rights within the city included

Parrott's Extended Family

IN ADDITION to her own family, "Granny" Abigail Parrott had two stepchildren, Tiburcio and Magdalena Parrott, the illegitimate children of her husband John, to whom she gave her love and affection as if they were her very own. For a quarter of a century or more Tiburcio lived in the Parrott household, both in San Francisco and at the estate in San Mateo. It was only in later years that he had a home of his own.

Tiburcio Parrott was born in Mazatlan, Mexico, in 1840, when his father was the United States Consul there. When John Parrott removed to San Francisco at the time of the Gold Rush he brought the child along. He was still a bachelor, and being unable to take care of the youngster placed him in a Catholic boarding school near Boston at the age of twelve. From there he was sent to France and Spain to further his education. Tiburcio completed his studies at Sandhurst College in England.

In 1860 he returned home to America, where his father was happily married, the father of four children and reluctant to meet with him. Finally he was invited to join Parrott & Company, and he returned to San Francisco. A big, handsome fellow, warm-hearted, refined and well read, he proved to be an asset to his father. He was then invited to reside at the family residence on Folsom Street where he helped in raising his half-brothers and sisters, all of whom appeared to worship him. While there he established a close relationship with his half-sister, Magdalena, the illegitimate daughter of his father and a Mexican woman, Carmen Barrera.

John Parrott obtained permission to bring Magdalena to the United States. She was placed in a Catholic boarding school at Saint Joseph's Academy in Emmitsburg, Maryland, where she met Abigail Meagher, her future step-mother. Magdalena, a sophisticated young lady of nineteen, came to San Francisco, where she met and married Doctor Robert Newhall, one of the city's most eligible bachelors. They became the parents of six children. Tiburcio, or Tio, as he was known by his nephews and nieces, became the idol of both families, the Parrotts and the Newhalls

Over the years Tiburcio became a successful businessman, taking control of Parrott and Company and other well established corporations. In time he achieved a popularity that even his wealthy father never had, as a flamboyant dandy, a first-class ballroom dancer, and a leading yachtsman.

Tiburcio's "Villa Parrott"

IN 1855 Tiburcio acquired eight hundred acres in the Napa Valley near Saint Helena, where he was heartily welcomed by the residents in the belief that he was one of San Francisco's wealthiest inhabitants. He built a showplace known as "Villa Parrott," but which he called "Miraville" because it afforded a commanding view of the valley.

Visitors flocked there to gaze upon the massive structure with wrap-around verandas and a seventy-five foot tower, with stained glass windows in the design of a parrot. Nearby was a two-story barn and a wine cellar drilled into solid rock with a capacity of twenty thousand gallons.

Within five years Tiburcio had over one hundred twenty acres of producing vineyards. His specialty, the Margaux grapes, won acclaim as one of California's finest. His award-winning wines were exhibited at the San Francisco Mid-Winter Fair in 1894. His well-appointed grounds were a virtual Garden of Eden; with thousands of rose bushes to perfume the warm air, beds of showy chrysanthemums and countless orange, lemon and tangerine trees interlaced with persimmons, walnuts, almonds, and even bananas.

With his handlebar mustache and well-groomed beard, he cut a dashing figure on the wine country scene. The young ladies about were alerted to his coming to town by blasts of his coachman's hunting horn. At age 48, Saint Helena's most eligible bachelor met and married Theresa Tuffy of Carson City, Nevada, whose father was Nevada State Treasurer. The marriage ceremony was performed by Reverend Fathers Daniel Slattery and Charles Becker. It was witnessed by Tiburcio's stepmother, Abby, who shared her love and affection with "Tio" as if he were her own son.

Like Abby, Tiburcio shared his bounty with everyone who came his way. He would give things away with both hands to anybody whom he thought it might give pleasure. A gentleman of refined and cultured habits, of high honor and integrity, he entertained lavishly and enjoyed the companionship of his many friends. They were shocked to learn of his death on November 11, 1884, at age 54, a victim of lung cancer. His married life lasted a mere six years. Theresa out-lived her husband by 57 long years, dying in 1951. They had no children.

The Parrott-Jesuit Connection

ONE OF Abby Parrott's lesser-known acts of benevolence was her way of helping the Jesuits acquire a more suitable location for Saint Ignatius College in San Francisco. The land had been purchased by the Jesuit Order in 1855 from Thomas Larkin and his wife Rachel for $11,500. At that time the site was but a hollow between the sand hills, commonly known as Saint Ann's Valley. In order to help them pay off their debt and move to larger quarters, Mrs. Parrott bought the old property at 841 Market Street. This enabled the Jesuits to move and build on a larger site at Van Ness Avenue and Hayes. And there they remained until 1906, when the college was badly damaged in the earthquake and fire. They subsequently moved to their present location on Fulton Street at Parker; the institution's name is now the University of San Francisco.

In 1874, the venerable Father Joseph Neary, S.J., a professor of Natural History in old Saint Ignatius College, acquired from the Compagne L'Alliance in France a large electro-magnetic generator that had been used by the defenders during the siege of Paris in the Franco-Prussian War. The apparatus was a gift to the college from Tiburcio Parrott. When it was installed, Jesuits could boast of being the first in San Francisco to enjoy the miraculous invention of electric light, the brainchild of Thomas Edison.

In 1896 the Emporium department store was erected on the former Jesuit property at 841 Market Street. Although the store's interior was burned out in 1906, the beautiful façade was undamaged. Abby Parrott insisted the store be rebuilt as before, with its beautiful central court covered with a stained-glass dome. The store celebrated its hundredth anniversary in 1996, and then closed a few months later. At this writing its fate is still undetermined, but the façade of the store, a city landmark, will be preserved.

The closing decades of the 19th century were the days of cobblestone streets and wooden sidewalks. They were also the age of letter writing, an art which has gone the way of the slate and chalk and the quill pen. Abby's letters to her scattered flock are an example of the gilded age of communication.

Abby wrote to Helen Meagher, her sister-in law, on February 10, 1861, just before the outbreak of the Civil War:

My Dear Helen,
Why are you & Byrnes so silent? It is a very long time since I have heard from you or any one from the South, and I fear there may have been sickness or some serious cause to occasion such an unusual cessation of all tidings. Do write and let me know how you all are, Willie and my dear little namesake, Abby.
I have still another daughter, baby Grace, not yet two months old, but well and strong like all my little ones. I feel myself very matronly with a family of four and my time, as you can imagine, is fully occupied. I have not sent you the promised photographs, for the simple reason I have not had them taken. My children, the oldest excepted, are like untamed deer, no persuasion can take them into strange houses, but I hope soon to overcome their foolishness, and then I will redeem my word. I would love dearly to have little baby's picture, will you not send it to me, dear Helen? The children know "Cousin Willie" from his Ambrotype.
Best love to Byrnes; tell him to write to me when he has time. Hoping to have the pleasure of a letter from you before long, ever, dear Helen.
                                    —Your affectionate sister, Abby.

A second letter on October 10, 1865, brought no response:

My Dear Helen,
So many years have elapsed, since I have had the pleasure of hearing from or writing to you, that I feel almost as if we were becoming strangers. Now that peace has once more blessed us, I trust our

correspondence may be a little more satisfactory. With me, during the past four years, the only change has been the addition of two more babies, making my little flock number six in all, five daughters and one son. A goodly number of olive branches, is it not?. The more the merrier—say I—since God has blessed them with perfect health, but I begin to feel matronly indeed, now that Minnie, my eldest is standing up to my shoulder so rapidly.

Your Willie must be quite a man now. Have you sent him to school yet?. And my namesake, is she strong and well? I should love to see all the tiny strangers that have strung up since I left Alabama now almost thirteen years since. I enclose one of my "cartes," also one of my only son Johnny, taken yesterday. Will you not send me a picture of my namesake in return? Best love to Byrnes. Do write immediately, and tell me all about yourself and family and whether the war has affected you. How are Mr. and Mrs. Eames? Please give them my affectionate regards when you see them.

I have no letters from anyone in Alabama, since April 1861 —and I long for tidings of all of you— [words illegible] is your children for Aunt Abby, and believe me, with love.

—Ever Yours, A.M. Parrott.

Abby waited a full six months, and with no response forthcoming, decided to write one more time. On May 24, 1866, she penned a more appealing letter:

My Dear Helen,

I am going to make one more attempt to elicit some news from you all in Alabama, which I pray may be successful. It was five years last month, since a letter from there reached me, and I feel exceedingly anxious to know how the time has passed with you, about the children, and in short, everything. As for myself there has been no change during that long interval save the addition of two baby girls, making my family now reach the goodly number of six, five daughters, Minnie, Daisy, Grace, Edith Isabelle and Regina May, whose second birthday we celebrated two days since—and my son—John—seven years old. With so large a flock to look after, you can well imagine that my life is far from an idle one or at all wanting amusement. I have besides Mr. Parrott's grown son, Tiburcio, who is in business here, and his nephew Louis Parrott, both young gentleman of about 25, making, taken altogether, a goodly household. We are at present in our country home at San Mateo, some twenty miles by railroad from San Francisco, where we will remain until Oct.1st.

Now if you will in turn, tell me about yourself & Byrnes and Mary Clara, Tim & their children, it will give me much pleasure. I had a sad letter from poor dear Sarah some time since, which did not surprise me, though it pained me greatly. Her life had had little sunshine apparently. I have had no news from home very recently, and almost dread to receive [a letter], for poor old mother is growing very old.

I send one of my pictures to my little namesake, Abby, with a kiss. Johnny sends one of his to his cousin Willie, also with a kiss and love. What a big boy Willie must be, does he go to school?

How are Mr. and Mrs. Eames and their children? Give them my love when you see them. Best love to Byrnes, Tim and Mary Clare, to whom I wrote months since, but had no line in return.

Do write soon, dear Helen, and believe me.

Your affectionate sister.
A.M. Parrott.

ALL OF ABBY'S CHILDREN married well, and those who remained in California established their homes in or near the family residence in Baywood. Mary Catherine (Minnie) married Christian de Guigne and lived across the street in a place appropriately called Minnehaha. Abby Josephine (Daisy) married Captain Albert Payson, S. A.; their house stood across the lawn from the de Guigne home. John Jr. wed Marie Emilie Donahue and lived in a bungalow nearby. Grace Almaden married Judge Robert Hayne and their house adjoined Baywood. Edith Isabelle married Archibald Douglas Dick; they made their home at Pitkero House, in Dundee, Scotland. Regina May married Auguste de Lande and went to live at Nenvillars in the Department of Haute Vienne, France. Noelie Christine married Joseph A. Donahue Jr., and resided at Holm Grove, Menlo Park.

As a rule married couples prefer to live apart from their in-laws, but such was not the case with the Parrott family of San Mateo. They preferred to live within shouting distance of each other, and made the Baywood grounds their recreation park. Every day was like Christmas at Baywood, with all the comings and goings, christenings, confirmations, birthdays, weddings and parties celebrating this and that. As the families grew in number so did the gatherings at Baywood. Granny Parrott had a heart big enough to love them all. If there were a contest for "Babysitter of the Century," Granny would win hands down.

It goes to show what a loving, charitable and forgiving person Abigail Parrott was. She went beyond the virtue of forgiveness by accepting the illegitimate children of her husband John as if they were her very own. When Tiburcio, the oldest, came to dinner at Baywood she always placed him at the head of the table. Who amongst us can match such virtue?

The only known photograph of Davey Brown,
from an old newspaper. Courtesy Jim Norris

– 20 –

THE MYSTICAL IRISH

MUCH HAS BEEN WRITTEN about the Irish, the Fighting Irish, the Lace Curtain Irish, the Shanty Irish, the Bog Irish and the Carousing Irish, but not a whisper about the Mystical Irish, who brought joy to the world with their beguiling antics.

There is a yearning in every Irishman to be different from other nationals, especially in matters of courtship, marriage and home life. From this yearning, and from a preoccupation with ancient myths, he has enriched the world. Take Irish plays for example; they are masterpieces of the dramatic art. Irish poetry is in a class all its own. An Irishman is equally at ease with saints and rascals, and takes delight in confusing his most ardent listeners. At a party he shines with his proverbial wit, pleasing Irish brogue and the gift of blarney.

In courtship, he is charming to his lady love and generous to a fault, but let her take the lead in wooing and he's off in a flash to seek a more mannerly woman who knows her place. His ideal woman has one noble virtue, tolerance of his ways; she expects but little from her husband in return for her good deeds. She graciously obeys his orders, cleans his clothes, makes his bed and bears him as many children as he wants.

The old adage "Truth is stranger than Fiction" is even more pronounced when and where the Irish are involved. So pull up your chairs and forget your cares as the story of the Mystical Irish begins to unfold.

Davey Brown, The Mysterious Man of the Mountains

A PIONEER in the wilderness, Davey Brown brought an aura of mystery when he arrived in Santa Barbara County in 1875. He carried the secrets of his past to his grave in Guadalupe Cemetery, where he was interred in 1898. One of the most popular camping grounds in the back country, high in the Figueroa Mountains, is named in his honor. It was there that the mysterious Irish frontiersman built a cabin and lived the life of a hermit in days long gone.

David Brown was born in 1800 at Mount Charles, County Donegal, a scenic area overlooking Donegal Bay and the turbulent Atlantic Ocean. In ecclesiastical records Mount Charles is listed in the Parish of Inver, Diocese of Raphoe, midway between Ballybegs and Donegal Town.

At the age of twelve, Davey shipped out on a British privateer which had as its purpose the harassment of Yankee commerce during the War of 1812. It was not long until the privateer was captured by the American Navy and taken to Charleston, South Carolina for interrogation of the crew. What happened to the ship remains a mystery to this day. However, when it came Davey's turn to account for himself, the American authorities released him forthwith as being too young for sea duty.

When he was set free, Brown gathered up his meager belongings and headed west to Missouri, and from there to Texas, where he met a fellow countryman, Tom Fitzpatrick, the "Pathfinder" and Kit Carson, who joined him in hunting and trapping on the unexplored western frontier. Eventually he parted company with these adventurers and set out on his own.

He became involved at the Alamo confrontation between Mexico and Texas, and came out without a scratch. He then enlisted in the Texas Rangers and took part in the Indian wars of the late 1840s. He was off again in 1850, this time to California in search of gold. There were rumors at the time that Davey Brown had killed a man some years before, and that he fled to California to escape punishment. That story was never confirmed.

Upon arrival in California he went into the foothills to hunt deer, which he butchered and sold to the miners. This venture proved to be very lucrative; he garnered enough money to strike out for greener pastures.

While visiting an Irish friend in San Francisco, Pat Regan, whom he had not seen in some years, Davey noted with astonishment that Pat's once shoulder-length hair had vanished, leaving him bald as a goose egg. "It's the kind of whiskey they're distilling now," Pat told Davey. "Two snorts, and all my hair fell out." Davey Brown, proud of his own curly locks and bushy beard, heeded the warning, and swore that he himself would never drink another drop. And by all accounts he never did.

Davey Brown's cabin, which he built in 1879.
Courtesy Jim Norris

A restless man by nature, Davey removed to Watsonville, in Central California, where he eked out a living working for ranchers for some two years. From there went to Guadaloupe, where he bought a few acres of land, some of which he leased out, so that the rent money and his few cattle provided him with a good living. As Guadaloupe began to develop, he disposed of his land holdings, gathered together his cattle and chickens, and moved into the isolated Figueroa Mountains.

Although he was now over eighty, he was still a hale and hearty man. During his first winter there, he made his home in the hollow of a chestnut tree in the sheltered Sunset Valley beneath the mountain. The following spring he was joined by another recluse, George Wills, whom Davey called "the boy," although Wills was 64 at the time. The two mountain men took a shine to each other, and working together they built a rugged cabin for themselves near Monzana Creek. The area is known to this day as Davey Brown Canyon.

At the age of ninety, Davey entered a race in nearby Lompoc, which was having a great hometown celebration. The race was between Davey, on his old mule, Captain Jinks, and a young lad on a pony. The pony balked, and Davey won the race and the ten-dollar prize. He spent some of the prize on a box of candy, which he presented to Grandma Gewe, who was also ninety at the time.

Although Davey Brown was considered a recluse in the community, he actually welcomed visitors whenever they came to his humble abode in the canyon. When the temperance crusade was sweeping the country in 1890, Davey Brown, a total abstainer himself, agreed to sit on the platform while Mrs. Mattei, the founder of the W.C.T.U. chapter in Santa Barbara County, lectured on the evils of John Barleycorn. When asked to testify on the matter, Davey said, "I never let liquor touch my lips." Then he spoiled it all by adding, "But I was drunk for sixty years."

Jeannette Lyons speaks of Davey with great affection in an article she wrote for the *Santa Inez Valley News* in 1975: "When I was a little girl, I saw Davey Brown at a Fourth of July picnic in Oak Grove opposite Alamo Pintado Road in Ballard. He patted my head and gave me an orange. He seemed to me incredibly old at the time."

Little is known of his early years. It was said as a young man he worked on a slave ship and, like other sailors, was paid in slave wages. Davey, who at the time was a heavy drinker, is said to have remarked. "Many a slave has slipped down my throat."

When his buddy George Wills died, Davey forsook his mountain retreat and returned to Guadalupe, where he lived with friends until his death in 1898, just a few days shy of his ninety-eighth birthday.

David Brown, the "Mysterious Man of the Mountains" is buried in Guadalupe Cemetery, Section 3, Lot 77.

The Legend of Grandma Hurley (1783-1891)
"Robert Emmet kissed her almost a century ago."

GRANDMA Hurley (Mary Sullivan) was born near historic Bantry Bay, County Cork, on August 11, 1783. The Sullivans were near neighbors of the Hurleys. Young Hurley marched off with his "pike" beside Mary's own brothers when General Hoche came over from France to lead the Irish Rebels in the fight for liberty.

Mary was then a pretty girl of fifteen, and in later years she never tired of telling how she watched as the brave young Irishmen, in their green uniforms trimmed with white, marched away to meet the enemy. The Sullivan boys, with pikes as their weapons, were felled by well-equipped British soldiers, but young Hurley got away, though badly wounded. His friends nursed him back to life in the hills, where they were safe from the enemy, who went about murdering Irish rebels at will. When young Hurley was well and strong again he married his dead comrades' pretty sister.

Mary was one of the O'Sullivan-Bares, whose names are associated with Ireland's belated struggle for freedom. There were two things which Grandma Hurley prided herself in all the days of her long and challenging life: one was that she belonged to this famous Irish family, and the other was that she had been kissed by Robert Emmet, who stopped at the Sullivan farm on his way to join his daring comrades in that ill-fated rebellion of 1798.

She also met the noble Earl Fitzgerald, for it was in his company that her brothers and her young lover marched off to war. All went well for her while her husband lived and worked, but his death apparently left her impoverished. In desperation she set out for America in 1871 with her children and somehow travelled all the way to California, where she remained for the rest of her life.

All of her children preceded her in death. In 1887, her second son, who had supported his mother and widowed sister, died at the age of eighty in San Francisco. Then the burden fell to his sister, Mrs. Dennis. She cared for the old lady as best she could until she also died. The death of her daughter, the youngest of her children, affected Grandma Hurley deeply, and she never fully recovered. "My boys died and I hoped that I'd be next" she used to say when she was mourning over her departed daughter.

Mrs. Dennis' daughter, Mary Parker, a widow with five children to look after, cared for her grandmother in the last years of her life. Five children and eighteen grandchildren, some of whom lived on the East Coast, mourned her passing; she was well over a hundred at the time. The Masonic Society, to which Mrs. Parker's husband belonged at the time of his death, made his widow an allowance of thirty dollars a month. This, in addition to the earnings of a young son, had to support old Mrs. Hurley, Mrs. Parker and her five children. However, there were other kindly souls who took care that Grandma had a roof over her head and a bite to eat. Their home for all those years was a quaint old cabin on Sherwood Place, in the shadow of Mount Davidson in San Francisco. When Grandma Hurley's son died, the Clay Street Bank, which owned the property, lowered the rent to five dollars a month. This was paid by a lady who wished to remain anonymous, but every month the rent money was given by her to the clergy of Saint Patrick's Church.

Jim Maloney's chicken coop

Near the end the old centenarian lay resting on a couch that filled one side of her bare little room. The neighbors kept the death watch in turn with the granddaughter, herself a woman of middle age. Grandma Hurley used to tell with pride and humor how strong she had been all her life. Yet before she died, she was little larger than a child. Her hair was snow white, but surprisingly her face was not much wrinkled.

"My grandmother was always a healthy woman," Mrs. Parker said. "She was a moderate in everything and that is why she lived so long. Her one solace was her pipe. She took up smoking when there was nothing unusual about a woman using tobacco, and she was fond of saying that she was too old to quit. She had to stop about six weeks ago, however, because she was too weak to hold the pipe. One of the very last things she said was, 'I'll be strong enough tomorrow, please God, to try the pipe again.'"

Jim Maloney's Chicken Coop in Old San Francisco

JIM MALONEY'S bizarre enterprise was located in the area known in pioneer days as Temescal Prairie, a barren wasteland in the East Bay. It is now a densely settled area in the vicinity of 48th and Telegraph Avenue, bordering on Emeryville. Land was free for the taking, so the Irish immigrant was quick to take advantage of it. Thereon he build his humble cottage and settled down to married life. When his neighbors began snatching up his prime plump chickens, he conjured up a plan to thwart their conniving tactics. In a nearby yard of a bankrupt saloon he spied a number of abandoned steam beer barrels, and seeing no one about, rolled one of the barrels all the way to his home. He returned to the abandoned property to pick up a telegraph pole on which to hoist the monstrous beer barrel he planned to use as a chicken coop.

On the top rim of the beer keg Maloney fashioned portholes for ventilation and at the bottom he made an entrance for his prize chickens. He then inserted the pole through the center of the barrel and fastened it thereto. After he raised the pole with the barrel on top he anchored it firmly to the ground with wooden braces. And finally he put a ladder in place for the use of the coop's new tenants.

The chickens balked at climbing the ladder until they discovered that this was the only way to reach the food basket. Pretty soon they were scrambling up the ladder, one after the other, like sheep jumping over a fence. Only then could Jim Maloney light up his old dudeen (pipe) and puff away, knowing that his prize chickens were safe and secure in their lofty perch.

Tragedy and Triumph on Ruby Hill

IN THE SPRING of 1887, Mike Lyons and Pat O'Keeffe leased the Dugout Mine at Ruby Hill, near Eureka, on Highway 50 between Austin and Ely. Together they faithfully worked their claim, until O'Keeffe was called to Eureka for jury duty in July. After talking it over the men decided that Lyons would go it alone for a few days and O'Keeffe would remain in town for the duration of the trial. As it so happened, the case was dismissed on July 16, and O'Keeffe ambled back to their cabin on Ruby Hill late that afternoon. Lyons was not home when his partner returned, but that didn't matter at the time, as he thought Mike was off visiting friends or had gone on a brief prospecting trip in the hills.

When Lyons did not make an appearance on Sunday morning, O'Keeffe became alarmed and headed out to their mine, only to discover that a cave-in had occurred a short way inside the tunnel. He shouted "Mike, Mike!" at the top of his lungs, and was relieved to hear his partner's voice behind a pile of rocks and clay.

There was little he could do on his own, so he ran breathlessly back to the cabin, grabbed a large frying pan and printed a message on its black bottom with the stem of his clay pipe: "MIKE LYONS HAS BEEN CAVED IN ON THE DUGOUT MINE! I have gone to dig him out. He has been in there since Thursday. Tell A. Jackson and others." He then hung the big black pan on the cabin door and made haste for Ruby Hill. On the way he rounded up three friends, Dennis Crowley, Charlie McDonald and Martin Pantoni, and together they rushed to the mine to free their entombed brother.

Harry Mitchel, a mining friend, happened by the cabin and saw the sign on the door. He grabbed the pan and raced his faithful steed towards Ruby Hill, shouting the word at each mine and dwelling. Another swift rider was dispatched to Eureka; from there men rode on the double to the mine, arriving just as O'Keeffe and his crew were at the point of exhaustion. The fresh crew took over ripping rocks, earth and timbers from the narrow tunnel. Encouraged by Lyons' faint voice inside, cheering every time they heard it, they cleared rock with renewed inspiration.

The men broke through about six o'clock in the evening, and Lyons scrambled out, little the worse for the frightening experience. Other than suffering from hunger and thirst, he appeared in good physical condition. A drop of Irish whiskey provided by one of his friends was all he needed. He hastened back to his cabin, saying that he thought it was about time to get a bite to eat. The rescue crew, led by his partner Pat O'Keeffe, set out for Eureka to celebrate. The story of the rescue of Mike Lyons became the occasion for a general thanksgiving.

Lyons and O'Keeffe vowed never again to break the miners unwritten code; "Men should always work in pairs."

A Gala Day in Old San Francisco

A TRULY HILARIOUS event in San Francisco resulted from a wager between two beguiling Irishmen, Michael Hayes and William Higgins, in September 1867. The conditions of the bet were that if Henry Haight, a candidate for Governor of California, received 1,500 more votes in the City and County of San Francisco than his opponent Mr. Gorham, Higgins was to take a hand-organ, play it in front of every house on Montgomery Street as indicated by Michael Hayes, and collect funds to be distributed equally between the Catholic Orphan Society and its Protestant counterpart. If Haight failed to receive the advantage indicated above Hayes was to carry the organ under the direction of Higgins. Haight won by a large margin, and Higgins had to shoulder the big barrel organ.

A multitude of revelers converged on Montgomery Street. At the appointed time, when the column was seen departing from Jackson, it was the signal for action by the gaping multitude. The strange procession moved with a measured tread, led by a band playing patriotic airs, and followed by the hero of the occasion, William Higgins, a handsome Irishman cranking a barrel organ that was rumored to be a hundred years old. The gaily adorned van of the column was led by

The Celebrated Hayes-Higgins Hand-organ Procession.
Author's collection

Miles Sweeny, one of the most influential Irishmen in early San Francisco, and one of his peers, William Badger, each of whom bore a canvas bag with the inscription, "REMEMBER THE ORPHANS."

In the rear of the van towered the stalwart William Higgins, playing a series of operatic arias, and sustained by Pat Bloomer with a diminutive monkey in tow. Another brawny individual staggered under the weight of an immense bouquet, which was afterwards presented to the hero of the day, William Higgins. As the procession moved along, crowds lined the streets and people crowded the windows and balconies above, throwing down handfuls of coins, which led to scrambling by idlers standing about. Hayes and his right-hand man, counselor Tim Murphy, were too agile for the scavengers, grabbing up the showers of gold and silver so fast that the spectators roared in admiration.

The amount collected for the orphanages, together with the mercantile donations, reached the amazing total of seven thousand dollars, an example of the generous character of the people of San Francisco then and now.

The worthy yet hilarious affair brought together the noblest and best in old San Francisco. In their midst was governor-elect Henry Haight, the first Democrat since the Republican sweep of 1862, wiping perspiration from his shiny brow, with his outstretched hat half full of coins, loudly calling for more. He looked as contented and as well-fed as the boarders at Mrs. Murphy's rooming house on Kearny Street. There too, was the attenuated figure of the defeated candidate Higgins, soliciting donations in a most energetic fashion. Michael Hayes, the lucky winner, sat in the rear of the carriage, shaking his tin box and crying out for alms. Near him was the portly Jim Ward, the policeman, better known as "Big Ward."

Up front was the organ-grinder, William Higgins, and in back of him Pat Bloomer, embracing his monkey. In the carriage one could see the profile of Miles Sweeney, the banker, with his peer, W.G. Badger, city treasurer, watching over the money-sacks fastened on either side of the vehicle. Other illustrious Celts included Sheriff-elect P. J. White, Ed Leonard, Joe Fogarty, Steve Story and James Lowe. Little wonder they were called the Good Old Days.

Irish Shenanigans on a San Francisco Trolley Car

A RIDDLE once went the rounds: "Why do the San Francisco Trolley Cars resemble the Map of Ireland?" The answer was "There's a harp on either end," meaning an Irish motorman and an Irish conductor. A hilarious incident involving an Irish conductor on the midnight run down the Peninsula has kept the story alive to this day.

This last trolley car, dubbed the Owl, left the depot in downtown San Francisco, ran all the way out Mission Street to the county line, where it lay over for about ten minutes, giving midnight revelers and others time to board. Every night the conductor would call out at the top of his voice, "ALL ABOARD, FOR LOMITA PARK, SAN BRUNO, BURLINGAME AND SAN MATEO!" And did the tipplers come running! For if they missed that last car they were stuck in the city until morning.

Among the passengers one night was a sophisticated lady from the posh community of Burlingame, who moved into the enclosed compartment of the trolley car and took an inside seat by the window. Along came an inebriated character and plopped down beside her. He tried to engage her in conversation in a very abrupt and surly manner. The lady, very disturbed by his antics, bided her time until the conductor came around to collect the fares. It seemed forever until the door opened and in walked the big harp conductor and

The Old Irish Fiddler:
Robert S. Thornton,
pioneer resident
Courtesy Jim Norris

cried out "Have your fares ready please." Now was the time to get rid of this bum, she thought.

When the conductor came to her seat she jumped up and called out, "Mister conductor, do you allow drunks on this car?" The big fellow hesitated for a moment and then in a kindly manner replied, "No ma'am, no, we don't. But sure now, if you'll just sit down and keep quiet no one will notice you."

Red Patrick McKenna

MOST MINING CAMPS had their characters, but the Royal Mine in Old Calaveras had the dandy of them all, Patrick McKenna (alias Red Pat), a roustabout who could out-work, out-walk, out-eat, out-drink, out-run, and out-sleep any man in the Mother Lode. He was born in County Clare, Ireland, and was appropriately named Red Pat, his hair being red, unkempt and curly. His skin too, shone red between big red freckles and the red hair that covered his powerful body.

One Fourth of July in the afternoon he displayed his capacity for edibles when a crate of eggs and a case of beer were set before him by his fellow miners. He began to eat the eggs, shells and all, washing them down with copious draughts of beer, to the amazement of the holiday revelers. After he had eaten a number of eggs and gulped down a few beers, Pat wiped his chin, looked at the crowd and remarked, "There was a burrd in that," and continued eating until he had consumed sixty eggs and ten bottles of beer.

On one occasion Red Pat McKenna was called to San Andreas as a witness in a lawsuit. The Womble brothers, Will and Clave, were also called as witnesses in the case. On the top of the hill leading out of Hudson mining area they overtook Big Pat on foot and offered to give him a ride, but he declined, saying he was in a hurry to get to San Andreas. With that they drove on and left him. It took three or four hours to get there. Pat, who knew the territory well, cut across Bear Mountain, and by walking and running he beat the Womble boys by about half an hour. When they arrived Pat greeted them in a friendly manner outside a saloon where he had refreshed himself with a goodly number of beers. On another occasion when a man was injured in a mine accident and no medics were on hand, Pat went on foot to fetch a doctor in Angels Camp, a distance of eight miles or more. He made the round trip in just under four hours.

The big Celt took delight in showing his strength by picking up a trained colt that was tied to the hitching rail in town and carrying the animal to the opposite side of the rail. If a saddle horse broke his tether, Pat would run him down and hold him firm until the animal calmed down, and then would lead him back to his station.

Evidently a man of high principle, he was never known to be involved in a fight, knowing it would be unfair, there being no man his equal in height, girth or weight. He liked alcohol in any form and yet was never known to be intoxicated.

Red Pat was once severely stabbed in the abdomen when he tried to break up a fight between two one-time friends. He was also blown up by a mighty blast in the diggings, and was almost smothered in the underground workings of the mines, but somehow he always managed to survive.

Alas, one Sunday morning he was engaged in tightening the fish plates that held together the rails of the high trestle over which ran an electric train transporting ore from the mine to the stamp mill. Because of the roar of the mill he did not hear the train as it was backing to the hoist, and he was run over and critically injured. It was some time before he could be removed. Despite his intense suffering he remained conscious during the ordeal and even aided the men at their work without a word of complaint.

One of his friends offered him a shot of whiskey, which he refused for the first time in his life, saying "No thank you, boys, Pat hasn't long for this world and he is going to die sober." That very night, without uttering a word of complaint, Red Pat McKenna passed away, certain that he would end up where all good Irishmen go.

McGreevy Park

WHEN George McGreevy stepped out his front door at 1311 Filbert Street, on a November morning in 1899, he found himself peering down into a large hole. The sewer under the crossing at Larkin Street had collapsed in the night, causing a 20-foot-square of macadam to cave in and settle a couple of feet. The rains washed dirt into the hole, turning it into a muddy lake, a menace to the neighborhood children. For four months, property owners begged City Hall to fill the cavity, but their pleas were ignored.

So the cunning McGreevy sodded the depression, build a wooden fence around it, and planted in the middle. Then he nailed a few signs to the fence. One said, "Goats, dogs and people, keep off the grass under penalty." Another read, "Our New Panhandle," although most people called it McGreevy Park.

His neighbors pitched in, taking turns watering the grass and the tree, which proved to have a healthy disposition. Birds perched in the branches, giving the park a homely feeling.

Then, just as McGreevy was considering making a bid for a Robert Aitken statue called "Life's Flowing Bowl" to serve as the centerpiece of his little park, and petitioning the Street Department for a lawn mower, a street inspector pulled up in a red buggy and proceeded to wipe the park off the map, pulling up the tree and tearing down the fence. A barrel of asphaltum and a wheelbarrow of crushed rock arrived on the scene soon after.

That spelled the end of McGreevy Park. That night there was great rejoicing for blocks around, with many a pint of steam beer knocked back in the corner grocery saloon.

Bridget Cunningham and Her Old Rocking Chair

THAT DELIGHTFUL old Irish ballad, "All Granny left me is her Old Armchair," is but an introduction to the life story of Bridget Cunningham, who lived to be 107 and had no money for her burial, although she was heir to over half a million dollars. Like Granny, what she did have was her old horse-hair-covered, weather-beaten rocking chair, which, according to her son Tim, looked natural there, right up "forninst the chimbly." And now that she was gone Tim thought it best to keep his mother's chair for her spirit to come and rest in, and besides, the big black cat with the white breast could sleep on it and think it was as always. Only poor old Bridget herself would never come back and say "whisht" and hustle him out of it.

Bridget Cunningham was the mother of Kate Townsend, the Dandy of New Orleans, a lady of the evening who, when one Trevile Sykes murdered her in 1883, was worth over a half million dollars. Because she had made it dishonorably, her wealth was money that neither Tim or his aged mother would have touched in the days when the Girl Bridget was still living—for Kate Townsend's name was, in fact, Bridget Cunningham, the same as her mother's.

The wolf was at the door when old Mrs. Cunningham died, and Tim, who was past seventy himself, was hard put to find the money to pay the undertaker. He did, however, own the little plot and the shanty standing on it across the bay in Alameda; but it would be a sad and sorry day if he ever had to mortgage that to pay for his mother's funeral, knowing that Kate Townsend's wealth was lying ownerless in New Orleans.

Bridget Cunningham was the mother of two sons who were killed in the American Civil War, whose lives and deaths brought endless sorrow to the mother who bore them, in contrast to her dearest daughter, Bridget, who as Kate Townsend made a name that was notorious on three continents. There were other children, twelve in all, five of whom died young. The others made it to America in the wake of the famine of 1847. Daughter Bridget was brought over the sea by some womenfolk who paid her fare to New York. Two weeks later three of the boys followed her in one of the so-called Coffin Ships bound for Boston.

The old folks remained at home in the little town of Balleyhaunis, in County Mayo. When her husband George died, leaving her all alone, old Bridget packed her meager belongings, went to Liverpool and from there to America to be with her children. Though little is known of her life in America, one can assume that she settled first in New Orleans, where she took to matchmaking for her daughter, Bridget.

According to Tim, "My mother made the match. She said, 'He is well-to-do and I would learn to love him by living with him.'" This did not prove to be the case. The mother regretted giving that advice for the rest of her life, making a match that ended so disastrously.

And yet she did just what parents and guardians were doing every day in that period. Nowadays parents stand aside and let their children decide for themselves.

The Cunninghams were certainly a long-lived family. Tim Cunningham's mother died at the age of 107. Both of his grandfathers were named Tim; they lived to be over a hundred, and his great-grandfather died in Galway at the age of 105. As was the Irish custom, the first born son was named after his father's father, which accounts for three Tims in succession.

And when Tim was asked if his mother has been ailing long, he said, "No sir, she never ailed at all. Just one night I seen the end was coming; for the brightness seemed to be dying out of her eyes, and they seemed more like glass, and she couldn't call back things to her mind like she used to. Then I told my wife that my mother's time was coming; and the next morning I called the priest.

"He came around that day and talked with her; but the old lady was hard to make believe her time had come. But the father did it, sir; he talked to her and comforted her—though its no comfort she wanted, for she was ready to go when God called her.

"Then my wife and I took to watching her, and her own daughter could never have done more for her, than that wife of mine. But it was no good minding and caring for her, sir. She was burned out, and when Friday night came she just passed—passed away, sir, just as the wind is moving the cypress there."

And old Tim Cunningham, with all his two and seventy years, made a gesture at the cypress in the corner that told more than his words.

"No, she was gone, sir," he continued, "and there was no money in the house but a very little. But still the undertaker took care of her, and would have buried her yesterday, it being Sunday, only he had a richer folk's funeral to look after. And he came and took her this morning, and we, my wife and I, and a few friends, went with her to Saint Joseph's Church and then after saying the prayers took her to Saint Mary's Cemetery.

"That's all, Sir. Her chair's lying there at the back of the house. That's all that's left us of her. That's all."

James Cummins
Courtesy Cummins family

– 21 –

JAMES CUMMINS
THE PRIDE OF KINSALE
1909 - 1986

JIM CUMMINS WAS THE EPITOME of Irish super-achievers who rose to fame and fortune in the Golden Land of California. At the age of eighteen he arrived in New York with only $25 in his pocket, went west and eventually became a millionaire. But that's getting ahead of the story; life for the young immigrant was no bed of roses.

As fate would have it, Cummins arrived in San Francisco on the eve of the Great Depression and was fortunate in having an aunt, Johanna Kelly, to live with until he found gainful employment and was able to fend for himself. He also had a cousin, Mark Hurley, an executive with the Southern Pacific Railroad, who got him a job in the company's freight department office. He held on to that position despite the meager wages and considered himself lucky to escape the lay-offs that took place in the 1930s.

When this writer met Jim Cummins in 1934, during the celebration of the fiftieth anniversary of the Gaelic Athletic Association, staged at Ewing Field, University of San Francisco, he was still working in that low-paying job and had little to show for all his hard work. In fact, when Harry McCue arrived at Ewing Field with his sound truck to broadcast the Gaelic Games, and casually asked for his $20 fee, Jim and I, who had helped organize the games, had to share the cost by putting up ten dollars each.

Moneywise we were not alone; wages were so meager in Depression days that the average worker could scarcely make ends meet. Irish immigrants were particularly hard hit, since many had arrived in America with little formal education and no trade to fall back on. In that respect Jim Cummins fared better than most, having acquired an education equal to that of young Americans.

For Jim, the nicest thing that happened during his stay with the railroad was that he met and married Betty Andrus, the charming daughter of the company vice-president, who advised him to "get the hell out of the railroad business." Jim took his father-in-law's advice. In 1938 he quit the railroad and bought a half-interest in a small trucking business run by a fellow countryman from County Kerry. Four years later he bought out his partner and became the sole proprietor.

As time went on he built up the business and became an associate of the Allied Van Lines, a huge co-op of nationwide haulers, and went on to become company president. When he retired from active participation in the firm in 1968 it employed over 25,000 people. At the time it was said to be one of the largest and most successful co-ops in the world.

Rather than take it easy as he could well have done by then, Jim Cummins' retirement seemed merely to whet his appetite for further involvement in the field of transportation.

The Orient Beckons

IN 1955, Cummins removed to Cambodia to help evacuate the French, who were fleeing the war zone. It was a tense situation at that time but Cummins was determined to fulfill his agreement with the French authorities, come what may. He was still active in the Cambodian affair when America got involved in Viet Nam, after the French pulled out and left the country at the mercy of the marauding communists from North Viet Nam.

The involvement proved to be a tragedy for America, but for Jim Cummins it became a windfall because of the escalation of the war in South Viet Nam. As a start he oversaw the construction of eleven warehouses in the war-torn country and transported thousands of American troops and supplies to bolster the South Viet Namese. He also flew home coffins containing the remains of countless Americans killed in action, which earned him the nickname, "The Coffin King."

Cummins was in Saigon when the North Viet Namese launched their attack and captured that city. Though seriously ill at the time and running a temperature of 105 degrees, he was fortunate in getting on one of the last planes leaving for Hong Kong. From there he flew to India, to London and on to Cork City, where he was hospitalized and made a splendid recovery.

The Kinsale entrepreneur had other business ventures in the Far East, including a shipping company in Hong Kong and another one in Singapore. Despite his many business involvements in lands afar, Jim's Irish heart was with his loving family back in San Francisco. He named a ship the *Betsy Cummins* for his wife and another the *Peggy Cummins* for his only daughter.

Never a man to put all his eggs in one basket, Cummins, in partnership with a Chinese investor, in 1969 purchased the Elsey Station Ranch in western Australia, a massive 2.2 million acre spread, eighty miles long and forty miles wide—more arable land than in all his native County Cork. Six years later however, he sold his interest at a profit, at the urging his partner, Mr. Wong, a shipping magnate who was being pressed by the Narodny Bank in Singapore. Wong needed the ranch as security for other deals in which he was involved.

The Kinsale adventurer had many close calls in the far corners of the earth. On one occasion, as he and a friend were having dinner with the Governor of the Falkland Islands on the night before the invasion, they received a warning of the impending attack, which enabled them to get on the last plane leaving the airport that night.

At the age of sixty, when most men would be thinking in terms of retirement, Jim Cummins became even more involved in the business world. In 1969, he bought into the Goodwin Marine Steamship Company in Singapore. As he had done when he became president of the Allied Van Lines in 1942, he developed the Marine Company into a diversified conglomerate specializing in tankers. When the firm went public some eight years later, he was the major stockholder. He presciently sold his interest just prior to the crash in the world tanker market. With a chuckle, he remarked, "More luck than anything else."

On the local scene Cummins is best remembered for his part in the development of World Airways, the company that instituted charter flights from California to Ireland. It created a sensation in competitive world travel when the Oakland-based company undercut Aer Lingus, the Irish airline, by almost $100 on the roundtrip fare. This unique travel arrangement provided an opportunity for Irish-Californians to visit Ireland at a price they could afford. In the ensuing years, eager travelers took advantage of the cheap fares and the ease of flight arrangements, creating a boon for Irish tourism, which is a primary source of Ireland's national income.

World Airways was founded by an Irish-American named Edward Daly, who served as its one and only president at the Oakland Airport. As President of the Board of Directors of the Fine Arts Museums of San Francisco, Daly endeared himself to the Irish community by providing for an exhibition of the Treasures of Early Irish Art (1500 B.C. to 1500 A.D.) at the DeYoung Memorial Museum in Golden Gate Park in 1970.

During the exhibition Daly and his associates put on a most elaborate banquet and provided first class entertainers, including the world-famed Bunratty Singers from Ireland, all at his own expense. The invitations and banquet menus were works of art in themselves.

The charter flights were largely all-Irish affairs, as the passengers were either Irish or had close friends among the Irish. It was also a congenial way to travel as passengers chatted and made new friends along the way. This ease of air-travel caught the attention of Americans of Irish descent who had never before harbored the idea of a visit to their ancestral homeland. More Californians traveled to Ireland than from any other state in the Union.

On one occasion this writer was appointed tour director by the proprietor of a travel agency in San Francisco. In that position I had access to the microphone of the plane's loudspeaker system to greet the happy travelers and make occasional announcements in the interests of all aboard. With over two hundred or more Irish, young or young at heart, on hand, the thought occurred to me, "Why not stage an Irish party?" To this the Irish-American head stewardess agreed wholeheartedly.

Having met a number of the travelers on previous occasions I was well aware of their capabilities in the way of Irish entertainment. One in particular stood out, Father Jerry O'Sullivan, a priest in the Diocese of Monterey, a latter-day John McCormack if you will. Father Jerry had a delightful Irish tenor voice, and did he ever like to sing. He was also an accomplished fiddle player ("violin" was rarely a part of the Irish vocabulary) and acted as his own accompanist as the need arose. He had a repertoire of Irish songs and old time ballads which were conducive to audience participation.

All during the hour-long entertainment, Father Jerry stayed close to the mike to lend his voice and give encouragement to the more timid performers. This may have been the first in-flight concert in the history of aviation. The passengers proclaimed it as the most delightful plane trip they had ever experienced.

The impromptu entertainment was so well received that we decided to put on a more flamboyant performance when we landed at Shannon Airport. We all fell in behind the Piper, Jack Jordan, and marched in a body to the airport terminal. No one could fill the bill better than the dapper San Francisco Native Son, who was an accomplished piper and a staunch member of the San Francisco Irish Piper's Band.

The balconies surrounding the terminal were lined, as if on cue, by men and women who had come from distant areas to meet their kin from the States. The crowd rose to the occasion when they realized what it was all about, cheering and waving Welcome Home banners. It was a scene that could never again be duplicated. Regrettably, the only ones missing were two leading performers, Jim Cummins and Edward Daly, who made it all possible.

A Noble Birthright

Abraham Lincoln's birthday means more to Jim Cummins than to any other Irishman who immigrated to the United States, for on that day of days, February 12, 1909, he too was born at Kinsale, in Ireland's County Cork. Besides that link with the great President and national symbol, the one-time immigrant was destined for an involvement in American affairs far beyond his expectations. But it was a long way to an uncertain future, from old Kinsale to contemporary San Francisco, for the big soft-spoken man who always found time for the other fellow and his problems.

Born to a seafaring family, Jim Cummins lent a dutiful ear to his mother: "The sea was not for her boy, so I became a school teacher instead." Too young to take part in the Irish War of Independence and the tragic civil war which followed, he, with other members of the family, sailed for America, hoping for a better life.

His sister, Nora, born in 1902, also a schoolteacher, was the first to leave the nest. She emigrated to San Francisco, where her aunt, Johanna Kelly, cared for her and helped her find work in the big city. Nora worked for the telephone company for a couple of years until she secured a position at the Saint Francis Hotel, where she became assistant housekeeper. She held that trustworthy position for forty-five years, a record unmatched in that day and age. Nora had a delightful singing voice and was an accomplished pianist as well. She died in 1986 at the age of 84.

Eileen, the next in line, was born in 1904. After completing school in Kinsale she went to London to study nursing, and after graduation returned home and bided her time in preparation for the long journey to America. In 1925 she traveled to San Francisco to join her sister, Nora. Eileen worked in San Francisco for some six years until she married John O'Brien and went to live with him in Portland, Oregon. Following a long period of much suffering, John

*Donald Cummins, Battalion
Chief of the San Francisco
Fire Department*

died of cancer in 1945. Eileen continued to live in Portland, where in addition to taking care of John's mother, she worked for the county recorder. Like her sister, she was 84 years old when she died. Eileen also had a lovely singing voice and played the piano with ease.

Jim, our plucky subject, was born in Kinsale in 1909 and died in Sonoma, California in 1986. Donald, Jim's younger brother, was born in Kinsale in 1912. He was educated at Saint John's parochial school, which was run by the Brothers of the Presentation Order. In 1925, at age thirteen, he went to Dublin to compete for a scholarship at the renowned Saint Enda's School, founded by Patrick Pearse. The school was run by Frank Burke, assisted by Pearse's brother and two sisters. Donald stayed on in Dublin and continued his classical education at Saint Enda's until he emigrated to San Francisco in 1927, accompanied by his widowed mother and a sister, Maureen.

It was the eve of the Great Depression; things were bad and getting worse by the day. Don was lucky to find work in a local warehouse, which called for hard work at meager wages and had small prospects for advancement. Despite the disadvantages he hung on to the job for over seven years.

At the height of the Depression, Donald, with ten thousand other applicants, took an examination for the fire department and passed number ten on the list.

Donald served for 35 years in the department and retired with the rank of assistant fire chief in 1970. In the meantime he had served four years in the U.S. Army on active duty, in the United States, North Africa and Europe. He was discharged from the service with the rank of captain.

He married Edna Ward of San Francisco at the ordinance proving grounds in Maryland, where he was stationed at the time. They were blessed with six children, all now well-educated, married and working in fine jobs. His oldest son Jim is an electronics specialist; Paul is a senior assistant District Attorney in San Francisco; Raymond is a doctor, and head of the radiology department at California-Pacific Hospital; Kathleen is a registered nurse; Mary is a school teacher; and Teresa is a certified public accountant.

Paul's appointment as head of the office's criminal division was the first order of business by newly elected District Attorney Terence Hallinan in 1996. It was an honor he truly deserved, having spent his entire career in the DA's office, and the past five years as head of the Municipal Court operations. He has prosecuted many homicide cases and worked diligently for the past years to get an accused serial killer extradited from Canada.

The Cummins Family Tree

ON JUNE 7, 1900, Captain James Cummins of Kinsale married Catherine Desmond of Castlepark at the Southern Parish Church in Cork City. His parents were Captain Timothy Cummins and Bridget Kiely Cummins of Kinsale. Like his father before him, James was captain of a schooner plying the route from Kinsale to England and Wales, carrying timber in both directions and bringing back coal from the Welsh coal mines. They also transported fish and farm produce to the English markets and occasionally brought ice from Norway.

James and Catherine had seven children, two of whom died young in Kinsale, Timothy, an infant, and Bridget, who died at age fifteen from scarlet fever. The other five, two boys and three girls, Jim, Donald, Nora, Eileen, and Maureen, all emigrated to America at different times.

According to Edward MacLysagh, the renowned Irish genealogist, although Cummins is a Gaelic Irish surname distinct from the English Cummings, it has many variants, such as Comyns, Commons and Commaine, and as such it is devoid of a coat of arms.

From his arrival in San Francisco in 1927, Jim Cummins was active in Irish affairs. He was elected president of the United Irish Societies in 1935. He was also an active member of the Rebel Cork Benevolent Association and the Cork Athletic Club. An ardent sportsman, he played hurling, Gaelic football and handball, and was a distance swimmer of considerable merit. As a life member of the South End Rowing Club he swam across the Golden Gate on eight different occasions. He was the first Irishman to win that particular event.

*Catherine Desmond and James Cummins, married in
Kinsale, County Cork, June 1900.
Courtesy Cummins family*

*Catherine Desmond Cummins wearing the famous
Kinsale cloak, about 1902.
Courtesy Cummins family*

Teresa Cummins, daughter of Donald Cummins, as "Rose of Tralee." Courtesy Cummins family

Cummins served as a director of Seton Hospital, formerly Mary's Help, and co-chaired its $6 million funding drive. He was an active member of the Olympic Club and a supportive member of the Family Club and the World Trade Center. He contributed generously to many worthwhile Irish causes in the San Francisco Bay area. One of his pet projects was San Francisco's All-Irish Library and Archives. To Jim, the library was the epitome of everything Irish; it put the word "Culture" in the Irish Cultural Center. When we met at different times he didn't wait to be asked. "Whenever you need money for the library, just let me know," he would say. Without his encouragement and financial support the library might never have reached fruition. His final contribution was a check for $25, written in a feeble hand shortly before his death in 1969, a gesture that speaks for itself.

M Y OWN FRIENDSHIP with Jim Cummins began at the onset of the Depression in 1929 and lasted for over half a century. I also have many fond memories of the Cummins family and of Mrs. Cummins, "Ma" to her family and friends. In those days it would not have been considered proper to address the lady of the house by her first name. "Ma" Cummins was a very kindhearted person who offered solace to those in need and none were sent away hungry or thirsty.

Because of Jim Cummins's charisma and leadership the Saint Patrick's Day celebrations in 1935 were by far the most spectacular of any staged up to that time. An elaborate two-day program was planned for Saturday, March 16, and Sunday, March 17. The grand celebration opened on Saturday evening with a reception and grand ball in the Civic Auditorium, with over five thousand revelers in attendance. On Sunday the grand parade was led by Police Chief William Quinn as Grand Marshal.

Jim Cummins was most instrumental in bringing the famed Abbey Players from Dublin to perform at the Curran Theater in San Francisco as a prelude to the 1935 St. Patrick's Day festivities. He also helped organize the San Francisco-Irish Choral Society, which brought together the most talented groups of singers in the Bay Area. About that same time he co-sponsored the Daughters of Erin, a theatrical company in which his family were principal players.

At household gatherings the Cumminses were the life of the party, with Jim in the lead. One of his favorite numbers was "I Am a Man You Don't Meet Every Day." My own favorite was his rendition of "A Daring Young Man on a Flying Trapeze," while acting as his own accompanist on the fiddle.

I THINK I KNEW Jim Cummins better than most. I knew him when he was a struggling railway clerk during the Depression, and also in the ensuing years when he became a man of wealth and influence. Despite his rise to fame and fortune, he cherished his humble upbringing and the friendships he had acquired in his less affluent days. He was a friend for life, regardless of one's station in life.

Jim Cummins was called to his reward on February 24, 1989, leaving his wife, Betsy, and three wonderful children to mourn his passing: Donald "Casey" Cummins, a prominent San Francisco attorney, with six children; Patrick, a truck driver with two sons; and Margaret Mary, who never married. Jim Cummins, "The Pride of Kinsale," was a man I admired and will long remember.

Eamon DeValera, President of the Irish Republic, circa 1920
Courtesy United Irish Cultural Center Library

OUT OF CHARLEVILLE

NATURE SEEMS to have taken special efforts in California, carving mountains and valleys beyond compare, allowing the Pacific and the west winds to create sculpture along the coast. Humanity has done the rest, building a crossroads where people from afar gather to mingle, often to strike sparks, and always to contribute to a remarkably combustive energy, whether they stay put or move on.

Four of those who stayed hailed from a small corner of County Cork, a place called Charleville, where they received their early education in the Brotherhood of Christian Schools. Little Ireland has shared so many of its sons and daughters with the Golden State that common origins among the Irish are never unusual.

Charleville brothers Cornelius and John Daly settled where giant redwoods tower over Humboldt Bay and became merchants of regional renown. Eamon DeValera and Daniel Mannix were latecomers on different missions. But in San Francisco in 1920 each experienced a welcome resonating with personal esteem and with love for an Ireland struggling to be free of foreign rule over state and church.

DeValera, Ireland's leader, would leave knowing that the Irish were with him all the way. Australia's Archbishop Daniel Mannix, enroute to Rome, was both impressed and inspired at how firm California's Irish were in their faith

The Dalys

CON AND JOHN DALY emigrated to America and thence to California where they founded the first department store in Eureka over a century ago. Con was the first one of the Dalys to leave home, traveling all the way to San Francisco where he found immediate employment in the firm of O'Connor, Moffat & Company, the

John Daly, an early photograph, original cropping. Courtesy Daly family

predecessor of Macy's in Union Square. He held that position for five years, when he removed to Eureka and went to work for the Crocker Drygoods Company.

About that time, his brother John left Ireland for America where he, too, first settled in San Francisco. He worked as an apprentice in drygood stores in the Bay Area and later in Grass Valley, in the gold country. In the meantime, he kept in touch with his brother Con in Eureka, who was planning to go into business for himself. After some discussion, Con succeeded in getting his younger brother to join him in his department store venture.

In September 1895 their plans became a reality when they opened Eureka's first department store, which they sentimentally named the Arcade, after their parents' establishment back in Charleville. This first store was located on lower F Street in a narrow building, twenty feet wide by one hundred feet deep.

By 1900 the business had increased to the extent that the brothers decided to expand their operation at the first opportunity. They searched around and found a larger building at Fourth and F Streets, ideally suited for expansion if the need arose.

Not long after, a third brother, Patrick, came to Eureka and went to work for his brothers. Patrick was of a more quiet disposition and didn't want the responsibility that would accrue if he were to become a part owner in the firm. He preferred to work as a hired hand and leave the decision making to his older brothers.

The inspiration for their venture in California can be attributed to their hard-working parents, John and Bridget Daly, who owned a three-story building in Charleville, with a drapery store on the ground floor and a small farm nearby. John ran the farm while Bridget looked after the store and took care of their sixteen children.

The Daly Brothers' store in Eureka
Courtesy Daly family

All the Daly boys served their apprenticeship in the Arcade, working after school and on Saturdays until they reached maturity. And each one in turn became proficient in the drapery business, which they used to good advantage when they settled in California.

Wife Hunting in the Old Sod

WHILE his business was prospering in Eureka, Con paid a return visit to his birthplace in Charleville, in search of an Irish wife. While there he met and fell in love with a lovely lass named Annie Murphy. The Murphys and the Daly families lived not far from each other, and when Con returned to his home town he needed no formal introduction to his neighbor.

After a brief courtship John and Annie became engaged, and made plans for their wedding in America. When Miss Murphy arrived in New York City, Con was there to meet her at Ellis Island. Soon thereafter they were married in New York City; they spent their honeymoon on the tedious journey to California.

After a brief stay in San Francisco, visiting with friends and taking in the sights, the newlyweds traveled to Eureka and settled down to married life. Their first home was at Seventh and I Streets, where their two oldest children were born, John in 1901 and Charles in 1902. In 1905 the Dalys moved into their new home 1125 H Street, a Colonial revival style mansion set amid beautiful gardens. Con built the house to accommodate his growing family and he and Annie lived there for the rest of their lives.

SOME YEARS LATER, John Daly returned to Charleville on a mission similar to that of his older brother, but as all of the Murphy girls were so charming, he was unable to make a decision on his first visit. According to his daughter Marion, who lives in Eureka, her father made three trips back to Charleville before he decided which one of the Murphy sisters he wanted to be his wife. Finally his favor fell on Eileen, the second youngest, who was only 19 at the time. Following their marriage in Charleville, John and Eileen spent their honeymoon in Europe and shopped in New York on the homeward journey to California.

Evidently John wanted an equally elegant residence for his new bride. When it was completed several months later, the two Daly homes stood side by side on H Street. Although Annie and Eileen were sisters, they scarcely knew each other when they came together in Eureka because of the age difference of some fourteen years.

Seeing how well his older brothers fared on the matrimonial trail, Patrick set out for the old hometown in high spirits. If he had in mind another one of the Murphy girls, no one will ever know, for when he met a young lady by the name of Marie Bandel, an exchange student from Munich, Germany, it was love at first sight.

Pat and Marie were married in 1910, and for a third time Eurekans had the opportunity of meeting a new Daly bride. Since they were such a close-knit family it came as no surprise when Pat and his new wife bought a big Victorian house across the street from Con and John. Four children were born to them, all boys, assurance that the Daly name would survive for years to come.

That Dalys did all things well was fully manifest in Con's famous gardens, featuring roses, daffodils, chrysanthemums and a variety of plants and shrubs. Little wonder his home was dubbed the showplace of Eureka.

The Dalys purchased a vacation resort in Englewood, south of Eureka, and had it converted into comfortable living quarters to accommodate the ever-increasing clan. As time went on, they built a number of guest cottages on the property, some of which were set

The Daly brothers: John, Father Michael, Con, and Pat.
Courtesy Daly family

aside for the married children and their siblings. The numerous Dalys flocked there to revel in their own playground, a home away from home. With all of the comings and goings of family and friends, and as proprietors of Eureka's leading business establishment, the Dalys became one of the most renowned families in the history of Humboldt County.

The Daly enterprise was an ideal partnership with Con minding the store and supervising the staff, and John as buyer, traveling throughout the United States to find the best products. He made a number of trips to New York, a week each way by rail and boat. At its height Daly Bros. of Eureka was the oldest of clients, world wide, served by the wholesale merchandising firm of McGreevey, Howell and Werring, which was contacted by John Daly on his first buying trip to New York. As the business increased, the firm employed additional buyers who called on leading wholesale establishments and purchased the latest in ladies' fashions from all over the United States and from foreign markets as well. The Daly firm opened a second buying office in Los Angeles, employing twenty full-time buyers to call on the many wholesale establishments in Southern California.

In 1920 the Dalys bought a larger building at Fourth and F Street and spent $75,000 remodeling and expanding the store and the upstairs offices. It was in that progressive period that the name Arcade was changed to Daly Brothers, and eventually to Daly's. This name change was followed by opening branches in Crescent City and Fortuna.

FOLLOWING THE DEATH of Con Daly in 1928, John and Con's widow, Annie, became partners in the operation of the department store. During that period their sons also became involved in the business. John S. and Charles Daly began work in 1924, followed by their brother Con in 1927. Jack F. Daly, John's son, joined the firm in 1939.

In 1940 John F. died suddenly, and shortly thereafter Charles was appointed as general manager, a position he held until the firm went out of business in 1995.

Con's oldest son, John, born in 1901, was educated in the local schools and spent three years in the study of retail merchandising in San Francisco and Los Angeles. Returning to Eureka in 1924, he joined the firm and got married shortly thereafter. He and his wife, Edna, became the proud parents of five children. They named their first born son John, in the Irish tradition, followed by Barbara, Kevin, Michael and Patricia.

Jack Daly, the son of John F. Daly, was born in Eureka in 1913. Jack was educated at the University of Santa Clara, where he earned a Bachelor of Science degree. He joined the firm in 1939, but his business career was cut short by the outbreak of World War II. Jack enlisted in the Army and served for four years in the South Pacific.

On graduation from officer candidate school in Australia, he joined the 5th Air Force in New Guinea. When the war ended in 1945, Jack Daly married Mary Jane Burns in Albuquerque, New Mexico. They became the parents of five robust children, Daniel, Timothy, Kerry, Erin and Mark.

Jack was a member of the Rotary Club, treasurer of the California State Automobile Association of Northern California and a Fourth Degree Knight of Columbus. He was also a member of the State Fair Association and Eureka's Saint Joseph Hospital board, as well as the Eureka chamber of commerce. But the honor he treasures most is being named Knight of Saint Gregory by Pope Paul VI.

The Daly sisters, Mrs. Catherine Mathewson, Mrs. Marion Biord and Mrs. Annette Falk were also involved in the family business until the late 1960s, making it a family enterprise from beginning to end.

Alas, the days of independent, family-operated stores were numbered. California had at least twenty of such emporia in cities from San Diego to Eureka, including Riley's in San Luis Obispo, Ford's in Watsonville, Levee's in Vallejo, and Levy Brothers in San Mateo. One by one they closed their doors.

Daly's held on until 1995, when it too fell victim to suburban shopping malls, chain stores, and internet vendors. The closing was a sad day for Eurekans, for Daly's was not only fine store, but an integral part of Humboldt County's history as well. Even the Great Depression had failed to put a damper on the Daly enterprises in Humboldt County.

Way back in 1885 the firm had only five employees in addition to the Dalys themselves, but at their height in the 1990s the three stores had more than two hundred steady workers. Many of the employees had been with the firm for years. Fred Crone and George Phraner had been with Daly's for fifty years. Mathilde Atwell and Ann Reid had served for 44 years; Gladys Meline and Lily Sampson, 37 years; and Cornelia McCloskey, 35 years.

The thirteen children born to John and Bridget Daly in Charleville were exemplars of the highest order, who brought joy and love and hope to the world in which they lived and worked. Besides Con, John and Patrick, who settled in Eureka, Charles went to Australia, Michael became a priest and served in his native diocese, Dennis came to California and settled in Watsonville. Robert stayed in Charleville, where he took up farming. Kitty Daly married a man named McCarthy and immigrated with him to America. Margaret (Daly) Condon went to Australia. Bridie (Daly) O'Donnell stayed in Charleville. Nelly owned the Blackwater Farm near Charleville, where she lived and worked for the remainder of her life. Agnes Daly became a nun and served for life in Rhodesia. Mary Daly also became a nun, taking the name of Sister Mary Dumpre in the Mercy Convent in Charleville.

THE DALY NAME is perpetuated in Cornelius Daly Inn, a bed-and-breakfast establishment at 1125 H Street in Eureka, run by Sue and Gene Clinesmith. This is the ornate Colonial Revival residence built by Con Daly for his wife Annie and their growing family almost a hundred years ago. The inn is in Eureka's Old Town, a quiet, romantic district rife with memories of a renowned clan.

Eamon DeValera visited Boys Town in Nebraska en route to San Francisco. The five men at center are (l-r) Father Flanagan, Archbishop Mannion, Bishop Harty Eamon DeValera, and Bishop Foley, of Ballarat, Australia.

Eamon DeValera, an Irish-Californian at Heart

NO FOREIGN DIPLOMAT ever made such an impression on the people of California as Eamon DeValera when he arrived in San Francisco July 17, 1919, to plead for recognition of the Irish Republic. Eamon DeValera, the most widely-known Irish patriot of his generation, was tendered a reception and ovation the memory of which he cherished to his dying day.

There was a broad smile of appreciation and satisfaction on his usually stern countenance as the Sinn Fein chieftain stepped off the ferryboat. Doffing his hat, he bowed and acknowledged the cheers of the multitude assembled on the waterfront. The gathering was so dense that the San Francisco police detail had a difficult time making a passageway to the automobile waiting to take DeValera to the St. Francis Hotel.

Many thousands of men, women and children brought traffic to a halt and blocked the entrance to the Ferry Building. They were there to catch a glimpse of this noble Irishman, a task which to their delight proved easy, for DeValera towered a full head above the members of his official party. "Up DeValera, Up DeValera! Hurray for the Irish Republic! Long Live Sinn Fein!" they shouted as he nudged his way to the automobile.

No distinguished visitor to these parts ever received a more spectacular welcome than this dauntless leader. Then and there, DeValera realized that he was no stranger in California but at home among his very own, and that all the good things he had heard and read about San Francisco were true indeed. The liberty-loving people of the city came forward to affirm their support for the Republic of Ireland. DeValera was so overjoyed with this gesture of good will and cooperation that he declared, "If ever I had to live outside of Ireland, San Francisco would be my first choice."

The Municipal Band was on hand to make DeValera feel at home, rendering such stirring airs as "The Star Spangled Banner," "The Wearing of the Green," and other popular American and Irish songs. The reception for President DeValera at the St. Francis Hotel was informal and friendly, but as surprising to the Irish President as his spontaneous welcome at the Ferry Building that morning.

AT TEN O'CLOCK on Friday morning DeValera was taken to City Hall, where he was received as the city's guest by Mayor Jimmy Rolph and the Board of Supervisors. He was presented with a beautifully engraved gold card with the following inscription:

> Presented to Eamon DeValera, President of the Irish Republic, by Mayor James Rolph and the members of the Board of Supervisors as a testimonial of esteem for his services in the cause of Irish Freedom.

From there he proceeded to an exposition, where he was welcomed by President McLaughlin of the Ancient Order of Hibernians; he addressed the national delegates for about half an hour.

San Franciscans by the thousands poured out their hearts to President DeValera at a huge meeting that evening, Friday, July 18, in the Exposition Auditorium. No man who ever visited the Golden Gate City ever received a more memorable reception and no orator ever drove home his well-chosen words with greater effect.

This mass meeting, which was held in the city's greatest gathering hall, was but one of the many outstanding demonstrations which followed in succession for the twenty-four hours after DeValera's arrival in the city, and it was the magnet that drew Irish-Californians from all over the State.

Every nook and corner in the auditorium was jammed. Try as

they might, the police were unable to keep the aisles clear. More than twelve thousand pushed their way into the spacious arena while thousands more, unable to gain admittance, waited outside in the hope of catching a glimpse of Ireland's hero as he emerged from the meeting place.

DECLAN HORTON, attired in the uniform of a Spanish-American war veteran, was on hand to blow his bugle announcing the arrival of President DeValera escorted by the League of the Cross Cadets. This was the signal for the gathering to arise and let loose its flood of applause and welcome. Amid the din that followed, DeValera, smiling, cheerful and happy took his seat on the stage.

In attendance were many of the most distinguished men in San Francisco and other cities in the Bay Area. Among them were: Mayor James Rolph; Archbishop Joseph Hanna; Joseph Tynan, the ship building wizard; Bishop Gallagher of Detroit; the Rev. Peter C. Yorke; Doctor Healy of the Catholic University, Washington D.C.; and scores of other dignitaries of Church and State.

Andrew J. Gallagher, one of the most renowned Irish-Americans in San Francisco at the time, served as chairman. He opened the meeting with an appropriate address and called on Mrs. Hortense Gilmore Kelly, who sang the "Star Spangled Banner" with such verve that the great audience rose en masse and joined in the chorus. In his introduction Chairman Gallagher said:

> President DeValera comes to us in America asking our help. Throughout our long history, no matter what else can be said concerning our characteristics, surely we have never fought save for a high and a spiritual ideal—for independence, for freedom, and for the rights of men throughout the earth. And never before have we been so idealistic as in the last struggle (the Great War so-called) . . . when thinking not of self, we went forth to bring freedom not only to ourselves, but to all men worthy of freedom throughout the earth.
>
> Now that the war is over, shall we be told that this was simply talk to encourage our men? Shall we turn from the idealism that drove our soldiers, not only into battle but on to victory? And shall we trample under foot this mighty charter of liberty and freedom which we have won by our arms for the world?
>
> If we are true to this ideal, if we stand for the things that have been voiced by our President, if we stand by this

mighty charter of our liberties, then we must do all in our power to aid battling Erin, that she may become a nation once again.

O N SATURDAY MORNING DeValera paid a visit to the University of St. Ignatius where a Doctor of Philosophy was conferred upon him by that institution's president, Rev. Patrick J. Foote S.J.

The following week he hosted a special reception for the priests of the archdiocese at the St. Francis Hotel, followed by another for the sisters at the headquarters of the Young Men's Institute. At noon on Sunday the President was called upon to unveil the statue of Robert Emmet in Golden Gate Park, which had recently been presented to San Francisco by United States Senator James Duval Phelan, and to deliver an open-air address on the martyred patriot. In the afternoon he attended the Irish Festival in Shell Mound Park for the benefit of the Jesuit Fathers and at 8 o'clock in the evening he addressed a mass meeting in the Oakland Auditorium.

Eamon DeValera was born in New York City October 14, 1892, of a Spanish father, Juan DeValera and an Irish mother, Kate Coll. Kate was born in the townland of Knockmore near Bruree in County Limerick December 21, 1856. She was given the name Catherine at baptism but was known by everyone as Kate

In 1874 Kate's father Patrick died, leaving four youngsters, including Kate, the oldest, for his widow to care for. At the age of twenty-three Kate set out for New York at the urging of an aunt who lived in Brooklyn. Eventually she found work as a domestic at the home of a French family named Girard. While there she met Vivian Juan DeValera, a Spaniard whose father was engaged in the sugar trade supplying the United States. Their courtship continued after she quit working for the Girard's and moved to New Jersey. On September 19, 1881, they were married at St Patrick's Church in Greenville and moved into an apartment at 61 East 41st Street, Manhattan.

Some twelve months later their first child was born. At baptism he was given the name Edward (Eamon in Gaelic) which he used until he became involved in public life. In 1885 Eamon's father fell sick and died. There was no way out but for Kate to put little Eamon in the care of another Bruree native, Mrs. Doyle, and go back to work. This arrangement did not work out as expected, however, and when Kate's brother Ned, who was living with her at the time, decided to return home she prevailed on him to take little Eamon with him to live in Knockmore.

Eamon DeValera

BY 1888 Eamon was old enough to attend school a mile away in Bruree. To the schoolboys he was not Eamon DeValera but Eddie Coll of Knockmore. After school he worked on his uncle's farm, where he fed and cared for livestock. He evidently enjoyed life on the farm; in later years he said his only regret was that he never learned how to plow.

Eddie received his primary education in the local schools and at age fourteen enrolled in the Christian Brother's school in Charleville, where he learned Greek and Latin, arithmetic and algebra, English and French. While there, despite their differences in age, he came to know Daniel Mannix, a future pillar of the church in Australia, with whom he would enjoy a lifelong friendship.

DeValera was accepted at Black Rock College in Dublin at the age of sixteen. He won honors in a number of subjects and a scholarship of £60 for two years. This paved the way for his entry into University College in Dublin, where he again took honors in mathematics and received a grant of £24. To meet his expenses he taught part-time at Blackrock.

At the age of 22 De Valera got his first full-time job at Rockwell College in County Tipperary. While in his second year at that institution he heard of an opening at Our Lady of Mercy Training School in Carysfort, Dublin. He applied for the position and began work in the training school in 1906 at the age of 24. He held that position until he received an appointment to St Patrick 's College in Maynooth in 1912 as a lecturer in mathematics and physics

About that time he met a young lady, Sinead Flanagan, a schoolteacher who had taken up the study of Gaelic in her spare time. By all indications it was love at first sight. Eamon and Sinead were united in marriage in St Paul's Church, Aran Quay, Dublin, on January 8,1910. Sinead retained her youthful charm over the years, captivating people many years her junior. She even caught the attention of President John F. Kennedy, who gave her a big hug when he was leaving Dublin Airport in 1962.

It seemed only a matter of time until DeValera would become involved in Ireland's fight for freedom. He had listened with rapt attention to the speeches of Patrick Pearse, Owen McNeill and an earnest Land Leaguer named Michael Davitt. When the volunteer enrollment forms were handed out, DeValera was troubled by the decisions he had to make, but was never a man to turn down a responsibility which would be for the good of dear old Ireland. He was then a married man and the sole provider for his wife and three young children.

In 1915 DeValera was raised to the rank of Commandant and given charge of one of the four Dublin Battalions. On Easter morning took his stand at Boland's Flour Mills in Westland Row. The rest is history.

Irish Bond Drive Led by Eamon DeValera in California

CALIFORNIA'S Irish Bond Drive was divided into twelve districts stretching from San Diego to Siskiyou County so as to enable everyone in the state to contribute. The California goal was set at $1,500,000.

Presiding Judge Bernard J. Flood of the Supreme Court in San Francisco and chairman of the American Commission on Irish Independence, which was floating the bonds in the United States, was appointed to direct the California campaign. In his opening statement Judge Flood declared:

> California friends of Ireland have never been found wanting when that liberty loving nation across the sea required a helping hand. Now that the Republic of Ireland is proving to the world that she has self determined to guide her own political destiny, and seeks to negotiate a loan to continue functioning towards complete independence and international recognition, her California friends are prepared to stand in the front line of her allies among the American States. California's quota will be oversubscribed.

The Los Angeles Bond Drive was chaired by P. P. McCarthy, with such able assistants as Joseph Scott, Dermot Kyne and W. Joseph Horan. The Los Angeles district included Ventura, Santa Barbara, San Diego, San Bernardino. Riverside, Orange and Imperial counties. They were called upon almost immediately by the state president, Judge Flood, to organize a group of qualified speakers to make clear the reason for President DeValera's visit and the purpose of the Irish bond drive. This was followed by a request to form local committees of the American Commission on Irish Independence in Los Angeles, Glendale, Hollywood, Santa Monica, Pasadena, Redondo Beach, San Pedro. Anaheim, Fullerton, Oxnard and Santa Ana.

In the Central Valley, Fresno was the first county to organize. This district included Tulare, Kings and Kern counties.

Merced District 5 included Madera, Mariposa, Stanislaus and Tuolomne counties. A .J. McGinnis was listed as county chairman and Edward Howard as city chairman. The regional headquarters was in Hollister, and included the counties of San Benito, Monterey, Santa Cruz and San Louis Obispo. Doctor James O'Donnell was district chairman, assisted by P. J. Doherty, Mayor of Monterey. P. B. O'Mahoney, a noble San Francisco Hibernian, paid a visit to Hollister to assist in organizing the bond drive. That flamboyant and wonderful Hibernian sponsored this writer's application for membership in Division 2, following my arrival in San Francisco in 1926.

Sonoma County chairman William Mooney said his organization would contribute its quota in record time. The Sacramento district included the surrounding counties of Amador, El Dorado, Plumas, Sierra, Yuba and Sutter. Chairman Alden Anderson declared that his district would be covered by a splendid force of volunteer workers, and would be enthusiastic enough to sell a bond to Lloyd George!

Eamon DeValera greets Jackie Kennedy in Ireland

And so went the Irish Bond Drive all over California from San Diego to Yreka and everywhere between. Californians opened their arms to Eamon DeValera, President of the Irish Republic.

> I thank the good people of California from the bottom of my heart," said DeValera as he stood on the ferryboat, waving a fond farewell to the City by the Golden Gate. "No other spot reminds me of my dear Ireland. I feel that my mission has been a success, and that the people who listened to me believed in me. May God bless California, and may God save Ireland!

Those simple words were uttered by as staunch a patriot and as true a son of democracy as the world had ever produced, endearing him further to the freedom-loving people of California

DEVALERA'S ARRIVAL in California could not have come at a more appropriate time. San Francisco was hosting two national conventions: the Democratic Convention to elect a candidate for President of the United States; and the Hibernians, the pillars of the Irish movement in America, who were gathering for the greatest session in the history of the order.

A committee of representative citizens was appointed by Mayor Rolph, headed by Supervisor Andrew Gallagher and P. B. Mahoney, County President of the A.O.H., to co-operate with the Hibernians in the reception and entertainment of the Presidential Party. DeValera's acceptance of the invitation stimulated interest in the convention like never before. Some 1,500 delegates took part in the convention, and more than ten thousand visitors came to participate in the weeklong program. The St. Francis Hotel was booked as the headquarters of the delegates under the auspices of the Ladies Auxiliary.

DeValera's official visit to San Francisco and his reception in the grand Rotunda of City Hall were moments that DeValera cherished for the remainder of his life. The address of welcome by Mayor Rolph held thousands of listeners in rapt attention. The spacious Colonial Ballroom of the St. Francis Hotel was decorated with the Stars and Stripes, which contrasted colorfully with the green, white and gold of the Irish Republic. Flowers of every color were in great profusion

The grand affair was presided over by Mrs. Hanna Malloy, State President, and Mrs. Mary Lyness, County President, of the Ladies Auxiliary. The guests of honor were Joseph McLaughlin of Philadelphia, National President of the Order, and Mrs. Mary McWorther of Chicago, National Chair of the Ladies Auxiliary.

At about that time the Ancient Order of Hibernians had reached the zenith of its power in America. San Francisco could boast of nineteen divisions (numbering from one to twenty, minus thirteen, the unlucky number), all of which were more active than the two, Divisions 5 and 7, that are still active today. Division 4 folded up a few years ago, because, some said, of the lack of enthusiastic officers.*

Suffice to say that the bond drive in California and San Francisco in particular was a resounding success, and was often oversubscribed.

This author's Alma Mater, Division 2, held its 26th annual picnic on September 9, 1895, at Harbor View Park. The Emmet Guard Band of San Francisco provided the musical entertainment and admission was 25 cents. Oh, for the Good Old Days!

Daniel Mannix was welcomed in San Francisco during his visit in 1919.

Archbishop Daniel Mannix

CHARLEVILLE is also renowned as the birthplace of Daniel Mannix, a raw-boned youth who became a priest and went on to become Archbishop of Melbourne, Australia. Daniel Mannix and Eddie Coll (Eamon DeValera), although not boyhood chums, grew up in Charleville and attended the same schools some years apart. They were destined to meet again in San Francisco, the most Irish city in America and the core of Irish nationalism on the Pacific Coast.

Daniel was born in the townsland of Deerpark to a family of five children, four boys and one girl, on March 4, 1864. His parents were Timothy and Ellen (Cagney) Mannix. The officiating Priest at his baptism was the Very Reverend Thomas Croke, whose nephew, Dr. Croke, served as the first President of St. Colemanís College, Fermoy, and later as Archbishop of Cashel. Another priest nephew ministered in Oregon and California and might well have become Bishop of California if ill health had not caught up with him

Little wonder Daniel would one day answer the call of "Come Follow Me," having attended Mass and listened to the sermons of the great Father Croke, the longest-serving parish priest in the history of Charleville. Eventually, Daniel did leave home, family and friends and set out on a life's journey in the manner of St. Paul and St. Patrick.

The year 1920 was an historic one for Archbishop Mannix and for Ireland as well. Sinn Fein won big in the general election in 1918; the first Irish Parliament since the infamous Act of Union in 1801 convened in Dublin; and the proclamation of 1916 declaring Ireland a republic was reaffirmed.

At that same time Archbishop Mannix was due for his first "Ad Limina" visit to Rome. It was seven long years since he had left Charleville for Australia. While his goal, as was required of prelates of his rank, was to confer with the Pope, his most fervent wish and prayer was to visit Ireland and his aging mother. In reality, he had grave doubts that his wishes would be fulfilled, given Ireland's sad state in 1920 with the imposition of martial law and British troops stationed all over the country, particularly in his native County Cork. His skepticism was confirmed when he was forcibly prevented by the British Navy from landing on Irish soil a few months later.

But in San Francisco the stately Archbishop was given a tumultuous welcome by freedom-loving Californians, Ireland's exiles and a host of Irish-American clergy.

Following his arrival in New York, DeValera made contact with Dr. Mannix in California through Judge Fawsett, the newly appointed envoy of the Irish Republic to the United States. Judge Fawsett was authorized to arrange a meeting of the two distinguished visitors at a convenient location during Dr. Mannix's stay on the West Coast.

As it turned out, the two former Charleville neighbors met in Omaha, Nebraska, at the Columbian Fathers' headquarters of the Irish Mission to China. There is little doubt as to the subject of their conversation. But what is not generally known is that their meeting was the turning point in Eamon DeValera's life. Following the advice of Archbishop Mannix, his trusted friend and lifelong confidant, DeValera decided to return to the Dail at the first opportunity.

DeValera returned forthwith to San Francisco and relaxed, a continent apart from the British constabulary who had been on his trail since his daring escape from jail in England. In Irish circles, to escape from an English prison is considered a badge of honor. This held particularly true in the case of such a world figure as Eamon DeValera, whose arrival in San Francisco in 1919 drew a larger audience than the Democratic Convention which was in session at the time.

IN THE MEANTIME, Archbishop Mannix stopped for a visit in New York on his way to Rome. He was officially welcomed by Mayor John F. Hyland and state and city dignitaries, and given a thunderous reception by New Yorkers from street sweepers to bankers.

Archbishop Daniel Mannix

However, as he was ready to set sail from New York on the liner *Baltic*, bound for Liverpool, a tense situation developed. Some ill-minded seamen let it be known that they would strike if Dr. Mannix was allowed to stay on board. But the longshoremen, who were pre-dominantly Irish by birth or descent, threatened every English ship in the big harbor with strike action if the *Baltic* was not allowed to sail.

That ended the stalemate. The *Baltic* set sail with the Archbishop and his assistants on board, amid the din of ship sirens and flag-waving throngs assembled on the docks to see off the travelers.

On the other side of the Atlantic, the Liverpool Irish were preparing to welcome the Archbishop. They made known their delight by sending a cablegram to Dr Mannix, which read:

> Ireland's exiles in Liverpool will accord you a hearty welcome, Maynooth priests presenting address, organizing reception. Others from Irish Self-determination League of Great Britain, United Irish Societies of Liverpool, and the Gaelic League, Lord Mayor of Dublin and deputation. Also representatives of other Irish bodies, here to greet you. If landed at any other place please come to Liverpool. Further, kindly notify time of arrival.

About that time a grim Prime Minister Lloyd George decreed in the House of Commons that Dr. Mannix would not be allowed to land in England or in Ireland. And on August 9, 1920, when the *Baltic* arrived off Queenstown Harbor, Ireland, the Archbishop was taken aboard a British naval ship and put ashore at Penzance in Wales.

From there the Archbishop made his quiet way to London and thence to Rome, to give an account of his stewardship in Australia.

Following his return to Australia in 1921, Dr. Mannix settled down to be a "good Australian," as he put it, and concentrated on his religious duties as Archbishop of Melbourne. Although he did not speak openly of Irish affairs, his detractors accused him of putting Ireland ahead of Australia, and politics before his religious calling. Such criticism was no surprise, there being a strong pro-British element in Australia at the time

There is no denying that Dr Mannix was a staunch Irish Nationalist, having championed the cause of Sinn Fein since its inception. "God bless the men who put their hands to Sinn Fein," he declared. During those tumultuous years of 1919 to 1922 and through the tragic Civil War that followed, he had little to say except to offer prayers for a just end to Ireland's plight.

Archbishop Mannix's love for Ireland and for his hometown Charleville never waned. His most ardent wish was to revisit his homeland even though his aged mother, whom he was prevented from visiting in 1921, went to her eternal reward in 1924.

During his long delayed visit to Ireland in 1925, the Archbishop lived with his sister, Mrs. Wallis, at her home in Maryville, on the outskirts of Charleville. In the quiet community he was a striking figure in his long purple and black cassock and purple-winged biretta as he strode every morning to celebrate mass at the Sisters of Mercy Convent Chapel. It was an opportunity to relive his childhood days and pray with the good Sisters where he had received his primary education, and more importantly, his religious inspiration.

Archbishop Mannix's influence on three continents was so powerful that his birthplace in old Charleville was thrust into the limelight of world history.

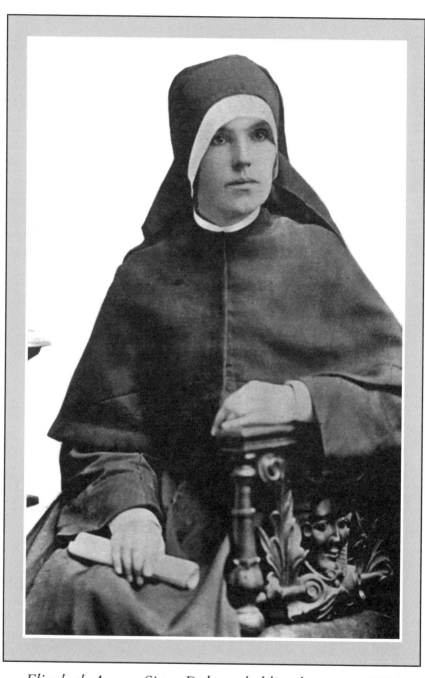

Elizabeth Armer, Sister Dolores, holding her vows, 1880
Courtesy Sisters of the Holy Family

– 23 –

Irish-Californian
Women of Distinction

OMEN HAVE LONG held a prominent place in Irish history, society and patriotic causes. With the advent of the Brehon laws—the ancient laws of the Celtic people—the Milesians, a learned race, ruled over Ireland diligently and honorably until the Anglo-Norman invasion in 1169 A.D. Once married, the woman was a partner with her husband, and not the property of her husband, which was the case in most civilizations in ancient times. If a man took unto himself a wife who owned property it was hers to keep after marriage. While women sought to be more beautiful by painting their cheeks with herbs and darkening their eyebrows with blackberry juice, they were also as warlike as their men.

A visiting Roman historian described the gentle sex: "A Gaelic woman fighting beside her man is a match for a whole troop of foreigners. Steely-eyed, she swells her neck, gnashes her teeth, flexes her huge biceps and rains wallops and kicks as from the twisted cords of a catapult." In the year 60 A.D., a fiery Queen Boudice carried the war to her enemies, riding in a chariot. She laid low the rampaging Roman Legions and burned Roman London to the ground.

Women are noted in Irish history far away in the mists of time, beginning with the warrior queen of the Milesians. When the Druid prince Amergrin arrived in Ireland he sought the protection of the three reigning queens, Erin, Fotla and Banba. The most noble warrior of all, Cuchulain, learned the art of war from a woman warrior named Aoife and went on to defeat Queen Maeve of Connaught fame.

In the Christian era we have St. Brigid, the Mary of the Gael, and Mother Mary Aikenhead, founder of the Sisters of Charity, the first woman to be honored on an Irish postage stamp.

Lady Gregory, who co-founded with W. B. Yeats the world famous Abbey Theater, and Siobhann McKenna, "Ireland's first lady of the theatre," are world famous. Modern Irish women writers have kept the spirit of the Gael alive and flourishing: Kate O'Brien, Mary Lavin, Edna O'Brien, Honor Tracy and Helen Concannon, who later served as a member of Dail Earinn, the Irish Parliament.

Irish women have a proud tradition of aiding their men on their own turf and more especially on the field of battle. And none more so than Mollie Reilly, who at the age of fourteen hoisted the flag over Liberty Hall at the onset of Irish Rising of Easter Week, 1916. Mary was a conspicuous youngster with gold-tinged red hair and smiling blue Irish eyes, who waited breathlessly for every chance to carry messages for James Connolly.

At the appointed time the Citizen Army, four companies strong, formed a square facing Liberty Hall. The drums rolled as James Connelly appeared for the first time in uniform. Standing erect, the noble leader presented young Mary Reilly with the flag, which she then raised aloft, and escorted a color-guard, who went in turn to each of the assembled companies, standing tall while they presented arms as the bugles rang out. One of the four buglers, Chris Halpin, lived to tell the tale that inspired future generations. It was the fulfillment of the Fenian's dream.

Irish-California women were as meritorious as their counterparts in Ireland, especially in matters of culture, religion and home life.

ELIZABETH ARMER, born in Sydney, Australia, in 1851, came to San Francisco as a small child with her parents. Her mother died soon after their arrival, and the little girl was taken in as a foster child by Mr. and Mrs. Richard Tobin. He was president of the Hibernia Bank, and was noted for his philanthropies. Elizabeth, or Lizzie, as she was then known, was deeply religious, even as a teenager. She would gather small waifs from the streets and take them home to teach them about God for a few hours each day. "In fact," Tobin said, "Lizzie is turning our place into a kindergarten."

When Lizzie was eighteen she went one day to Mission Dolores cemetery, where she met Father John Prendergast, a native of Ireland. She told him of her love for teaching small children. He sent her to see Archbishop Joseph Sadoc Alemany, to discuss her wish to become a Carmelite nun. The Archbishop said, "Have you never thought that there might be other work to consider? There are children in San Francisco to be cared for while their mothers are off to work. Someone must teach them the ways of faith. Someone must visit the poor. Father Prendergast tells me that this is work you could do well."

"I can try, Your Excellency," she said. She had no idea then that the work suggested by the Archbishop would lead her to become the founder of a remarkable Sisterhood.

Elizabeth and another young woman moved into a rented flat on Pine Street on November 6, 1872, a date which is regarded as the founding day of the Holy Family Sisters. The two girls began a program of social relief work for which they had little or no preparation.

On their daily rounds to visit the homes selected by Father Prendergast, the two girls found many pitiful, even tragic cases of human misery. They sought to help families where drink had wrought havoc. They were often baffled or frustrated by moral issues and severe illnesses. All they could do was try to improve the conditions they found in people's homes.

The two worked long hours, and often forgot to eat regularly. Elizabeth's companion suffered a breakdown and was replaced by a second helper, who found she could not work under such conditions. After she left, Mrs. Richard Tobin came to Elizabeth's aid, accompanying her on her housecalls. In April 1873 a young woman named Ellen O'Connor arrived to work with Elizabeth, and stayed on. As Sister Teresa, she became Elizabeth's close friend, and eventually succeeded her as Mother General of the Holy Family Sisters.

GRADUALLY OTHER WOMEN came to join and help in the never-ending tasks, working long hours among poor, ignorant, often hostile people, and sitting through night watches with the sick and dying in a city that had little concern for anything besides money and pleasure. In 1878 they began taking care of children of working mothers in their flat on Pine Street, as many as they could accommodate. Archbishop Alemany was deeply appreciative of their work with the unfortunates.

All this time they had been going to the Dominican convent in Benicia for their novitiate. On the feast of St. Joseph, in 1880, they all pronounced their vows. Elizabeth, age 26, became Mother Dolores, Mother General of the new order, whose official purpose was to visit the poor, teach religion to children, and care for children who otherwise would have no care.

In 1881 Archbishop Alemany dedicated the first convent for the sisters, who soon began traveling to hold religious classes and minister to the poor wherever they could, after pastors of outlying parishes asked for their help. Before women drivers were a common sight, the sisters were driving their own cars across the Sierras, the deserts of Nevada, and the salt flats of Utah. In some remote locations the Holy Family Sisters of San Francisco dispensed a kind of chuck-wagon Christianity, gathering groups of children together to feed and teach them.

In 1959 the motherhouse and novitiate was moved from Hayes Street in San Francisco to old Mission San Jose, fifty miles to the south.

Mother Dolores died in August 1905. At Mission Dolores cemetery one can see the Tobin family monument near the spot where Elizabeth Armer first met Father Prendergast, a fateful meeting that has resulted in care and education for countless thousands of children from Texas to Hawaii.

SISTER MARY IGNATIUS MEEHAN forms the last link in the chain of pioneer sisters who were privileged to serve with Mother Baptist Russell, Founder of the Sisters of Mercy, known all over California as "The Mother of the Poor." Sister Mary was born Helen Meehan on September 6, 1873, in Columbia Hill, in the Mother Lode country. Her parents, Martin Meehan and Honora Phelan Meehan, were both natives of Queen's County, now known as County Laois. It was presumed that having an aunt who was a Sister of Mercy attracted her to that religious community. On August 15, 1897, she entered St. Mary's Hospital, then located on Rincon Hill, as the last postulant to be received as a novice by Mother Russell.

Sister Mary made her vows according to tradition on November 3, 1900, and was assigned to that pioneer institution where she graduated with the Hospital's first class of nurses. She was still there when the 1906 earthquake and fire destroyed St. Mary's Hospital; she helped to evacuate the patients to the steamship Modoc, anchored on the San Francisco waterfront, to Oakland, and to the tent hospital in Golden Gate Park.

Sister Mary Ignatius served at hospitals for a total of 58 years of her religious life: six years at Saint Mary's Hospital in San Francisco, four years at Saint Mary's Hospital in Modesto and the remaining forty-eight caring for the sick and the aged at Our Lady's Home in Oakland. Her life was one of self-sacrifice and total dedication to the sick and the aged. She spent her last five years at St. Mary's Hospital Infirmary, where she endeared herself to the religious community and to all who came to pay her a visit in her declining years.

Sister Mary Ignatius passed away in St. Mary's Hospital in the seventy-fifth year of her religious profession and at the ripe old age of 101. Her remains were removed to the Mother house in Burlingame, where a Requiem Mass was celebrated in the Sisters' Chapel, followed by burial in the Sisters' Plot in Holy Cross Cemetery.

*Sister Mary Ignatius Meehan (center) with nurses and babies at
St. Mary's Hospital, about 1914. Courtesy Sisters of Mercy*

EMMA FOSTER DONAHUE of Solvang occupies a proud place among
her peers with a background of pioneer ancestors harking back to
the American Revolutionary War. A historian of no mean ability,
Emma Donahue put her knowledge into writing about the customs
and traditions of life in early California.

Her father, Marion Sumpter Foster, was a direct descendant of
General Francis Marrion, the canny Swamp Fox of South Carolina
fame, who during the War for Independence served directly under the
command of George Washington.

Marion Foster served as a soldier in the Civil War, became a successful cattleman and rancher, and in later years was one of the trail-
blazers to California. Marion Foster operated the first stagecoach lines
across the prairies and over the mountains to the West Coast, for a
period of seventeen years. As one of the earliest settlers in Santa Inez,
he fell in love with new country and the simple way of life in
California.

In Montreal, Canada, Foster met and married an Irish lass named
Ellen Burke, from County Galway. Miss Burke, a qualified nurse, was

a graduate of the French Hospital in Montreal. The newlyweds traveled to California and settled down to married life on the San Marcos Ranch. Because of her humanitarian work in nursing, Ellen Foster endeared herself to settlers for miles around. She gave birth to three girls, one of whom Emma, the subject of this vignette, married John Donahue, a son of the pioneer Donahue family of Santa Barbara.

Emma Donahue carried on the noble traditions of humanitarian and charitable works begun by her mother. She was constantly active in Catholic welfare causes and served as a member of the Altar Society of Santa Inez Mission in Solvang. During World War I she worked diligently in the Red Cross and Liberty Loan drives.

The Donahues lived out their lives on a 78-acre ranch, raising their three children, John Jr., Mary Ellen and Kathleen. In addition to her literary activities Emma Donahue was a noted horsewoman with a keen interest in the breeding and raising of prime stock

JULIA COFFEY began her career as an educator in 1895. Like the indomitable Kate Kennedy, women's suffragist and educator, her name and her accomplishments are destined to go down in the history of education in San Francisco.

Miss Coffey began her inspiring work in 1895 and went on to become principal of Emerson School in 1917. An Irish-Californian whose great and lasting work for humanity was truly outstanding, she came from a family who had been part and parcel of this city since 1860.

Her parents were James Coffey, from County Cork, and Julia McHugh Coffey, of County Galway. In later life her father was a well-known contractor and builder and held various civil and political positions in the city. Their roots go deep in old San Francisco; they once lived on the site of the world renowned Palace Hotel. When the new section west of Van Ness Avenue was created 1870, James purchased a site and built one of the first new homes to house his growing family. His fine residence escaped destruction in the 1906 catastrophe, as did almost everything west of that broad thoroughfare.

Julia Coffey graduated from the old Pacific Heights Grammar School. She won an award at the Denham School, established by the leading San Francisco educator, J. Denham. This was the highest honor granted to a girl student in that period. She graduated from the Normal School with the class of 1895. That distinguished class led to the beginning of the San Francisco Teachers' College.

Julia Coffey graduated at the head of her class and was one of six out of eighty students who passed the examination and were given teaching positions in the San Francisco School Department. Her name was entered on the substitution list September 11, 1895, and nine months later she was assigned a permanent place as a primary teacher. Her great work began in 1896, in the old Spring Valley School, where she taught for ten years.

She had for long been a student of the fundamentals of child-training and character development. As an active member of teacher's associations, she attended meetings and conventions, and lectured on the subject of "The Coming Teacher" following her graduation from the teachers' training course.

After ten years at the Spring Valley School she was called upon by the Department of Education to engage in a new work of studying the individual child in an "Opportunity Class" at Hamilton Grammar School on Geary Street. Despite this important assignment and the time consuming work-load, Miss Coffey took up the study of school administration at the University of California, and made many independent investigations as well.

Following the 1906 earthquake and fire, she was given such important assignments as reorganizing the old Lincoln School at Fourth and Harrison Streets. When the School Department was reorganized in 1909, this enterprising teacher applied for the principalship of a new school being built in the Potrero District. In the meantime the School Board appointed her principal of the historic Daniel Webster School. What was then six class rooms with Miss Coffee as principal, grew into one of the most modern school buildings in the city. Assisted by her teachers and others, she established a completely equipped social center, the first of its kind in San Francisco. She also created the Jackson Playground in the district, which is still functioning. With the encouragement and support of Mrs. Lowell White, the head of the Playground Commission, the new Daniel Webster School building was completed in mid-summer, 1917.

MARYFLO RYAN was another Irish-Californian deserving of special mention in California annals. She brought to California the distinct flavor of Mother Ireland, not only in her bright and entertaining personality, but also in a unique business enterprise at 683 Sutter Street, conducted under the title The Crock of Gold from Ireland. Anyone familiar with Irish Literature and particularly with the enchanting works of James Stephens, will immediately recognize this title.

Born Maryflo Gogarty in Dublin, she was the daughter of Doctor Henry Kelly Gogarty and Margaret (Oliver) Gogarty. Her parents were of profound Gaelic nobility, her father a prominent

Dublin surgeon and her mother a celebrated beauty during the Dublin Castle regime. Her only brother, Doctor Oliver St. John Gregory, was an eminent poet, author and medical specialist in Dublin.

Maryflo Gogarty acquired a classical education in private schools in Dublin and in colleges in England and in Germany. Upon graduation with high honors she met and married Dr. W. A. Ryan, a surgeon in the Colonial Medical service. She had one daughter, Maureen Florence Ryan, who was also educated abroad, graduating from Sacred Heart College in Rochampton in London; from thence she returned to San Francisco to live with her mother.

Mrs. Ryan's establishment in San Francisco was an exclusive business dealing only in imported goods, a forerunner of today's Irish Import shops. Her leading line was Trist Belleek China, unsurpassed in its line in the United States. The name of her establishment was quite unique; taken from the best known writings of James Stephens, an intimate friend of the Gregory family in Dublin, who had received a literary prize in Paris for his book, *The Crock of Gold.*

MARGARET MCGUIRE was another exponent of the Irish influence in California. A native San Franciscan whose parents were Thomas and Annie McGuire, she became a substantial and highly esteemed citizen of the city. Margaret received her primary education in the parochial and public schools and thereafter completed a course in prestigious St. Vincent's Convent, from which she was graduated in the late 1870s.

A devout Catholic, Miss McGuire was employed as a stenographer in the office of Archbishop Patrick Riordan, who succeeded California's first Archbishop, Joseph Sadoc Alemany. She later took a similar position with the renowned San Francisco law firm of Dunham, Carrigan and Hayden. In 1912 she accepted a position with the newly formed State Industrial Accident Commission, where she remained for a number of years.

In the meantime Margaret McGuire attended law school, graduating in the class of 1921 with a degree as Bachelor of Laws. She became an even more valuable employee as a referee because of her comprehensive and accurate knowledge of all phases pertaining to the workings of the Industrial Accident Commission.

Miss McGuire served as a member of the San Francisco Bar Association and the California Bar Association. A constant and devout communicant, she was invested in the San Francisco Archdiocesan Council and in the National Council of Catholic Women, in which she acted as secretary. She was also an active member of the San Francisco Professional Women's Club, the Young Ladies Institute and the Women's Safety League of Northern California.

FLORENCE DONNELLY, nee Holland, is another Irish-Californian woman who deserves a prominent place in California history. She had a noble heritage, as the granddaughter of two pioneer California families, to guide her along life's way. Her paternal grandparents, the Franklin Hollands, could trace their ancestors to the minute men who fought in the American Revolutionary War.

The Hollands were married in Boston and spent their honeymoon traveling to California by way of the Isthmus of Panama and thence by ship to San Francisco. Franklin Holland and his bride settled in the coastside hamlet of Tomales, where he engaged in business with his brother-in-law, Warren Dutton, whose wife was the former Martha Holland. Franklin served as Assistant Master of Transportation in Butler's Department during the Civil War.

In the ensuing years Franklin bought the Dutton interest in a general merchandise store in Tomales and became the sole owner. He also served the community as a school trustee and postmaster. The Hollands had five children, one son and four daughters: Frank S., Julie, Mabel, and Gertrude. Frank married Alice Conmy, whose parents, John and Maria {Cherry} Conmy, were both Irish born, he in County Galway and she in County Clare.

The Conmys had met in Australia and soon thereafter traveled to California at the onset of the Gold Rush. They were married in the historic St. Francis Church in San Francisco, by Father John Scanlon on July 11, 1852. Shortly thereafter they went to Weaverville in Trinity County, where John had a mining claim. A printer by trade, John became associated with the Trinity Journal. During their stay in Weaverville three of their children were born.

In 1859 the family moved to Shasta, where John was now the owner and publisher of the *Shasta Courier,* a position he maintained for eleven years. During that period he also served as Collector of Internal Revenue at the behest of President Abraham Lincoln. Their youngest daughter, Alice, was born in Shasta in 1868, and a year later the Conmys moved to San Jose so that their children would have a better education.

In the meantime Mr. Conmy was engaged by the firm which published the *San Jose Mercury,* still being published. Alice attended the Notre Dame Convent school and graduated from that prestigious institution while it was still located in San Jose.

Florence Holland was the only child of the Frank and Alice Holland. She attended public schools in Marin County, San Francisco State College, and later did post-graduate work in English and journalism at the University of California in Berkeley. She married Hugh Donnelly in 1910.

Florence Donnelly began her great work as a newspaper reporter early in life and in 1930 became the only reporter on the San Rafael *Independent,* now the *Independent-Journal.* In 1935 she co-founded the Marin County Historical Society with Miss Belle Brown. These two ambitious women worked together on the Marin committee of the State Landmarks Commission.

One of the Historical Society's most urgent projects was the establishment of a historical museum, followed by the publishing of a history of Marin County. In the meantime they sketched and built a replica of the old San Rafael Arcangel Mission, which had fallen to pieces.

In 1950 Florence Donnelly took a leave of absence from the newspaper in order to serve as executive producer of the Marin Centennial Pageant, titled "The Golden Span." In 1952 she became society editor of the *Independent-Journal* and the recipient of an award for the best women's page in newspapers of the *Independant-Journal* class. She was honored for Outstanding Community Service in 1953.

The Donnellys had one son, James Holland Donnelly, born in 1912, who was educated in San Rafael and at College of Marin in Kentfield. Early in life he was a Marin county correspondent for various San Francisco newspapers. Later he took a position as field representative for the California Wine Institute. He enlisted in the U.S. Infantry in World War II, retiring with the rank of Major. The James Donnellys had three children, Franklin, Eileen and Sheila.

.

Edward P. "Slip" Madigan
Courtesy St. Mary's College of California Archives

"SLIP" MADIGAN, JOE "CLUTCH" CRONIN, "LEFTY" O'DOUL

IRISH KINGS OF SPORT

SOME OLDER CALIFORNIA football fans relate that every so often they are awakened by "the roar of the crowd," reminiscent of the days when the Galloping Gaels of St. Mary's took on the mighty California Golden Bears. On one momentous occasion in 1927, the victory-hungry Gaels, led by "Slip" Madigan, defeated the Bears by a score of 26 - 7. Madigan's men had come a long way since their ignominious defeat, 127 - 0, by the Bears, six years earlier.

On taking over as coach at the age of 25, Madigan almost singlehandedly transformed an unskilled football squad into one of the most exalted teams in America. Highly revered as a coach, he was equally renowned as a showman who thrived on an uproarious atmosphere at games played with wild abandon. Confrontation on the playing field provided an opportunity for the flamboyant coach to showcase American football on a grand scale.

A protege of the great Knute Rockne at Notre Dame, where he was honored as a leading lineman, Madigan came to St. Mary's College in 1921, when it was located in Oakland. That fall, after the disaster against the Golden Bears, college administrators cancelled the remainder of the schedule, and gave serious thought to dropping the sport, for the time being at least. However, at the insistence of Brother Gregory Mallon, the college president, it was decided to hire a new coach in hope that he would be able eventually to field a winning team.

What convinced Brother Gregory to hire Madigan was his achievement at Notre Dame. By all accounts, the terms offered by the president were generous, and Madigan had no qualms about accepting them. In addition to his yearly salary he was to receive ten percent of the gate receipts.

Slip Madigan with Knute Rockne
Courtesy St. Mary's College Archives

During the first two years of his tenure, while the college was known as the "Old Brickpile" in Oakland, his share of the gate was barely enough to keep clothes on his back. But when the new campus in Moraga opened for business in the 1930s, his take increased a hundredfold. In addition to his salary of $7,000 a year, he earned nearly twice that amount in gate receipts and commissions, not counting his liberal expense account for food, rent and transportation.

Within a few years Madigan put together a formidable football squad, competitive with any in the nation. His Galloping Gaels defeated such leading teams as the University of Southern California, Oregon, the California Golden Bears, and mighty Fordham. Little wonder that St. Mary's was touted as the Notre Dame of the West, and Madigan himself as the "Wonder Coach."

Off the field it was the flamboyant Irishman's phenomenal promotional schemes that garnered the attention of sports fans all over the country. Madigan engaged his own publicity agents to glamorize the prowess of his athletes at press conferences and sporting events. He traveled to New York City, staged lavish press parties and gave his publicists a free hand to invent sensational stories about the giant-killer Gaels.

It was an era of free-style recruiting and rough and tough football, which suited Madigan to a T. He even outdid his mentor, Knute Rockne, in many respects. Although Slip was only 26 at the time, he was at his best in coaching his raw recruits. With skill and precision he molded a squad that attracted the public and the press from Kezar Stadium in San Francisco to the Polo Grounds in New York, and at noteworthy stops along the way.

Since there was no television and radio was still in its infancy, Madigan had to rely on newspapers and magazines to make known the exciting story of the gridiron Gaels. The fall practice was begun with considerable fanfare. Following a sumptuous lunch, sports writers and photo journalists were escorted to the field, where the uniformed squad was lined up to meet them. Each player introduced himself to each writer as cameras clicked in an hour-long ceremony. At a time when jerseys were one drab color, the St. Mary's squad, togged out in red, white and blue jerseys and red silk pants, created a sensation in footballdom.

TOM FOUDY, the leading college publicist at the time, remembers one occasion when the publicity was especially creative. He informed newspapers in the South that the the St. Mary's Special, coming their way, had on board "Miss Gael," who was more beautiful than Miss America. The response by return wire caught Foudy unprepared to back up his sensational announcement. Having no such person in the entourage, he was hard pressed to find a young lady who might fit the bill—but he did. No Miss America, surely, but to her credit the young woman went along with the ploy and gave all the correct answers at the ensuing press conference.

Foudy could not remember her name. However, he had everything else down pat as if it were yesterday. He insisted that the publicity would have been nothing without Madigan's charisma, Irish wit and infectious laughter.

While passing through New Orleans, Slip met a man from Syndicated Ratings at a time when St. Mary's was way down on that list. After their meeting the Galloping Gaels were moved up to the Top Twenty. There was strong rivalry between two leading Catholic institutions, New York's Fordham and St. Mary's, and the competition was always tough and close. Under Slip Madigan, St. Mary's three wins and a tie in nine games with Fordham were enough to keep the rivalry at a high pitch and the fans in an excited mood.

By the late thirties Madigan was a familiar face to Gotham crowds as he strode down Broadway and through the Bowery. His annual Eastern trip was as much a transcontinental revel as a football excursion. "The Bells of St. Mary's" was Slip's theme song. Although he couldn't sing it like the polished crooner, Bing Crosby, he could recite it with a flare that caught everyone's attention.

After one big win over Fordham, the homebound train full of celebrants was scheduled to depart New York City at 1 a.m. But Madigan couldn't leave without saying goodbye to his friends. With a newsman in tow he taxied to a famed Long Island restaurant, a number of Irish bars and Broadway night clubs. At each visit business came to a standstill as the delighted owners, maitre d's and bartenders greeted him with a cheery, "Hello Slip!"

The last goodbye was at White's, a famous nightclub, where the stage show stopped to greet Madigan. In the manner of a seasoned entertainer the exuberant coach jumped onto the stage and led the entire gathering in a ringing rendition of "The Bells of St. Mary's." Little the worse for wear, Madigan and the newsman arrived at the train station at 3 a.m., two hours late.

Coming or going, Slip Madigan never missed an opportunity to promote the exploits of the Galloping Gaels. On one return journey, following a win over Fordham, he posed for photographers surrounded by team members, holding aloft a part of the Fordham goal post. To hometown critics who questioned whether being three weeks away from studies was conducive to higher learning, Madigan replied, "We play in New York, and that is an experience in itself. Our players join the alumni in visiting the most interesting sights, stopping or dining at the best hotels. Three weeks across America is worth two semesters. This is something they don't teach in class."

Ireland's National Game on the Moraga Campus

THE DISTINCTLY Irish character of St. Mary's has been quite obvious since its founding. Coach Madigan was staunchly Irish, as were most of the Christian Brothers on the faculty: Brothers Gregory Mallon, Leo Meehan, Jasper Fitzsimmons, Albert Austin Crowley and James Shanahan.

A primary factor that enabled St. Mary's to draw big crowds at the games was the all-out support of Catholic ethnic groups in the greater Bay Area, especially the Irish, Italians and Hispanics. The exploits of the Galloping Gaels became the principal topic of conversation at Irish gatherings, and were argued over backfences and rehashed in Irish saloons, at christenings, weddings and wakes.

St. Mary's College proved its Irishness as a willing sponsor of "Hurling," Ireland's age-old competitive sport. The Irish spirit flowered when hurling took root in Moraga, and students became fans with all the fervor normally devoted to American football. The Irish community reciprocated by sitting on the St. Mary's side of the playing

The Hurling team at St. Mary's, ready to play Ireland's national sport, 1934. The author is second from right in the second row. Author's collection

field, and the United Irish Societies invited the leading Gael players to participate in the St. Patrick's Day Parade in San Francisco. All along the line of march toward the reviewing stand at City Hall, they were cheered on by thundrous applause.

Hurling's most ardent proponent on campus was Brother James Shanahan, a member of the teaching faculty. Brother James, a champion hurler himself, was born in County Tipperary, where he joined the Brothers of Christian Schools order and was eventually sent to the western province based in Moraga.

Something akin to ice hockey, and even more spectacular, hurling is a fast and fascinating game when played by skilled participants. Hurling, however is not new to San Francisco. It was played in Hayes Park, the city's first public recreational grounds, (the site of the present Civic Center) more than thirty years before the Gaelic Athletic Association was founded in Ireland in 1894.

When hurling got underway at St. Mary's in the glory days of the Galloping Gaels, it brought new life to the Gaelic Games in San Francisco. The newly formed St. Mary's hurling team for the most part was made up of teaching brothers and athletic-minded students, most of whom were Irish by descent. A lesser number were Irish born, like Brother James, who had competed in the old country. Francis

Prenderville, Brother James and Tim Ryan, another Tipperary man, were the principal organizers. Hurling balls and instruction manuals were shipped from Ireland to the Moraga campus at the appointed time; training sessions got underway immediately and were well attended from the beginning.

The Opening Round at Ewing Field

THE CLASH between St. Mary's and Cork, the reigning Pacific Coast champions, brought out the largest gathering ever assembled at Ewing Field at the foot of Lone Mountain. Many came not just to see a hurling match, but to cheer for the St. Mary's team, whom they equated with the Galloping Gaels of American football fame.

They didn't have long to wait. When the ball was thrown in and the game got underway, one of the St. Mary's players got possession and in the manner of an All-Ireland champion drove the ball between the uprights for the first score. The fans simply went wild, jumped to their feet and let go with a roar that reverberated all over Lone Mountain. In wild delight, they pounded on the old wooden stands which shook and rattled as though a temblor had hit them.

Pat O'Neill, the "Voice of the G.A.A.," was also at his best on that occasion in 1934. Although a Corkonian by birth he was also a St. Mary's fan, calling every player by name. From start to finish it was either side's game to win, with the score even at half-time. Both sides played the game in a sporting manner, devoid of roughness and keeping injuries at a minimun.

Toward the end St. Mary's took the lead, and when the final whistle blew the entire gathering converged on the playing field and serenaded the winners, a scene reminiscent of those at Dublin's Croke Park, but with a Yankee touch. The following week the players, managers and supporters were invited to the college campus, where they were wined and dined and given a heroes' welcome.

In a three-way competition, St. Mary's next outing was against the Clare team. Unlike the game against Cork, it was a rough and tumble match that did little to enhance hurling or please the spectators. Clare had only a limited number of skillful players and had to call on others of lesser experience to make up the team.

As a result the game was not played in a sporting manner. The referee was hard put to control the antics of the newcomers, who played with wild abandon and disregard for their more skilful opponents. Little wonder a number of the St. Mary's team were injured, some seriously enough to require medical attention on the field.

Joe Cronin
Courtesy Baseball Hall of Fame

Worse yet, when the teaching brothers showed up in the class-rooms the next morning, all bandaged up, it was too much for the educational authorities to condone. They immediately called together all those in positions of responsibility to explain what had happened and why so many injuries had occurred, in contrast to the outing against Cork. Unsatisfied with the explanation, the authorities decided to withdraw from any further involvment in the promotion of hurling at St. Mary's College.

For Irish hurling enthusiasts, and the promoters in particular, it was a tragedy. One can only assume that if hurling had been adopted by St. Mary's on a permanent basis, other Catholic colleges would have followed, and Ireland's national game would have become an intregal part of American sports. The least that can be said is that it was good and exciting while it lasted.

Joe Cronin - Baseball Immortal

JOE CRONIN'S ENTIRE LIFE was one of challenge and commitment in the world of sports. At the age of fourteen he won the junior tennis championship of San Francisco, and four years later he led the Fighting Irish of Sacred Heart to victory over the St. Ignatius Wildcats. In 1956, following an outstanding career as a player, coach and manager, Cronin was elected to Baseball's Hall of Fame.

Joseph Edward Cronin was born in the Excelsior District of San Francisco in October 1906, six months after his family emerged from the devastating earthquake and fire that almost destroyed the city. Cronin's immigrant Irish father, Jeremiah, worked as a teamster in the Mission District, which thousands of his countrymen called home.

Joe, the only athlete in a family of three boys, developed a passion for baseball while practicing after school at the Excelsior Playground. In 1920 he entered Mission High School, where he played basketball, baseball and soccer. While there he shared the infield with Wally Berger, who later won fame in his rookie year with the Boston Braves, pumping out 38 home runs. When Mission High burned down in 1923, young Cronin transfered to Sacred Heart, which proved the turning point in his baseball career

One cloudy day in 1924, lanky, pink-cheeked Cronin, recently injured, sat on the bench at Commerce High School ballfield on Van Ness Avenue wearing the Irish pin stripes, his long legs loosely extended from his big frame. A pair of crutches leaned aimlessly alongside. The stands were packed with the spirited supporters of Sacred Heart and the equally dedicated fans of their arch-rival, the St. Ignatius

Wildcats. The overflow gathering had come to witness the outcome of the San Francisco Catholic high school league championship.

It seemed that the Irish had reached the end of their rope. The scoreboard read 1 - 0 in favor of the Wildcats in the bottom of the ninth inning; two men were on base as two others came to bat and struck out. Sacred Heart needed a miracle, and it seemed unlikely to come from the injured Joe Cronin as he struggled to his feet amid jeers from the Wildcat boosters.

Joe Cronin
Courtesy Baseball Hall of Fame

Reaching for a bat, Cronin cast a wary eye on the enemy pitcher. Throwing aside his crutches, he hob-bled to the plate and stood tall with a look of determination in his Irish eyes. The confident pitcher grinned, raised his arms and prepared to throw, little fearing the half-cripple at the plate. Cronin belted out a two-run pinch double that won the game and the championship for the Fighting Irish.

When Cronin graduated from Sacred Heart in 1924 he was offered an athletic scholarship at St. Mary's College. He declined the offer because his family needed all the money he could bring in. At the time he was working as a part-time instructor for the San Francisco public playgrounds, filling in for regular instructors as the need arose.

An Humble Beginning

JOE CRONIN began his baseball career playing semi-pro ball for the little town of Napa. Every Sunday morning, rain or shine, he would get up to attend Mass at Epiphany Church, then board a Mission Street trolley car to the waterfront to catch the ferry bound for Vallejo, thence a train to Napa. Before long, Charley Graham asked him to play for his home professional team, the San Francisco Seals.

While thinking it over Cronin was also solicited by Joe Devine, a team scout who wanted him to play for his club, the Pittsburgh Pirates. He signed up forthwith and played 36 games with the Pirates in 1926. The following year he was sent to the New Haven club in

Connecticut, affiliated with the Eastern League. While there Cronin was sold to Kansas City, which sent him on to Wichita.

As it happened, Clark Griffith, owner of the Washington Senators, was on the lookout for a hard hitter to replace the injured Goose Goslin. Griffith's cagey scout, Joe Engel, saw Cronin at practice and was so impressed he wired Griffith that he had found a suitable replacement. Determined to sign up the peppy infielder, Engel wired Griffith to be prepared to pay the full asking price of $7,500 that the Blues' owner insisted on. The wire included a note for Mildred Robinson, Griffith's niece, telling her to pretty up, that he would be bringing home a "real sweetheart."

Engel contacted Kansas City Blues owner George Muehlbach, figuring the price for the little-known hitter could be negotiated. But Muehlbach refused to compromise. Knowing the talent he'd found, the Washington scout was not about to let Joe Cronin go. He handed over the full $7,500 then and there.

Engel arrived in Washington in high spirits, bringing Cronin to Griffith's house for dinner. The cagey owner was dismayed to learn that his new infielder was batting only .245. His winsome niece didn't seem to mind the low average at all.

All went well for Cronin in the 1928 season. He played 63 games at shortstop for the Washington club. Under the guidance of Walter Johnson, the ex-pitcher supreme, Cronin raised his batting average to .283, hitting safely 193 times out of 492 attempts.

Wedding Bells on the Potomac

AT THE CLOSE of the baseball season in 1934, Joseph Edward Cronin married Mildred Robinson, Clark Griffith's niece, after a lengthy courtship by present-day standards. They had known each other for seven years. The honeymoon plans called for a sea voyage to end in San Francisco, Joe's native city. An urgent message awaited their arrival, one that would have a tremendous influence on their lives.

Cronin was to call Griffith as soon as possible. In a phone call later that day Joe was informed that Tom Yawkey, new owner of the Boston Red Sox, wanted him and was willing to pay $50,000 (equivalent to $1 million today). Even at that astronomical figure Griffith was reluctant to give up his prized shortstop, let alone his brother's son-in-law. Nonetheless he told Cronin if he decided to go, he would be assured $50,000 a year as player-manager. With Cronin's consent Griffith finally agreed to Yawkey's proposition.

As leader of the Red Sox, Cronin was convinced that he could shape the squad to his form of the game. The team's board of directors went along with him, even though they were unsure of his strategy and his handling of the players. No doubt there were other compelling reasons—like a chance to beat the "unbeatable" New York Yankees.

During his years with Boston, Cronin earned the respect and admiration of the fans, although he never matched his top Washington batting average. During the 1938 season his fans honored him with a "Joe Cronin Day" at Fenway Park, presenting him with a $1,250 purse and an Irish Terrier.

With his batting average on the decline, Cronin was about to hang up his uniform, but the war and the resulting shortage of players forced the aging star to stay on the active list. In 1945 he fractured his right leg, putting an end to his playing career. The following season he returned to the club, this time as a non-playing manager. For Joe it was "the luck of the Irish" when he led the rejuvenated Red Sox to their first pennant in 28 years. With that record to his credit, Cronin retired from the playing field in 1948 and moved to the executive offices in Boston, where he served as vice president, treasurer and general manager. He held those positions until he was named President of the American League on January 31, 1959.

IN 1956 CRONIN was elected to baseball's Hall of Fame. Boston fans celebrated by dedicating a day to their idol and presenting him with a new Cadillac, license plated "HF-56." He was also given plaques and clocks and a sizable purse that he turned over to charities. He then resumed his position as head of the American League.

His achievements included leading the Washington Senators to a pennant at the age of 27, winning the American League's most valuable player award in 1930, and seven times in succession being recognized by the Sporting News as the best shortstop in the major leagues.

Cronin's legacy as a player is one of remarkable inspiration to the youth of America:

A .302 batting average over a twenty-year playing career.
Eight seasons with 100 or more runs batted in.
Five pinch-hit home runs in 1943.
The youngest major league manager at 26.

As Connie Mack tells it, "Oh my, yes, Joe is the best in the clutch, with a man on third and one out. I'd rather have Cronin hitting for me than anybody I've ever seen, and that includes Ty Cobb, Simmons and the rest of them." In Boston the Cronin legend lives on. Old-timers claim they can still hear that salute from the stands to the old clutch-hitting kid from Sacred Heart, "Oohh, isn't he a sweetheart!"

But Joe Cronin was more than a player or a plaque in the Hall of Fame. He was a dedicated family man, a loving husband and a wonderful father whose children were the joy of his life. True to his Irish upbringing he was a devout Catholic and didn't mind talking about it. "When I was in the minors in Kansas City, I was hitting only .239; it was hot and humid, and I didn't like the place. I went to Mass for thirty days straight and asked the Lord to get me out of there, and He came through."

Cronin first visited Osterville on Cape Cod in 1944; he resided there permanently following his retirement. He loved the Cape and its enchanting panorama and took delight in calling it "the California of the East." In retirement he attended Cape Cod baseball games and allied functions and threw out the ball on opening day whenever possible.

Following a long battle with cancer, he passed away at his Osterville home on September 7, 1984, at the age of 77. Some twelve hundred mourners attended his funeral mass in St. Francis Xavier Church in Hyannis, while outside stood a throng of spectators, some wearing Red Sox caps and other emblems of their departed idol. The roster of mourners included baseball commissioner Bowie Kuhn, Red Sox owner Haywood Sullivan, team president Jean Yawkey, manager Ralph Houk and coach Johnny Pesky, former Red Sox star Dominic DiMaggio, brother-in law Calvin Griffith, former NBA commissioner Larry O'Brien, New England Patriots owner Billy Sullivan, and Thomas "Tip" O'Neil, Speaker of the House of Representatives.

Honorary pall bearers included baseball commissioner Kuhn, former American League president Lee McPhail and former Red Sox stars Ted Williams and Bobbie Doerr, who were unable to attend.

A moving eulogy was delivered by longtime family friend Father Joseph Scannell of the Mission Church in Roxbury, who said that Joe did his dying triumphantly. A burgundy-colored oak coffin bearing Cronin's remains was followed down the center aisle by his grieving wife Mildred, daughter Maureen and sons Tom (Minnesota Twins public relations director), Michael and Kevin.

During the obsequies Bishop Daniel Cronin (no relation) of Fall River praised Joe Cronin as a model for young people.

"Joe brought to the youth of today magnificent accomplishments," said the Bishop. "The wonderful qualities that youth possess today are because heroes such as Joe Cronin have made our country great."

Frank "Lefty" O'Doul

ASIDE FROM his rise to fame on the baseball diamond, Frank "Lefty" O'Doul is best remembered as the Butchertown Boy, a moniker that carried a lot of weight in old San Francisco. Outer Third Street is where life began for the sandlot slugger who posted a lifetime batting average of .349 in the major leagues. He was a brash young Turk who set his sights on becoming a merchant prince in his native city, and quit school in the seventh grade to pursue his rags-to-riches dream.

In later years when someone mentioned to Miss Rose Stolz, his grammar school teacher, that it was too bad he had to quit school after only seven years, she replied, "I know Frank never went beyond the seventh grade, but just remember this, he was the only boy in school who always took off his hat when speaking to a lady."

O'Doul was born in 1897 in San Francisco's Butchertown, a rough neighborhood but also a productive one with its livestock compounds, feedlots and packing houses. The jumbled community spawned such illustrious citizens as Robert "Believe it or Not" Ripley, Gentleman Jim Corbett, and Eddie O'Dea, a sandlot slugger turned policeman.

When O'Doul quit school he went to work for Joe Rosenburg, a wholesale butcher, whose premises were within walking distance of Frank's home. He got up at 5 a.m. to herd and feed livestock, and to deliver meat in a wagon to San Francisco's downtown merchants. It was tough work for a grown man, let alone a lanky youngster just turning fifteen. He was so tired from the long work hours that he had no heart for baseball.

In time Frank got used to the hard work, although he never really liked it. He did, however, have an affinity for horses and dogs, which which were plentiful in Butchertown at the time and which helped sustain his interest in the work at hand. He had a particular liking for one old horse, Milky, who belonged to a teamster named Charlie Turner. O'Doul and his pals would gladly deliver meat for Mr. Turner if he'd let them ride Milky bareback.

Back To Baseball

In spite of his hard work, O'Doul found time for his first love, baseball. In the Bayview Turner League he pitched for the Mohawks. Among his teammates, all Butchertown residents, were Eddie O'Dea, catcher, and Denny Desmond, pitcher, both of whom became policemen, and Fred Nicholson, who later worked for the Bank of America. With the battery comprised of two Harps*, the Mohawks won the city title in 1913.

That was the turning point for O'Doul. From that day on it was all baseball for the Butchertown boy. He practiced at every opportunity, developing a good curve ball at the age of sixteen, when he graduated out of the old Turner Barn League.

In 1916 O'Doul joined the South San Francisco parlor of the Native Sons of the Golden West. (South San Francisco referred to the southeast corner of San Francisco, not to its San Mateo county neighbor of that name.) This membership paved the way for his entry into professional baseball. The Native Sons had an elimination tournament, with South San Francisco and Stanford parlors reaching the final. Stanford won but were required to forfeit the game because Splash Kennedy was ruled a professional by the authorities. Irish Jack Regan, manager of the South San Francisco club, encouraged O'Doul to enter organized baseball without delay.

The timing was just right. When someone told Hughie Smith about the nifty pitcher, he signed him up to play for the home team, the San Francisco Seals of the Pacific Coast League. Smith, a seasoned catcher for the Los Angeles Angels, devoted his remaining years to the betterment of the Seals and to the nostalgic Old Timers Day at Seals Stadium.

Early in 1917 O'Doul reported to manager Harry Wolverton, reputed to be one of the greatest in the minor leagues, for spring training. Lefty had played for the Seals only five weeks when he was shipped to Des Moines, Iowa. As he related in later years, this was his first long train ride. "I thought I had travelled for a million miles. I was pop-eyed," he said. "Soon after I arrived I pitched against St. Louis and got a broken finger. Blood poisoning set in, and I had to enter a hospital. As I lay in bed I was awfully lonesome for old "Butch." Some of my pals in Butchertown wrote to me, and I reread their letters until I almost wore the ink off."

That winter O'Doul was returned to the Seals and was delighted to be home again. Then, in a morning game the Seals were playing down in Vernon, O'Doul overslept, and Spider Baum, the club's oldest player, had to fill in for him. Believing that O'Doul had overslept deliberately, Spider complained to Charley Graham, the manager. "This O'Doul is the youngest kid on the club, but he can't get up on

---

*The Irish were called "Harps" by sportswriters and commentators, as well as by some of the general public.

Frank "Lefty" O'Doul,
the pride of the San Francisco Seals.
Courtesy Don Figone

time. He's too fresh." And there the matter stood, when the baseball schedule was cut short in midsummer because of America's entry into World War I. Lefty O'Doul enlisted in the Navy as an electrician.

For the next few years after the war was over, Lefty's baseball career took a nosedive. He failed as a pitcher with the Yankees and the Red Sox in the early 1920s, and returned to the Coast League.

On the strength of his being named the most valuable player in the Pacific Coast League in 1928, the New York Giants took O'Doul into the majors. Almost immediately he snapped his ankle, and Manager John McGraw, fearing he had an unsound player on his hands, sold O'Doul to the Philadelphia Phillies the following year.

The Wearin' of the Green

DURING HIS STAY in Philadelphia, O'Doul bought his famous Kelly green suit. He wore it to the Phillies' Baker Bowl one day and got three hits, including a home run. The next day he put on a green shirt and tie and got four hits, including a homer and a triple. He then added green socks and green underwear, and got two home runs, a triple and a double. The next year he bought a new green suit and immediately fell into a slump, whereupon he got out the old one and started to hit well again.

In 1931 O'Doul was traded to Brooklyn, despite his batting averges of .383 and .398 in his two years with the Phillies. One of his sensational hits was a pinch home run off Pat Malone in 1930, which knocked the Chicago Cubs into third place and out of pennant contention.

The handsome O'Doul was as much hero in Brooklyn as he had been elsewhere. He was admired for outfitting a youth team in green uniforms at his own expense. Hundreds of his admirers once stormed down from the stands to escort him around the the bases, after he had slammed his third home run of the day against Pittsburgh.

In 1932 he won the the National League batting championship again, his overall prowess moving one sports columnist to write:

> If a great catch is needed to save the game, who comes galloping across the sod to spear the wicked drive? Frank Merriwell O'Doul. If a homer is needed to tie the score, whose big bat hoists the ball over the far-flung wall? Larruping Lefty of San Francisco. With the teams locked in an extra-inning scramble, who slides over the plate in a whirl of dust with the winning run? Fearless Frank, the hero of Flatbush.

O'Doul was traded to the New York Giants in 1933, amid mutterings of revolution in Brooklyn. Alas, O'Doul's long legs had started to weaken, but he still had his Irish heart and his bat, and in 1933, in the twilight of his playing career, he achieved his supreme triumph.

It was the second game of the World Series between the Washington Senators and the New York Giants. The Giants had won the first game. O'Doul no longer played on a regular basis, and was crouching in the shadows of the dugout beneath the howling mob. Stewart "Goose" Goslin had hit a home run for the Senators, making it 1 - 0, when O'Doul turned to pitcher Hal Schumacher and said "Don't worry, Hal, I'm good luck for you. If [manager] Bill Terry will put me in I'll win the ball game."

In the sixth inning, with Hugh Crits on first base, Mel Ott was walked, filling the bases. Then from the dugout came the booming voice of Terry, shouting "O'DOUL! O'DOUL!"

Into the sunlight strode Lefty O'Doul, blinking a little and swinging his big bat. He took his stance at the plate and gazed at the enemy pitcher. Alvin Crowder raised his brawny arms and pitched the first ball. O'Doul swung and fouled it away. Another pitch, another foul. Joe Cronin, manager of the Senators, ran over to Crowder to discuss the tense situation.

Crowder threw an outside ball as O'Doul dug in. Lefty managed to check his swing with a Trojan effort as the ball sailed high over the outside corner. The umpire hesitated and then called it a ball. The spectators sighed nervously.

O'Doul, a seasoned pinch-hitter, tipped Crowder's next pitch. Catcher Luke Sewell tried desperately to hold it, but the ball got away for what would otherwise have been the third strike. With two balls and two strikes on the batter, Crowder came in with his mysterious curve.

The mighty O'Doul was ready, and swung with all his might, launching a streak of white into center field. The Senators caved in, and the Giants eventually scored six runs and then took the series, four games to one.

Home Among His Own

WHEN HIS DAYS in the big leagues were over, O'Doul returned home to take over as manager of the San Francisco Seals in 1935. To a dyed-in-the-wool San Franciscan, managing the Seals was the most prestigious position in the minor leagues. The Seals set an all-time attendance record in 1946 when they drew 714,000 fans.

O'Doul led the Seals to two Pacific Coast League pennants, one in 1935 and one near the close of his managerial career in 1951. O'Doul also served as manager of the San Diego Padres, 1953-54, Vancouver in 1956 and Seattle in 1957.

There may have been better natural hitters than Lefty, but no one ever studied the science of batting more diligently. He put his experience to good use, teaching rookies how to swing with the rope trick, after the manner of Marty Maher, the Irish-born army sergeant who became the inspiratiom for the film "The Long Grey Line," about West Point. Maher taught the Army cadets how to swim with a rope to keep them afloat until they swam off on their own, and then he would cut the rope loose without their knowing it.

O'Doul cured Ferris Fain and others of a tendency to lunge at the ball by simply tying a rope around their waists. Every time they swung he yanked the rope and righted them. As an avowed perfectionist, O'Doul had the rare knack of being able to make a ball player play better than he knew how. To that, players like the great Joe DiMaggio would say "Amen."

More than a ball player of note, O'Doul was a showman in every sense of the word. Of all those who admired him, the late and great journalist Arthur Brisbane said it best:

> The name Lefty O'Doul is a precious thing, perfect, a name that could not have been invented. Anybody named Lefty O'Doul could not possibly be commonplace or fail to make his mark in some direction. Lefty O'Doul is a finer name than Rory O'Moore or Tam O'Shanter. It is a marvelous name and with it goes a marvelous smiling face.

San Franciscans used to welcome O'Doul home with a triumphant parade up Market Street to City Hall and an appropiate speech by the mayor. O'Doul, elegantly attired in an expensive camel-hair jacket, would make a brief answering speech in which he modestly shrugged off his baseball heroics. He sniffed the salubrious air and said with simple feeling, "It's good to be back in San Francisco."

Few ballplayers leave their sport so acclaimed as O'Doul. Damon Runyon called him the "Beau Sabreur of baseball." Ford Frick, a sports writer who became president of the National League, said rapturously, "Sing if you will of the glory of Schumacher and Ott, for they deserve it. But for myself, strike up an Irish melody, maestro, and make it lively and quick and twitching, for I would fain lift the lilting lyric to the man in the green suit."

Thomas William Sweeny
from a daguerreotype, taken at Mathew Brady's New York studio
at the start of the Civil War in 1861. Courtesy Richard J. Coyer

– 25 –

THOMAS WILLIAM SWEENY
THE FIGHTING IRISHMAN

1820 - 1892

THOMAS SWEENY WAS BORN on Christmas Day, 1820, in the picturesque village of Dunmanway, County Cork, to William and Hanora Sweeny. County Cork had been the ancestral homeland of the Sweenys since the 13th century. In 1827 his father died, leaving a wife and four children to fend for themselves. Five years later, in 1832, Hanora took Thomas, his older sister and two younger brothers to Liverpool and boarded the *Augusta,* bound for America.

In later years Sweeny claimed that during a storm in the voyage he was washed overboard. In order to attract attention he threw his cap into the air hoping someone would see it; then he crossed his arms over his chest and, lulled by rocking waves, fell asleep. As luck would have it a crewman spotted the cap, and a boat was lowered to rescue the young Irish lad in the nick of time. The Sweenys arrived in New York without further mishap and settled down in the big bustling city.

Thomas acquired his primary education in New York and at the same time became involved in military and literary clubs that would have a lasting effect on his future. Sweeny then received an apprenticeship with a publisher who specialized in law books. Following the outbreak of war with Mexico, Sweeny enlisted in the First New York Regiment. His involvement with the various military groups in the city led to his appointment as a second lieutenant in the famed regiment.

On March 9, 1847, the spiffy regiment took part in an amphibious landing at Veracruz, but Sweeny himself was spared the action as a result of a heat stroke. However, when fully recovered he took part in engagements at Cerro Gordo, Contreras and Churubusco under the command of General Winfield Scott. At Churubusco the First New York suffered over one hundred serious casualties, among whom was Sweeny himself. A bullet ripped through his right arm, which had to be amputated to save his life.

After a period of convalescence in Mexico City, he was evacuated to the coast and then returned to New York City to await a new assignment. As a gesture of appreciation, Lt. Sweeny was chosen as the guest of honor at the Printers' Ball in New York on January 17, 1848, celebrating the birthday of Benjamin Franklin, the patron saint of printers.

In March 1848 Sweeny received a commission as Second Lieutenant in the 2nd U.S. Infantry. And two months later, on May 15, 1848, he married Ellen Swain Clark, a distant descendant of Benjamin Franklin.

On November 8, 1848, Sweeny's regiment boarded ships in the New York harbor, bound for California around the coast of South America. Lt. Sweeny was assigned to Company D, commanded by Captain and Brevet Major Samuel P. Heintzelman, a strict military enthusiast. Almost immediately a personality clash developed between Sweeny and his commanding officer. Heintzelman sought to have Sweeny transferred as a way out of the dilemma. But, for whatever reason, he failed in the attempt and had to put up with Sweeny's antics.

The regiment arrived in Monterey on April 6, 1849. Company D and two other companies changed ship and sailed southward, reaching San Diego on April 20. Sweeney was not impressed with the small Mexican pueblo, calling it "a collection of dilapidated adobe buildings." At first the enlisted men lived in tents near the town, while the officers rented quarters from local residents.

Four months later Heintzelman took possession of the old San Diego Mission for his troops, despite the fact that Philip Crosthwaite had a lease on the land and buildings. This did not sit well with the residents of long standing in the old town.

Sweeny stayed in San Diego until April 1850, when he took up living quarters at the Mission. Shortly thereafter Major Heintzelman left San Diego to attend a court-martial in Oregon, leaving the one-armed officer in charge. On the night of June 22, Private Lawrence Kearney, a fellow Irishman, got drunk, took a horse from the stable and went on a wild late-night ride. He was found the next morning sleeping it off on a grassy mound, but the horse was nowhere about.

Sweeny ordered the sergeant of the guard to personally escort the soldier to the guard tent. A short while later, while sitting in his tent reading a book, the sergeant heard a voice exclaim, "Lieutenant Sweeny, that damned son of a b—, pity he didn't lose the other arm too." That was more than such a high-spirited Irishman could bear. Sweeny stormed out of his tent as Kearney was asking permission to finish his breakfast before being placed in the guard tent. Sweeney would have none of it; he ordered the soldiers to seize Kearney and drag him over to the tent. During the confrontation, Kearney swore at Sweeny in threatening tones.

When they were in front of the guard tent the one-armed officer had the offending soldier "bucked," a common practice in the Army at the time, in which the offender is placed on his stomach with his arms and legs brought back and bound together behind his back in the form of a horseshoe. While this was being done the prisoner sneered at Sweeny, saying, "Is this all the punishment you can give?" In a fit of Irish temper Sweeny ordered the men to tie the ropes tighter and had Kearney placed in the hot sun and denied water. Kearney yelled at Sweeny, "I'll pay you for this you damned rascal!" In the evening the prisoner was untied and placed in the guard tent, but the next morning Officer Sweeny had him bucked again, even though his limbs were swollen

Kearney had a change of heart and apologized to his commanding officer for the nasty things he had said the day before. He was untied forthwith, examined by the post surgeon and placed in the infirmary. When the surgeon visited him a few days later he found that gangrene had set in. On the following day Private Kearney died.

MAJOR HEINTZELMAN learned about this unfortunate event when he returned to San Diego some weeks later, but was unable to give it his full attention, having received orders to establish a military outpost at the junction of the Colorado and Gila Rivers. He appointed Sweeny as assistant quartermaster for the expedition, and the one-armed lieutenant was kept busy in his new assignment. His work enabled him to forget about the Kearney incident, but this affair was far from over.

Two months later Heintzelman received a dispatch from headquarters saying that the death of the Private Kearney was considered murder, and that Lieutenant Sweeney would have to face a civil court. Heintzelman replied, saying he was too busy getting his command ready for the march to the Colorado and could not be bothered with this matter.

Finally, on October 25, 1850, Heintzelman led his companies out of Mission San Diego on the first leg of the expedition. After many days' marching the men reached the desert outpost of Vallecito and camped there waiting for supplies to catch up with them.

Shortly thereafter a deputy sheriff from San Diego arrived with a subpoena for Lieutenant Sweeny. Sweeny agreed to go, but insisted that all the officers and a number of the non-commissioned officers accompany him and serve as witnesses at his trial. Seeing his mission in jeopardy, Heintzelman wrote to headquarters asking them to send another officer to him; otherwise "we might be left without an officer at the post." The deputy sheriff, with Sweeny and one sergeant, headed out to San Diego, while Heintzelman led his troops in the opposite direction. On November 27, the commanding officer chose a site on the west bank of the Colorado River to establish his new outpost, which he named Fort Yuma, after a local Indian tribe.

IN THE MEANTIME Sweeny stayed in San Diego with his wife, awaiting his trial. On December 9, 1850, he was brought before a civil court judge on a writ of habeas corpus. The judge heard the testimony of Sweeny and the sergeant and ruled that there was no need to detain the accused officer any longer. So the same day he entered court, Lieutenant Sweeny left a free man.

Sweeny spent the next several weeks with his family in San Diego and then left for Fort Yuma with the next supply train, arriving at his destination on January 22, 1851. But his relations with Major Heintzelman were still tense, and would become even worse in the following month. The senior officer made Sweeny assistant quartermaster, his first duty being to help get ready to move the outpost to a hill overlooking the junction of the two rivers. In addition to his regular duties the devilish Irishman found time to criticize his commanding officer.

In late February a traveler called at the post saying he had met a family, the Oatmans, stranded in the desert and needing help. Heintzelman sent along a small party with some food and other essentials, but the men returned a short time later saying that the Indians had killed the family except for one boy, who escaped by feigning death, and two girls, who were taken captive. One girl died in captivity a short time later, but the other remained a captive until her release four years later in 1855. That disturbing incident became known as the "Oatman Massacre."

Sweeny and other officers pressured Heintzelman to send troops out to rescue the girls, but he refused to do so. This riled the fighting

Irishman no end. Sweeny gave vent to his anger in a letter to his wife in San Diego: "Yes! there was a whole family murdered under Heintzelman's very nose, two girls taken into captivity by the Indians; and there was nothing done to avenge the murder or rescue the captives from worse than death. And what was the gallant Major's excuse for his inglorious inactivity? Why, that he had not sufficient force at his disposal to accomplish anything."

Tempers also flared between the two officers during the course of moving the Fort; they got into many arguments over how things should be done. Heintzelman wrote in his diary, "It is impossible to count on Sweeny."

At last, with Fort Yuma moved to its hilltop location, life at the base settled into a dull garrison routine. About that same time, Major Heintzelman became involved in the Colorado River Ferry Company, which had a lucrative business ferrying people and livestock into California. He invested in the operation until he owned one half of the business, but then word came from headquarters that jeopardized his investment.

On May 9, 1851, the Army decided that Fort Yuma should be temporarily abandoned because of the high cost of sending supplies. With the troops being withdrawn from the area, the ferry transport company would also leave rather than stay put, unprotected from possible Indian attack. There was a loophole in the order: if the commanding officer was unable to remove all of the equipment and supplies from the post, he could leave a small detachment consisting of an officer and ten soldiers to guard the items left behind.

HEINTZELMAN DECIDED to leave some material and men at the Colorado Post and surprisingly picked Lieutenant Sweeny to command the detachment. The one-armed Lieutenant received his orders, which said, in part, that he and his men should "prevent hostile incursions of our Indians into Mexican Territory and also any hostilities between the Indians themselves. "In short," Sweeny told his wife, "to accomplish with a corporal and nine men, what he, himself was incapable of accomplishing with three companies of infantry and five commissioned officers."

Despite their differences, Heintzelman leaned on his controversial junior officer in all his military undertakings. He had Sweeny set up camp next to the ferry company; his ramparts consisted of a ditch dug around the camp behind a fence made out of brush. The few tents which served as command quarters Sweeny dubbed "Camp Independence," not for patriotic reasons, but because he would be free of his commanding officer. The enlisted men were at odds as to who was in command, Major Heintzelman or Lieutenant Sweeney.

The next day, June 5, Heintzelman and his command headed west for Santa Isabel, where the Army had a supply depot. But before the troops left, Sweeny gave them a letter to his wife. It explained, "I have just time to write a line, to inform you it is very uncertain how long a time may elapse before you will hear from me again. The command leaves Yuma today—and I am to remain—for God knows how long, with a pleasant prospect of being starved to death and no means of informing my friends of the facts."

To make matters worse, a month later Heintzelman's command would withdraw all the way to San Diego, too far away for rescue should anything threaten Sweeny and his men. Meanwhile Sweeny and his troops had to live under the searing heat of the desert, giving what little aid they could to travelers while keeping a wary eye on the neighboring Indians.

ON NOVEMBER 12, five months after Heintzelman had left the Colorado River base, a relief column made up of an officer, ten men and a wagon train bearing five months' worth of supplies arrived at Camp Independence. Sweeny was told he and his men were being relieved; they were to escort the wagon train back to San Diego. Sweeny may have been delighted to meet his replacements, but the stories he had to tell them were cause for concern by the new arrivals.

In fact, a few days before the relief column arrived, the Indians had attempted to overrun the Army post. They entered the camp under the pretext of trading with the soldiers, but as their numbers increased they refused to leave. Sweeny was equal to the challenge and chased them out by aiming a 12-pound howitzer at them. Then, on the night before the replacements came, a party of sheepherders encamped nearby were attacked in their sleep and all but two were killed.

Both officers agreed it would not be safe for Sweeny and his men to cross the desert back to San Diego, so they decided to keep all the troops at Camp Independence for the time being. This more than doubled the number of men at the outpost, providing good protection against Indian attack, but it placed twice the strain on the food supply. To compound that problem, the Zuni River expedition led by Captain Lorenzo Sitgreaves arrived eighteen days later, asking for supplies so they could fulfill their mission.

Before the latter party's arrival, an express rider had been dispatched from Camp Independence to tell Major Heintzelman about the decision not to send Sweeny back to San Diego. The Major was not pleased with this news, and in short order he outfitted another relief party, this time with an officer and eighteen men, with orders to take charge of the outpost, to send Sweeny and his command back with the wagons, and also to investigate the murders of the sheepherders. Despite Heintzelman's orders to maintain Camp Independence, all the officers decided to abandon the post and withdraw entirely to San Diego.

On December 6, 1851, the troops gathered up what equipment and supplies they could transport, buried the rest, and headed west. Before reaching San Diego they met up with a large body of troops under the command of Heintzelman and Lieutenant Colonel John Magruder, who were on their way to attack the Indian village of Los Coyotes and bring an end to the uprising led by Antonio Garra. They took most of the soldiers from Camp Independence with them and sent Sweeny back to the coast with Captain Sitgreaves's party. Heintzelman and Magruder were victorious at Los Coyotes, which broke the back of the uprising.

ANTONIO GARRA was captured and turned over to the militia in San Diego. During his confinement he was placed in Sweeny's custody. Sweeny claimed that Garra admitted to him that he was behind the murder of the sheepherders and the attempt to overrun Camp Independence.

The militia asked Sweeny to attend the Indian's court-martial, but he refused on the grounds that the trial was not under the jurisdiction of the United States Government. And when Garra was found guilty and sentenced to death, the militia asked Sweeny to carry out the sentence of the court. Again he refused on the same grounds, but as a matter of duty, he provided weapons for the firing squad.

During the Garra uprising a group calling themselves the "San Francisco Volunteers" came to San Diego, offering their services in quelling the revolt. Ironically, these men were troublemakers themselves. They were the so-called Sydney Ducks, Australians who had been chased out of San Francisco and came south looking for excitement. By the time they arrived, however, the revolt had petered out and nobody wanted their help.

On New Year's Eve, 1851, Philip Crosthwaite, the sheriff, caught two of the "volunteers" stealing horses, and threw them in jail. Their leader demanded that the men be turned over to him to be dealt with, or the rest of his men would tear San Diego apart. Fearing the worst, the sheriff told Lieutenant Sweeny about the threat. Then another member of the gang confronted Crosthwaite in the Town Plaza and asked if he was going to release the men. When he said no, the man threw a punch at him, which the Sheriff easily ducked. The man then pulled out a gun and fired point blank at the big lawman. Fortunately, the weapon misfired. With that the sheriff drew his own gun and shot the assailant in the leg. Just then others came forward, and seeing their comrade being shot, opened fire on the Sheriff. Caught in the middle of the plaza with no protection, Crosthwaite ducked bullets while firing back. Then a slug caught him in the pelvis, knocking him down. A courageous bystander braved a hail of gunfire, picked up the lawman and carried him into a building. The mobsters dashed across the plaza to finish off the sheriff.

Just then the fearless one-armed Irishman dashed into the plaza, drew his sword, confronted the onrushing mob and ordered them to disband immediately. They could hardly take him seriously. Here he stood, a lone one-armed man, wielding only a sword, ordering them to leave. They ignored him and kept coming. What they didn't know was that Sweeny had eighteen well-armed soldiers hiding behind one of the buildings. When the gang refused to obey him, Sweeny yelled out an order; his men came out of hiding and took aim. The trouble-makers quickly surrendered. Crosthwaite eventually recovered from his wounds, and the notorious gang was forced to board a ship headed for San Francisco.

DESPITE THEIR DIFFERENCES as to how the Army should conduct its affairs in California, Major Heintzelman called on Sweeny time and again when he needed a capable officer. For example, in February 1852, during the march across the desert to re-establish Fort Yuma, Heintzelman received word that a number of his recruits were quartered in San Diego. He delegated Sweeny to go back and get them.

Sweeny did as commanded and found the recruits encamped near Mission San Diego. While there he heard terrible tales of their behavior from their commanding officers. He was told that when their ship stopped at Jamaica they had fought with the natives, and that the same thing happened while they were crossing the Isthmus of Panama. In San Diego, it was said that they attacked their own officers, and Magruder's troops had to intervene, placing some of them in irons. But Sweeny found the new recruits, who were mostly Irish, quite respectful. He had the irons removed. He then took command and marched them all the way to Fort Yuma without incident.

The Indians in that area were still on the warpath, and it fell to the lot of Sweeny and other officers to deal with several tense situations. On May 12 Heintzelman ordered Sweeny to proceed into the territory of the Cocopas tribe. The Cocopas fled as the troops advanced. When the troops came across a settlement they overpowered it. A few Indians appeared bearing a white flag. They told Sweeny that they were ready to surrender and make a treaty with the Army. He agreed, but insisted that their warriors would have to accompany him back to the post. Two days later Sweeny returned with 125 Cocopa warriors and chiefs in tow. Heintzelman was especially pleased when the Indians agreed to Sweeny's demands and offered their services in controlling the other tribes living along the river.

JUST TWELVE DAYS LATER Sweeny was assigned to lead a similar expedition that would have dire consequences. On May 26 he was dispatched north of the fort to break up a suspected Indian encampment. His detachment contained some of the troublesome recruits he had picked up in San Diego two months earlier. The patrol marched further and further north but found no trace of encampments. Meanwhile their water supply dwindled. Exhausted from heat and thirst, the men made their way wearily back to Fort Yuma. A roll call revealed that a number of men were missing, which necessitated sending a mounted patrol to round up the stragglers.

This was more than the most vocal of the recruits could bear. Late on the night of June 1, two of the recruits, William Hayes, a native of Dublin, and John Condon, of Queen's County, stole food, wagons and ammunition and deserted. Next morning a patrol was sent out to apprehend the men. That evening a party, under the command of Sweeny himself, set out to catch up with them. Because of the intense heat, they headed towards Sackett's Wells, where they figured the deserters would go to get water. By riding fast they hoped to get there before Hayes and Condon.

When they arrived at their destination Sweeny saw a large gathering of men, horses and wagons, that turned out to be government boundary surveyors, led by Lieutenant Colonel Louis Craig, who was in charge of the military escort. Sweeny asked Colonel Craig to be on the lookout for the two deserters and capture them if possible.

The next day Sweeny met up with an express rider who told him that Colonel Craig was dead. Craig had approached the two deserters on foot, disarmed himself, and tried to persuade them to give up. Instead Hayes drew his gun and shot the officer at point-blank range, and Condon shot a sergeant who came to his aid. Then the two men mounted Craig's horse and rode off. Some local Indians captured them and turned them over to Colonel Magruder at Mission San Diego. The deserters were charged with desertion and murder, court-martialed, and found guilty. They paid for their crimes by hanging on January 31, 1853, in what was said to be the first military execution in the United States Army in peacetime.

Heintzelman continued to send Sweeny on patrols against the Indians. Finally, the defeat of the Yumas at the confluence of the Colorado and Gila rivers put an end to the Indian uprising. The Indians surrendered, and their chiefs signed a peace treaty on October 2, 1852.

A LTHOUGH THE WAR with the Indians was now over, the clash between Sweeny and his commanding officer continued unabated. Things came to a head when the junior officer received a box addressed to him filled with magazines. Heintzelman claimed the magazines had been ordered by the post treasurer and belonged to everyone. He ordered Sweeny to surrender the materials. The latter said he would if Heintzelman could produce evidence that the magazines indeed belonged to the post.

That was the last straw; the stubborn Celt was placed under arrest and confined to his quarters. A week later Heintzelman found an easy way out; he suspended the charges and assigned Sweeny to lead a patrol looking for stolen cattle. Within a few days Sweeny found the missing livestock but not the thieves. Sweeny would be called on to lead other patrols, but his problems with "Old H," as he called Heintzelman, were not over.

On May 16, Sweeny celebrated his fifth wedding anniversary by eating brandy peaches his wife had sent him. He felt quite homesick all day. The next day he had the biggest confrontation yet with Heintzelman:

> While at drill the Major Heintzelman told me to caution my company what to do. I told him I had. He said I didn't speak loud enough for him to hear me, & insisted on my doing so. Upon my complying, he said I spoke too loud, and said I must evince a different spirit from what I did that morning; I said it was my wish to evince a good spirit if permitted, upon which he ordered me to silence in a loud & peremptory manner. I then reminded him that I had a commission, and would not submit to be talked to in that way; upon which I was arrested. During the day I was compelled to go to the officer's sink and to the

mess room to get my meals. I received my charges on the 23rd [of May] among which is one for Breach of Arrest, for the above causes.

A short time later Heintzelman resurrected the charges concerning the magazines. For the rest of 1853 Sweeny remained under arrest and confined to the post. Good news finally came on November 10, when an order came relieving the men from duty at Fort Yuma. Twelve days later Sweeny himself got an order transferring him out of Heintzelman's company. Heintzelman released Sweeny from detention on December 12, and the very next day the fiery one-armed officer, along with a number of others, left Fort Yuma for the last time. Thus ended one of the most petty and hilarious confrontations in the history of the United States Army.

A Happy Reunion in the Big City

ON JANUARY 29, 1854, Sweeny reached New York City and was reunited with his adoring family after a three-year separation. Although he would never again serve in California, this did not mark the end of his services on the frontier. After a seven-month stint on recruiting duty in New York, he was sent to Carlisle Barracks in Pennsylvania, and from there removed with his regiment to Fort Pierre in Dakota Territory as part of General William Harney's Sioux Expedition. Sweeny spent two years in this former trading post on the upper Missouri River. Evidently it was a rewarding experience for the daring lieutenant, who spoke of it in a personal manner: "[Harney] complimented me very highly, and said it was a damn shame to compel an officer circumstanced as I was, to do Company duty so many years, and the greater part of that in the field; that, as far as he was concerned, there was nothing in his power he would not do for an officer who had lost an arm in defense of his country."

Sweeny left Fort Pierre on June 6, 1856, for another tour of recruiting duty in New York. Then he turned his hand to writing, setting forth his hectic adventures in Southern California in an article entitled "Life on the American Desert." He sold his story to the *New York Atlas*, which serialized it over a period of sixteen weeks, beginning with the December 7, 1856, issue.

In April 1857 Sweeny once more said a fond good-bye to his growing family and headed for Dakota again, this time serving at Fort Randall. Six days after his arrival, he was made acting quartermaster of a 300-man expedition against the Indians who had perpetrated the Spirit Lake massacre. Besides many settlers losing their lives in the incident, four women were taken captive. By the time Sweeny's expedition marched out of Fort Randall, two of the women had died and the others were subsequently released.

After this gruesome episode Sweeny and his men settled down to their rather boring garrison duty. On June 4, 1858, Sweeny left Fort Randall and frontier duty for the last time to spend the next two years recruiting in New York. His stay was not all that he had yearned for. His wife had been in poor health, and now was getting worse. On August 30, 1860, Ellen Sweeny died, leaving her husband to look after their four children. A Civil War was looming on the horizon. As a result Sweeny was forced to send the older children to boarding school and leave the youngest in the care of his wife's relatives.

IN THE FOLLOWING YEAR, 1861, having finally been promoted to Captain, Sweeny took command of the federal arsenal in Saint Louis, Missouri, where there were many pro-secessionists to contend with. A group of men asked Sweeny to surrender the weapons and ammunition in the arsenal to them. He replied that before he would do that, he would take a match and "blow the arsenal to hell."

Shortly thereafter, Sweeny was joined by Captain Nathaniel Lyon, whom he knew from his sojourns at San Diego and Fort Pierre. Together they worked diligently to keep Missouri in the Union. Although the incumbent governor wanted his state to secede, the pro-Union politicians were able to keep Missouri from joining the Confederacy when the issue came up for a vote.

These same politicians helped Lyon and Sweeny keep a close watch on secessionist groups in the city. In this way the Army was able to thwart the plans of Missouri's governor. As a result of his efforts in this crisis, Lyon was promoted to Brigadier General. After securing Saint Louis, Lyon sent Sweeny on a mission to the southern part of the state to arrest the governor, who was fleeing to safety in Arkansas. Despite their efforts, the governor reached Arkansas, a confederate stronghold, and set about organizing Confederate troops to move into southern Missouri.

Several officers advised General Lyon to withdraw, but Sweeny convinced them all to stand and fight. Although they were outnumbered in the battle at Wilson's Creek, the Union troops withstood several assaults until General Lyon fell mortally wounded, thus becoming the first Union general to be killed in the Civil War. About the same time, Sweeny was felled with a bullet in his leg. Having lost their commander and running low on ammunition, the Union troops retreated back to Saint Louis.

While recovering from his wounds, Sweeny did office work and served on court-martial boards in Saint Louis. Eventually he joined a division that was part of General John C. Fremont's campaign to free southern Missouri from Confederate influence. But Fremont was later recalled by President Abraham Lincoln, and the campaign accomplished nothing worthwhile.

In January 1862 Sweeny left Missouri for an inspection tour in Illinois, where he was made colonel of the 52nd Illinois Infantry, the regiment he would serve during the Civil War.

Colonel Sweeny and his men arrived too late to take part in General Ulysses Grant's smashing victory at Fort Donelson, but they were given custody of the prisoners taken at the battle, whom they escorted to prison compounds in Illinois.

At the battle of Shiloh, however, they saw action aplenty. Sweeny had a horse shot out from under him, and then was shot twice in his good arm. Luckily his wounds were superficial and his recovery was quick. During his brief confinement in a field hospital, an officer from Grant's staff paid him a visit. During their conversation Sweeny said, "Ah, someone should be punished for this," referring to the fact that the Union Army had been caught off guard at Shiloh. The officer apparently repeated this to Grant, who held it to himself.

When he was fit and ready for duty, Sweeny rejoined his regiment at Corinth, Mississippi, this time under the command of General William Rosecrans. After the two-day battle General Rosencrans criticized the way some units fought, except those on the right flank, which were commanded by the one-armed Irishman. The general, impressed by Sweeny's performance, decided he should be rewarded. "Such a record should not remain unnoticed, and it is not only a duty but also a pleasure for me to testify to his worth and to urge his nomination to the rank of Brigadier General." General Grant also made known his feelings in glowing terms, "A more gallant and meritorious officer than Colonel Sweeny is not in the Service — the rank should be given [to] him at once."

Thomas William Sweeny as Brigadier General

AND SO IT came to be, on November 29, 1863, the "Fighting Irishman" was made a Brigadier General in the United States Army. During Grant's campaign to take Vicksburg, a strategic town on the Mississippi River, Sweeny commanded a division protecting the supply depots and warding off Confederate incursions. Whenever the Union Army needed a proven leader, Sweeny was their man.

And sure enough, in the spring of 1864, Sweeny was chosen by General Sherman to become part of his Atlanta campaign. On July 22, he stopped a massive Confederate counter-offensive that could have destroyed Sherman's left flank. Sweeny came through all those tough battles with his honor intact, but he became a victim of the Battle of Atlanta in another way.

A short time after that successful engagement, Sweeny was visited by Major General Grenville Dodge, his commanding officer. During their conversation, Sweeny remarked that a nearby division had broken and run, and he had had to move in and save them by deploying his artillery. Dodge vehemently denied that this happened, and intimated that Sweeny was lying. Sweeny lost his temper and began hurling threats at his superior, calling him a "God damned political general!" Dodge flew into a rage and slapped Sweeny across the face. The Irishman retaliated by punching Dodge in the nose and challenging him to a duel.

Sweeny was placed under arrest and sent to Kentucky to stand trial before a court-martial. Although he was acquitted of all the charges, none of the Army brass wanted him in their command any longer. He was honorably discharged from the Volunteer Corps and transferred to the regular Army with the rank of Major. The War Department, not knowing what to do with him, sent Sweeny to New York to await further orders. This turned out to be a mistake on the Government's part and a turning point in Sweeny's rambunctious life.

Sweeny's Involvement in the Fenian Movement

WHILE ON LEAVE in New York, Sweeny became involved with the Fenian Brotherhood, an organization that had as its purpose the freeing of Ireland from English rule by force of arms if necessary. He befriended John O'Mahony, its founder, and William Roberts, one of its most ardent proponents. Well aware of his daring exploits during the Civil War, the shrewd organizers prevailed on Sweeny to join the movement as their Secretary of War. Without a moment's hesitation, he agreed.

Now that he held a lofty post in the Fenians, Sweeny was reluctant to return to duty in the U. S. Army. He stayed on in New York, hoping to get more leave. At this same time, political newspapers asked why Sweeny was allowed to remain in the Army while at the same time serving as a military advisor to a political movement. The War Department finally decided that their charge had been absent without leave for too long and had him dismissed from the Army.

Sweeny refused to devote himself entirely to the Fenian cause. He also became involved in a power struggle with the leadership, which was nothing new for him. While O'Mahony wanted all the money and military equipment to go directly to Ireland to fight the British, Roberts wanted to invade Canada, the closest target. Sweeny sided with Roberts and they were able to wrest control of the organization from O'Mahony and his aides.

Roberts and Sweeny, supported by the vast majority of the membership, pushed their plan to invade Canada at the opportune time. Sweeny was convinced Canada was more vulnerable in the winter, with the roadways covered with snow and the rivers frozen stiff, which would deter the opposition, allowing the Fenians to take control of Canadian cities, one at a time. At that juncture, Canada would be bartered in exchange for Ireland's freedom. The Fenians accepted this plan and became impatient for winter; the more vocal members wanted immediate action. To Sweeny's aid came a powerful figure from his military past.

General Winfield Scott, the man Sweeny served under during the war with Mexico, died on June 1, 1866. Andrew Johnson, who had replaced the martyred President Abraham Lincoln, declared a state of mourning for General Scott and ordered all government offices closed. Sweeny, seasoned military strategist, took advantage of the situation and launched an invasion into Canada.

Groups of armed Fenians crossed into Canada from upper New York State and Vermont, with the largest contingent coming from Buffalo. Most of them met little or no resistance. The force from Buffalo, under Sweeny's leadership, was able to defeat a regiment of Canadian Volunteers and British Regulars. But soon their supplies ran out, and with larger forces bearing down on them, were forced to return to the United States.

When word of the invasion got out, the American authorities were furious. General George Meade, still elated by his victory at Gettysburg, lined up his troops and headed for the Canadian border. At the same time, Sweeny lost no time in organizing more men, and he too hastened to the border with re-enforcements to bolster the invasion. Ironically, both men were on the same train, Meade getting off at Malone, New York, while Sweeny continued on to Vermont.

Meade and his troops were successful in keeping more Fenians from entering Canada, and arrested others who were returning to the States. As fate would have it, a regiment of U.S. soldiers reached Vermont just as Sweeny was about to lead a group of Fenians across the border. He was arrested and held prisoner in a local hotel. At the same time, O'Mahony and Roberts were also arrested in New York. Supporters stepped forward to post bail for the latter, but not for Sweeny, who had planned the invasion. Eventually, the government dropped its case against Sweeny and released him forthwith. This was a wise move; had they maligned the Fighting Irishman in any way, the country might have been torn apart. In the minds of most Americans, Sweeny was a hero who had turned the tide in favor of the Union Army at Arkansas, Corinth and Shiloh.

W HEN A GLUM Sweeny returned to New York, he discovered that the Fenians had turned against him because of his failure to conquer Canada. Even Roberts, whom he had supported, turned his back on him. To save face, Sweeny resigned his office.

All was not lost, however. A grateful nation was not going to turn its back on an Irish immigrant who put his life on the line in the war with Mexico and again in the Civil War. President Andrew Johnson reinstated Sweeny in the Army with his former rank of Major, on November 8, 1866.

Sweeny was sent to Georgia to take command of the troops stationed in Augusta. Here he met and courted an Irish lass, Eugenia O'Reagan, more than twenty years his junior. They were united in marriage on September 30, 1867. In December of that year, he was transferred to Atlanta, which was a triumph for him, since he had been arrested there before the city surrendered in 1864.

After nine months commanding the troops in Atlanta, he was sent again to Augusta. Then in January 1869 he and two infantry companies were ordered to Savannah to put down an uprising of former slaves at Ogeechee Creek, south of the city. Sweeny cautiously led his men into the trouble spot and successfully restored calm to the area without any violence or firing a single shot.

Two months later, Sweeny received word that his name had appeared on the Army list of retirees, although he had heard nothing official up to that time. He was by then a senior Major in the Army. The following month he was ordered to report to New York to be examined by Army surgeons. After waiting over a year, his retirement became official on May 11, 1870. The citation read as follows:

> A board of examination having found Major Thomas W. Sweeny, United States Army, unassigned, incapacitated for active service , and said incapacity is due primarily to a wound received in the battle of Churubusco, Mexico, which occasioned

the amputation of his right arm—and, secondly, to a gunshot wound received in the right leg at the battle of Wilson's Creek— and, thirdly, by a gunshot wound in the flesh of the left arm received at the battle of Shiloh, these and several other wounds being aggravated by long and faithful service and exposure in the line of duty. The President [Grant] directs that his name be placed on the list of retired officers of that class in which the disability results from long and faithful service, or from wounds or injury received in the line of duty . . . Major Sweeny is, by direction of the President, retired with the full rank of Brigadier-General.

SWEENY SPENT the rest of his life in quiet retirement. He refused to seek political office because he felt "a general in the United States Army should never meddle in petty politics." In his last years he divided his time between New York and Augusta, Georgia, having two children by his second wife, Eugenia. He also gave of his time to various veterans' organizations.

General Thomas William Sweeny died at his home in Astoria, Long Island, New York, on April 10, 1892. His memory is perpetuated in his American army career which spanned a period of some twenty-five years of faithful service, and as an Irish-Californian in the landmark "Sweeny's Pass" in San Diego County.

Frank McCoy
Courtesy Santa Maria Historical Society

– 26 –

FRANK MCCOY
THE REAL MCCOY OF SANTA MARIA

W HEN THIS WRITER SET OUT in a Model T Ford on the tedious journey to Los Angeles over a half a century ago and stopped overnight at the fashionable Santa Maria Inn, it never occurred to me that it was founded by a fellow Irishman named Frank McCoy. It was the first time I had slept in such luxurious surroundings since my arrival in California in 1926. Having little interest in history in those days, I gave no further thought to the matter at the time. The hotel porter called me at the appointed time, and following a sumptuous breakfast I set out for Los Angeles to see firsthand what the City of Angels had to offer.

I well remember all that happened along the way. It was customary in those days to pick up anyone in need of a ride going your way. As I approached the highway leading south there stood a young lad waving a hand-made sign, "Santa Barbara." I pulled aside to give him a lift, knowing his company would help minimize the tedious journey. As it turned out he, too, had a story to tell, of his upbringing in Ohio, his industrious family and why he had come to California with little but adventure in mind.

It was all so interesting that I didn't notice the time until a road sign, Santa Barbara, appeared in the distance. When my traveling companion gestured where to stop, I pulled over and decided to let the old steaming engine cool off in the shade. As a token of appreciation the rider insisted on buying hamburgers and soda pop, which we both enjoyed during the brief respite.

Santa Maria Valley and the barren slopes were a wilderness when the Portola Party journeyed through the area in 1769 on their way to find Monterey Bay. The friendly Chumash Indians were the first tribe to settle there, where there was little to suggest that anything but the hardy sagebrush and weeds would survive. In time man and nature, working together, helped change all of that. The Franciscan

Fathers planned well and built a chain of Missions and trading posts connected by El Camino Real (The Highway of the King), each within a day's ride in California's cradle days.

The Spanish were followed by Swiss dairymen, Danish and Portuguese farmers and Irish adventurers in search of land. Little is known of the first Irish settlers in these parts who went as they came, leaving no written record of their exploration. In their later travels, however, they spoke glowingly of a land richer and fairer than any they had previously beheld. This startling account lured countless others in search of this worldly paradise, a trend which continues to this very day.

Santa Maria, originally known as Central City, was laid out in 1874 on land donated by four early settlers, surveyed and recorded at the county seat on April 12, 1875. When water became available to supply the developing farms and orchards, other adventurers from all across the country flocked to the valley in search of a better way of life. The arrival of the Pacific Coast Railroad from San Luis Obispo in 1892 coincided with the name change, from Central City to Santa Maria, for mail addressed to the township had a way of showing up in Central City, Colorado.

It was only in later years when I became involved in recording California's Irish contribution, that I learned about Frank McCoy of Santa Maria and his many exploits and accomplishments. For here indeed was an Irishman who left a lasting imprint in the heartland of sunny California.

The McCoy Family

FRANK MCCOY was born in County Tyrone on May 25, 1872. His parents were both natives of St. Louis, Missouri, which already boasted a sizable Irish population. In the spring time they paid a visit to their ancestral homeland in the old country, and during their stay Mrs. McCoy gave birth to a son, whom they named Frank, after his grandfather, in the age-old Irish tradition. The McCoys returned home to St. Louis with their newborn son, and took up where they had previously left off.

The McCoys were no strangers in America. Frank's great-grandfather, James McCoy, had braved the stormy Atlantic on a sailing vessel bound for Philadelphia in 1837. On the maternal side his great-grandfather was a descendant of the O'Neills of Ulster, pottery makers by trade, who came to America to promote the sale of their product in the New World. Their mission proved so successful that they decided to settle permanently in the United States and in due course disposed of their holdings in the old country.

Like many other Irishmen, Frank's father, Hugh, proved his loyalty to America by enlisting the Union Army after the outbreak of the Civil War. Following his discharge in 1865 he returned to his native city and married his childhood sweetheart, Miss O'Neill.

Frank McCoy was reared in Mound City, a suburb of St. Louis, and educated in the public schools in that city. After graduating from high school he enrolled in the University of Missouri at Columbia. But when his father died suddenly, he had to leave his studies and return home to take care of family matters.

California Bound

IN 1893, at the age of twenty-one, Frank McCoy journeyed to San Francisco in search of a more promising way of life. In order to be better prepared for all that California had to offer, McCoy took a refresher course in business administration at a local college. Upon completion of his studies he found a suitable position with the Union Sugar Beet company, headquartered in Betteravia, close by the city of Santa Maria. In that position he gained considerable experience in the housing and feeding of company employees on the premises where they worked. This in-house system, catering to the needs of the workers, was quite common in that early period. As more and more workers acquired homes of their own, company boarding houses became a thing of the past.

In his work for the Union Sugar Company McCoy did quite a bit of traveling, during which time he discovered to his discomfort the total lack of hotel accommodations for the ordinary traveler. In 1915 he resigned his position with the company and took a year's vacation to assess the situation. He traveled around the country looking for a suitable location for the hotel he intended to build. During his stay at the Bradley Hotel he heard about the Blockman property outside Santa Maria, and decided on the spur of the moment to look it over. The following day he began negotiations with the intention of purchasing the property.

When the deal was finalized in 1916 McCoy had the old Blockman house moved off the land and began construction of the first section of the Santa Maria Inn. When the building was completed on May 16, 1917, the Inn opened for business, and with considerable fanfare, registered its first tenant, James Cooney, a longtime friend of Frank McCoy and highly respected District Manager of the

The original Santa Maria Inn, begun by Frank McCoy in 1917 and expanded over the years. Courtesy Santa Maria Historical Society

National Supply Company. (As fate would have it, Mr. Cooney passed away at the famous Inn some thirty-six years later.)

In 1919 twelve rooms were added to the original structure, bringing the total to 24 bedrooms with baths, an airy kitchen and pleasant dining room. In 1923 another 21 rooms were added, and a final addition in 1928 brought the total to 85 rooms in all.

The hotel became famous during the case of Universal Oil Company versus the Standard Oil Company of Indiana, as the headquarters of the Washington lawyers involved in the belated trial. The elegant Tap Room that Frank McCoy had envisioned in his original plans put the finishing touches on the grand hotel. It was designed to provide the atmosphere of pubs reminiscent of the British Isles, with plank or flagstone floors and rich mahogany paneling.

An avid floriculturist, McCoy capitalized on his love of flowers by placing them everywhere in the Inn. The windows were adorned with colorful potted plants which blended with fresh-cut flowers from the hotel's own gardens. No visitor could doubt the legend of Sunny California.

The sun-latticed patio of this quiet retreat blends with the murmuring sound of water cascading from the antique fountain. Little wonder Santa Maria Inn has become the showplace of the Inland Valley, the hub of local society and a retreat for the weary traveler.

It was the Luck of the Irish which McCoy relished throughout his engaging life, and took delight in speaking about in later years: the idea that you can work hard and earnestly and still accomplish little if Luck refuses to enter the picture.

Santa Maria was presently enhanced by James Goodwin, who initiated the planting of over forty thousand eucalyptus trees as wind breaks in the area. These plantings changed Santa Maria from a wind-blown desert into the entrancing place it is today. Palm trees, flowering magnolia and dazzling silver trees adorn the entrance to the Inn. A pittosporum hedge over twelve feet high around the front gives the guests a feeling of seclusion at all times.

An Irish Enclave

AT THE TIME there was already a thriving Irish community in the Santa Maria Valley, among whom was the prosperous Black family. Patrick Black, the patriarch of the clan, was born in 1827 in County Limerick, where he studied for the priesthood. Apparently the religious life was not for him, for he left the seminary and set out to see the world. He never stopped until he reached the California Gold Fields. The rough way of life in the mines did not appeal to him in the least, so he returned to San Francisco hoping to find more suitable employment.

In San Francisco he felt quite at home among his many countrymen. He found employment immediately as a teacher in the San Francisco School District. Then he acquired a more lucrative position with the Hudson's Bay Company as a bookkeeper. On the move again, he came to Huasna, near Santa Maria, where he engaged in sheep raising for a number of years.

In the meantime he met and married Maria Morris, a sister of Judge I. J. Morris of Santa Maria. They became the proud parents of eight stalwart sons. In later years the eight Black boys and their father became members of the local Elks Lodge, setting a precedent in numbers unequaled in the history of that renowned fraternity. A longtime reminder of the Irish presence in Santa Maria was Black's Candy Store, which was destroyed by fire in 1908.

Another prominent Celt was Cornelius Donovan, a native of County Cork, and an early settler in Santa Maria. Donovan became a leading contractor and land developer. He married Mary Hourihan from the same county, who came directly from Ireland to California and settled in Nipomo. Their union was blessed with three robust children, Daniel, Eugene and Mollie.

Other noteworthy Irish settlers were the McMillan brothers, who constructed the landmark, old McMillan Hall; Dean Loughlin, the pioneer Chief of the newly formed Santa Maria Fire Department; and the Gibson, Smith and Humphrey families.

Over the years the Santa Maria Inn, with its Tower of Elegance, lured the great and near-great: Ex-President Herbert Hoover, newspaper magnate William Randolph Hearst, William Jennings Bryan, California Governor Goodwin Knight, and Senator William Knowland. Hollywood luminaries Cecil B. De Mille, Charlie Chaplin, Jean Harlow, Jack Benny, Bing Crosby, Barbara Hutton, Clark Gable, Cary Grant, Mary Pickford, Rudolph Valentino, John Wayne, Joan Crawford, Gregory Peck, Bette Davis, Robert Young, Doris Day and Shirley Temple all stayed there. William Randolph Hearst, the sage of San Simeon, while stopping at the Santa Maria Inn, whispered to Marion Davies, "Honey, this would be a nice place to stay if we ever sold the castle."

The picturesque valley and ocean dunes provided the setting for such spectacular epics as "The Ten Commandments," "The Spirit of Saint Louis," "Morocco," and the "Thief of Baghdad."

Santa Maria was an exciting place to be in those days. There was such a need for extras because of the remote location, far removed from Hollywood, that all those who showed up found work in one production or another. During the filming of "The Ten Commandments" everyone in sight was given a part. Cecil B. De Mille, the Director was so overwhelmed by the enormity of the filming project that he exclaimed "Thank God we don't have to part the Red Sea every day!"

A report in the *San Francisco Chronicle* sheds further light on Santa Maria and Camp De Mille, where thousands of actors, extras and production crews lived and worked during the filming of the "Ten Commandments." The article gave a descriptive account of the colossal undertaking: "It took workmen a month to build the set, using 500,000 board-feet of lumber, 50,000 pounds of nails, uncounted buckets of plaster and paint and 75 miles of steel cable. During the shooting 2,500 extras were employed, which included 250 Orthodox Jews brought up from Los Angeles by De Mille to lend authenticity to the story of the Israelites flight from Egypt."

Alas! the historic setting was lost to posterity when De Mille, apparently strapped for money, ordered it dynamited, the great structures knocked down, broken to pieces and buried on the spot. To hasten the demolition he allowed local residents to take all the lumber they could haul away within a given time. Then he headed for San Francisco to prepare for additional filming called for in the script.

The End of an Era

When Frank McCoy, a man of many talents, passed away on December 10, 1949, his nephew, Edward McCoy, fell heir to the fabulous Santa Maria Inn. Following the lead of his ingenious uncle, he added a swimming pool and recreational area in 1955 and a coffee shop and banquet room in 1956. Edward also built 22 motel units close by the main building. The grand re-opening was held appropriately on May 25, 1958, the birthday of the founder, Frank J. McCoy.

In time all good things come to an end. When the old El Camino Real was widened in 1950 to become Highway 101, travelers no longer drove past the Santa Maria Inn on their way through the town. The glory days of the Inn were numbered. The palatial building with its grand amenities closed its doors.

And so it remained for several years until the Channel Islands Development Company acquired the property in 1981. Under the supervision of Martin Smith, company chairman, and its general manager, Victor Marzorati, the Inn was painstakingly restored to its former grandeur. Tradition was rekindled with the restoration of the historic Santa Maria Landmark.

The spacious lobby, the Garden Room and the exquisite dining rooms are reminiscent of a bygone era. And the McCoy Room, with its memorabilia, brings back the days when Frank McCoy was the idol of weary travelers along El Camino Real. The Ranchero Room's array of photos depict the trail riders, past and present, including President Ronald Reagan and the First Lady.

The fabulous "Tower of Elegance" on the sixth floor was built in 1984, with eighty spacious suites, splendidly furnished, bringing the Inn's room count to 166. The ground floor was refurbished and renamed Tower Lane Shoppes. Downstairs are the wine bar and cellar, along with offices, banquet rooms, and health and fitness facilities.

Frank McCoy would feel justly proud if he could see the final result of his untiring efforts.

Don Timoteo Murphy
from a sketch made after his death
Courtesy California Room, Marin County Library

VIGNETTES OF IRISH CALIFORNIANS

ORDINARY PEOPLE

WHO LED EXTRAORDINARY LIVES

THE IRISH HAVE CONTRIBUTED to the development of California in every region of the state, in areas as remote as Calexico and Modoc, and such little known places as Gaviota, Napoma, Lompoc, Coyote and Elk. A full account of their aspirations and achievements would take volumes. This chapter spotlights only a few of the thousands of Irish who led interesting or exemplary lives and deserve a prominent place in California history.

DON TIMOTEO MURPHY was a giant of a man, physically, mentally and in the extent his holdings, commanding instant attention wherever he went. He stood six feet two inches in height and almost three hundred pounds in weight, erect, handsome, fair-haired and with a pleasing personality to match.

Murphy was one of first *extranjeros* (foreigners) to receive a land grant from the Mexican government, an enormous one to be sure, comprising the Santa Margarita, Las Galinas and San Pedro ranchos in Marin County. In his position of administrator of the Mission lands, Don Timoteo proved worthy of it all, in his treatment of the Indian neophytes in particular. More than any of the previous administrators, he made an earnest and sincere effort on their behalf at every opportunity. He learned the Indian tongue, and this, coupled with his friendly nature and commanding presence, gained the respect of the Coast Miwok tribe.

During Mission days some of the neophytes (natives who had adopted Christianity) had become good mechanics and craftsmen. The younger Indians had acquired the rudiments of education, and they in turn had imparted their knowledge to their families and others.

As time went on the big Celt secured for them a grant of arable land, which embraced much of Nicasio Valley, northwest of San Rafael.

Under Mexican law the Indians could not sell their products directly to traders. Don Timoteo helped change that rule for the best interests of his wards. He then helped them promote the sale of their wares, and with the proceeds he bought tools, clothing and other necessities for them. He often rode on horseback to their *rancherias* in Nicasio to learn what supplies they needed. Under his caring and wise administration the Indians led relatively contented, carefree lives in their beloved homeland.

Contemporary historians are wont to speak only of how badly the Indians were treated under the rule of white men, which was evidently true in many cases. However that was never the case where Don Timoteo was involved. He had a keen sense of the Indians' abilities, and always claimed that, given a decade of fair treatment, they would develop into a fine trustworthy people.

On the land that had been granted to him by Governor Micheltorena, Don Timoteo built a large two-story adobe hacienda on what is today C Street between Fourth and Fifth in San Rafael. He erected stables for his Norman horses and pure-bred cattle, both of which he brought all the way from Ireland. He also had a kennel for his prize greyhounds and Irish setters. Indians and others from distant ranchos were all made welcome when they called at the Murphy hacienda. They and their mounts were fed and feasted, and with a hoot and a holler set on the return journey to their *rancherias* in the hills of Sonoma county.

Irish Roots

DON Timoteo (Timothy) Murphy was born in County Wexford about 1800. His father was a well-to-do farmer who provided his son with a good education, despite the fact that every Irishman, named Murphy was under suspicion by the British Constabulary following the rebellion of 1798.

After leaving school young Murphy went to Dublin, where he found employment in a commercial establishment. He remained there until he was offered a more lucrative opportunity with an English firm operating in Lima, Peru. He lived in Lima for two years, until he was sent to Monterey, California, where the English firm, Hartnell and Company, had a northern branch. By this time he had learned to speak Spanish fluently, an accomplishment which endeared him to the populace in his new environment.

Don Timoteo Murphy's hacienda in San Rafael
Courtesy California Room, Marin County Library

Following his arrival in California in 1828, Murphy, an expert rifleman and hunter, started otter hunting, a prosperous enterprise at a time when otter skins were fetching fifty to eighty dollars each. He continued in this business until 1838, when he joined Governor Alvarado's forces against those of Don Carlos Carrillo. In appreciation of his support Alvarado, the victor, appointed Don Timoteo administrator of Mission San Rafael Archangel. In 1839 Don Timoteo became a naturalized citizen of Mexico, and lived in Marin County for the remainder of his life.

Under the rule of California by Mexico, Don Timoteo was Marin County's most trustworthy citizen, serving as Alcalde (Mayor) of the pueblo of San Rafael, Indian agent, Land Commissioner and Justice of the Peace.

The arrival of General John C. Fremont in San Rafael in June 1846 spelled trouble for Murphy. Fremont's troops took over the Mission for their headquarters. Then Fremont ordered the killing of three unarmed Californios—twin brothers Francisco and Ramon de Haro and their aged uncle, José Berryessa—who were on their way to Sonoma. Fremont also took sixty of Murphy's fine horses, as he had done at other ranchos along the way, and made no effort to compensate the owners.

DON TIMOTEO was held in high esteem by the Americans after they took over the government in California. In fact, he was appointed to a committee of Americans in San Francisco, along with such prominent men as Robert Semple, Richard Sherman, Jasper O'Farrell, Thomas Leese and Nathan Spear, to protest to the President of the United States against the proposed appointment of General Fremont as governor of California. The authorities in Washington got the message, and there the matter ended.

The Irish Don was by now a wealthy man, owner of three land grants in Marin County, totalling some 22,000 acres. But he was also generous to a fault. On the spur of the moment he deeded to the Catholic Church a large section of his property on Market Street in San Francisco, not far from where the Palace Hotel now stands, as a site for a school and orphanage.

Now in middle age and still single, he yearned to have some of his relatives in Ireland come to live with him. One of the first to arrive was a nephew, John Lucas. Lucas was much like his colorful uncle, and they enjoyed a few wonderful and rewarding years together in San Rafael before Timoteo's death in 1853.

Don Timoteo is best remembered for the hilarious celebrations he staged at his adobe in what is now the heart of San Rafael. Nothing like them had ever before been seen in Marin county: A Celtic Feis and Spanish fiesta, all in one, lasted for three exciting days. There were bull-and-bear fights, calf roping, greased-pig wrestling, and hayrides for young and old. Irish guests danced to the music of Big John Kelly, the fiddler, perched atop a rickety old stagecoach which had seen better days on the trek to California.

When day was done, Don Timoteo wooed his listeners in the manner of an Irish Seanachi (story teller) as they gathered around a huge bonfire. His tales were of Ireland long ago, of the Little People, the Leprechauns, the Banshee, and the Giant Finn mac Cumbaill, of whom he could claim to be a descendant without batting an eye.

Eventually John returned to Ireland to fetch his fiancee, Maria Sweetman. They were married and returned to California together in 1865, settling down on a section of the Murphy rancho that Uncle Timothy had deeded to them in his will. The McNear property, including the secluded McNear's Beach, Peacock Gap and China Camp, were once part of the Murphy holdings.

John and Maria were blessed with a fine family. In later years they took delight in relating tales of the good life on the Murphy ranch, where their friends stayed for weeks as houseguests and enjoyed lavish feasts and sporting events. They had the privilege of flagging down the train, which had a right-of-way over the Lucas property, to ride to Tiburon to catch the ferry for San Francisco.

The Murphy heirs were also generous, bequeathing to the Catholic Church a vast section of land for an orphanage and school for motherless boys, known today as Saint Vincent's School. Saint Vincent's is now State Historic Landmark No. 630. John and Maria Lucas also donated the hillside property for a cemetery, named Mount Olivet, reserving a family plot where they and their uncle are interred. The beautiful Lucas Valley, north of San Rafael, is named for the family.

SENATOR JAMES D. BYRNES was a longtime public servant who represented both San Mateo and Santa Cruz counties in the California Legislature. There was never an instance when his party pledge was dishonored.

Senator Byrnes was a man of imposing appearance, standing six feet four inches in height. His manly bearing and genial countenance attracted attention wherever he went. He became involved in local politics when San Mateo County was in its

Senator James D. Byrnes
Courtesy San Mateo County
Historical Association

infancy, in 1853, and became one its first and most popular supervisors. His hearty good nature and prescient objectives won him a sizable following, which he was able to retain throughout his long political career. In later years he was nominated for a seat in Congress but declined the offer because of ill health.

Born in County Tipperary in 1831, Byrnes came to America at an early age. When his parents died, and with few prospects for a livelihood in Ireland, he sailed for America and settled in New York. During his stay there he met and married Margaret Crowley, a recent

Senator Byrnes's house, built in 1875, was a showplace where the family entertained many visitors. The building still stands, at 703 First Avenue in San Mateo. Courtesy San Mateo County Historical Association

arrival from the Old Sod, in 1851. They spent their honeymoon on the tedious journey to California.

Following a brief stay in San Francisco they moved to San Mateo and settled down to married life. Determined to make good on his own, Byrnes established a country store and stagecoach stop which over the years became the most popular stopping place in San Mateo County. The couple became the proud parents of six children: James E., Thomas, Mrs. M. T. Bigley, Mrs. E. Hosing and Misses Annie and Mary Byrnes.

As a legislator James Byrnes served his adopted city and state with honor and dignity until forced to resign because of ill health. His son, Thomas, took over in business and politics where his father left off and was appointed postmaster of San Mateo by President Benjamin Harrison in 1889. His name had been submitted by Senator Leland Stanford. On February 15, 1893, he received official recognition for outstanding service from Postmaster General Jonathon Wanamaker.

On May 11, 1903, Senator James D. Byrnes died at his home in San Mateo following a brief illness. He was survived by his wife of fifty years and their children and grandchildren.

The funeral took place May 15 at Saint Matthew's Church, where a Requiem Mass was celebrated by Father Timothy Callaghan who paid high tribute to James Byrnes' exemplary life and labors. A large group of relatives and friends followed the remains to St. John's cemetery where the last rites were performed. Distinguished mourners from San Francisco, San Mateo, Santa Clara and Santa Cruz counties were in attendance at the obsequies.

WILLIAM O'CONNOR was one of the most noteworthy of the early Irish settlers in Pomona. His extensive orange groves were the showplace of the citrus industry in early California. In addition to oranges he grew peaches, apricots, prunes and pears.

O'Connor was a native of County Sligo, as were his parents, Michael and Mary (McTige) O'Connor. In 1847, when William was only five years old, his father, an experienced gardener, moved with his family to Manchester in search of employment. Evidently things did not go as planned, and as a result William was put to work at the age of seven in a textile factory as a spinner. He began working half days and eventually became a full-time employee in that humble occupation.

In 1859 the family emigrated to the United States and settled in Pennsylvania, where William found work in the coal mines. With little formal education, the only work he could find was that of a common laborer, which was the lot of many an Irishman in that period. At the age of twenty he went to Omaha, Nebraska, where he was employed by Union Pacific during the construction of the transcontinental railway. From there he moved further west to work for the Central Pacific Company laying the rails through the Sierra Nevada mountains into California.

In 1875 he moved to Southern California where he was employed in construction projects in and around Anaheim. Later he worked in railroad construction as an independent contractor and was one of the leading builders of the line to North Pomona.

O'Connor compensated for his lack of education with his energetic and industrious habits, coupled with an Irish wit and the will to win. Like many of his fellow countrymen, he was a diligent supporter of churches and schools; he took a leading role in the construction of the first Catholic Church in Pomona.

In 1873, at the age of 31, he married Bridget O'Reilly, whose parents hailed from County Cavan. Of that union came seven children: William J., Edward H., Catherine, John P., Ada Madeline, Grace, and Francis L.

JOHN FRANCIS POWELL was another Irishman who left his imprint
on the Inland Empire. He eventually owned a big spread between
Los Angeles and San Bernardino. A native of County Galway born in
1839, he came with his parents, Mathias and Della (Burke) Powell to
Charlestown, Massachusetts, where he grew to manhood in the shadow of the famed Bunker Hill Monument.

John attended the renowned Winthrop School, which was run by
the venerable old school-master, Mr. Griffin, who was also a drama
instructor and critic. Seeing that his young pupil possessed a talent for
the stage, Griffin secured passes for him to the National Theater and
the Boston Museum, so as to enable him to prepare for the upcoming
school exhibitions.

In the meantime Powell caught the attention of Edwin Forrest,
the renowned tragedian, and became one of his leading pupils. When
Forrest was leaving Boston he wanted to take Powell with him and
educate him for the stage, but this his mother would not allow.

In 1859, at the age of twenty, Powell enlisted in the U. S. Navy
and served on the gunship *Constellation* whose missions were the suppression of slavery and the capturing of slave-trading ships. In 1861,
following the outbreak of the Civil War, he returned home to Bunker
Hill and enlisted in the First Massachusetts Infantry regiment. He saw
action against the Confederates in the Carolinas, at Whitehall,
Goldsboro, Blintz Creek and Rainbow Bluff. In 1864 he was mustered out at Camp Wenham, Massachusetts, and two years later re-
enlisted in the regular army.

Almost immediately he was given charge of a company of recruits
stationed at Devil's Island in New York. From there he was sent to
California and assigned to the Second U.S. Artillery in San Francisco.
Shortly thereafter he was placed in Command of Goat Island (now
called Yerba Buena), which the U.S. Army had seized from Thomas
Henry Dowling, its rightful owner for some nineteen years.* Powell
held the position for only five months.

He had caught the attention of General Halleck, who sent him to
Sacramento to open a recruiting office for the regular army. While
there he received orders to open a branch office in Marysville. After
ten years of faithful service in both the U.S. Navy and the U.S. Army
he was honorably discharged from the service in December, 1869.

Free of military duty and in search of a new way of life, Powell set
out for Los Angeles, where he joined his brother Michael at his Big
Rock Creek Ranch. While living there the Powell brothers made a

---

*Had Abraham Lincoln still been alive, this take-over would never have happened.

treaty with the Indians, who were hostile to the white settlers at the time. By so doing they helped to make that section of the country safe for immigrants and longtime residents as well. After three years the Powells sold out and re-invested in nearby Castro, where they took up sheep raising as a livelihood.

In 1875 John Powell was elected Justice of the Peace for Soledad Township and was re-elected to that same office in 1877. In 1879, at the age of forty, John was united in marriage to Miss Dora Lake of Jamestown, New York. They became the parents of three children: Francis M., Alfred C. and Florence M. John Powell was an active participant in politics, a member of the Republican Party, and a proud member of the Grand Army of the Republic, Stanton Post No. 55, Los Angeles.

JAMES MCCAFFERY was one of the earliest and most successful horticulturists in Santa Barbara County. Born January 6, 1818, in Aughnamullen, near Castleblaney in County Monaghan, his life story reads like an Irish fairy tale. His formal education was very limited on account of the restrictions placed on Irish Catholics in that period. It was all the more difficult for young McCaffery, who had to walk three miles to the nearest school, a crudely constructed stone building with an earthen floor and no heat save a little peat fire at one end of the room. In winter he brought along sods of turf as his contribution to the heating system. Despite these obstacles, however, he learned to read and write.

Upon leaving school McCaffery went to England, where he became a tailor's apprentice. When qualified as a journeyman tailor he returned to Ireland at the age of 25 and married his childhood sweetheart, Miss Mary Brady.

Shortly thereafter the newlyweds returned to England, and James went to work for the firm where he learned his trade. However, the work environment was so injurious to his health that he had to quit and rest in bed in order to recuperate. As Irish luck would have it, McCaffery was a member of the Saint John's Consolidated Union of Tailors, who provided medical assistance at their expense. The treatment was so successful that within four weeks' time he was out and about and ready to start working again.

However, his doctor had informed him that the climate in England was not conducive to his future health, and that he should seek a more agreeable one if possible. The McCafferys hastened to Liverpool and booked passage to Australia. All went well in Sydney, where James found employment and saved enough money to purchase income property.

In 1844 misfortune became his lot when he lost his wife and their oldest child. Three years later, James opened a saloon in Sydney and re-married. His new wife, an Irish lass named Katie Ryan, came from County Tipperary. Her family, the Ryans of Drumwood, were closely related to the Prouts of Watergrass Hill in County Cork, including Father Prout of the "Bells of Shannon" fame.

When word of the discovery of gold in California reached Sydney, the McCafferys disposed of their holdings down under, and with two children from his first marriage, set sail for San Francisco on June 1, 1849. Following a brief rest the family removed to Mission San Jose, where they were given quarters which they refurbished to suit their needs.

On his way to work one day James was injured by a runaway horse, fracturing his arm, and as result had to quit work for the time being. While recuperating he met Doctor Richard Den, an Irish-born physician practicing in Santa Barbara, who offered to assist him if he were to come to his part of the country. When he accepted the offer the good doctor provided him with horses and wagons for the journey down the coast, which took sixty days over rough trails.

In 1852, with help from Doctor Den, James took up farming on 52 acres of rented land. He grew potatoes and hay, which he sold to residents in and around Santa Barbara.

In 1856 McCaffrey rented the San Jose Vineyard from Bishop Thaddeus Amat and commenced making wine, a venture that proved quite profitable. He continued to work the Mission lands, which he stocked with cattle and sheep. However, 1863 was a disastrous year because of a drought which nearly exterminated the herds of cattle in Santa Barbara County. Had it not been for the vineyard which yielded bounteously, he would probably have lost everything.

But hard work and perseverance paid off, and McCaffrey eventually became a man of considerable wealth and influence. This allowed him to spend his remaining years in quiet retirement surrounded by his family and friends.

McCaffrey's pride and joy was his large and loving family, two children by his first wife, Mary, and seven by his second wife, Katie, five sons and two daughters—nine in all to comfort him in his declining years.

THOMAS CLOYNE, from County Longford, was one of the early pioneers who settled in Oxnard, Ventura County, long before the construction of the transcontinental railway. It was due in no small way to the collective endeavors of men such as Cloyne that the bounteous resources of Ventura County were used to benefit the land owners and to enrich the state coffers.

Born on May 10, 1840, Thomas was a working member of the Cloyne household on their Irish farm. This experience instilled in him the courage to strike out on his own at the first opportunity. But it took some time. Finally, in 1866, at the age of 26, he emigrated to America and joined a wagon train headed west for California. He settled among his own in San Francisco, where he lived and worked for two years. While there he was hired by Peter Donlan, his brother-in-law, who was also from County Longford, to bring Donlon's livestock to Ventura County.

For seven years, Cloyne worked on the Donlon ranch in the manner of the biblical Good Shepherd, tending his flocks day and night. He saved up enough money to purchase a hundred acres on Xavier Road, near the present city of Oxnard, and with that as a nucleus he increased his holdings and became a prosperous farmer and businessman in Ventura County. It was a rags-to-riches experience for Tom Cloyne, who came to the county almost penniless in 1868 and at the time of his death on January 2, 1917, owned 700 acres in the Los Posas section, and 270 acres near lovely Round Mountain. He also owned stock in both Oxnard banks, and numerous other securities.

Unfortunately, he didn't live to see his magnificent estate converted into a plantation for the production of lima beans, which in time became the largest segment of agriculture in the county. During the Great Depression "Ham Hocks and Lima Beans" were on the menu of family-type restaurants and cafeterias all over California, providing a substantial meal at a price the ordinary working man could afford. For those who had to subsist on one full meal a day the dish was a Godsend.

Thomas Cloyne was an active and enthusiastic member of the Pioneer Society of Ventura County. He also served as county roadmaster for many years, at a time when the position involved the laying out and building of some of the first roads in the area. He was also one of the leading contributors to the newly constructed Santa Clara Catholic Church; both he and his wife gave generously to its maintenance over the years.

On May 8, 1876, Cloyne married Miss Mary Reilly, a native of County Cavan, at Mission Santa Barbara. By all accounts it was a happy marriage that lasted for nearly 35 years until Mary's death on December 21, 1910. Of that union came nine children, six sons and three daughters.

James, Joseph, Charles, Edward and Peter received their primary education in the local schools and later at St. Vincent's College in Los Angeles. All of them shared in the work of the Cloyne family farm and plantation. Thomas Jr. attended Ventura Business College, but fell sick and died at age nineteen. All the sons were staunch adherents to the Catholic faith and active members in the Knights of Columbus. Little is known of the three girls, Mary, Clara and Katie, other than that they lived at home on the farm.

FRANCIS JOHN MAGUIRE was a man whose family came from a long line of Irish patriots and statesmen, some of whom had given their lives in the age-old struggle for Irish freedom. Born in Cork City in 1816, Maguire had only to give allegiance to the English rulers in order to acquire wealth and honor, and to have lordly titles bestowed on him.

But with a heart and conscience deeply committed to his people he refused to become a tool in crushing still further his downtrodden countrymen. After being trained in the law, he joined the Patriotic Party and advocated its principles so openly that he drew the wrath of the British authorities, who had him arrested, imprisoned and tried for treason.

He managed somehow to escape under cover of darkness and was not heard of again until he surfaced in New York City in 1848. He traveled to California soon after that date. A brilliant scholar and linguist, he became a master of the Spanish language and consequently the counselor and trusted friend of many of the Spanish descent on the Pacific coast. He was also instrumental in negotiating matters pertaining to land laws which were introduced by the Americans when they took possession of California. He taught the Spanish-speaking residents the duties as well as the privileges to be gained as American citizens, which would benefit them in due course.

In 1863 Maguire was elected county judge and was twice re-elected to that exalted position, serving until his death on June 17, 1879. A meeting of the bar was called to pay full respect to his memory. Resolutions were passed by that august body, extolling his virtues as a man, his talents and honor as a counsel and judge, and his high principles as a citizen of his adopted state and country, and extending sympathy and condolence to his grieving family.

Francis Maguire was liberal and yet compromising in his views, warm hearted and extensive in charity, a public benefactor always willing to promote any worthwhile project. He took the lead in the erection of a permanent wharf and in the construction of a railroad. Ever prudent in his discourse, courteous but firm, as a presiding officer he tempered all his judicial sentencing with mercy and compassion.

THOMAS J. DONAHUE was another Irish-Californian who left his mark on this state. Trained as a stonemason, he settled first in Dubuque, Iowa. At the first opportunity he returned to his home town in Ireland to marry his longtime sweetheart, Mary Agnes Condron. He brought her back to live with him in Dubuque. Tom and Mary Agnes became the parents of ten children: Patrick, Jim, John, Ed, Kate, Annie, Thomas, Nellie, Lizzie and Mary.

Following the birth of Patrick and Jim in Dubuque in 1865, Thomas traveled overland to Grass Valley by land, while Mary Agnes took the two boys with her to New York and boarded a steamer bound for San Francisco by way of Cape Horn. They were delayed temporarily in New York on account of the confusion surrounding the assassination of President Abraham Lincoln. This turn of events caused them to change their itinerary; they eventually reached San Francisco via the Isthmus of Panama. The Donahue family was finally reunited in Grass Valley a few months later.

After he had made his stake in the gold mines, Thomas, a stonemason by trade, worked in Sacramento, putting the finishing touches on many buildings, including the State Capitol, and later at the Santa Inez Mission at the behest of Bishop Mora of California.

The Irish were masters in the art of stonemasonry, as can be seen in the magnificent castles and monasteries (many in ruins) all over Ireland. There are countless examples of those intricate Irish designs all over America as well, such as the Bunker Hill Monument, which was constructed by Irish stonemasons including Michael Cahalan, an escaped Irish Rebel from County Tipperary.

Knowing Donahue's ability as a stonemason, Bishop Mora sent Father Lynch, the Rector of Santa Inez Mission, to Gilroy, to convince Tom Donahue that his skills were needed to save the crumbling Santa Inez Mission. Thomas accepted the invitation and set out with his livestock, including his prize Percherons, on the tedious journey to Santa Inez. Mrs. Donahue traveled down the coast by ship to Gaviota with their nine children in tow.

The family lived in the Mission as caretakers while Thomas began work to preserve the decaying Mission buildings. The Donahues and their numerous offspring were destined to play a major role in the future development of Santa Inez Valley. A goodly number of the Donahue children and grandchildren became schoolteachers in the public schools, thereby leaving a permanent Irish influence in that part of the state.

James left his imprint in Santa Barbara County as a surveyor, road- and bridge-builder. Patrick had seven children who married and added to the Donahue family tree in Santa Barbara County. Ed was a dairy farmer and harvester operator and later became a county road-master like his brother, Jim.

Thomas Jr. farmed as the owner of a 3,000-acre ranch in Happy Canyon. He married Abby Keane, a daughter of Doctor J. W. Keane and Mary Lathrop Keane, a Mayflower descendant. Thomas and Abbey had five children, two of whom were schoolteachers: Thomas E., whose wife was also a teacher; and Coralyn Henning, who taught at local grade schools and Santa Inez Valley High School.

John was a foreman on the San Marcos ranch and a trustee of the Santa Inez High School. John and his wife Emma had three children, John Jr., Edna and Mary Ellen. Kathleen, a schoolteacher who never married, taught at many schools in California from Refugio to San Francisco. Annie married James Sullivan and became the mother of two children. Nellie, who never married, was also a teacher at the Pico Adobe Home in Refugio (now Ronald Reagan's retirement ranch) and later at nearby Las Cruces.

Mollie married Frank Mahoney, whose father, Jeremiah (Jerry) Mahoney, was a leading San Francisco building contractor who built such magnificent structures as the famed Palace Hotel, the Phelan Building, the Hibernia Bank, and the Saint Francis Hotel.

The Mahoneys acquired considerable Santa Inez property, including the former Sweeney ranch in Lompoc. The Frank Mahoneys had four children; William (Bill), Mary, Francis and Kathleen. Mary married Fred Hayes and lives on Sweeny Ranch in Lompoc. Still hale and hearty in her eighties, Mary has shown a keen interest in the history of Irish Californians and feels justly proud of her illustrious forebears from old County Cork.

Lizzie married Peter Roberts, a tailor from Bohemia, who settled in Santa Barbara. The Roberts had two children, Louise and Virginia (Jennie). Virginia married Anthony Days in 1937 at the Santa Inez Mission.

PATRICK MURPHY was another Irishman who, with his five sons, left his imprint on both San Luis Obispo and Santa Barbara counties. In 1859 the tenacious pioneer emigrated to America and settled in New York City. While there he married an Irish lass, Rose Ann McKane, whom he had known in the old country. In 1865 the Murphys traveled to California on the overland trail and settled briefly in San Francisco.

Unlike their counterparts who dug for gold, the Murphys moved to Southern California and chose farming as a livelihood. Little is known of their activities during the next few years. In 1879 they arrived in Guadalupe, where Patrick purchased the 160-acre College Ranch from the Catholic Church. The Murphys were well received by the Hispanic community, who provided them with living quarters while their home on the ranch was being built.

Murphy cultivated the fertile valley farm on which he raised bounteous crops of wheat and barley. His success caught the attention of the *Los Angeles Herald*, which reported on August 14, 1889, that "Patrick Murphy, threshing barley—5,000 sacks per acre, makes around a $1 a sack—he and his sons doing all the work."

The old pioneer, a native of Kings County (now Offaly), Ireland, lived out his life on the ranch and passed away on February 17, 1923. He was preceded in death by his wife, to whom he had been married for over 57 years. They left five sons, William, Edward, Thomas, Joseph, and John, to mourn their passing.

All the boys cherished their Irish upbringing and, like their parents, were active in church affairs. William married Albina Casserini at St. Agnes Catholic Church in Los Angeles on October 24, 1906. They had four children, Florence, Ruth, Margaret and William.

Edward died on November 3, 1930, and is buried in Calvary Cemetery in Santa Barbara.

Thomas married Palmira Franzina, who bore him four children; Lilian, Genevieve, Eileen and young Thomas. Thomas the elder died in Santa Inez and is interred in Hill Cemetery in Ballard. He and his wife had eleven grandchildren and thirty great-grandchildren, enough to keep the Murphy name alive for generations to come.

Joseph Murphy lived and died in the Santa Inez valley and is buried in Calvary Cemetery in Santa Barbara. John, the youngest boy, born in 1877, married Julia Collins. They had three children: Rose Ellen, Eugenia, (who died young) and John D.

The Murphy Brothers' store in Santa Inez, manned by Joseph and John, did a thriving business for years. The old Murphy farmhouse, the residence of the oldest son, William, still stands, a constant reminder of the tenacious Murphy clan who were so much a part of Santa Inez Valley in days long gone.

ANDREW J. MCKENNA was one of the most influential law enforcement officers on the West Coast as Chief Special Agent for the Southern Pacific Railroad. The four corners of his jurisdiction were Portland, Oregon; Tucson, Arizona; El Paso, Texas; and Ogden, Utah.

*Andrew McKenna (standing) guarded President Harry S. Truman on the
Southern Pacific Presidential Train. Courtesy McKenna family*

His charge was to protect life and property and to conduct any and all
investigations necessary to apprehend criminals.

The first train robbery on the Southern Pacific took place at
Verde, Nevada in 1870. The last robbery was on February 15, 1933,
at Ontario, California. All told, there were fifty-six train robberies on
the Southern Pacific system. In only six cases did the perpetrators get
away. All the other robbers were apprehended by the railroad police,
brought to trial and made to pay for their mischief.

The organizational structure of the Southern Pacific police force,
which was founded in 1901, is quite similar to that of any police
department, with specialists known as K-D officers and police dogs
trained in attack and search techniques. Many of the department's
vehicles have 4-wheel drive for use in mountainous areas. These vehicles are also equipped with mobile radios so that officers can commu-
nicate with all trains and station houses.

As was true in the San Francisco Police Department, railroad
police "chiefs" were unmistakably Irish: Charles Crowley, Patrick
Kendelon, Daniel O'Connel, Daniel Quillinan, William Stone,
George Barnett and our zealous subject, Andrew J. McKenna.

McKenna was born in San Francisco, a proud native son equally proud of his Irish heritage. His parents, Andrew and Ann Reddy McKenna, arrived in San Francisco from Ireland in the 1870s. By chance they met, fell in love and were married in Old Saint Mary's, which was then the Cathedral. They made their home at 2509 Post Street, where Andy owned two little cottages.

They became the parents of five children: Andrew, our subject, and Margaret were the only ones to survive childhood illnesses. Following her husband's death in 1906, Ann finished rearing the two children on her own by renting the two little cottages on Post Street. Following their primary education Andrew enrolled in Sacred Heart College while his sister attended St. Rose Academy. After graduation from Sacred Heart Andrew went to work for the Southern Pacific in San Francisco, beginning a life-long career. Having harbored the idea of becoming a lawyer, he relished challenge and rose through the ranks of the Southern Pacific Police Department to become its Chief Special Agent.

His duties included investigating all crimes on trains and railroad property. As chief he was responsible for the security of all Hollywood stars—such as Ann Blyth, Irene Dunne, Ann Sheridan and Lana Turner—who rode the trains to promote the sale of Liberty Bonds during World War II. He also had the honor of guarding President Harry Truman on the Southern Pacific Presidential Train

His nephew, William Joesten, tells it so: "I remember we were on vacation at our cabin in Boulder Creek, when a Plymouth sedan pulled up in the dirt driveway and a couple of men in suits came looking for Uncle Andy. They had just received word of a train wreck, and he had to leave to investigate the wreck."

Andrew never married; after his mother's death in 1934 he moved to San Jose to live with his sister, Margaret Joesten, and her family. He was a lover of all sports—baseball, football and horse-racing. When football was in season he travelled to Los Angeles to watch his favorite team, Notre Dame, play Southern California. He was a big fan of the Irish, and Irish to the core, himself.

MICHAEL DAVITT found both adventure and romance when he came to Oakland to establish branches of the Irish Land League in California. While he expected to be well received in California's free and open society, he never dreamed that he would also find a wife among Oakland's fair daughters.

When Davitt, Ireland's spokesman in those dark and evil days, arrived in Oakland in 1880, he was the house guest of James and

Mary Canning, prominent early and wealthy settlers. The Canning name, embedded in Canning Street in Temescal, has ensured its place in history. Three major Oakland institutions were largely financed through the Cannings' generosity: the splendid Victorian Gothic edifice of St. Francis de Sales (which in 1962 became the Oakland Cathedral), the First Providence Hospital at 26th and Broadway, and the now defunct St. Joseph's Home for the elderly poor at Fruitvale.

While staying with the Cannings, Michael Davitt met and fell in love with Miss Mary Yore, Mrs. Canning's charming niece and legal ward. Following a lengthy courtship Michael Davitt and Mary Yore were united in marriage on December 30, 1886, after a prenuptial Mass at St. Francis de Sales Church, by that church's founding pastor, Father Thomas McSweeny. Irish eyes were on Oakland that morning as congratulations by telegraph came from Irish Nationalists scattered all over the world. The *Oakland Tribune* was emphatic in its pronouncement: "The selection of a wife from amongst Oakland's fair daughters is also conclusive evidence that Michael had a level head."

As a matter of history, St. Francis de Sales was not the first Catholic Church in Oakland; that honor belongs to Old St. Mary's, founded in 1863 as a chapel-of-ease to St. Patrick's Church in San Francisco, whose first resident pastor was Father James Croke, a brother of the Archbishop of Cashel, co-founder of Ireland's Gaelic Athletic Association.

Convinced that Ireland's economic and social oppression was incurred by an unjust land system, Michael Davitt established the Land League in 1879 to secure for Irish tenant farmers the ownership of the land which was rightfully theirs, rather than the rackrenting landlords'. By bringing land reform to the core of Irish politics he sought to weld the land question to the political Home Rule Movement. And where else to preach the Davitt gospel than in California's free and open society?

In the meantime the California Irish came together as never before. Having done well for the state and for themselves, they were now in a position to support every worthwhile Irish cause. Principal among the exiles was the old pioneer, James Phelan, who proudly proclaimed "Michael Davitt, you are no stranger in a strange land, but at home amongst your very own. We welcome you with all our hearts."

Irish communities all over California staged fund-raising parties, as they had previously done during the Fenian movement. Davitt's mission on behalf of the impoverished Irish tenant farmers—something akin to the American share-croppers of pre-Civil War days—was an outstanding success. Thus on St. Patrick's Day Oaklanders can drink a toast to one of Ireland's greatest advocates of social justice.

SAN LEANDRO was the second most important civic community in early Alameda County. This delightful enclave was co-founded by Irish-born John Ward and William Heath Davis, both sons-in-law of the late Don Jose Estudillo, for two specific purposes: to wrest control of Alameda County seat from Alvarado and to create a land boom on the Estudillo estate.

St. Leander's parish had two founding fathers, Irish-born Father Joe Quinn, former pastor of Old St. Mary's, and John Ward, who sold the site to Archbishop Alemany for five dollars, just enough to make it legal. In 1864 Father Quinn began the construction of a chapel in San Leandro, and a few months later the Archbishop decided to elevate St. Leander's to a parish church, and appointed Father James Callan as resident pastor.

As a result of Father Callan's untimely death in the explosion of a Sacramento River steamboat, St. Leander's was pastorless for quite a while. Among the earliest records of the San Francisco Archdiocese is a handwritten memo dated 1865 to Father Michael King, appointing him as the pastor of Oakland's Old St. Mary's, San Leandro's St. Leander's, and Old St. Raymond's in Dublin.

Alas, John B.Ward, who co-founded the city of San Leandro and St. Leander's parish, has no memorial in today's city of San Leandro. To make amends it would be well for St. Leander's parishoners celebrating their 125th anniversary to petition the city fathers to restore the name of Ward Street, which was changed a few years back to Estudillo Avenue.

THE NATIVE SONS OF LITTLE IRELAND: Away up on the rugged northern coast the little town of Elk deserves a prominent place in California history. It all began in Cuffey's Cove over one hundred years ago, when a group of young men, inordinately proud of their noble Irish heritage, founded the Native Sons of Little Ireland. Their names ring out like a litany of Irish Saints: Andrew Cooney, Edward Conway, John Conway, Charles Buchannon, Jack Doherty, William Doherty, Frank Donahue, John Kenny, Thomas Lynch, Peter Smith, John Rafter, Charles McMaster and James McMaster.

It was said that the foregoing young troopers got their inspiration from the song about Ireland's founding:

> Sure a little bit of heaven
> Fell from out the skies one day,

John Conway
1838-1918

Andrew Conney
1849-1932

Will Dougherty
1872-1916

John Kenny
1833-1904

Charles McMaster
1864-1934

Jack Dougherty
1877-1930

Thomas Lynch

Frank Donohue
?? - 1894

James McMaster

The Native Sons of Little Ireland

And nestled on the ocean
In a spot so far away.
And when the angels found it
Sure it looked so sweet and fair,
They said, Suppose we leave it
For it looks so peaceful there.
Sure they called it Ireland.

CUFFEY'S COVE—the name was later changed to Greenwood—was a little bit of Ireland in many respects, with a total population of between three and four hundred, mostly Irish, who had a strong voice in everyday affairs. Those proud Native Sons of Little Ireland have sponsored and perpetuated the annual observance of St. Patrick's Day since the late 1890s. The spirited celebrations were enhanced by the Elk Altar Society, whose members Anne Daniels and Lila Lee are justly proud of the tradition.

However, it fell to the lot of Mary Berry to keep alive and promote this century-old tradition when its founders passed away. Mary Boyle Burk's St. Patrick's Prayer adds luster to the ecumenical spirit and social goodwill that it would be well for all of us to emulate:

> A perennial feature of the St. Patrick's celebration is the splendid cooperation of non-Catholics in the production of a church benefit which, though under Catholic patronage, they have benevolently adopted as their own. Their generous donation of labor and goods is an inspiring and edifying example of religious tolerance and good will. God grant that the spirit will never cease! In days when few are unaware of the sad need for "man's humanity to man", the world may well look to a little town on the Mendocino County coast of California, not for oratory but for guidance.

In the older, more carefree days each community had to provide its own entertainment; the village of Greenwood and the Native Sons of Little Ireland were not found wanting. Greenwood, like other remote communities, had its share of acting talent for staging hometown plays. When the need arose for a charitable function or other worthy cause, the community got together and staged a concert in the village, just as had been done in Ireland.

In the author's home town in Ireland, lacking a building large enough to accommodate a crowd, the organizers had to wait until springtime, when Tynan's big hayshed was empty. Everything needed for the concert was provided by the local community with an assist where needed from adjoining communities, at no cost to those involved. The big hayshed was enclosed with sheets of burlap fastened to the upright with ropes and wooden staples.

A stage was built at the upper end, and a dressing room of sorts to accommodate the cast. Seating consisted of wooden benches, with high-backed chairs for the elderly and infirm. With Guiness Stout and Jameson whiskey flowing freely, stage-fright was of little concern. However, those who imbibed too freely tended to forget their lines, which drew more laughter than the best performers on stage.

The Native Sons of Little Ireland in Cuffey's Cove, six thousand miles removed from their ancestral homeland, kept alive the Irish tradition through music, dance and merriment on St. Patrick's Day and at other times throughout the year. Hometown talent shows allowed the residents of little Greenwood to proclaim their Irishness in a humorous way. The three most popular events were the New Year's Masquerade, the St. Patrick's Dance and the Fourth of July Parade, which lured visitors from coastal communities far and wide. Mary Berry, who has organized the St. Patrick's Day bash for the past 45 years, says, "Oh, years ago we just danced all night until the wee hours of the morning."

In 1893, and for years thereafter, the Native Sons of Little Ireland sponsored St. Patrick's dances as a benefit for St. Mary's Star of the Sea parish in Cuffey's Cove. When the Blessed Sacrament church was built in Greenwood and the Cuffey's Cove abandoned, the Altar Society vowed to continue the century-old tradition.

In 1910 there was a grand reunion of the old Irish pioneers of Cuffey's Cove in Greenwood Hall. The event was sponsored by young men, sons of the Irish immigrants. The extent of the participation showed that the Irish were still active in Mendocino County. The reception committee listed John Conway, Sr., J. Rafferty, Charles Brien, and C. J. Buchannon. The arrangements panel included Jack Dougherty, Elk; Dave Crockett, Albion; Ed Boyle, Mendocino; Ed Conway, Fort Bragg; J. P. Connor, Point Arena; and Jack Walsh Miller.

Eight years later, in 1918, the Native Sons of Little Ireland were still active, according to an announcement touting the 30th annual St. Patrick's Ball in Greenwood. The Sons invited the newly formed Civic Club to join them in promoting the celebration. Invitations stated that Wood's Orchestra would furnish the music, and "only a very serious excuse could keep the lovers of a good time and good music away from Greenwood March 17th."

As old Ireland was still under foreign rule in 1918, the Native Sons of Little Ireland sang the mournful anthem at various gatherings during those "Dark and Evil Days":

Oh, Paddy dear, and did you hear the news that's goin' round!
The shamrock is by law forbid to grow on Irish ground.
No more Saint Patrick's Day we'll keep, his colors can't be seen,
For there's a cruel law ag'in the Wearin o'the Green.

EVEN THE GREAT DEPRESSION failed to put a damper on the Elk/Greenwood St. Patrick's Day celebration. The 1929 bash brought together the largest gathering ever assembled up to that time. The fame of Greenwood's Hometown Harmony Boys lured revelers from San Francisco all the way to Point Arena.

The celebrations continued unabated during World War II, but the hours were changed on account of the curfew. Despite the uncertainties of that period, people came from all over the state to Greenwood to celebrate St. Patrick's Day. For example, in 1944 a San Jose doctor won a sack of potatoes, and a woman from Los Angeles garnered the winning ticket on the treasure chest and contents.

The Centennial Celebration, put on by the Elk Altar Society on Saturday, March 13, 1993, was a fitting tribute to the good people of Elk/Greenwood and Cuffey's Cove, where it all began in days of yore.

ERIN GO BRAGH!

Mayor Richard J. Riordan (left) is introduced as Los Angeles 1997 Irishman of the Year by Irish Fair Foundation President Terrance Anderson during the 122nd Irish Day ceremonies at City Hall.

– 28 –

THE IRISH IN LOS ANGELES

THE HISTORY OF THE IRISH in Los Angeles is analogous to that of the Ancient Order of Hibernians, which was organized there on September 17, 1875. Unlike the bustling cities to the north, San Francisco, San Jose and Sacramento, Los Angeles had not garnered the attention of the argonauts and immigrants. As it so happened elsewhere in California, it was the Irish who charted the future course of the City of Our Lady of Angels, from a sleepy pueblo to a vibrant metropolis.

The Ancient Order of Hibernians is an integral part of Irish history dating back to the days of the Penal Laws, when fearless Hibernians stood guard for the priest as he said Mass in a cave or remote hideaway in the woodlands of Ireland. It is also a living part of American history, as witness the Massachusetts Hibernians, who stepped in to protect Catholics after a frenzied mob had burned down a Catholic convent.

The Ancient Order of Hibernians was founded in Ireland by Rory O'Moore, a sagacious warrior of that noble clan, the O'Moores of Laoghise (Leix), who ruled over the Fortress Kingdom of Dunamase. Their lineage is one of the strongest links between pagan and Christian Ireland. It was an O'Moore who commanded the Irish who under Roderick O'Connor, the last High King of Ireland, and besieged the Norman invaders in Dublin. Annie O'Moore gave birth to the noble Patrick Sarsfield, who carried on the long war for faith and fatherland.

The A.O.H. had its roots in the Order of the Golden Collar, whose purpose was patriotic and whose members were knights. When Ireland was Christianized, the Knights were committed to protect the Catholic clergy in the performance of religious duties. As historian

471

John O'Dea tells it in his *Glories of Ireland*, "There is no stranger story in all history than the intimate connection of the O'Moore family with the Annals of the Ancient Order of Hibernians."

Unlike the O'Neills and the O'Donnells, who left Ireland following their defeat at the battle of Kinsale in 1601, the O'Moores stayed to engage in continual rebellion against the English mercenaries. They not only held the English confined to the Pale but laid low the last of the notorious Crosby gang at the Battle of Glenmalure in County Wicklow.

Rory O'Moore well understood the fate that awaited Irish Catholics in that dreadful period of relentless persecution and genocide. He called together a Catholic confederation, and in measured words exhorted them to stand together or suffer the consequences: "Friends, we must all hang together or we will undoubtedly all hang separately." The assemblage took his words to heart and linked arms to found the Ancient Order of Hibernians.

The people's trust in Rory O'Moore is manifest in these stirring lines:

> As to the future, while none can be sure,
> Our trust is in God and Rory O'Moore.

In America the A.O.H. acquired its charter in New York City in 1836, where every parish had a division. From the dark and evil days of the Know Nothing Party, the Ancient Order, under the guidance of Archbishop John Hughes of New York, proved its worth as a tenacious defender of civil and religious liberty. During a wave of religious bigotry, a mob calling themselves "Native Americans" burned down the Ursuline convent in Boston. Whenever a member of this association was arrested for acts of violence against Catholics and questioned, his stock answer was "I know nothing." To combat these blatant activities the A.O.H. was committed to the same mission as in Ireland: To protect the priests at Mass and the Catholic churches they served.

In May 1844 Know Nothing zealots physically attacked Catholics in New Jersey and burned the churches, rectories and convents in two parishes.

In the early 1890s, when the ghosts of bigotry took form again under the name American Protective Association, the Hibernians for a second time became the defenders of their ancient faith and second fatherland. In various states, the A.O.H. was the one and only Catholic society which provided opposition to the prevailing intolerance. The Order even bore the expense of court costs and legal advice, in a face-off that left the A. P. A. de-fanged.

The Hibernians in Los Angeles

A CONSIDERABLE number of Irish had been living in Los Angeles for decades before the arrival in 1875 of the Honorable Michael Ward, the A.O.H. State President from San Francisco, who came south with the intention of forming a chapter in Los Angeles. The historic event took place in the chambers of Judge Gray, a short distance from the "Old Plaza," the center of the Mexican town.

M. J. Golden was installed as president and William Farrell as recording secretary, along with Daniel Doherty as Los Angeles County's first delegate. The charter membership included Danny Desmond, whose "Desmond Band" was the first Irish musical group in Southern California. Others of the original membership included Daniel Cunningham, co-founder of Cunningham and O'Connor Mortuary, and Walter Desmond, whose pioneer general store evolved to become the leading chain of men's clothing stores in the Southland.

With the Hibernians leading the way, the Irish in Los Angeles were destined to become as successful and noteworthy as their counterparts in the San Francisco Bay Area. The debut of the Hibernian Order in Los Angeles was proudly heralded by the two leading newspapers of the day, the *Daily Herald* and the *Evening Express*. What the Irish on the East Coast lacked at a crucial period in time, the Irish in California had from day one, a favorable press.

The work of the A.O.H. was greatly enhanced by Judge Gray, who allowed them to hold weekly meetings in his chambers until they found a place of their own at the corner of Main and Arcadia Streets, the approximate site of the present Los Angeles City Hall. At the time the Irish were the best-organized ethnic group in Los Angeles. Dues collections had reached a point which enabled the A.O.H. to provide for members sick benefits of eight dollars a week, the services of a professional nurse in the case of severe illness, and a funeral assistance of seventy-five dollars.

Just six months after its founding, the A.O.H. organized the first St. Patrick's Day celebrations in Los Angeles. March 17th, 1876, was heralded as a great day for the Irish. It started with a Mass in the Old Mission Church. According to newspaper accounts, the Hibernians took over several front pews and were most impressive in their colorful regalia.

The route of the original parade led from the town center to St. Vincent's College, where the Hibernians were greeted by the clergy, and a stirring oration by Father Flanagan from Ireland. That was followed by the first St. Patrick's Day Hibernian Ball at the old Turn

Verein Hall. The mayor, the grand marshal and county judges were present as countless Hibernians and their ladies fair danced to the stirring music of Desmond's Irish Band.

From those humble beginnings the Los Angeles Hibernians grew and flourished, as the minutes of the monthly meetings year after year indicate. The brothers cherished their Catholic faith and proudly proclaimed their loyalty to their Irish heritage. Brotherly love and Christian charity were their creed, which they affirmed in word and deed

In the 1898 Christmas edition of the archdiocesan newspaper, *The Tidings,* an article relates how the A.O.H. had come a long way since its modest beginning: "From a division small in numbers this branch has grown until it has today the largest membership and strongest financial standing of any Catholic organization in Southern California."

Dear to the hearts of every true Irishman was the issue of Irish freedom, "A free and united Ireland." This was especially true of the A.O.H. in Los Angeles, where the brothers spearheaded fund-raising campaigns for the relief of poverty in Ireland and provided a constant source of funds to bolster the cause of Irish Nationalism.

The glory days of the A.O.H. in Los Angeles began at the close of World War I in 1918, under the leadership of Joseph Scott, Judge Thomas White, Peter Murray and Edward Tynan. In the early 1920s the A.O.H., led by the indomitable Joe Scott spearheaded the first major archdiocesan drive to raise funds for the construction of parochial schools. The campaign was a resounding success, and from that day forward Catholic education flourished in Los Angeles.

In the ensuing years, the Los Angeles Hibernians caught the attention of the National Catholic Welfare Conference for their strong campaign against taxation of Catholic schools, as well as their powerful efforts to root out anti-Catholic and anti-Irish textbooks in public schools.

In July 1927 the Hibernians took the Hollywood film industry to task over their blatant portrayal of the stereotype of drunken, carousing Irishmen, as in the movie "The Callahans vs. the Murphys." Their timely outcry forced Metro Goldwyn Mayer to modify the most objectionable portions of that film. From then on the A.O.H. was a force to be reckoned with in Southern California.

The Los Angeles Hibernians were in the forefront of fund raising to initiate and support a chair of Celtic Studies at the Catholic University of America. This literary program continues as one of the principal centers of Irish history and culture in the nation.

The resurgence of ethnic interest is notable in Los Angeles today, as elsewhere in America. The local Hibernians hope it will enable them to realize their century-old dream: the building of a Hibernian Hall that will serve as a social and cultural center for Irish and Irish-Americans.

With Terry Anderson in the lead anything and everything is possible. Terry was the founder of Division Two and revived the A.O.H. from dispirited decline. The A.O.H. has four active divisions in the Southland to build on: two in Los Angeles, and two more in Anaheim and Mission Viejo. As the saying goes, "The Irish may be slow to start, but when they do there is no stopping them."

The Irish Fair in Los Angeles

THE GRAND NATIONAL Irish Fair and Musical Festival, the largest celebration of its kind in Western America and one that annually attracts over 50,000 patrons, was established in 1974. It was sponsored by the Irish Heritage Foundation, Inc. under the Anderson brothers, Terence and Allyn, president and vice president.

The foundation is dedicated to the promotion and preservation of Irish and Irish-American history and culture in Southern California. Its primary goal, however, is to erect a Hibernian Hall to accommodate the various Irish social and cultural activities in and around Los Angeles.

With more than 1.5 million Irish-Americans in Southern California, the Heritage Foundation also provides a communications network for about 250 Irish social, benevolent, sports and other clubs. Activities are monitored by a volunteer board of directors.

For over twenty years, Tom McConville, the radio "Voice of the Irish" in Los Angeles, has provided the local community with the latest news from the old sod, live interviews with Irish entertainers and political figures, coverage of sporting events, and, especially, promotion of the spectacular annual fair, all interwoven with traditional Irish music.

Irish dancing is a must for fair-goers, whether its competitive high-stepping or just an old-fashioned Ceili. Strolling through the fair is like a visit to Ireland, amid minstrels playing harps, fiddles and flutes, and others singing old Irish ballads and traditional airs.

A long line of booths purvey Irish-made goods, books and magazines of Irish interest, Irish jewelry and the music of Ireland, from reels and hornpipes to the latest in rock.

One of the principal attractions is "Tara," which evokes singular memories: the heart and soul of the Irish nation and the seat of power of the Gaelic nobility in Ireland's Golden Age, "Tara of the Kings" is the home of the Brehan Laws, which form the basis of all modern law and order. For centuries the High King sat on his throne surrounded by the Kings of Ulster, Munster, Leinster and Connaught, dispensing justice to his subjects all over the land. The Los Angeles Irish Fair and Festival rekindles that tradition.

No musical instrument in the world so quickens the pulse or stirs the blood as the bagpipes, and no Irish Fair would be complete without the colorfully arrayed pipers. All eyes are on them in their resplendent best, as they lead paraders and performers through the fairgrounds, displaying the skill it takes to squeeze stirring music from a grotesque and difficult instrument.

HOWEVER, it was the 1989 annual Grand National Irish Fair and Musical Festival at the Burbank Equestrian Center that put the icing on the Irish cake in Los Angeles. The 1989 extravaganza was by far the most spectacular celebration ever staged since its debut 1n 1974. As fairgoers stepped into the shady courtyard and beheld the performers decked out in their colorful regalia and smelled the mouth-watering aroma of cooking over open fires, it was only the harbinger of things to come.

Across the terrain, running at breathtaking speeds, came the wolfhounds ready for the chase, Irish hurling and soccer players working out on the grassy mound, and costumed step dancers practicing before going on stage. While strolling in the cool shade of the trees, along the ways skirted by bales of hay, visitors were entertained by roving musicians and an occasional seanachai (storyteller).

In the distance a grand parade wound its slow way through the immense crowd with Ireland's checkered history on view: flag-bearers, pipe-majors, kilt-clad pipers, clansmen, kings and queens, politicians and dignitaries, standing tall, to see and be seen. There too was the newly crowned "Rose of Tralee," lovely Colleen Cutler, with tears of joy spilling out of her blue Irish eyes

Hollywood, the mecca for actors and actresses, displays its share of Irish talent at the Fair, often producing plays by famous Irish writers, such as James Joyce and Sean O'Casey, as well as works re-enacting Ireland's legendary past.

This Fifteenth Annual Grand National Irish Fair provided an opportunity for the Irish in Los Angeles to showcase their achievements in the southern metropolis in a manner befitting a noble race

In 1985 the Greater Los Angeles St. Patrick's Day Committee was formed at the behest of the Los Angeles City Council. The committee's avowed purpose was to present the annual "Official" St. Patrick's Parade. In recent years the parade has developed into one of the largest celebrations of its kind and the fastest growing in America.

In 1989 the Parade Committee joined forces with the Irish Fair Association, merging three outstanding Irish cultural events under one banner: The Irish Fair, The Rose of Tralee Pageant, and the St.Patrick's Day Parade.

As a consequence the St.Patrick's Parade remains an official Los Angeles event that calls for an appointed city liaison with the Irish community.

Edward L. Doheny, Oil Baron

No HISTORY of Los Angeles is complete without an account of the life and legends of Edward L. Doheny, who rose from a penniless adventurer to become one of the wealthiest men in California. Born in 1856 of poor Irish immigrants in Fond du Lac, Wisconsin, he ran away from home as a teen-ager, traveling through Kansas, Texas, Arizona and New Mexico while eking out a living along the way.

At the age of 36 he arrived in the still raw city of Los Angeles with just the clothes on his back and a few coins in his pocket. While browsing around the inner city he spotted a gurgling tar pit, which he judged from previous experience as a prospector to be a sign of crude oil.

Somehow Doheny managed to borrow enough cash to take out a lease on the land. Within a couple of months he was able to harness the first oil gusher to flow in the city of Los Angeles. Encouraged by this immediate success, he proceeded to drill wells in and about Los Angeles and other areas of the state until he controlled practically the total oil production in California. By 1922 his total worth reportedly topped that of John D. Rockefeller, who was known as the richest man in America.

Having acquired wealth in such abundance, Doheny decided it was time to live the part, sporting a walrus mustache, British tailoring and an autocratic mien. As further proof of his state in life, he spent money freely and purchased a property in what is now the heart of Los Angeles. With the land surveyed and mapped, he set aside a large section for a city park and developed the remainder into a grand estate which he named Chester Place.

When the ornate mansion was completed, Doheny engaged an entourage of servants and bodyguards, enough to be the envy of any potentate, prince or sultan. Not content with in-house grandeur

Edward L. Doheny

alone, Doheny acquired a luxurious yacht, the Casiana, which he used to showcase his standing in the community.

A self-made man turned philanthropist, Doheny gave very generously to worthwhile Irish causes, particularly to the Irish Freedom movement. His wife, Estelle, decked out in chains of sapphires, diamonds and rubies, ruled over Chester Place in the manner of an empress. And why not? She had recently been appointed a Papal Countess, and delighted in using the formal title "Countess Estelle."

It was the custom at Chester Place for footmen and maids to line the long marble staircase, waiting to usher in visitors for a greeting from Madame Doheny. For all her grand airs, however, Estelle had a very humble way of showing off her home, leading visitors along the shimmering marble corridors into the Pompeian Room, where she pointed out the vaulted ceiling with gold leaf, and her priceless collection of antique watches, or her prize-winning display of orchids in the conservatory.

Countess Estelle's proudest treasure was her private chapel, with its magnificent tabernacle where the Eucharist was reserved. Outside the chapel entrance stood two Spanish armoires containing ladies' hats and scarves in various colors, so that hatless women could cover their heads before entering, as was the Catholic custom.

Edward Doheny had his share of troubles. He was caught up in the Teapot Dome scandal during the administration of President Grover Cleveland and that of President Warren Harding as well. However, it was not until President Calvin Coolidge took office that the scandal came to a head.

The Senate Committee on Public Lands, having agreed to look into Naval oil reserves, held its first hearing on October 23, 1923. Senator Thomas Walsh of Montana was appointed as chief examiner. Doheny made his first appearance on December 3. His testimony concluded on a humorous note. When Walsh said, "I was told that Senator Smoot handed you a note when you were coming into the room," Doheny hesitated, and then agreed that it was true. "Let's see the note," Walsh demanded. "Certainly," replied Doheny. Reaching into his pocket, he pulled out a handful of shredded papers and slapped them on the hearing table. The contents, he said laughingly, would make very painstaking reading. In disgust, Senator Walsh dismissed the witness.

Finally, in late 1926, Doheny and his associate Albert Fall had to stand trial on criminal charges in Washington, D.C. However, Doheny and his legal team were better prepared than they had been at the civil trial in Los Angeles. His lawyer, Frank Hogan, a flamboyant Irishman, had a particular gift for oratory, coupled with flashing Irish eyes and a thunderous voice that filled the courtroom.

For hours and hours Hogan held the jury spellbound with his rhetoric, appearing so overcome with emotion at times that he had to wipe tears from his eyes. He invoked the memory of the dead, calling President Coolidge "as able and loving and as fine-hearted a President as the nation ever had or would have." In closing, Hogan compared his clients' plight to the Crucifixion and Edward Doheny to Jesus Christ Himself.

Having deliberated for seven hours without agreement, the jurors were locked up for the night. At fifteen past ten the following morning the jury came in with their verdict: not guilty. This set off a wild demonstration in the courtroom; tables and chairs were overturned in sheer delight. Lawyers on both sides and friends stood in line to shake the defendants' hands. Doheny, old and worn from the ordeal, wept with joy. In her hotel room Lady Estelle burst into tears and declared "My prayers have been answered!"

THE DOHENY FAMILY returned triumphantly to Los Angeles, where a welcoming crowd of some four hundred friends and well-wishers, including clergymen, dignitaries, naval officers and motion picture stars, had gathered to meet them. Doheny was treated to a sumptuous banquet by the city to celebrate his acquittal. Principal speakers were the mayors of Los Angeles and San Francisco and Doheny's triumphant lawyer, Frank J. Hogan.

Before his death Edward Doheny was confined to his residence at Chester Place for some three years, almost completely bedridden. Weak and worn, he passed away on September 8, 1935, at the age of 79.

Countess Estelle survived her husband for a number of years, living on in their fashionable Los Angeles estate, surrounded by house-

hold servants, guards and occasional film stars. When she was suddenly taken ill, she was rushed to a Los Angeles hospital, where doctors
agreed she had only hours to live. A priest was called to administer the
last rites of the Church. She succumbed while his prayers still echoed.

Edward Doheny contributed very generously to churches,
schools and charitable institutions. While exploring the oil fields in
Mexico, he and Estelle were very impressed by the beautiful Santa
Prisco church in the city of Taxco. According to Monsignor Francis
Weber, in his "Vignettes of California Catholicism," when Doheny
was asked by Bishop John J. Cantwell to assume the burden of financ-
ing the proposed St. Vincent's Church on the land adjacent to his
home in Chester Place, Doheny agreed, on condition that the design
of the new church be based on Santa Prisco.

Doheny was so determined to emulate Jose de la Borda that he
allowed a statue of his patron saint to be incorporated in the base, one
bearing a striking resemblance to himself, a meager indulgence for the
gift of such a beautiful church. The placing of St. Vincent's is unique.
The axis is at a 45-degree angle with both Figueroa Street and Adams
Boulevard, to ensure that there would be no danger of adjacent commercial structures detracting from the church.

Opposite and right: St. Vincent's church, at Figueroa and Adams Streets in Los Angeles, was completed in 1925. Built in the Spanish Revival style popular in the 1920s, of reinforced concrete with an exterior of stucco, Indiana limestone trim, and decorative tiles on the dome, the church is one of the most beautiful in the state. Courtesy St. Vincent's church

In St. Vincent's the designers refined and enhanced some of the artistic features in such a way as to retain the basic design. The exterior is in the manner of Spanish architecture, with stucco walls and Indiana limestone trim, shipped all the way from Bedfort, Indiana. Ornamental tile covers the dome and Spanish red tile the roof.

CAPTAIN MICHAEL MURRAY was one of the most prominent Irishman in early Los Angeles, where he served as quartermaster of the National Soldiers Home in Sawtelle.

Captain Murray was born in the Province of Ontaria, Canada, on September 13, 1861. His parents were Patrick Murray from County Clare and Mary (Broderick) Murray, a native of Quebec. Patrick, Mary and their children came to the United States in 1861 and engaged in farming near Geneva, Ohio. The Murrays had seven children besides Michael. Michael received his primary education in the parochial schools in Cleveland, and following his arrival in San Francisco in 1882 he enrolled in St. Mary's College, which was then located in the city's Mission District.

Following graduation from St. Mary's he enlisted in the Fifth United States Cavalry and rose through the ranks to become a first lieutenant of engineers. In that capacity he was in active service during the Spanish-American war, and in the army of occupation in Cuba. He served for a period in New Mexico, whence he received an appointment as commissary officer at the Soldiers' Home in Sawtelle.

In November 1889, at the age of 28, Captain Murray was united in marriage to Mary Quinn, an Irish immigrant whose family had settled in Fort Supply, Indian Territory. Two children were born to Michael and Mary: Josephine, who never married, and Irene, the wife of James O'Brien, a longtime resident of Hollywood. The O'Briens had two children, Jean and William, a graduate of the U.S. Military Academy at West Point in 1920. William served as an Army first lieutenant in Nogales, Arizona, on the Mexican border.

WILLIAM IGNATIUS FOLEY had a distinguished career as a member of the Los Angeles bar, practicing law in the Southland for over a third of a century. He was a native San Franciscan, born February 19, 1861, whose father Francis Foley crossed the plains on a wagon train, reaching San Francisco in the gold rush of 1849. In 1878, William enrolled in St. Ignatius College, then located on lower Market Street. From there he went east to Columbia University in New York for his bachelor's and master's degrees in law. He was admitted to the New York Bar and practiced for a time in San Francisco and Seattle before moving to Southern California. He opened his first office in Pomona in 1884.

After a permanent move to Los Angeles, he became associated with Henry T. Gage, the future governor of California. On Mr. Gage's election in 1899, Foley traveled with him to Sacramento as his private secretary. Offered an appointment to the State Supreme Court, Foley declined. Later he accepted the post of attorney for the State Board of Health. While serving in that office, Foley drafted a number of measures that are still an integral part of the health laws of California, the healthiest state in the nation.

A lover of books, Foley had an extensive private library in his home on 751 South Catalina Street: Latin and Greek classics, contemporary works and volumes dating from the seventeenth century. He was also a lover of music and song, and a versatile composer whose works included popular poems and lyrics.

Foley married Sarah Dolores Sepulveda of the distinguished California family of Palos Verdes Rancho. Mrs. Foley shared her husband's abiding interest in music; she charmed family and friends with her melodious voice.

William Ignatius Foley passed away at his home in Los Angeles on April 19, 1921, in his sixtieth year. Sarah had died in 1906. The Foleys had four children. Their oldest daughter, Viola, and her husband lived out their lives at the old family home on South Catalina Street.

JOHN W. CUSHING was another Irishman who left his mark in Los Angeles County. He was born in Belfast June 23, 1830, to Patrick and Mollie (Stewart) Cushing, natives of that industrial city, where the elder Cushing was a leading contractor.

John was educated in the schools of Belfast, where he resided until the age of eighteen. He emigrated to New York City in 1848, working there for the next five years. Determined to become an American citizen, he won naturalization on August 29, 1857. By then he had moved to San Francisco, where his citizenship papers finally caught up with him.

For an interval he worked at gold mining before returning to the city to contemplate his next move. His favor fell on Southern California, where he purchased a 160-acre parcel and began raising grain and livestock. He added to his holdings by purchasing 180 acres of prime land north of Savannah, in the San Gabriel Valley, known as the Primrose Ranch.

In 1861, at St. Mary's Cathedral in San Francisco, Cushing married Mary Carr, a recent immigrant from County Donegal. The wedding ceremony was performed by Father James Croke, who had served in the Oregon and California missions before being recalled to duty in San Francisco.

The Cushings had eleven children: Mary, Elizabeth, Anne, Patrick. Cecilia, Catherine, John (who died young), James, Joseph Emmett, Eileen and Margaret. Patrick, born on the family ranch on January 31, 1866, became a noted leader in the community and with his brother, Joseph Emmett, farmed successfully on the home ranch.

Patrick was baptized in the old San Gabriel Mission Church as were his brothers and sisters. He married Ellen Grean of Portland, who was a member of an illustrious Irish family. Ellen gave birth to four children, all in the old Cushing home in which their father was born: John (1905), Catherine (1907), Mary (1909) and Richard (1911). They too were baptized in the quaint old mission church at San Gabriel.

Eugene Dowling, Sr.
Courtesy Siskiyou Historical Society

– 29 –

EUGENE DOWLING

THE GREENING OF THE SISKIYOUS

T HE NAME DOWLING takes pride of place in communities all over the United States, but nowhere more so than Siskiyou County, the birth place of Eugene Dowling, its favorite son and renowned raconteur. 'Twas he who founded the Siskiyou Historical Society to preserve and perpetuate the legends of pioneer days in one of the most remote areas in California.

Yreka, the principal city, has a unique history all its own, with a bit of the Wild West thrown in. Gold was discovered in 1851 on the flats of Yreka, then known as Thompson's Dry Diggins. When the town took shape in its present location the name was no longer used. For a short spell it remained nameless, until a bill was introduced in the state legislature to create Siskiyou County, and the name Yreka became official. Yreka is a derivative of "I-e-k-a," meaning "the white," the Indian name for Mount Shasta.

A proud native son, Eugene Dowling was born in the hamlet of Humbug, near Yreka, on August 14, 1864. His parents were John and Catherine (Shea) Dowling, tenacious pioneers of those early days. John was born in County Kerry in 1826. In 1858 he came to California, where he met his future wife, a native of Canada.

John Dowling mined for gold in Humbug, northwest of Yreka. He was killed in a mining accident when a big boulder rolled down on top of him. The place he met his death was named Dowling Gulch in memory of him. He left his widow and five children, ranging in age from three months to ten years. Eugene, our subject, was the oldest.

Catherine Dowling had a hard time raising the children on her own. To make ends meet she pawned her jewelry, and then took in washing and did other chores as well. While Gene was still a young-ster, the family moved to Yreka and purchased a house on Oregon Street. There Gene grew to manhood and set out on life's way, imbued with the spirit of his noble ancestors. His brother, John B., and sisters, Cissie and Nellie, stayed on in the old home in Yreka until his death. Little is known of the other brother, Edward. John B. was a prominent businessman in Yreka, where he owned a number of properties.

At an early age, Gene went to work for the *Yreka Journal* and learned the printer's trade, which he applied with considerable success in the ensuing years. Later on he accepted a position with the firm of Jones & Company in Hornbrook, where he worked for a number of years. While there he met and married Gertrude Smith, who bore him two children, Eugene S. Jr., who settled in Medford, Oregon, and Mrs. Glen Johnston, of San Francisco

As a result of the esteem in which he was held, Dowling was elect-ed Siskiyou County Auditor and Recorder in 1898, a position he held for sixteen years. Shortly thereafter he became an associate of the First National Bank of Yreka. Eventually he returned to the County Recorder's office, where he worked as an assistant to his sister, Miss Cissie Dowling, then County Recorder.

A Noble Clan

DOWLING is one of the oldest names in Irish history and is also renowned in American history. One branch of that tenacious clan in Ireland can trace its roots to one Noah Dowling, who reigned as King of Leinster in the year 144 A.D. Noah had nine worthy sons; Ross Faly (Ross of the Kings), Darby, Prince Brassel, Catach, Feaghus, Crevan, Angus Nic, Euchy Timin, Oillol Cadach and Fiacha, enough to sire the royal clan for generations to come.

The Dowlings are one of the "Seven Septs" (Tribes) of ancient Laoghise (County Laois) headed by the fearless O'Moores and includ-ing the O'Dorans, O'Lalors, O'Kellys, Devoys and Mackaboys (McEvoys). The O'Dowlings multiplied in their home territory and spread to the adjoining counties of Kilkenny, Kildare and Wicklow, where they are still numerous. Towns named Ballydowling (Dowling's Town) help preserve their memory and accomplishments.

In the year 1607, some of the leading members of the clan were banished from their ancestral homeland by English mercenaries and transported to a more barren area in North Kerry. From that branch came our subject's father, John Dowling, who came to California in 1858 in search of his Pot of Gold.

County Kerry was also the birthplace of Bartholomew Dowling, a leading historian and author of the "Brigade of Fontenoy" and other leading literary works. Bartholomew immigrated to California and eventually became editor of The Monitor, the official publication for the Archdiocese of San Francisco. He died in San Francisco and was laid to rest facing the rising sun in Holy Cross Cemetery in a towering granite mausoleum.

The Dowlings in America

The Dowlings were among the first settlers in Colonial America, having arrived in Georgia in the year 1638. However, little is known of their exploits in that early period. A more precise account is that of the Dowlings who arrived in Virginia on August 1, 1683, on board the ship *Samuel Mathews*. From that branch came the celebrated "Dowlings of the South," including Robert Dowling, born in Virginia in 1730. Robert married a Virginian and fathered a son, William, whose mother died in childbirth. Robert married a second time, taking for his wife Sarah Guinn, a native a Virginian of Irish descent. They had five children: James, John, Maryann, Elizabeth and Sarah.

In 1773 Robert and his family moved to South Carolina, where they became known for their ingenuity and patriotism. When the call to arms came during the American Revolutionary War, Robert enlisted in the 6th Regiment of the North Carolina infantry. He fought in a number of decisive battles, two of which, King's Mountain and Cowpens, are well known to every student of American history. His pay for eight years of military service was only $186.

William, Robert's son by his first marriage, joined the most dreaded band of guerrillas, led by General Francis Marion, the celebrated "Swamp Fox." As a result of William's part in the conflict he became a marked man by the Tories. When they learned of his whereabouts, they followed him to his home at night and shot him dead in front of his twelve-year old son.

This malicious act incurred the wrath of his two half-brothers, James and John Dowling, who enlisted forthwith in Benton's Regiment, also under the command of General Marion. Spurred on by the Dowling brothers, the Carolinians fought valiantly against the cold-blooded British. Proof of their faithful service can be found in vouchers and other military records.

The three Dowlings, Robert and his sons, were at Yorktown on that glorious day when Lord Cornwallis surrendered and the Union Jack bit the dust for the first time on American soil. As far as can be determined, they were the only three-member family to witness one of the most historic events in the history of America.

By fate, the O'Moores and the O'Dowlings were destined to come together again in the Carolinas during the struggle for American Independence. Brigadier General James Moore (O'Moore] commanded all the forces of the Carolinas. Under his leadership the Carolinians routed the British troops in Charleston and engaged them in battle as they retreated northward, eventually to Yorktown, where they met their doom. According to Dr. Ramsey's history of Carolina, troops under the command of General Moore defeated a well-armed, well-entrenched Scottish Regiment at Moore's Creek Bridge near Wilmington in North Carolina.

While on his way to meet and be honored by General George Washington, General Moore caught the dreaded yellow fever and died at New Berne on the intercoastal waterway route. It was a sad ending for such a courageous soldier with the royal blood of the O'Moores in his veins.

The Dowlings of Siskiyou County

EUGENE DOWLING worked continuously for the betterment of his native city and county. According to Dr. Roy Jones in his book, *Land of Remember*, Eugene Dowling was a kind and warm-hearted man who had a deep understanding of life, his own as well as others. To him the world was full of brightness and good cheer. He had known difficulties and privations. Evil and insolence were antagonistic to his ideals, but realism and justice were his constant companions.

He learned the hard way that the world around him did not embrace his lofty ideals. Siskiyou was "Black Bart" country, the scene of a number of stagecoach robberies. Black Bart was a legend in his time; the mere mention of his evil actions and contempt for the law brings to mind the hair-raising encounters of Wild West days. Black Bart had a deep, resonant voice, and when he commanded the stage-driver to "Throw down the box," that was enough to frighten the bravest man.

A Touch of the Wild West

IN 1898, Gene Dowling went to work as a clerk at Thomas Jones's general store in Henley, a short distance from Yreka. Still unmarried at the age of 28, Gene slept in a back room at the store to save on rent. Quite often local gamblers would come to the store at ten or eleven o'clock at night seeking provisions for a midnight meal. Most of them knew the congenial clerk, who it seems was always willing to accommodate them. Thomas Jones tried to dissuade Gene from this practice, with the admonition,"You work all day, they sleep. Their purchases are minimal in any event, and some night one or more of them will take advantage and rob you." But Gene, who wanted to oblige, paid no heed.

And sure enough, on August 2, 1893, at around 9:00 p.m., as Dowling, with his shoes and shirt removed, sat in his room reading, he heard what he thought was someone drawing water from the well in back of the store. He assumed it was either Lee Man or Susan, his wife, a Chinese couple who lived nearby, and who generally came at night for their next day's supply of fresh water. Then there was a knock on the door, and thinking that it was some late night revelers, Gene unlatched the door.

Instead of a friendly face, he was confronted by two revolvers held by two masked men, one tall and one short, each one striving to disguise his voice. Dowling was warned to be quiet, and was told take them into the store and open up the safe. With no shoes on his feet and blindfolded, he asked them to remove the sack. "I can't see, and the rocks are hurting my feet. I shan't try to get away." They removed the sack.

While one of the culprits held Dowling by the arm, the other was trying to unlock the iron doors to the store. Gene recognized his captors by their stature and their voices. He knew them well enough, and he knew that neither of them was possessed of any sympathy whatsoever. He decided to make a run for it at the first opportunity.

Unlocking the big front door was a bit tricky, requiring the attention of both perpetrators. When one of the captors relaxed his grip on Dowling's arm, he bolted, running up the street and yelling at the top of his voice. The robbers drew their revolvers and shot at him. At a distance, revolvers are rarely accurate, so both bullets missed their target. Mrs. Thomas Jones, who was sick at the time, heard the screams followed by the gunshots. She opened her door and let Gene come inside. Trying not to excite her, he told her who the robbers were.

Search parties were organized at once, and spent the whole night searching for the rogues, who were finally caught. They were never prosecuted, however, because one of the characters was related to a family highly regarded in the area.

Some years later, when Eugene Dowling was serving as county auditor and recorder, one of the robbers appeared in Dowling's office in Yreka. This man had been drinking, enough to bolster his courage, to seek a quarrel and somehow to clear his guilty conscience. In a fit of temper, he accused Dowling of "talking out loud that I was one of the two who held you up in Henley." If he thought he was going to intimidate Dowling, he was picking on the wrong man; Gene was cautious but never fearful.

Dowling leaned forward in his chair and looked pointedly at his accuser. "No, you are wrong, but I did tell Mr. Jones the names of the two, told him immediately after the holdup. You were one of them, and you know it. So do I. You are carrying a gun; I have none. You took one shot at me when I had no chance to defend myself. I'll tell you what I'll do. You meet me at the fairgrounds (the county fair was then on) in the gulch nearby. I will then have a gun with me, and you and I will settle this affair once and for all." Dowling arrived at the specified time, but his challenger failed to keep the appointment. And that was the end of the affair.

Thomas Jones's store was the social center in Klamath River and Cottonwood Basin. Sitting around the Franklin stove, the citizens deplored the fact that thieves and robbers sometimes went scot-free. At the end of the nineteenth century, people had grown tired of the lawlessness of mining days. They were outraged when they heard of the shooting and subsequent death of George Sears and Casper Meierhaus at Cole's Station, close to the Oregon border. It happened about midnight, August 25, 1895, when Sears, the owner of a saloon, and Meierhaus, a German customer, were surprised by two men who entered the saloon with robbery in mind. Sears was shot in the side of the head. The elderly German, who was sitting in a back room when he heard the noise, came out to see what happened, and was shot in the forehead at close range. Witnesses claimed to have seen the two men, one a dark Spaniard and the other an American of light complexion, both about 25 years of age.

Eugene Dowling set out immediately by coach for Yreka to inform Sheriff Hobbs, arriving at 2:00 a.m. Hobbs, accompanied by a constable and others from the community, set off in search of the culprits. Sears' son had seen the two robbers hurrying away in the direction of Hungry Creek Road. The posse soon caught up with them. Louis Marino, who after the robbery had consumed a bottle of liquor to stifle his conscience, was still under the influence when picked up. Marino had no gun; his only weapon was a pocket knife. He claimed he was on his way to Hungry Creek in search of work.

Marino's companion, an American named Garland Stemler, was also arrested and jailed in Yreka. Stemler was then taken to the county hospital, where Meierhaus, in critical condition, was being treated. The German identified Stemler as the man who shot him. When Stemler was arrested, he had the evidence on him: a pistol with three empty chambers. The matching three empty shells were found at Sears' saloon, the scene of the robbery. George Sears died at Cole's Station August 8, 1895, at age 67, and Casper Meierhaus, age 60, passed away six days later.

Just a short time earlier, two other murders in Siskiyou County had been solved with the arrest of William Mull and A. H. Johnson, the latter an ill-tempered blacksmith. Now there were two more murderers in jail. There was no question as to the identity of the four, but to bring them to trial and get convictions would take weeks, even months. And besides, the cost to Siskiyou County would drain the county treasury. There was widespread distrust of the courts, with their tardy justice, and county residents yearned to take the law into their own hands. Newspapers carried editorials deploring a crime wave and the ineptitude of law enforcement. Too many criminals, especially those able to pay high-priced attorneys, walked away free.

August 26, 1895, was a sad day in Yreka. A determined group of men from all over the county arrived there at noon, stopping everyone they met and demanding that they join the mob. They stormed the jail, took Stemler, Marino, Johnson and Mull outside, and hanged them in the Courthouse Square. Then the group rode off, leaving four corpses dangling in the darkness of night. The frightful incident was a closed book. For many years thereafter Siskiyou was free of murder.

As for EUGENE DOWLING, he wanted no part of mob justice. He believed in the law and in the courts, despite their many failings. Fidelity was in the blood of the Dowlings—at home and abroad. In their impoverished ancient homeland they championed the cause of their downtrodden countrymen, quite often at the peril of their lives. And in America they were renowned as patriots in wartime and community activists in peacetime

The Dowlings in California and in remote areas like Siskiyou County fared much, much better than their counterparts in the old sod. They were active in political and cultural life of their communities, and became financially independent in the process. At that same time back in Queens County (County Laois) we learn that one Philip Dowling conducted a pay school in Branra Townsland, near Abbeyleix; his income was £25 (about $125) a year. Classes were held in a wretched cabin built with sod and stones which cost less than two pounds. Another teacher, John Dowling, from Clonaslee in the

Barony of Tinahinch, Queen's County, also conducted a pay school at a yearly salary of £7 ($35.00). The fact that they were both Catholics may account for their meager pay, as was the custom under English rule.

Their relations in San Francisco were doing much better, according to a partial list gleaned from the 1867 city directory:

> James Dowling, manager of the Metropolitan Theater
> Richard Dowling, harness maker
> Patrick Dowling, stonecutter
> Michael Dowling, hackman in Portsmouth Square
> Edward Dowling, retail liquor dealer
> Annie Dowling, San Francisco teacher
> James Dowling, carpenter
> Richard Dowling, livery stable owner
> Thomas Dowling, bootmaker
> Madison Dowling, miller
> Daniel Dowling, hotel clerk
> Edward Dowling, landscape gardener
> Edward Dowling, hotel porter
> James Dowling, furniture dealer
> Jennie Dowling, teacher
> William Dowling, bricklayer

IN HIS DAY Eugene Dowling was so popular that he was endorsed by both the Republican and Democratic parties when he ran for the office of Siskiyou County Recorder. When it came election time, he didn't have to campaign at all, except for meeting some of his many friends who by their constant support made his nomination tantamount to election.

Siskiyou, one of the largest counties in the state, is unsurpassed in scenic grandeur. The landscape changes from low rolling hills to forests of stately pines, oaks and maples and many other trees and shrubs peculiar to the Siskiyou highlands. The magical Marble Mountains can only be reached by the steepest and most perilous trails. The eastern portion of the county has something even more unusual: the Modoc Lava Beds, a national monument, caused by a prehistoric volcanic eruption. Further east, Mount Shasta rears its snowy head over fourteen thousand feet into the blue heavens.

In truth it was more than the lure of gold that brought the pioneer adventurers like Eugene Dowling to the enchanting wilds of Siskiyou county.

THE FIRST STORE AT CALLAHANS
ERECTED 1854.

RESIDENCE OF A.H.DENNY.
— CALLAHAN'S RANCH, SISKIYOU CO., CAL.—

This old engraving shows the home of the A. H. Denny family, where
six children and a dog are playing in the front yard. The small inset in
the sky shows "The first store at Callahans, erected 1854."
Courtesy Siskiyou Historical Society

THE WILDLY BEAUTIFUL country of Siskiyou County has lured
adventurers and settlers for many years. However, it was the Irish,
including Irish missionaries, who led the way, morally and otherwise,
in the development of this fascinating domain The Irish had their
"Little Ireland" in Callaghan, in the Scott River Valley, famed for its
coarse gold and nuggets. The first religious service was held in the
home of Mr. Callaghan, where many Irish people in the area received
the long-awaited comforts of their religion.

As of 1854 there was no resident priest in Siskiyou County.
However, in the fall of that year Father Hugh Gallagher returned from
Ireland to San Francisco, bringing with him Father James Cassin and
Father Thomas Cody, destined for the missions in Northern
California. Their journey north was a memorable one, full of hard-
ship. They traveled by steamboat up the Sacramento river to

Two early Irish residents of Siskiyou County were Joseph and Ann Cavanaugh. He came to the county in 1852 to look for gold. By 1858 he had given up mining to farm and raise cattle on a fine ranch at Edgewood. They were married in 1860 and had four children.
Courtesy Siskiyou Historical Society

Marysville. Then a stagecoach, bumping along for over a hundred miles, let them down, tired and worn, in the sun-baked hamlet of Shasta. But the worst was yet to come: a 120 mile jaunt by muleback over one of the crookedest and most hazardous trails in the whole mining region.

Fortunately, a period of respite awaited them when they descended Scott Mountain and arrived at the ranch of the Irishman named Callaghan. In later years the two clerics recalled with delight that a baptism was performed at Callaghan's on July 4, 1858.

Fifteen years later, their brother priest, Father Patrick O'Kane, celebrated a high mass at the Church of St. John and St. Paul on Christmas Day, 1873, at a fond farewell celebration to his ministry in Siskiyou County.

From Callaghan, Father Cassin and Father Cody went to the mining camp of Rough and Ready, and then on to Fort Jones, in both of which they ministered to a number of Catholic families, mostly Irish. With so many Irish around and about, the two clerics were no longer strangers in a strange land. They went about their priestly duties with renewed vigor. With those two Irish missionaries serving in Siskiyou County in the year 1855, Archbishop Alemany was satisfied that his priests were reaching all the Catholics throughout the far-flung Archdiocese.

THE DOWLING CONTRIBUTION to Siskiyou County was further enhanced by Eugene Dowling's son, Eugene Smith Dowling, born in Yreka on March, 29, 1902. Eugene was educated in the local schools and attended the University of California at Berkeley, where he graduated with a degree in business administration. He began his career with the California-Oregon Power Company until his appointment as auditor of Siskiyou County, a position he held for ten years. He was one of the founders of Siskiyou County Historical Society, along with another Yreka native, Waldo Joseph Smith.

Eugene S. had an abiding interest in the history of his native county and won election as the Siskiyou Historical Society's second president. He also worked on various committees and contributed articles for many publications. In later years he served as chairman of the Museum Board of Governors. Eugene Jr. died while still a young man, on March 14, 1958, at age 56, leaving a wife and an only son James, now an ophthalmologist in Walnut Creek.

Eugene Sr. passed away in 1934. The old pioneer was survived by his wife, Gertrude, daughters Catherine (Mrs. Glen Johnston) and Nellie and sons Eugene S., John and Edward. They were all lifelong residents of Yreka except Mrs. Johnston, who resided in San Francisco.

Funeral services were held atSt. Joseph's Catholic Church where he worshipped for many years. Friends gathered to pay their last and loving respects to one of their own. All of the county and city officials and people from all walks of life were present at the obsequies.

Following a Requiem Mass the old pioneer was laid to rest in Yreka. A man of high principle and integrity, Eugene Dowling Sr. left a legacy of honest endeavor, trustworthiness and achievement rarely equaled in the history of Siskiyou County.

Sources

Books, Pamphlets, and Scholarly Manuscripts

—Arsenal Museum and Historic Society of Watervliet N.Y. *History of Watervliet Arsenal,* 1989.

—Blue and White News. Sacred Heart Graduation Class of 1889 Sacred Heart College. San Francisco.

—Carlson, Wada F. *This is our Valley,* Santa Maria Valley Historical Society, 1959.

—Casey, Father James (Pastor of Red Bluff). *Life and Works of Father John F Quinn,* 1988.

—Coyer, Richard J., "Thomas William Sweeny." A thesis submitted by Richard Coyer to the University of San Diego, 1973.

—Coyer, Richard J., "History of the Irish in San Diego." A thesis submitted to the University of San Diego, 1977.

—Days, Mary Louise. *Irish Settlements in Santa Inez Valley.* Santa Barbara, February 1991.

—Delury, John Francis, "Irish Nationalism in Sacramento, 1850-1890." Thesis, University of San Francisco.

—Donahue, Barbara J. *Selected Papers of a Western Pioneer 1811-1884,* San Francisco 1972.

—Dowling, Captain Patrick (Irish-born American Privateer): A handwritten dispatch to Benjamin Franklin in Paris. American Philosophical Society of Philadelphia, April 3, 1780,

—Earl of Longford and Thomas P. O'Neill. *Eamon DeValera.* Hutchingson and Company, Ltd., London, 1970.

—Felker, Reverend Joseph. *Sacred Heart Parish, Redlands 1894-1994.* Riverside, California, 1994.

—Fresno City and County Historical Society. *M. Theodore Kearney, Prince of Fresno.* 1988.

—Fresno City and County Historical Society: *Fresno Past and Present.* 2 Vols., March 1975 and June 1976 "Thomas E Hughes, the Father of Fresno"

—Friedman, Leon, and Fred Israel. *The Justices of the Supreme Court, 1789-1969.*

—Galindo, Vincent, Sacramento Office of Senator Bill Lemann. "The History and Rich Tradition of the National Orange Show in San Bernardino." January 25, 1993.

—Hansen, Warren D. *San Francisco Water and Power, 1985-1987.*

—Harley, H. Bruce Ph.D. Archivist, Diocese of San Bernardino. *Readings in Diocesan Heritage 1862-1890.* Vols. 1 to 10

—Herring, Mary Porter. *Family History of Senator John Barry Curtin.* Newton Highlands, Massachusetts 1985.

—History Room, San Francisco Main Library. "Mayor Twelve, Frank McCoppin, December 2 1867-December 6 1869."

—Hruby, Daniel D. *Mines to Medicine. The Exciting Years of Judge Myles O'Connor.* San Jose 1965.

—Hunt, Rockwell D., *California and Californians,* Vols. 1-4. Lewis Publishing Co., 1932.

—*Illustrated History of Los Angeles County.* Lewis Publishing Co., 1887.

—Jones, J. Roy. *Land of Remember.* Hornbook, Humboldt County, 1910.

—Kopp, Senator Quentin. *Political History of Senator John B. Curtin,* Sacramento, November 19, 1993.

—Lee, Thomas Z. *The Journal of the American Irish Historical Society.* New York, 1897.

—Long, Charles. *Who's Who in Los Angeles County.* Lang Publishing Co. 1928-29.

—MacLysagh, Edward (Chairman, Irish Manuscript Commission). *Irish Families, their Names, Arms and Origins.* Dublin, Ireland, 1957.

—McCoy, Edward. *Santa Maria Inn History,* Santa Maria, September 1955.

—McDevitt, Brother Mathew. *Associate Justices of the United States Supreme Court.* San Francisco 1946.

—McGowan, Joseph. *History of the Sacramento Valley.* 3 Vols., Lewis Publishing Co., New York, 1961.

—McMaster, John Bach. *Benjamin Franklin.* Chelsea House Publishers, 1980.

—*Memoirs and Genealogy of Representative Citizens of Northern California,* Standard Publishing Co. Chicago 1901.

—Monahan, Father John, C.M., *History of Our Lady of Angels Seminary,* Niagara, New York.

—O'Doul, Frank "Lefty", as told to Will Connolly. *Turner's Butchertown Boys and Lefty's First Trip Away From Home.*

—O'Shaughnessy, M. M., *Hetch Hetchy; its Origins and History.* San Francisco, 1934.

—Schmidt, Earl F. *Who were the Murphys?* Mooney Flat Ventures, 1992.

—Sofranco, Eleanor, & Catherine Ross. *Upon this Rock: The History of St Peter's Parish,* Lovilla, Iowa.

—St. Mathew's Parish Archives. "Centennial Jubilee of St Mathew's Church, San Mateo, 1863-1963." San Mateo, 1963.

—Toland, James Robert. *History of the Tolands in America, With Roots in County Donegal.* San Francisco State University, June 1988

—Trick, Patricia P. *Santa Maria Inn,* June 30, 1990.

—White, Sister Winifred Mary. "Eugene Casserly, his Political and Legal Career." A dissertation given at the Catholic University of America, San Rafael Branch. July 1952.

—Whitridge, Arnold. *Rochambeau.* Reprint of the 1893 edition published

by Houghton, Mifflin, under the title, Benjamin Franklin, A man of
    Letters. A series: American men of letters.
—Woodroff, Jacqueline McCart, "Benicia, the Promise of California"
    thesis, University of California, 1946, on the life and times of Justice
    Joseph McKenna.
—Young, Father John E., C.M., *History of Niagara University.* Jamaica,
    New York, December 1980.

ARTICLES IN PERIODICALS:

—"Daly's Department Store Celebrates its 75th Anniversary in Eureka."
    Eureka Times Standard, September 13, 1970.
—"Joe Cronin, Hall of Fame Player and Executive." *Sporting News,*
    September 17, 1984.
—"Profiles in Progress," *San Francisco Examiner*, July 28, 1964.
—"The All-American Maverick." *San Jose Mercury News* California Today,
    July 27, 1980.
—"The Amazing Madigan," *Sports Illustrated Magazine*, Fall issue 1992.
— "The Oldest and Newest Hospital in the Valley." *O'Connor Foundation*
    Quarterly. Christmas Edition, 1980.
—"The Sun-Maid Raisin Story." *Fresno Bee*, Country Life Section,
    February 1958.
—"When Irish Power Came to the City." *San Francisco Examiner-*
    Chronicle, Sunday Edition, April 1, 1979.
—Duffield, Isabel McKenna. "Washington in the 90s," *Overland Monthly,*
    San Francisco, 1929.
—Fontes, Marsha, "Carville: Odd City on Ocean Beach," *San Francisco*
    Independent, October 7, 1987.
—Gleason, Father Joseph. "Lone Mountain History," *San Francisco*
    Monitor, May 18, 1929.
—Hovey, Jan. "Annual Calaveras Grape Stomping at Murphys." July 1997.
—Lockwood, Charles, "The Victorian Way of Death," *San Francisco*
    Sunday Examiner & Chronicle, August 12, 1979.
—McDonagh, Will. "Joe Cronin, a Man for One Season Every Day of his
    Life," *Boston Globe*, September 9, 1984.
—McDonald, Jack. "Slip Madigan Story" *The Daily Review* September 26,
    1983.
—Murphy, Frank. "Most Reverend Daniel Mannix, Archbishop of
    Melbourne, Australia," *The Capuchin Annual*, 1965.
—Renaud, Renee. "Colma's Dead Once Rested at Foot of Lone
    Mountain." *Richmond Review*, 1987.
—Robbins, Millie. "Legendary Doctor Hugh Toland," *San Francisco*
    Chronicle, March, 25,1970.
—Robbins, Millie. "Tracing the Parrott Line," *San Mateo Times,* October

24, 1980.

—Rosenbaum, Art. "Lefty O'Doul was More Than Just a Player," *San Francisco Chronicle*, October 10, 1991.

—Rosenbaum, Art. "Slip Madigan and St Mary's Football Tours," *San Francisco Chronicle*. 1991.

—Rosenbaum, Jack. "There'll never be another 'Slip'," *San Francisco Independent*, August 25, 1992.

—Smith, Red. "Lefty O'Doul, Student of Hitting and a Sincere Teacher." *Boston Globe*, December 9, 1969.

—Wood, Richard Coke. "Murphys, Queen of The Sierra." *Calaveras Californian*, Angels Camp, 1948.

ORAL HISTORIES AND INTERVIEWS

—Coman, Betty: Oral History of Father John F. Quinn, Pastor of Winters. Winters, California, 1995.

—Cunningham, Louise.: The life and times of her late husband, James Earl Cunningham of San Bernardino," 1995.

—Dowling, Patrick: A recorded interview with Senator Tommy Maloney at the age of ninety six.

—Maloney, Warren R.: An oral History of the Maloney clan in Ireland and America.

—O'Shaugnessy, Beth.: Oral History of the O'Shaughnessys in Ireland and California. San Francisco 1995.

Index

RANCH PREMISES OF JAMES B
6 MILES NORTH OF ETNA,